All You Can Eat!

one-pot cooking

More than 600 delicious dinners in just one pot!

Lisa Rogak & B.J. Hanson

JG PRESS

Published by World Publications Group, Inc.
140 Laurel Street, East Bridgewater, MA. 02333
www.wrldpub.com

ISBN 10: 1-57215-722-4
ISBN 13: 978-1-57215-722-4

Printed and bound in the United States of America.

10 9 8 7 6 5 4 3 2

Many of the designations used by manufacturers and sellers to distinguish their
products are claimed as trademarks. Where those designations appear in this
book and Adams Media was aware of a trademark claim, the designations have
been printed in initial capital letters.

This publication is designed to provide accurate and authoritative information
with regard to the subject matter covered. It is sold with the understanding that
the publisher is not engaged in rendering legal, accounting, or other professional advice. If legal advice or other expert assistance is required, the services
of a competent professional person should be sought.
    —From a Declaration of Principles jointly adopted by a Committee of the
American Bar Association and a Committee of Publishers and Associations

Previously published as the *Everything® Soup Cookbook* and the *Everything® Slow Cooker Cookbook*.

Contents

Introduction

After a hectic day, it's easy to reach for the same old takeout menus to have dinner delivered in thirty minutes. After all, you don't have the time or energy to make a meal, and your family is hungry *now*! Wouldn't you like to give your family a satisfying, healthy dinner without spending your night standing at the stove, keeping track of when the chicken is ready to come out of the oven, the rice is fully cooked, and the broccoli perfectly steamed? Thanks to *All You Can Eat: One Pot Cooking*, you can!

The first collection of recipes covers soups––but don't expect Grandma's bland chicken soup. From simmering broths to thick, rich stews, you'll be thrilled with your options.In the mood for soup bursting with ethnic flair? Try the Vietnamese Crab and Pineapple Soup. Want to keep your family fit? You'll find a whole chapter of healthy—and delicious—recipes. And for the nights when you have only a few minutes to spare, try one of our Quick Soups recipe—perhaps the Hearty Ground Turkey and Vegetable Soup, or maybe the Tuna Chowder No matter what you're in the mood for, you'll find a quick, one-pot recipe that'll fill you up.

The second part of our volume moves beyond soups into the realm of slow cooker recipes. Slow cookers aren't just for overcooked beef stew anymore—in Part 2, you'll find recipes for tasty appetizers, entrées, kids' favorites, desserts, breads, and more! You'll be thrilled with the intense and delightful flavors slow cooking reveals—all with few utensils and simple ingredients. And the best part is—the meal makes itself while you're at work! You'll find a complete meal ready to eat within minutes of stepping through your door.

So save the takeout menu for another day, and enjoy the mouthwatering flavors—and simple recipes—that the meals in *All You Can Eat: One Pot Cooking* have to offer.

Introduction to One-Pot Soups

Why soup? Soup entices the senses as it simmers, warm and fragrant. Served, it tastes sumptuous. And it is just as vivid in food value: vitamins in ample variety, proteins from grand grains to tasty meats, fiber from vegetables to fruits to nuts, everything. The beauty of soup lies in the way it can introduce or anchor a meal. A small cup is an appetizer. Or a bowl can buttress a sandwich, a small platter of cheeses or nuts or fruit slices, a salad, a plate of rolls, a warm cottage loaf.

Different Soup Families

The following are a few of the different categories of soups. Most varieties are based on texture, ingredients, and, very commonly, thickness. By understanding the different varieties of soup, you will have a better understanding of what a recipe will be like before you even make it!

BISQUE—A soup made with vegetables, fish, or shellfish that is thick, smooth in texture, and opaque (this is usually done by pureeing vegetables or adding cream).

BOUILLABAISSE—On the French Mediterranean coast, a list of specific fish/shellfish, garlic, and spices creates the classic bouillabaisse ("bool-ya-base") (classic stewed with saffron). Most people define it most flexibly, to contain a good variety of different kinds of fish/shellfish.

BOUILLON—A clear, thin broth.

CHOWDER—A thick, chunky soup made with potatoes. There are a large variety of chowders that can include vegetables, seafood, chicken or virtually any other ingredient.

CONSOMMÉ—A very clear soup or stock.

GAZPACHO—A vegetable soup served cold, often made with tomatoes as a key ingredient.

GUMBO—These are soups filled to the gills with a variety of seafood, vegetables, and meat chunks of all kinds, thick broths, and sometimes Creole seasonings (filé and/or okra).

PANADE—Soups thickened with bread, either diced pieces or rounds placed on the bottom of the individual soup bowls.

POTAGE—A French word for soup in general, now used to refer to especially hearty soups.

STEW—A very thick soup based on chunks of meat or occasionally fish.

STOCK—Basically a broth, but sometimes used to refer to broths made using meat bones that have been preroasted.

Basic Soup-Making Equipment

The one crucial piece of equipment you'll need for whipping up some soup is a nice big soup pot. A minimum of two gallons in size will ensure that you'll be able to make most soup recipes in this book and won't have to worry about boilovers. The ideal choice of material for an all-purpose soup pot is stainless steel with an aluminum core or an aluminum disc on the bottom (aluminum helps ensure even heating). All-aluminum pots are not a good choice—aluminum will react to acidic liquids which can create off-colored and off-tasting soups.

Some other things you will want or need to make and serve your favorite soups include:

- Ladles
- Tureen or large serving dish
- Bowls, crocks, soup cups, and soup spoons
- Blender, food processor, hand-held immersion blender, or food mill
- Basic set of cutlery
- A saute pan (you can often just saute in your soup pot before you add liquids as well)

Simmering Broths

Basic Beef Broth

1 medium potato
3 large carrots
1 large onion
2 stalks celery, including leaves
1 large tomato (optional)
½ pound lean beef trimmings
4 pounds beef soup bones

8–10 whole black peppercorns
5 sprigs fresh parsley
1 bay leaf
1 tablespoon salt
3 cloves garlic
13 cups cold water

1. Preheat oven to 450 degrees. Clean the potato and carrots thoroughly (do not peel). Chop the potato, carrots, onion, celery, tomato. Cut the beef into medium-sized chunks (around the size of a golf ball).
2. Place the beef bones, onion, and carrots on a baking sheet and bake for 30 minutes or until bones begin to brown. In the meantime, place all the other ingredients *except* ½ cup water into a soup pot. Put the pot on medium heat; do not let the broth boil.
3. Remove the baking sheet and allow it to cool. Place the bones and vegetables in the soup pot and turn the heat up to high. Pour the remaining ½ cup water onto the baking sheet and swish it around for a few seconds; drain the water into the soup pot.
4. Bring to a boil and then simmer for 4 hours, covered. Strain the mixture through a cheesecloth-lined colander into another pot. Freezes well.

Safe Handling of Broth

Bacteria can begin to grow on broth quickly, so it is important to handle it with care. Strain the broth and discard all solids as soon as the stock is done cooking. If the broth is not going to be used immediately, chill it to room temperature by immersing it in a bath of ice water; then refrigerate or freeze it promptly. Always cool broths to room temperature before refrigerating or freezing them. Hot broth can take up to a day to cool in the refrigerator, allowing bacteria to form.

Basic Chicken Broth

3 pounds chicken (whole **or** parts)

16 cups (1 gallon) cold water

1 teaspoon salt

1 pound onions, coarsely chopped

½ pound celery, coarsely chopped

2 whole cloves

½ pound carrots, coarsely chopped (cleaned but not peeled)

2 cloves garlic, sliced in half

1 bay leaf

½ teaspoon black peppercorns

½ teaspoon fresh thyme

3–4 sprigs of parsley

Yields 12 cups

This broth can be kept in the fridge for 2 to 3 days and will be ready for immediate use.

1. Wash the chicken under cold running water. Place it in a soup pot with the water and bring to a gentle boil. Simmer for 1 hour, frequently skimming off the fat that rises to the top.

2. Add salt, onions, carrots, and celery and continue to simmer for an additional 1½ hours.

3. Add the remaining ingredients and simmer for another 30 minutes. When finished, remove the pot from the heat and cool immediately. Chicken stock is highly susceptible to spoilage, so the temperature needs to be reduced quickly. This can be done by setting the pot in the sink in 5 to 6 inches of cool water.

4. When cool enough to handle, strain the soup through a sieve or colander into another pot or large container. Straining a second time through cheesecloth will get you a much clearer broth.

Buying Garlic

When buying fresh garlic, look for heads that are plump, firm, and heavy for their size. Any green shoots or spouts indicate that the garlic is old and will have an off flavor. Store whole bulbs in an open plastic bag in the vegetable drawer of your refrigerator. Markets now carry a variety of processed garlic options, from peeled cloves to fully chopped pastes. They are a great convenience, but buy these in the smallest containers possible, since they lose their fresh taste and become stale very quickly.

Dashi

Yields 4 cups

This traditional Japanese clear broth is used extensively for soups, sauces, and as a delicate seasoning.

1 piece kelp (kombu), about 5 inches square
5 cups cold water

⅓ cup dried bonito flakes (also called smoked fish flakes)

1. Place the kelp and cold water in a soup pot; bring to a boil. Remove from heat and stir in the bonito flakes. Let it stand for 2 to 3 minutes.
2. Using a slotted spoon or tongs, remove the kelp and discard. Strain the broth into a new container. Use it now, in any Japanese-inspired soup, or cool it to room temperature by immersing it in a bath of cold water, then refrigerate immediately. (This broth does not freeze well.)

Basic Vegetable Broth

Yields 5–6 cups

Feel free to make additions, subtractions, and substitutions in your vegetable broth. Leeks, spinach, turnips, mushrooms, and tomatoes are all good choices.

4 large onions, peeled and quartered
6 large carrots, peeled and quartered
3 large stalks celery, peeled and quartered
1 medium potato, peeled

1 cup cabbage, cut into eighths
5–6 peppercorns
1 bay leaf
3 sprigs of thyme
3 sprigs of parsley
8 cups cold water
Salt

1. Place all the ingredients in a large soup pot. Bring to a boil, then immediately reduce to a simmer. Cook for 1 hour.
2. Allow the pot to cool, uncovered, off the heat for an hour or so. Strain the soup through a sieve or colander; then squeeze the solid ingredients so that the extra broth is collected (squeezing inside a cheesecloth works really well). Strain again through cheesecloth for clearer broth. Salt to taste. Freezes well.

Potato and Vegetable Broth

3 baking potatoes
1 large leek
6 carrots
6 stalks of celery
3 medium zucchini
4 large onions
½ pound fresh mushrooms
  (any kind)
1 whole head of garlic

10 peppercorns
8 sprigs fresh thyme
  (**or** 1 tablespoon dried)
8 sprigs fresh flat-leaf parsley
3 bay leaves

> **Yields 8 cups**
>
> If broth is not going to be used immediately, cool it to room temperature by immersing the pot in a bath of cold water; refrigerate or freeze promptly.

1. Without peeling them, clean, then chop the potatoes, leek (white light green parts only), carrots, celery, and zucchini. Quarter the onions and mushrooms; do not discard any parts. Slice off the very top of the garlic head, just enough to expose the tops of the cloves.
2. Place all the ingredients in a soup pot. Add enough cold water to cover the vegetables; then add more water until its level is about 6 inches higher.
3. Bring to a boil, then reduce to a simmer. Cook for about 1¾ hours. Squeeze the liquid out of the vegetables, adding the liquid to the broth. Strain.

Broth—the Foundation of Soups

Many soups start off with a broth, or stock. Broths are basically the liquid remnants of boiled meat, poultry, seafood, and/or vegetables along with some seasonings. The finished product is often robust and rich in flavor. Broths are also used in a lot of sauces and other dishes. In supermarkets, broths can be bought in the form of cubes, powder, or liquid in cans or jars.

Fish Broth

2 onions
½ head of celery
4 pounds fish heads and bones
1 bay leaf

6 sprigs parsley
3 sprigs of thyme
Pepper

1. Chop the onions and celery. Rinse off the fish parts; then place them in a large pot and cover amply with cold water. Add all remaining ingredients.
2. Bring to a boil, then reduce to a simmer; simmer uncovered for 30 minutes. Strain and discard all solids. If broth is not going to be used immediately, allow it to cool to room temperature by immersing it in a bath of cold water; then refrigerate it promptly.

Vegetable Broth with Apple

4 medium onions
2 apples, cored
3 large carrots
3 parsnips
6 leeks
3 celery stalks
2 whole heads garlic
4 shallots

3¼-inch piece ginger
½ bunch thyme
½ bunch chervil
½ bunch parsley
2 bay leaves
1 tablespoon peppercorns
24 cups cold water

1. Core the onions and apples. Chop the carrots, parsnips, leeks, and celery into large pieces. Leave the garlic heads, shallots, and ginger unpeeled.
2. In a very large soup pot, combine all the ingredients. Bring to a boil, then reduce to a simmer. Cook for 2 hours.
3. Let cool slightly. Squeeze the liquid from the vegetables into the soup pot. Strain and discard solids. Re-boil and simmer for another hour.

Scotch Broth

1½ pounds lamb bones, rinsed
(shoulders are fine)
8 cups cold water
3 leeks, thoroughly cleaned
2 large onions, peeled and
quartered
½ bunch celery, chopped
3 carrots, peeled and chopped
2 bay leaves

¼ bunch of parsley stems
3 sprigs of thyme
½ cup pearl barley
Salt and pepper

Yields 5 cups

Next time you use parsley, freeze the stems. That way, you'll have them handy for your Scotch Broth.

1. Trim all visible fat from the lamb bones and cut or break them into the smallest pieces you can. Place the bones and vegetables in the water in a soup pot. Bring to a boil, then reduce to a simmer. Simmer for approximately 4 hours, skimming off the scum that rises to the top several times with a large spoon.

2. Stir in the barley and herbs. Bring to a boil again and reduce to a simmer for 1 hour, adding a bit more cold water as necessary to cover the bones.

3. Skim off the fat and season with salt and pepper. Strain, discarding all solids. (To store the broth for later use, cool it to room temperature by immersing the cooking pot in a bath of cold water; then refrigerate or freeze promptly.)

Roasted Vegetable Broth

Yields 4 cups

A bouquet garni is a small bag of mixed fresh herbs that often includes sprigs of parsley and thyme and a bay leaf.

1 teaspoon olive oil
1 bouquet garni
½ pound (8 ounces) mushrooms
4 carrots, peeled and chopped
8 cloves garlic, peeled

2 onions, peeled and quartered
½ head of celery, chopped
1 turnip, peeled and quartered
7 cups cold water
Salt to taste

1. Preheat oven to 400 degrees. Using the olive oil, lightly grease a baking pan that has sides. Prepare the bouquet garni using the fresh herbs of your choice. (A traditional bouquet with a few red pepper flakes added is a nice complement to the flavor of this broth.)
2. Place all the vegetables in the oven and roast for 1 hour, turning them over a couple of times.
3. Place the roasted vegetables in soup pot. Pour 1 cup of the water into the baking pan and use a wooden spoon to scrape up the remaining bits of roasted vegetables. Add this to the soup pot.
4. Pour the remaining 6 cups of water over the mixture and add the herb bag. Bring to a boil and reduce to a simmer for 1 to 1½ hours.
5. Strain, squeezing the liquid from all the solid ingredients. Discard the bouquet garni and all solids.

Bag o' Spices

A small bag of mixed fresh herbs, called a bouquet garni (or sachet d'épices), is often used in broth and soup recipes. A traditional bouquet garni includes a thyme sprig, parsley stems, and a bay leaf. To make a bouquet garni, simply place the fresh herbs of your choice on a four-inch square of cheesecloth and fold the sides up around the herbs to make a pouch, securing it closed with a piece of string. This bundle is then dropped into the broth or soup and left in throughout the cooking process to release the herbs' flavors. When the broth or soup is done cooking, this bag of spices is easily removed and discarded. You can also use a leek leaf in place of the cheesecloth; simply wrap the herbs in the leaf and tie a string tightly around the bundle.

Giblet Broth

2 tablespoons butter
Neck and giblets from an
    18-pound turkey
1 cup chopped onion
2 leeks, chopped
1½ cups chopped carrots
½ cup chopped celery
1 cup dry white wine

5 cups cold water
½ bunch parsley sprigs
1–2 teaspoons thyme
2 bay leaves
2 cloves
5 whole black peppercorns
Salt to taste

Yields 3–4 cups

If the broth is not going to be used immediately, cool it to room temperature by immersing the pot in a bath of ice water, then refrigerate or freeze promptly.

1. In a soup pot, heat the butter. Add the neck, giblets, and vegetables; sauté for 10 minutes. Pour in the wine, and let it reduce for 1 minute. Add the water. Bring to a boil and simmer for 30 minutes.
2. Add all the remaining ingredients to the pot. Bring to a boil again, then reduce to a simmer. Cook for 1 hour. Strain.

Mushroom Broth

2 pounds fresh mushrooms
    (a mix of varieties is nice)
½ bunch celery
½ pound carrots

3 large onions
3 cups cold water
Basic Chicken Broth (page 5)
1 tablespoon sherry

Yields 6 cups

If you are fresh out of chicken broth—not to worry! This recipe works well with beef broth, too.

1. Dice the mushrooms, celery, carrots, and onions. Place all of the vegetables in a soup pot with 3 cups of water. Bring to a boil, then reduce to a simmer and cook for 45 minutes. Strain.
2. Add enough chicken (or beef) broth to make a total of 6 cups of liquid. Reheat thoroughly. Add the sherry just before using the broth.

Lobster Broth

Yields 8 cups

Chill as quickly as possible if not using both immediately. After it has cooled, cover it tightly and refrigerate.

1 or 2 whole lobsters
   (about 2 pounds total;
   more is fine)
12 cups water
1 cup dry white wine
3 yellow onions, chopped
5 stalks celery, chopped
1 pound mushrooms (any type)
4 cloves garlic, minced or
   crushed

½ bunch of parsley
4 sprigs thyme
2 bay leaves
¼ teaspoon fennel
1 teaspoon peppercorns

1. Split the lobsters from front to back and remove the little sacs from behind the eyes of each lobster; discard the sacs. Break the lobster into pieces to make everything fit into the soup pot.
2. Cover the lobster pieces with the water and bring to a boil. Using a ladle, skim off and discard the white scum that accumulates on the top of the water.
3. Reduce the heat. Add all the remaining ingredients; cook for 1 hour, pouring in a bit more water as necessary to keep the shells covered.
4. Check flavor and seasonings, allowing the liquid to reduce and concentrate for 20 minutes longer if you desire a stronger flavor. Strain and discard all solids.

Veal Broth

2½ pounds veal bones
   (meaty ones)
6 cups cold water
2 cups chopped onions
1 cup chopped carrots
1 cup chopped celery

1 parsnip, chopped
1 bay leaf
½ bunch of parsley
5 sprigs of thyme
1 teaspoon peppercorns

> **Yields 3 cups**
>
> Refrigerate the broth overnight. The next day, skim off and discard the fat layer from the top.

1. Preheat oven to 450 degrees. Cut or break the veal bones into several pieces. Put into a baking dish with sides, in a single layer. Roast for 30 minutes. Add the vegetables and roast for 30 more minutes. Remove from the oven.

2. Using a slotted spoon, transfer the bones and vegetables to a soup pot. Pour 1 cup of the water into the baking dish and use a wooden spoon to loosen any cooked-on bits from the bottom of the dish; add this to the soup pot, along with the remaining 5 cups of water. Bring to a boil and simmer for 3 to 4 hours, uncovered. Add the herbs and simmer 1 hour longer.

3. Strain the mixture and cool it to room temperature by immersing the pot in a bath of ice water.

Taking Stock

Adventurous cooks who get into diverse cuisines look to broths that provide an appropriate palette on which to build their dishes. By adding one or two ingredients to the Basic Vegetable Broth recipe (page 4), you can make many stocks with just that one recipe. For Chinese stock, add one thinly sliced two-inch piece of fresh ginger and two sliced garlic cloves (in addition to the original five the recipe calls for). For Vietnamese stock, add one star anise and one chopped stalk of lemongrass (or ¼ cup dried). When making stocks for Mexican foods, add one ancho chili pod and one cinnamon stick. For Middle Eastern dishes, a stock with the zest of one lemon adds another dimension.

Wild Mushroom Broth

Yields 4 cups

Reconstitute dried mushrooms 20 to 30 minutes before cooking time.

1 ounce dried wild mushrooms
   (porcini, morels, or any kind)
2 pounds white button
   mushrooms
½ pound (8 ounces) fresh
   shiitake mushrooms
4 shallots, peeled and quartered

¼ head of celery, chopped
1 bay leaf
4 sprigs of parsley
1 sprig fresh thyme
  (**or** 1 tablespoon dried)
½ teaspoon black peppercorns

Without trimming or slicing them, place all the mushrooms in a soup pot. Add the seasonings and enough cold water to cover all the ingredients. Bring to a boil, then reduce to a simmer. Cook for 2 hours. Squeeze the liquid from the mushrooms, adding that to the liquid in the pot. Discard the mushroom solids.

Thai Broth

Yields 6 cups

Check with your guests before serving this broth made with fresh cilantro. Some people dislike the flavor of this herb.

2 small Thai chilies, seeded
3 cloves garlic
2 shallots
1¼-inch piece of ginger
4 kaffir lime leaves
5-inch piece of lemongrass
6 cups Basic Chicken Broth
  (see page 5)

1 scallion
¼ cup cilantro
3 tablespoons tamarind paste in
  ½ cup hot water (**or** use
  the juice from 2 limes)
¼ cup Thai fish sauce (nam pla)
White pepper to taste

1. Chop the chilies, garlic, shallots, and ginger. Thinly slice the lime leaves and the lemongrass. Place these ingredients in a soup pot with the broth. Bring to a boil, then reduce to a simmer and cook for 30 minutes.
2. Finely chop the scallion and the cilantro. Add them to the soup pot, along with all the remaining ingredients; simmer for 2 more minutes. Strain, discarding all solids.

Red Wine Broth

1 medium carrot
1 medium-sized yellow onion
1 small turnip
2 cloves garlic
1 pound raw meat (beef or
    pork is best)

1 bouquet garni (see "Bag o'
    Spices" on page 10)
2 tablespoons butter
4 cups other meat broth **or**
    cold water
3 cups dry red wine

> **Yields 4 cups**
>
> Other veggies and herbs may be substituted. Try parsnips, fennel, ginger, basil, or tarragon.

1. Chop the carrot, onion, turnip, and garlic. Trim the fat from the meat and cut the meat it into ½-inch cubes. Prepare the bouquet garni using your choice of fresh herbs. (A traditional bouquet garni with a few black peppercorns added complements this recipe well.)
2. In a soup pot, melt the butter. Add the meat and the vegetables and cook on low heat for 20 minutes until they are all completely browned. Add the ½ cup of broth or water and ½ cup of the red wine. Boil the mixture until the soup pot is almost completely dry and virtually all liquids have evaporated.
3. Add the rest of the red wine, broth, and the bouquet garni. Bring to a boil, then reduce to a simmer and cook for about 2 hours. Skim off the impurities with a spoon several times during this period. (Feel free to add cold water at this point to adjust the strength of the broth.) Strain and discard all solids. If the stock is not going to be used immediately, cool it to room temperature by immersing the pot in a bath of cold water before refrigerating.

Water Temperature

To maintain the clarity of your broth, always use cold water; adding hot water to broth will produce a less desirable, cloudy final product.

Asian Pork Broth

Yields 8–10 cups

Don't have any pork spare ribs handy? Substitute pork chops and still ensure a tasty broth.

2 pounds pork spare ribs
3 leeks
12 cups cold water
1 bunch celery, chopped

8 black peppercorns
1-inch piece ginger root
2 teaspoon soy sauce

1. Separate the spare ribs. Chop the leeks coarsely (white and light green parts only).
2. In a soup pot combine the pork, leeks and, water. Bring to a boil, then reduce to a simmer; cook for 1¾ hours, skimming off the impurities and the fat regularly.
3. Add the peppercorns, unpeeled ginger root, and soy sauce. Simmer for ½ hour. Discard all solids. Strain the broth thoroughly. Use some; freeze some. (Before freezing or refrigerating the broth, cool it to room temperature by immersing the pot in a bath of cold water.)

Soybean Broth

Yields 3 cups

Mung bean sprouts can be substituted for soybeans and sprouts, but they aren't as flavorful.

½ pound (8 ounces) soybean
  sprouts
2 cloves garlic
2 scallions

2 tablespoon soy sauce
2 teaspoon sesame oil
Red pepper threads

1. Cut the small threads from the sprouts and discard the threads. Place the sprouts in water to cover, bring to a boil, and reduce to a simmer; cook for 7 minutes. Meanwhile, mince the garlic and diagonally slice the scallions into small pieces.
2. When the sprouts have steamed, add the garlic, soy sauce, sesame oil, the white parts of the scallions, and salt to taste. Pour in 3 cups of cold water and bring to a boil; reduce to a simmer and cook for 15 minutes. Garnish with the green parts of the scallions and the red pepper threads in the individual bowls.

CHAPTER 2

Seafood Soups

Shrimp and Butternut Squash Soup

Serves 8

In this recipe, prepare the shrimp and chill that mixture while you oven roast the squash separately; then combine them.

2 tablespoons fresh-squeezed lime juice

6 tablespoons fresh-squeezed orange juice

1½ teaspoon ground coriander, divided

¼ teaspoon red pepper flakes

3 tablespoons vegetable oil, divided

½ pound (8 ounces) large shrimp

2 medium butternut squash

4 cups (1 quart) chicken broth

1 cup cream

2 teaspoon grated orange rind

4 teaspoons minced cilantro

Salt and pepper

1. Combine the lime juice, orange juice, ½ teaspoon of the coriander, the red pepper flakes, and 1 tablespoon of the vegetable oil in a large bowl and whisk thoroughly. Peel and devein the shrimp, then slice in half lengthwise. Toss together. Refrigerate this marinade for 2 hours.

2. While the shrimp is marinating, preheat the oven to 425 degrees. Cut the squash into quarters and remove the seeds, leaving the skin on. Using a large roasting pan, place the squash pieces face down and add enough water to cover the bottom of the pan, about ⅛ of an inch deep. Cover the pan loosely with foil; bake for 50 minutes.

3. Allow the squash to cool, then remove the skin. Using a blender, blend half the squash with about half the chicken broth. Pour the mixture into a soup pot. Prepare the other half of the squash the same way. Stir in the cream, orange rind, and remaining coriander. Cover and warm gently on a low heat.

4. In a large saucepan, heat the remaining oil. Drain the marinade from the shrimp. Place the shrimp in the pan and cook for 1 minute on each side.

5. Pour the squash base into serving bowls. Top with the shrimp, then the cilantro.

Shellfish Chowder

2 (6½-ounce) cans chopped
   clams
3 ounces salt pork
1 onion
1 pound red potatoes
2 tablespoons flour
1 cup water
2 tablespoons chopped dill

1 bay leaf
10 ounces scallops
3½ cups milk
¼ teaspoon white pepper

> **Serves 6–8**
>
> You can substitute 1½ pounds of fresh clams for each 6½-ounce can. Boil them in just enough water to cover for 10 minutes and reserve the liquid (discard the shells).

1. For this early American-style recipe, drain the clams, reserving the liquid. Dice the salt pork and the onion. Dice the potatoes into ½-inch cubes, peels on.
2. In a large saucepan, sauté the salt pork in its own fat over medium heat for 7 minutes. With a slotted spoon, remove the pork pieces to drain on paper towels. Discard all but 2 tablespoons of the fat.
3. Using this fat, sauté the onion for 3 minutes; then allow it to cool slightly. Add the flour to coat. Pour in the water and add the potatoes, dill, and bay leaf. Bring to a boil, then reduce to a simmer and cook for 15 minutes. Add the clam liquid and the scallops; cook for 6 minutes. Add the clams and simmer for 1 minute.
4. Stir in the milk and white pepper and serve.

Brothy vs. Thick Chowders

While generations of canned soups have conditioned us to believe that chowder is, by definition, a thick, pasty soup, some of the most delicious handmade versions of these chunky soups feature a thin, though rich, broth.

Saffroned Fish Soup

2 pounds Spanish onions
2½ pounds tomatoes
6 cloves garlic
¾ teaspoon saffron threads
3 tablespoons olive oil
1 teaspoon thyme
1 teaspoon fennel seeds
2 bay leaves
Black pepper
4 cups water

2 pounds firm fish, such as sea bass, snapper, pike, or trout
1 cup dry white wine
¼ cup mayonnaise
¼ cup plain nonfat yogurt
¼ teaspoon red pepper
12 small slices French bread
½ pound halibut **or** monkfish fillets
¾ cup grated Swiss cheese

1. For a Provençal delight, slice the onions, quarter the tomatoes and squeeze out seeds, then cut the flesh into large chunks. Finely chop the garlic. Break the saffron threads with a small knife.

2. Using a soup pot, heat the oil. Sauté the onions on medium for 3 minutes. Add the tomatoes, ⅔ of the garlic, the thyme, fennel, bay leaves, black pepper to taste, and half of the saffron. Sauté for 5 more minutes.

3. Cut the 2 pounds of fish into slices 1–2 inches wide. Add them to the soup pot along with the water and the wine. Bring the mixture to a boil, reduce to a medium heat, and cook for 25 minutes, stirring often.

4. Meanwhile, mash the rest of the garlic slightly. Place it in a bowl with the other half of the saffron, the mayonnaise, yogurt, and red pepper; mix well and refrigerate, covered. Toast the bread slices.

5. Strain the soup, squeezing the liquid from all the vegetable ingredients and discarding the fish heads if you have used them.

6. Cut the fillets into 1-inch cubes and stir them into the soup. Bring to a simmer and cook for 5 minutes; be careful not to overcook the fish. (Overcooking will cause the fish to lose its flavor.)

7. In 6 individual soup bowls, pour the soup and top with the cheese. Float 2 slices of the French bread on each bowl, spread with the chilled mayonnaise mixture.

Salmon Chowder

20 scallions (**or** 2 cups of any
    type of onion, chopped)
¼ pound (4 ounces) bacon
2 shallots
1 teaspoon thyme **or** summer
    savory (fresh, if possible)
1 teaspoon tarragon
    (fresh, if possible)
2 pounds potatoes
    (any kind but red)

3 pounds salmon
4 tablespoons butter
2 bay leaves
4 cups Fish Broth **or**
    Basic Chicken Broth (see
    recipes on pages 8 and 5)
1½ cups cream
Salt and pepper
Fresh chopped dill (optional)

> **Serves 4–6**
>
> To substitute fresh herbs for dried, double the amount called for and add them 5 minutes before the soup is ready.

1. Trim the scallions and cut into 1-inch pieces. Dice the bacon. Finely dice the shallots and herbs. Slice the potatoes into ⅛-inch-thick slices. Remove the skin and bones from the salmon and cut into 3-inch chunks.

2. In a soup pot, sauté the bacon to a golden brown in its own fat. Discard all but 1 tablespoon of the fat, leaving that much in the pot along with the bacon. Add the butter, scallions, shallots, and bay leaves, and cook for 2 minutes.

3. Add the potatoes and the broth, supplementing the mixture with enough water to cover the potatoes, if necessary. Bring to a boil, reduce to medium, and cook for 10 minutes only.

4. With the back of a spoon, mash some of the potatoes against the side of the pot and stir to thicken the mixture. Add the salmon and cook for 10 minutes. Allow the soup to cool slightly, then stir in the cream and add salt and pepper to taste. Garnish with chopped dill, if desired.

Common Fresh Herbs

Most supermarkets now carry a variety of fresh herbs including thyme, chives, rosemary, sage, and oregano. But even if they don't, you can almost always find fresh Italian (flat-leaf) parsley, the best kind for cooking. Dill and cilantro are now quite common, and I recently saw fresh flash-frozen herbs in the freezer section of a store.

Crab Chowder

2 pounds fresh crabs **or** 12
    ounces canned crabmeat
6 cups milk
1 bay leaf
1 pinch of saffron
2 leeks
1 stalk celery
2 small red potatoes

2 whole artichokes, cooked
    (**or** 2 artichoke hearts,
    canned or frozen)
1 cup water
2 tablespoons lemon juice
1 pinch of cayenne pepper
1 tablespoon chervil (optional)

1. If using fresh crab, boil in water for 3 to 6 minutes, depending upon the size. Remove the meat with a nutcracker and cut into large dice.
2. Combine the milk, bay leaf, and saffron in a soup pot. Over medium heat, bring to a boil; add the crab and cover. Take off heat, keeping it covered, and let it stand.
3. Finely dice the white part of the leeks, the celery, and the potatoes. Remove the leaves and the center choke from the artichoke and dice the bottom (the heart).
4. In a saucepan, melt the butter and add all the vegetables, the water, and the lemon juice. Bring to a boil, reduce to medium heat, cover the pan, and cook for 10 minutes. Take the cover off, turn the heat up, and cook until the liquids have evaporated. Turn the heat down to the lowest setting.
5. Add the fish and milk mixture along with the cayenne. Stir and warm thoroughly, but slowly. Garnish with the chervil.

Clam Chowder

8 pounds fresh clams
   (cherrystones, littlenecks,
   butters, or quahogs)
¼ pound (4 ounces) bacon
10 cloves garlic
3 scallions
4 tablespoons butter
2 teaspoons thyme

2 teaspoons dill
1 bay leaf
2 pounds potatoes
1½ cups cream
Salt and pepper
Flat-leaf parsley, chopped
   (optional)

> **Serves 6**
>
> Before chopping the clams, be sure to remove the skin around the neck of the clam.

1. Clean the clams thoroughly. Cover them barely with cold water in a large pot, and cover the pot tightly with a lid. Bring to a boil, remove from the heat quickly, and let stand covered for 10 minutes, or until the shells open.
2. Remove the clams from their shells and cool. Discard the shells, but reserve the cooking liquid, straining it through cheesecloth. Cut the clams into ½-inch dice and refrigerate. Clean the soup pot.
3. Cut the bacon into ⅛-inch pieces. Place in soup pot over low heat. Cook over medium heat until golden brown. Discard all but 1 tablespoon of the bacon grease, leaving the rest of the fat and the bacon in the pan.
4. Peel the garlic cloves and cut the cloves in half, lengthwise. Chop the scallions coarsely, including half of the green parts.
5. Add the butter, vegetables, and herbs to the pot and sauté for 5 minutes.
6. Dice the potatoes into a ½-inch cubes. Add them to the pot along with all of the reserved clam broth. Bring to a boil, reduce to medium, and cook for 15 minutes. Adjust the thickness of the broth by mashing some of the potatoes against the side of the pot with a wooden spoon. Stir for 1 minute. Remove from the heat.
7. Stir in the chopped clams and cream, and add salt and pepper to taste. Garnish with the parsley.

Lobster Chowder

Serves 6

To thicken the chowder, mash some of the potatoes against the side of the soup pot before adding the lobster, stirring for 1 minute.

3–4 fresh whole lobsters
3 ears corn
10 medium shallots
1½ pounds potatoes
¼ pound (4 ounces) bacon
4 tablespoons butter

1 teaspoon dill
⅛ teaspoon cayenne pepper
1½ cups milk
2 small green onions (green parts only), thinly sliced (optional)

1. Boil the lobsters in a large pot half-full of salted water for exactly 4 minutes. Remove the pot from the heat and set it aside to cool, then remove the meat from the tails and claws and dice into large cubes. Refrigerate the meat and save the shells.

2. Remove the innards from the inside of the shells. Place the shells in a pot and add enough water to cover. Bring to a boil, then reduce to a simmer and cook for 1½ hours. Strain the broth and discard the shells.

3. While the broth is cooking, husk the corn. Using a sharp knife, cut the kernels off the cobs. Peel and coarsely chop the shallots. Cut the potatoes into ¾-inch cubes. Chop the bacon into small chunks.

4. Using a soup pot, cook the bacon pieces on low heat until the fat begins to collect in the pot. Turn the heat up to medium and cook the bacon until it is golden brown. Discard all but 1 tablespoon of the bacon grease, keeping the rest of the fat and the bacon in the pot.

5. Add the butter, shallots, and dill to the soup pot. Sauté for 6 minutes, stirring now and then. Add the cayenne.

6. When the lobster broth is ready, add it to the soup pot with the bacon, along with the potatoes and the corn kernels. Add cold water to cover all ingredients. Bring to a boil and simmer for 12 minutes. To thicken the chowder, mash some of the potatoes against the side of the soup pot just before adding the lobster, stirring for 1 minute, to thicken the mixture a bit.

7. Add the lobster pieces, and simmer for 8 minutes. Cool slightly, then stir in the milk. Garnish with green onions.

Shrimp and Spinach Soup

1 large garlic head
1 pound (16 ounces) medium-
  sized uncooked shrimp
4 cups white rice, cooked
½ teaspoon lemon rind
1½ teaspoon lemon juice

4 cups Basic Vegetable Broth
  or Basic Chicken Broth (see
  recipes on page 6 and 5)
Salt and pepper
4 cups finely chopped spinach
  (stems removed)

> **Serves 4**
>
> If possible, get all of the ingredients fresh. This recipe will benefit greatly from this extra effort.

1. Roast the garlic first: Preheat the oven to 350 degrees. Cut off and discard the very top of the garlic head. Place the garlic (top up) in a small baking dish with a lid, and drizzle some olive oil over the garlic. Cover and cook for 35 to 45 minutes. Allow to cool. Squeeze out the roasted garlic pulp, discarding the rest.
2. Bring water to a boil in a large saucepan. When the water boils, reduce to a simmer and add the shrimp (shells on). Cook, uncovered, for about 3 minutes, or until the shrimp turns pink. Remove the shells and the veins from the shrimp. Cut the shrimp in half and reserve.
3. In a mixing bowl, mix the rice, the lemon rind, and the lemon juice.
4. In a soup pot, bring the broth to a boil. Season with salt and pepper if desired.
5. Place a large scoop of the rice mixture in 4 individual soup bowls. Top with the spinach, then the shrimp, and then the roasted garlic. Pour the broth around this.

Orzo
Orzo is a type of pasta shaped like a grain of rice. It has a delicate flavor and consistency that result in a totally new dish when substituted for larger pasta or rice. However, it tends to get mushy, so add it later in the cooking process than you would pasta or rice.

Gumbo

1 pound (16 ounces) medium-sized uncooked shrimp
12 cups water
3 bay leaves
2 stalks celery, chopped
3 cups sliced okra
1 large green bell pepper
1 large onion
4 cloves garlic
1 (28-ounce) can tomatoes
4 tablespoons oil

Salt (about ¾ to 1 teaspoon)
½ teaspoon pepper
½ teaspoon cayenne pepper
1 teaspoon dried thyme
1 pound (16 ounces) lump crabmeat
24 oysters, shucked, liquid reserved

1. Peel and devein the shrimp, reserving the shells. Place the shells in a large soup pot with the bay leaves and half of the celery. Add the water, bring to a boil, reduce to a simmer, and cook for 30 minutes.
2. Meanwhile, slice the okra into ¼-inch rounds, dice the green pepper and onion, and mince the garlic. Drain the tomatoes and chop them coarsely.
3. In a large skillet, heat 2 tablespoons of the oil and sauté the okra (on low to medium heat) for 20 minutes, stirring it constantly.
4. In another skillet, heat the remaining oil on medium and sauté the garlic, onion, green pepper, tomatoes, and the remaining celery with the salt and black pepper for about 5 minutes.
5. Strain the shrimp broth into a soup pot, discarding the shells. Add all the sautéed vegetables the cayenne pepper, and the thyme to the pot. Bring to a boil, reduce to a simmer, and cook for 30 minutes. Add the shrimp and crabmeat and simmer for 10 more minutes. Take it off the heat.
6. Stir the oysters and their liquid into the mixture. Cover and let it sit 5–10 minutes, or until the edges of the oysters begin to curl, before serving.

Swedish Shrimp Bisque

3½ pounds fresh, raw, white-fleshed fish fillets **or** whole fish (preferably halibut or cod)

3 onions

1 carrot, peeled

4 stalks celery

1 tomato

4 cloves garlic

3 tablespoons butter, divided

10 sprigs fresh dill

8 cups water

1 teaspoon lemon juice

2 bay leaves

10 black peppercorns

1 pound (16 ounces) raw shrimp, unpeeled

3 tablespoons flour

2 egg yolks

½ teaspoon salt, optional

¼ cup chopped fresh chives

½ cup cream

Serves 8

If you are using a whole fish, double-check to make sure you have removed all of the bones.

1. If you are using whole fish, trim the fish a bit, but retain the heads, bones, and skin if you like. Chop the onions, carrot, celery, tomato (discard the tomato seeds), and garlic.
2. In a soup pot, warm 1 tablespoon of the butter. Sauté the onions and garlic on medium heat for 3 minutes. Add all the other vegetables, the fish, dill, and water. Bring to a boil over medium heat, skimming off the impurities with a slotted spoon until no more form. Add the lemon, bay leaves, and peppercorns. Simmer for 30 minutes.
3. Add the shrimp and simmer for 5 minutes. Remove the shrimp, peel and devein them, and refrigerate.
4. Simmer the soup mixture for 30 more minutes. Strain, squeezing the liquid out off all ingredients, and discard all solids.
5. In a large saucepan, melt the remaining 2 tablespoons of butter and whisk in the flour. Gradually stir in 6 cups of the soup mixture. Simmer for 3 minutes. Meanwhile, beat the egg yolks slightly in a small bowl.
6. Stir the chives, egg, and cream into the mixture. Add the shrimp (whole or cut lengthwise). Serve.

Lobster Bisque

2 medium-sized fresh lobsters
4 stalks celery
2 cloves garlic
1 onion
*2½ cups Fish Broth **or** Basic Chicken Broth (see recipes on pages 8 and 10)*
2 bay leaves
6 black peppercorns

4 tablespoons butter
4 tablespoons flour
1 dash of nutmeg
1 cup cream
4 tablespoons sherry
Dill sprigs (optional)

1. Using a large soup pot, fill it about ⅔ of the way up with water. Bring to a boil. Pick up the first lobster by its back. Remove the claw plugs and drop the lobster, headfirst, into the pot. Let it cook for 6 minutes. Do the same for the other lobster. Set them aside to cool a bit.
2. Chop the celery and garlic coarsely. Slice the onion. Remove the lobster meat from the tails, claws, and body. Discard other inner parts. Crush the shells.
3. Place the shells, the broth, the vegetables, bay leaves, and peppercorns in a soup pot. Bring to a boil, then reduce to medium heat and cook for 45 minutes. Remove from the heat, strain, and discard all solids.
4. In a small saucepan, melt the butter and whisk in the flour. Cook for 2 minutes, stirring constantly. This mixture is called a *roux*. Add the nutmeg.
5. Stir the roux into the main broth mixture. In a small saucepan, heat the cream separately and thoroughly, but do not let it boil. Meanwhile, dice the lobster meat.
6. Place the roux-broth mixture back on low heat and simmer for 2 minutes. Add the cream and lobster; stir. Serve garnished with the dill.

Fish and Squid Soup

½ pound (8 ounces) whole
squid (calamari)
¾ pound (12 ounces) monkfish
fillets
1 pound (16 ounces) cod fillets
4 tablespoons olive oil
2 tablespoons minced garlic
1¾ cups finely diced onion
1½ cups finely diced leeks
(white and light green
parts only)
2 cups cubed tomatoes

½ teaspoon saffron threads
3 tablespoon tomato paste
½ cup dry white wine
1 teaspoon thyme
1 teaspoon fennel seeds,
crushed
Black pepper to taste
4 cups water
2 hot dried red peppers
½ cup finely chopped parsley
(optional)

Serves 4

Unless you're familiar with cleaning fresh squid, purchase it cleaned and ready to cook from your fish market.

1. Cut the squid's central body into ½-inch pieces. Cut the tentacles into bite-sized pieces. Cut the rest into 1½-inch chunks. Cut the monkfish and cod into 1½-inch cubes.

2. In a soup pot, heat the oil. Add the garlic and onion, stirring constantly for 3 minutes. Add the leeks, tomato cubes, saffron, tomato paste, wine, thyme, fennel, and black pepper. Pour in the water. Bring everything to a boil.

3. Add the squid and monkfish pieces and 1 of the red peppers; simmer for 15 minutes. Add the cod and the other red pepper, bring back to a boil, and cook for 5 minutes. Discard the peppers. Garnish with the parsley before serving.

Cooking with Fish

Fresh seafood should be used within one day of purchase. Check the smell. There should be no fishy odor. The flesh should be firm and the eyes on a whole fish should be clear.

Mussels and Wine Soup

Serves 6

Place up to ten peppercorns at a time on a flat, hard surface. Using a small saucepot or small skillet, apply pressure with the heel of your hand to break the seeds.

48 mussels
5 cloves garlic
5 black peppercorns
2 tablespoons oil

2 cups light Rhine wine
½ cup water

1. Wash the mussels and clean the shells well with cold water. Slice the garlic cloves and crack the peppercorns.
2. In a soup pot, heat the oil. Sauté the garlic on medium heat for 2 minutes. Add the wine, water, peppercorns, and mussels. Bring to a boil, cover, reduce heat, and shake the pot until the shells open.
3. Place a colander over a bowl and pour the mixture through the colander to collect the liquid in the bowl below. Pull off the top shells and the beards of the mussels and discard these. Keep the mussels, on the half shell, warm in a bowl.
4. Using a clean pot, strain the broth again using cheesecloth or a fine sieve. Bring back to a boil. Into each soup bowl, place some of the mussels. Pour broth over them and serve.

Cooking with Shellfish
To prevent eating spoiled shellfish, discard all mussels or clams that are open before cooking. Discard all that are closed after cooking.

Catfish Soup

2 pounds catfish fillets
2 onions
2 stalks celery
2 cups chopped tomatoes
4 cloves garlic
5 tablespoons minced parsley
½ of a lemon
6 tablespoons olive oil
½ cup flour
½ can tomato paste
½ cup full-bodied red wine

4 cups Fish Broth (see recipe
   on page 6) **or** water
1 generous pinch of thyme
1 generous pinch pf basil
1 pinch of cayenne pepper
Cooked rice (optional)
Fresh chopped green herb of
   your choice (optional)

> **Serves 8–10**
>
> Cooked rice can be frozen for up to six months. Make twice what you need and freeze the rest in an airtight container.

1. Cut the catfish fillets into 2-inch-thick pieces. Chop the onions, celery, and tomatoes. Mince the garlic and parsley. Cut the lemon into several slices.
2. In a soup pot, warm the oil. Whisk in the flour, stirring well on low heat. Cook it on medium for several minutes, until brown.
3. Add the onions, celery, garlic, and parsley to the flour mixture. Cook 3–4 minutes. Add the tomatoes, tomato paste, wine, broth (or water), lemon slices, and all the seasonings. Simmer for 1 hour, stirring occasionally.
4. Place the catfish pieces in a single layer in the pot. Bring to a boil, reduce to a simmer, and cook for 20 minutes.
5. Serve over the cooked rice and garnished with a sprinkle of any green herb.

Sea Bass and Shrimp Soup

Serves 6–8

For an elegant touch, replace the 8 cups of water with 4 cups of water and 4 cups of dry white wine.

8 cups water (**or** 4 cups water and 4 cups dry white wine)
1 onion, quartered
1 carrot, chopped
6 tablespoons chopped flat-leaf parsley
5 cloves garlic
5 black peppercorns
1 bay leaf
1½ pounds tomatoes
½ pound (8 ounces) shrimp
2 pounds sea bass fillets
5 tablespoons olive oil
6–8 slices toasted Italian bread

1. Pour the water (and wine, if using) into a soup pot; add the onion, carrot, 3 tablespoons of the parsley, 2 of the whole garlic cloves, the black peppercorns, and the bay leaf. Boil, uncovered, for 20 minutes. (This mixture is called *court bouillon.*)
2. While the court bouillon is cooking, mince the remaining 3 garlic cloves. Coarsely chop the tomatoes. Peel the shrimp and remove their veins, discarding everything but the shrimp themselves.
3. When the court bouillon is done cooking, remove it from the heat. Add the sea bass, cover, and simmer for 12 to 16 minutes, making sure not to let the liquid boil. (Be careful not to overcook the fish. It should be simmered for about 6 to 8 minutes per pound.)
4. Meanwhile, heat the olive oil in a large saucepan and simmer the minced garlic, the remaining 3 tablespoons of parsley, and the tomatoes for 6 minutes. Add the shrimp and cook for another 3 minutes, adding a little warmed water (or dry white wine) if you need more liquid.
4. When the sea bass is ready, remove it from the pot using a slotted spoon; cover the fish to keep it warm. Strain the court bouillon, discarding the solids. Keep it on low heat.
5. Add the sea bass to the shrimp mixture, stirring it very carefully. Rewarm. Add 3 cups of the strained court bouillon to the fish-shrimp mixture. Keep the remaining court bouillon on low heat.
6. Place a piece of the Italian bread in the bottom of each individual soup bowl. Ladle the court bouillon over the bread, then ladle the fish-shrimp mixture over that.

English Cod Chowder

1¼ pound cod pieces
2 onions
1 carrot
2 stalks celery
½ pound potatoes
1 bouquet garni (see "Bag
 o' Spices" on page 10)

2 tablespoons butter
2 tablespoons olive oil
1 teaspoon curry powder
3 tablespoons dry white wine
2 tablespoons corn flour
¼ cup milk
¼ cup crea

Serves 6

If you don't have any cream on hand, increase the milk to ½ cup and add an additional 2 table-spoons of butter.

1. Remove the skin from the cod and cut the fish into small pieces. Thinly slice the onions, carrot, and celery. Peel and dice the potatoes. Prepare the bouquet garni using your choice of fresh herbs.

2. In a soup pot, warm the butter and the oil. Add the onions, carrot, and celery, and sauté on medium heat for 5 minutes. Stir in the curry and cook for 1 minute. As that is cooking, boil 3½ cups of water in a separate pot.

3. Add the water, bouquet garni, and fish pieces to the main soup pot with the vegetables. Bring to a boil, reduce to a simmer, and cook for 5 minutes.

4. With a slotted spoon, and using a small, clean bowl, remove about a dozen of the neatest-looking fish pieces. Add some of the hot broth to cover them. Cover the bowl itself to keep it warm.

5. In the main soup pot, turn up the heat a bit and cook the mixture, uncovered, until its volume is reduced—15 minutes of reduction should be fine. Discard the bouquet garni and cool this mixture slightly; then place it in a blender or food processor and purée. Put it back into the pot, add the wine, and begin reheating it.

6. Meanwhile, whisk the corn flour into a couple of tablespoons of the milk; then add all the milk. Pour this mixture into the main soup pot, stirring constantly. Remove from heat, add the fish mixture to the pot, and stir in the cream. Serve.

Scallop Soup

1 large onion
½ pound carrots
1¾ pounds potatoes
3 tablespoons chopped parsley
8 tablespoons butter, divided
15 large scallops
1 sprig thyme
1 tablespoon dill

½ cup dry white wine
4½ cups Fish Broth (see
    recipe on page 8)
1 cup whole milk
1 pinch of cayenne pepper

1. Finely chop the onion and carrots. Peel and dice the potatoes. Chop the parsley.
2. In a soup pot, melt 6 tablespoons of the butter. Chop the other 2 tablespoons into small pieces and refrigerate. Sauté the onions and carrots on low for 10 minutes.
3. Add the scallops, thyme, dill, parsley, wine, and broth to the pot. Bring to a boil, reduce to a simmer, and cook for 10 minutes. Meanwhile warm a large bowl.
4. With a slotted spoon, remove the scallops, placing them in the heated bowl. Cover it.
5. Add the potatoes to the soup pot. Bring to a boil, reduce to a simmer, and cook for 15 minutes. Remove the thyme sprigs. Cool slightly. In a blender or food processor, purée the potato mixture.
6. Rewarm the soup gently, adding the milk gradually. Add the scallops, the chilled bits of butter, and sprinkle with the cayenne pepper.

Using Bouillon Cubes

Bouillon cubes will work in place of broth when necessary. When using them instead of homemade broth, be sure to add a little extra of the aromatic vegetables such as onion, celery, and carrots. You may also want to choose the low- or lower-salt variety so you can have more control over how salty your soup will be.

Tangy Shrimp Bisque

½ pound (8 ounces) raw
  shrimp
3 tablespoons bread crumbs
2½ cups Fish Broth, divided
  (see recipe on page 6)
4 tablespoons butter, divided
1 pinch of nutmeg

1 teaspoon lemon juice
½ cup cider
Pepper
1 egg yolk
½ cup cream

Serves 4–6

Looking to save yourself some time? Rather than discarding your shrimp shells, freeze them for making broth another day.

1. Place the shrimp (still in their shells) in a saucepan and add enough water to cover. Bring to a boil, reduce to a simmer, and cook them for about 3 minutes, or until the shrimp turn pink. Remove from heat, drain, and allow shrimp to cool.

2. In a small bowl, mix the bread crumbs with 1 cup of the fish broth. Set it aside to soak for 10 minutes.

3. Meanwhile, peel the shrimp and remove their veins; discard the shells and veins. Melt half the butter in a soup pot. Add the shrimp, nutmeg, lemon juice, the bread crumb mixture, then the rest of the butter. Toss and simmer for 2 minutes.

4. Remove from heat and allow to cool slightly. In a blender or food processor, purée the shrimp mixture. Return it to the soup pot. Gradually add the cider and the rest of the fish broth. Reheat on very low heat.

5. Meanwhile, in a small bowl, whisk the egg yolk and cream together. Mix a little bit of the soup into it, stirring well to incorporate. Then add the egg mixture to the main soup pot. Stir until it thickens.

Smooth Moves: Blender vs. Food Processor

They seem interchangeable sometimes, but they're not. Blenders and food processors are different tools with different strengths. For ultrasmooth purées, a blender is the first choice. For rougher purées, or chopping jobs with drier ingredients, use a processor.

Bar Harbor Fish Chowder

Serves 6

Poke the tip of a knife into the thickest part of the potato, then lift the knife up, handle first. If the potato falls off, it's done. If it hangs on, then it needs more time.

¼ pound salt pork, diced
4 cups diced potatoes
3 medium onions, peeled and
  sliced
2 teaspoons salt, divided
3 pounds white-fleshed fish,
  such as flounder, haddock,
  or cod

2 cups milk
1 tablespoon butter
¼ teaspoon freshly ground
  black pepper

1. Fry the salt pork in a heavy kettle and then remove the pork with a slotted spoon; set aside. Add the potatoes, onions, and ½ teaspoon salt. Cover with hot water and cook over medium heat, covered, for 15 minutes, or until the potatoes are just tender.
2. Meanwhile, cut the fish into large chunks and put it in another saucepan. Add boiling water to cover and 1½ teaspoons salt. Simmer, covered, until the fish is fork tender, about 15 minutes.
3. While the fish is cooking, scald the milk by placing it in a small saucepan and bringing it to just below the boiling point over medium heat; do not allow the milk to boil.
4. When the fish is done cooking, remove it from the heat. Strain and reserve liquid. Remove any bones from the fish. Add the fish and strained liquid to the potato-onion mixture. Pour in milk and heat through, about 5 minutes. Mix in the butter and pepper. Serve immediately.

Frying vs. Sautéing

Frying means cooking at moderate temperature (ususally 340 to 360 degrees) in a large amount of oil, such as a pan filled two inches deep, or a pot filled with oil for deep-frying. Sautéing is a cooking method using small amounts of oil, usually measured in teaspoons or tablespoons, and very high heat—nearly at the oil's smoking point.

Oyster Halibut Soup

2 pounds halibut
½ pound (8 ounces) clams
½ pound (8 ounces) uncooked
    shrimp
½ pound (8 ounces) tomatoes

1 onion
2 cloves garlic
¼ cup olive oil
4 ounces white almonds
    (shelled and skins removed)

Serves 8

Leaving the bones in the fish while cooking will add flavor. Halibut bones are large and easy to remove after cooking.

1. Using 3 pots, cook the halibut, clams, and shrimp separately, using all bones, shells, and so on, and enough water to cover in each case. For the halibut, bring the water to a simmer, reduce to low, and cook, covered, for about 12 to 14 minutes. Cover the pot containing the clams, bring to a boil, and remove from the heat immediately; let stand, covered, for 10 minutes, or until the shells open. Cook the shrimp, uncovered, over medium heat. As soon as the water begins to boil, lower the heat and simmer for about 2 or 3 minutes, or until the shrimp turn pink. Retain all cooking liquids.
2. Pour all of the cooking liquid into one pot. Peel and devein the shrimp. Shell the clams. Debone and skin the fish. Cut the halibut, clams, and shrimp into bite-sized pieces. Discard all bones, shells, and skins.
3. Chop the tomatoes coarsely, discarding the seeds. Dice the onion and garlic.
4. In a soup pot, heat the oil on medium heat. Place the vegetables in the oil and sauté for 3 minutes. Strain the vegetables, pressing the liquids into the pot. Discard the solids.
5. Add enough water to the retained cooking liquid to make a total of 10 cups of liquid; add to the soup pot. Bring to a boil. Mash the almonds almost to a paste. Add the almonds and the seafood pieces to the pot, turning off the heat. Let the soup sit for 5 minutes, covered, before serving.

CHAPTER 3
Poultry Soups

Turkey Chili

Serves 4

If you like your chili spicy, do not remove the seeds from the jalapeño chilies.

1 pound uncooked turkey
½ of an onion
2 cloves garlic
2 tablespoons chopped jalapeño chilies
1 (15- to 16-ounce) can white beans
1 (15- to 16-ounce) can chickpeas (garbanzo beans)
2 tablespoons olive oil
4 teaspoons ground cumin

1 teaspoon summer savory
1 teaspoon marjoram
½ pound ground turkey
4 cups Basic Chicken Broth (see recipe on page 5)
¼ cup pearl barley
Hot sauce
Salt and pepper
Cheddar cheese, grated

1. Cut the turkey into ½-inch cubes. Mince the onion and garlic. Seed and chop the jalapeños. Drain and rinse the beans.
2. In a soup pot, heat the oil. Sauté the onion and garlic on medium heat for 3 minutes. Stir in the cumin, savory, and marjoram and cook for half a minute. Add both kinds of turkey, sautéing them until browned slightly. Pour in the broth and stir in the barley and the jalapeños. Bring to a boil, reduce to a simmer, and cook for 30 minutes.
3. Add the beans and a dash of hot sauce, and salt and pepper to taste; simmer for another 10 minutes. Top with the grated cheese and serve.

Saffroned Chicken Soup

9 cups Basic Chicken Broth
   (see recipe on page 3)
1 (3-pound) whole chicken
2 cups chopped onions
1 cup diced carrots
¾ cup diced celery
3 garlic cloves
2 tablespoons minced parsley
   (optional)

¼ teaspoon saffron
3 tablespoons butter
¼ teaspoon thyme
2 ounces dried noodles
1 cup corn kernels

Serves 8

Use wide egg noodles for this soup. They tend to hold up the best.

---

1. Pour the broth into a soup pot. Cut the chicken into pieces, reserving the neck, gizzard, and heart. Place all the chicken pieces and parts in the pot. Bring to a boil, reduce to a simmer, and cook for 1 hour.

2. With a slotted spoon, remove and discard the neck, gizzard, and heart. Also remove the chicken pieces, allowing them to cool slightly on a plate. Remove and discard the skin and the bones, then cube the chicken meat until you have 1 cup of it. (Save the rest for another recipe.)

3. Strain the broth and cool it to room temperature by placing the pot in a bath of ice water. Refrigerate it for 6 hours or overnight. Remove and discard the hardened fat layer that will have formed on top.

4. Chop the onions, dice the carrots and celery, and mince the garlic and parsley. Crumble the saffron.

5. Heat the butter in a soup pot. Sauté the onions, carrots, celery, garlic, and thyme for about 10 minutes on medium heat. Pour in the broth you made earlier and bring to a boil. Reduce to a simmer and cook for 15 minutes.

6. Add the saffron. Heat to just before the boiling point and add the noodles. Simmer for 10 minutes. Add the chicken cubes and corn, simmering for another 5 minutes. Garnish with the parsley.

Chicken Gumbo

Serves 8

Serve with warm and crusty rolls.

1 (3-pound) whole chicken
½ cup chopped celery
½ cup chopped onions
½ cup chopped green bell
   peppers
3 cloves garlic
2 teaspoons cayenne pepper
2 teaspoons black pepper
1 cup flour, divided in half

7 tablespoons olive oil, divided
8 cups Basic Chicken Broth
   (see recipe on page 5)
¾ pound (12 ounces) sausage
   (chorizo **or** andouille)
4 scallions
Salt and pepper
Hot sauce

1. Cut the chicken into serving pieces (breasts, thighs, etc.). Chop the celery, onions, green pepper, and garlic.
2. Combine the cayenne and black pepper and ½ cup flour in a bag. Place each chicken piece in the bag and shake until coated. In a large saucepan, heat 3 tablespoons of the oil. Brown the chicken pieces on all sides, turning a couple of times. Remove them with a slotted spoon and set aside. Add the other 4 tablespoons of oil to the skillet, scraping up the browned chicken bits with a wooden spoon. Whisk in the second ½ cup of flour. Cook over medium-low heat for 5 minutes. Take the pan off heat and add the celery, onion, green peppers, and garlic, stirring them in for 1 to 2 minutes.
3. Scoop this mixture into a soup pot and add the chicken broth. Bring to a boil, reduce to a simmer, and add the chicken. Cook for 40 minutes. Meanwhile, thinly slice the sausage and chop the scallions (white and green parts).
4. When the chicken is done cooking, remove from the pot, discarding the skin and bones. Coarsely chop the meat and set aside. Add the sausage to the soup pot and salt and pepper to taste; simmer for 10 minutes.
5. Stir the scallions into the pot along with the chicken pieces and a dash of hot sauce. Warm thoroughly and serve.

Corn and Chicken Soup

4 cups Basic Chicken Broth
   (see recipe on page 5)
12 ounces corn kernels
1 tablespoon sake
1 tablespoon curry powder
1 teaspoon salt
1 teaspoon sugar
1 egg white

½ pound (8 ounces) uncooked
   chicken meat
1 teaspoon cornstarch
1 egg
1 teaspoon sesame oil
2 cups water
Scallions, chopped (optional)

Serves 4

Instead of scallions, try thinly shredded lettuce or cabbage.

1. In a soup pot, bring the broth to a boil. Reduce to a simmer and add the corn. Cook for 10 minutes.
2. Add the sake, curry powder, salt, and sugar, simmering for 5 minutes. Remove from heat.
3. Slice the chicken into thin shreds. Place the chicken in a bowl and stir in the egg white and cornstarch. Set aside.
4. In another bowl, whisk together the whole egg and the sesame oil.
5. In a small pan, bring 2 cups of water to a boil. Toss in the chicken mixture and cook for 20 seconds. Remove the chicken with a slotted spoon and drain the pan. Add the chicken to the broth-corn mixture. Gradually whisk in the sesame oil mixture. Take off heat and allow to sit briefly. Garnish with scallions and serve.

"Curry Powder" and "Garam Masala"

Curry powder is actually a blend of spices, invented by the British to resemble one of the famous masalas (spice blends) of India. In addition to ground coriander, cumin, mustard seed, turmeric, and other spices, good blends contain ground, dried curry (or kari) leaves, a typical spice of southwestern India. Garam masala (which means "hot spices") is also a mixture of spices used in Indian cooking, and is available premade in specialty stores and many supermarkets. It is usually a combination of spices such as cardamom, cinnamon, cloves, nutmeg, cumin, and peppercorns; but, like curry, there is no standard blend.

North African Chicken Soup with Fruit and Nuts

1 (4–pound) whole chicken
1 onion
3 cloves garlic (**or** 2 teaspoons roasted garlic)
1 cup diced dried apricots
   (unsulfured is best; they are
   dark brown)
4-inch piece ginger
4 tablespoons olive oil
1 teaspoon turmeric

1 teaspoon cinnamon
1 dash of ground cloves
5 cups Basic Chicken Broth
   (see recipe on page 5)
½ cup raisins (golden or brown)
1 teaspoon saffron
5 ounces uncooked couscous
½ cup sliced almonds
Harissa (optional)

1. Cut the chicken into serving pieces (such as breasts and thighs). Finely chop the onion and cloves. Peel the ginger (removing the thinnest layer possible) and finely chop or grate the root. Dice the dried apricots.

2. Heat the oil in a large saucepan. Brown the chicken parts for 10 to 12 minutes. Using a slotted spoon, remove them from the pan and reserve. Drain all but 2 tablespoons of fat from the pan.

3. Over medium heat, sauté the onion and garlic in the pan with the chicken fat for 3 minutes. Stir in the ginger, turmeric, cinnamon, and cloves, and cook for 1 minute.

4. Add the broth to the pan. Using a wooden spoon, scrape the bottom of the pan to loosen all the cooked-on bits. Add the apricots, raisins, saffron, and the reserved chicken. Bring to a medium simmer, cover, and cook for 45 to 60 minutes. Take off the heat.

5. Using a slotted spoon, remove the chicken pieces, discarding the skin and the bones. Remove all visible fat from the pan. Coarsely chop the chicken and set aside.

6. Add the couscous to the pan, replace the lid, and let stand for 5 minutes. Add the chicken and stir well. Replace the cover and let stand for 1 to 2 more minutes, off the heat.

7. Garnish with the almond slices and a very small dollop of the harissa, and serve.

Lime and Chicken Soup

3 limes
1 jalapeño chili
1 tablespoon minced cilantro,
*   plus 6 sprigs*
1 tomato
1 red onion
¼ pound (4 ounces) mild
*   yellow cheese*
2 corn tortillas
½ pound (8 ounces) uncooked
*   chicken breast*

5 cups Basic Chicken Broth
*   (see recipe on page 5)*
1 teaspoon oregano
1 teaspoon basil
1 bay leaf
Freshly ground black pepper
Salt

Serves 6

Chicken is perhaps the most dangerous raw meat. To prevent salmonella and other bacteria from being transmitted, thoroughly wash your hands and all utensils before and after handling it.

1. Juice 2 of the limes and cut the remaining lime into thin slices. Mince the jalapeño and the cilantro. Chop the tomato and the red onion. Cube the cheese. Cut the tortillas into strips.
2. Place the chicken in a large saucepan. Cover with water, bring to a boil, and cook for 5 minutes (blanching the chicken). Remove it to a plate and slice it into very, very thin strips, or shred it.
3. In a soup pot, combine the broth, lime juice, oregano, basil, jalapeño, bay leaf, and pepper. Bring to a boil, reduce to a simmer, and cook for 10 minutes.
4. Add the chicken, tomato, red onion, cilantro, and salt to taste. Bring to a boil, then reduce to a simmer and cook for 10 minutes. Remove the bayleaf.
5. Garnish with cheese cubes, slices of tortilla and lime, and cilantro sprigs.

Turkey Leftovers in Bread Bowls

Serves 6

Don't have time to make a bread bowl? Your local bakery should carry loaves to use instead.

2 teaspoons sugar
1⅓ cups warm water
1 envelope (or 2½ teaspoons) rapid-rise yeast
2 cups whole-wheat flour
1 cup bread flour (high gluten)
1½ cups white flour
2 eggs, separated
⅔ cup grated Monterey jack cheese

¼ cup cold water
4 cups chopped cooked turkey
4 cups Giblet Broth **or** Basic Chicken Broth (see recipes on pages 11 and 5)
Leftover vegetables, chopped (optional)
Salt and pepper

1. Using a small bowl, combine the sugar and the warm water. Shake in the yeast and let it sit at room temperature for 5 minutes.
2. In a large bowl, combine 1 cup of the wheat flour, all of the bread flour, and 1 cup of the white flour. Make a well in the center.
3. Whisk the egg yolks (reserving the whites); then add them to the yeast mixture. Add the cheese. Pour this mixture into the well of the flour mixture. Stir only enough to combine, adding more of the whole-wheat flour and white flour in equal measures until the dough is stiff. Punch it down.
4. Flour a wooden board. On it, knead the dough until it is smooth. Put it into a buttered or oiled bowl. Cover it with a towel and place it in a warm place to rise for 30 minutes. Punch down the dough and knead again for 5 minutes. Divide the dough into 6 portions. Refrigerate briefly (or up to 3 days).
5. Preheat the oven to 425 degrees. Roll out the dough into rough circles, about ¼-inch thick. Select 6 ovenproof soup bowls and butter the *outsides* of them. Put a bowl in the center of a round of dough. Pull the dough up around the bowl, completely covering the outside of it. Press the dough into place, but do not secure over the lip of the bowl (the bowls will be removed after baking). Repeat this process with each bowl and round of dough. Turn the bowls upside down on a cookie sheet.

(continued)

6. In a small bowl, whisk the egg whites and the cold water together. Brush half of this mixture lightly over all of the dough surfaces. Bake the bowls for 15 minutes.
7. Meanwhile, combine the meat, broth, and vegetables (if using) in a pot and bring to a simmer over medium heat. Add salt and pepper to taste.
8. Once the bread bowls are done cooking, slide the soup bowls out of the bread bowls. Return the bread bowls to the oven, empty side up, brushing the inside surface with the rest of the egg white mixture. Cook for 6 more minutes.
9. Fill the bread bowls with the turkey soup and serve immediately.

Chicken Chili

4 cups cooked chicken (**or** turkey)
1 large onion
1 tomato
2 tablespoons chopped cilantro
1 teaspoon chopped basil
2 cloves garlic
¼ cup olive oil

3 cups Basic Chicken Broth (see recipe on page 5)
2 teaspoons chili powder
1 pinch of ground cloves
2 (15- to 16-ounce) cans white beans, rinsed and drained
Tortilla chips

Serves 6

Garnish with the tomato and serve with tortilla chips on the side.

1. Cut the meat into ½-inch cubes. Chop the onion, tomato, and herbs. Finely dice the garlic.
2. Heat the oil in a soup pot on medium heat. Add the onion and garlic; cook on medium for about 3 minutes, lowering the heat as necessary to make sure the garlic doesn't burn.
3. Add all the other ingredients except for the tomato and the tortilla chips. Bring to a boil, reduce to a simmer, and cook on low for 1 hour (checking frequently to make sure the beans do not burn).

Turkey Chowder

Serves 10

To reduce fat, use flavored vinegars when sautéing meats and vegetables. They will add flavor to the dish and tend to blend well with almost any recipe.

1 onion
2 stalks celery
1 green bell pepper
3 carrots
3 russet potatoes
2 tablespoons butter
*2 cups Giblet Broth **or** Basic Chicken Broth (see recipes on pages 11 and 5)*
3 cups cooked turkey, cubed
1 cup corn kernels

3 cups milk
¾ teaspoon thyme
Salt and pepper
Fresh chopped parsley (optional)

1. Thinly slice the onion and celery, chop the bell pepper, slice the carrots, and dice the potatoes.
2. In a soup pot, heat the butter on medium heat. Add the onion and green pepper, sautéing for 4 minutes. Add the broth and the carrots, bring to a boil, reduce to a simmer, and cook for 5 more minutes.
3. Add the potatoes and celery, simmering the mixture for an additional 10 minutes.
4. Stir in the turkey, corn kernels, milk, and thyme; salt and pepper to taste. Heat gently, but thoroughly. Garnish with parsley and serve.

Lemon Chicken and Okra Soup

1 broiler chicken, (2½ pounds)
Juice of 2 lemons
6 cups Basic Chicken Broth
   (see recipe on page 5)
1 large onion, peeled and chopped
3 medium tomatoes, peeled and
   chopped

1 (6-ounce) can tomato paste
2 cups sliced okra
⅓ cup uncooked long-grain rice
2 teaspoons salt
¼ teaspoon pepper
½ teaspoon ground red pepper
1 teaspoon ground turmeric

> **Serves 4**
>
> Out of chicken broth? Not to worry, the chicken in this soup will flavor the water.

1. Cut up the chicken into serving pieces (wings, legs, etc.). Rub lemon juice over the chicken pieces. Put the chicken in a large kettle with the broth. Bring to a boil, then simmer covered for 15 minutes.
2. Add all the remaining ingredients and simmer for 30 more minutes, until the chicken and rice are tender. Remove the chicken pieces with a slotted spoon; skin and debone them. Dice the meat and return to the kettle. Serve.

Curried Chicken Soup

1 tablespoon butter
1 teaspoon curry powder
¾ tablespoon flour
1½ cups Basic Chicken Broth
   (see recipe on page 5)
Paprika

1 egg yolk
¼ cup whole milk
¼ cup cooked chicken, cut into
   small pieces
Fresh chopped chives
   (optional)

> **Serves 2**
>
> If you transfer the egg back and forth between your cracked shells, the yolk with separate itself out.

1. Melt the butter in a saucepan. Add the curry and the flour and stir, cooking for 1 to 2 minutes. Pour in the broth and bring to a boil. Add paprika to taste. Turn the heat down to low.
2. In a small bowl, beat together the egg yolk and the milk. Gradually whisk this into the broth mixture. Stir in the chicken and heat on low for 5 minutes. Garnish with chives and serve.

Thanksgiving Turkey and Bacon Soup

8 slices bacon
6 cups Giblet Broth **or**
  Basic Chicken Broth
  (see recipes on pages 11
  and 5)
½ cup uncooked rice (any kind)
5 scallions, finely chopped
½ cup butter
¾ cup white flour
Salt

¼ teaspoon pepper
2 cups milk (any strength)
1½ cups cubed cooked turkey
3 tablespoons sherry

1. Cook the bacon; then lay it on paper towels to absorb the grease.
2. In a soup pot, combine the broth, rice, and scallions. Bring to a boil, reduce to a simmer, and cook 30 minutes.
3. In a large saucepan, heat the butter on medium-low heat. Whisk in the flour, salt to taste, and pepper, stirring for 1 minute.
4. Remove from heat, drizzle in the milk, and return to low heat. Stir until the mixture has thickened slightly.
5. Gradually stir the milk mixture into the rice mixture; stir in the sherry. Add the turkey. Crumble in the bacon; mix well and serve.

Chicken and Coconut Soup

3 pounds chicken

8 slices galangal (also called Thai ginger)

3 stalks lemongrass

8 chili peppers (red or green)

1 lemon

½ of an egg white

2 teaspoons cornstarch

4 cups Basic Chicken Broth (see recipe on page 3)

3 cups coconut milk

4 tablespoons fish sauce (Thai **or** Vietnamese)

½ teaspoon sugar

Salt

1 cup peanut oil

1 teaspoon black pepper

Coriander leaves

> **Serves 6–8**
>
> To add a flavorful twist to this recipe, substitute Thai broth (see page 14) for a basic chicken broth.

1. Cut the chicken into thin strips. Slice the galangal. Slice the bottom 6–8 inches of the lemon grass, on the diagonal. Seed and coarsely chop the chilies. Juice the lemon.
2. In a bowl, mix together the chicken strips, egg white, and cornstarch. Refrigerate for 30 minutes.
3. Pour the chicken broth into a soup pot. Add the galangal, lemon grass, and chilies. Bring to a boil, cover, reduce to a simmer, and cook for 10 minutes. Remove the cover and stir in the coconut milk, fish sauce, sugar, and salt to taste, then simmer for 15 more minutes.
4. Meanwhile, using a skillet or wok, heat the peanut oil. Stir in the chicken pieces, separating them, and cooking just until they turn white. Drain.
5. Pour the broth mixture into individual bowls. Divide the chicken pieces among them. Sprinkle each bowl with lemon juice, pepper, and coriander leaves.

Low-Fat Chicken

Nearly all of the fat in a chicken comes from its skin. You can buy preskinned chicken breasts in the grocery store, but it's simple to peel the skin off yourself before cooking. Choose white meat over dark for the leanest meal.

Hearty Winter Chicken and Noodle Soup

3 chicken quarters
(about 2 pounds total)
4 cups water
½ cup chopped celery,
plus 2 stalks, thinly sliced
2 tablespoons fresh chopped
parsley
1 teaspoon salt
1 teaspoon dried thyme,
crushed
¼ teaspoon pepper

1 bay leaf
4 medium carrots, sliced
3 medium onions, chopped
3 cups packaged dried wide
noodles
2 cups milk, divided
1 cup frozen peas
2 tablespoons all-purpose flour

1. Skin the chicken. Rinse the chicken and pat it dry with paper towels. Place the chicken, water, ½ cup chopped celery, parsley, salt, thyme, pepper, and bay leaf in a large Dutch oven. Bring to boiling; reduce heat. Simmer, covered, for 30 minutes.
2. Add the sliced celery, carrots, and onions; simmer, covered, for another 30 minutes, or until the chicken is tender and no longer pink. Remove from heat. Discard the bay leaf. Remove the chicken with a slotted spoon; let cool slightly. Debone the chicken; discard the bones. Chop chicken and set aside.
3. Heat the soup to boiling. Add the noodles; cook for 5 minutes. Stir in 1½ cups of the milk and the peas. Combine the remaining milk and the flour in a screw-top jar. Cover and shake until smooth; stir into the soup. Cook, stirring, until thickened and bubbly. Stir in chicken. Cook for 1 to 2 minutes more, or until heated through.

Quick Turkey Cassoulet

3 slices of bread (**or** 1 cup
    premade bread crumbs)
2 teaspoons olive oil
2 onions, chopped
1 carrot, chopped
2 cloves garlic, finely chopped
¼ pound turkey kielbasa
    sausage, thinly sliced
1½ cups diced cooked white
    turkey
1 (16-ounce) can Great
    Northern beans, drained
    and rinsed

1 (28-ounce) can whole toma-
    toes, drained and coarsely
    chopped
1 cup Basic Chicken Broth
    (see recipe on page 5)
½ cup dry white wine **or** dry
    red wine
1½ teaspoons chopped fresh
    thyme
½ teaspoon salt
½ teaspoon freshly ground
    black pepper

> **Serves 4**
>
> Save yourself some time by substituting 1 cup of premade bread crumbs for your 3 slices of bread.

1. Preheat oven to 350 degrees. Tear the bread into pieces and spread them on a baking sheet; bake for 6 to 8 minutes, stirring occasionally, until crisp and lightly colored. Set aside.
2. In a Dutch oven or flameproof casserole dish, heat the oil over medium heat. Add the onions, carrot, and garlic; cook, stirring, until the onions begin to soften, about 5 minutes. Add the kielbasa and cook, stirring, until it is lightly browned, about 5 minutes longer. Add the turkey, beans, tomatoes, chicken stock, wine, thyme, salt, and pepper. Bring the mixture to a simmer.
3. Sprinkle the cassoulet with the bread crumbs and bake for 20 to 30 minutes, or until browned and bubbling.

Chicken Ragout

Serves 4–6

This recipe can also be used as a sauce for your favorite homemade pizza or eaten with pasta.

2 tablespoons olive oil
1½ pounds boneless, skinless chicken thighs, cut in ½-inch pieces
¼–½ pound (4–8 ounces) Italian sausages, casings removed
½ of a medium-sized white onion, chopped
2 stalks celery, finely diced
2 carrots, peeled and finely diced
1 large clove garlic, minced

1 bay leaf
1 cup dry Marsala wine
½ pound fresh mushrooms, sliced
1 (14- to 16-ounce) can crushed tomatoes
1 cup Basic Chicken Broth (see recipe on page 5)
1 tablespoon tomato paste
3 generous pinches of ground cloves

1. Heat the oil in a large skillet over medium-high heat. Add the chicken thighs and Italian sausage. Stir, breaking up the sausage into small pieces; cook until the chicken is browned and the sausage is no longer pink. Add the onion, celery, carrots, garlic, and bay leaf, and continue to cook until the onion is softened. Stir in the Marsala. Bring to a boil, scraping up any brown bits that are stuck to the bottom of the skillet. Reduce the heat and simmer until half of the liquid has evaporated (about 15 minutes).
2. Transfer this mixture to a Dutch oven. Mix in the mushrooms, tomatoes, chicken stock, tomato paste, and cloves. Bring to a boil, then reduce heat and simmer, stirring occasionally, for 45 minutes. Remove bay leaf.

German Potato Soup with Ha

Serves 6

Potato skins contain many vitamins not found in the "meat" of the potato. Unless your recipe calls for a clean, "white" look, leave the skins on.

1 onion
3 leeks
2 pounds potatoes (any kind)
3 tablespoons butter
1/4 teaspoon thyme
6 cups Basic Chicken Broth
   (see recipe on page 5)
   or water
1 meaty ham bone

1/2 pint cream
White pepper
Salt

1. Slice the onion, the white part of the leeks, and the potatoes.
2. In a soup pot, heat the butter on medium. Add the onions and cook for 3 minutes. Add the broth, leeks, potatoes, ham bone, and thyme. Bring to a boil, reduce to a simmer, and cook for 15 to 18 minutes.
3. Remove the soup pot from the heat and take out the ham bone. Cut the meat off the bone; discard the bone and shred the meat. Set aside.
4. Using a blender or food processor, purée the broth mixture. Return it to the pot, add the ham pieces, and reheat. Drizzle in the cream, season with pepper and salt, and serve.

 Common Vegetable Cuts
JULIENNE *are thin matchsticks, 1/8" × 1/8" × 1 1/2"*
BATONS *are larger sticks, 1/4" × 1/4" × 2"*
DICE *are cubes of 1/4" × 1/4" × 1/4" (small dice are called brunoise, and larger dice are usually just called cubes)*

Chinese Corn and Ham Soup

4 ears corn (white if possible)
½ cup minced ham
4 egg whites
3 tablespoons milk
5 cups Basic Chicken Broth
   (see recipe on page 5)
Salt

3 tablespoons cornstarch
3 tablespoons water
1 teaspoon sesame oil

> **Serves 6–8**
>
> Feel free to substitute canned or frozen corn in any recipe calling for fresh corn. It holds up well even over several hours of cooking.

1. Shuck the corn and remove the silk. Cut the kernels off the cobs with a sharp knife, discarding the cobs (or freeze them for use in making broth another day). Mince the ham.
2. In a bowl, beat the egg whites until they are frothy. Beat in the milk. Set aside.
3. Pour the broth into a soup pot and bring it to a boil. Sprinkle in some salt, add the corn kernels, and bring to a boil again. Simmer for 5 minutes, covered.
4. In a small bowl, whisk together the cornstarch, water, and sesame oil. Drizzle this mixture into the corn mixture and stir until the soup is both thick and clear.
5. Take off heat. Drizzle in the egg white mixture, stirring constantly. Stir in the ham and serve.

 Common Vegetable Cuts
CHOPPED items are cut roughly into small pieces, using a knife or food processor
SLICES are ⅛-inch thick unless otherwise specified

Scandinavian Pork and Pea Soup

Serves 8

To keep onions from making your eyes tear, peel the onions in the sink with cold water running over them.

1 pound yellow split peas, rinsed

6 cups water

2 pounds lean bacon

3 medium carrots, peeled and diced

1 celery stalk, finely diced

4 medium leeks, peeled and chopped (white and light green parts only)

2 medium onions, peeled and halved

½ teaspoon dried thyme

1½ teaspoons salt

¼ teaspoon freshly ground black pepper

1 pound pork sausage links, cooked and drained

1. Soak the peas in cold water according to package directions. Put the peas in a large kettle with 6 cups of water. Cook slowly, covered, for about 1½ hours, until tender.

2. Meanwhile, put the bacon, carrots, celery, leeks, onions, thyme, salt, and pepper in another kettle. Cover with water. Cook slowly, covered, for 40 minutes, until the vegetables and bacon are tender. Remove the bacon; slice and keep warm. Using a slotted spoon, remove the vegetables and add them to the cooked split peas; add some of the broth in which the vegetables were cooked, if desired, to thin the soup.

3. Reheat, if necessary. Ladle the soup, including the vegetables, into wide soup plates and serve the sliced bacon and the cooked sausage links separately on a platter.

Portuguese Kale Soup

1 pound kale
1 pound small red potatoes
1 cup chopped onions
½ cup chopped carrots
3 pounds tomatoes
2 cloves garlic
1 pound chorizo sausage
1 tablespoon vegetable oil

2 tablespoons butter
8 cups Basic Chicken Broth
*   (see recipe on page 5)*
Salt and pepper

Serves 6–8

For variety, feel free to substitute ½ pound of cabbage for half the kale, and 1 cup dry, red kidney beans (soaked overnight) for half the sausage.

1. Strip the kale leaves off their stems and cut diagonally into wide slices. Dice the potatoes. Chop the onions and carrots. Peel, seed, and chop the tomatoes. Mince the garlic. Prick the sausage and boil it in water for 5 to 10 minutes to release the fat; drain and cut it into ½-inch slices.

2. In a soup pot, heat the oil and butter together. Sauté the onions, carrots, and garlic for 3 to 5 minutes on medium heat. Add the broth and potatoes, bring to a boil, reduce to a simmer, and cook for 15 to 20 minutes.

3. With a masher or the back of a cooking spoon, mash most of the potatoes against the side of the pot.

4. Add the tomatoes and simmer for 10 to 15 minutes. Add both the kale and the sausage slices, cooking for another 5 to 10 minutes. Salt and pepper to taste.

Split Pea Soup

1 pound dried green split peas
2 tablespoons olive oil
1 medium onion, finely diced
2 carrots, peeled and diced
2 celery stalks, diced
2 cloves garlic, minced
½ teaspoon thyme
1 teaspoon black pepper
1 teaspoon Worcestershire
  sauce
½ teaspoon Tabasco sauce

2 bay leaves
2 whole cloves
2 pounds ham hocks
1 pound baking potatoes,
  peeled and diced
Salt and pepper

1. Rinse the split peas; soak them overnight in enough water to cover.
2. Heat the oil in a soup pot over medium heat. Add the onions, carrots, celery, garlic, thyme, pepper, Worcestershire, and Tabasco; sauté over medium heat for 5 minutes. Add the split peas along with their soaking liquid, the bay leaves, cloves, ham hocks, and potatoes to the soup pot and bring to a boil. Skim off any foam that appears on the surface. Reduce the heat and simmer gently for 2 hours.
3. Remove the ham hocks and allow them to cool. Cut the meat into small cubes and add to the pot. Add salt and pepper to taste. Remove bay leaves before serving.

Basque Bean Soup with Sausage

1 pound (16 ounces) white
   pea beans
1 onion
4 white turnips
6 potatoes
4 carrots
4 leeks
7 cloves garlic
1 small head white cabbage
½ pound (8 ounces) dried
   peas (green **or** yellow)

1 meaty ham bone
2 bay leaves
2 whole cloves
Basic Vegetable Broth
   (see recipe on page 6)
Salt
1 teaspoon thyme
12 small cooked sausages
Swiss cheese, grated (optional)

Serves 6

For a quicker soak, put all the beans in approximately 6 cups of water, bring it to a boil, and then set aside for 1 hour.

1. Soak the beans overnight in cold water, then drain.
2. Chop the onion. Cut the turnips and potatoes into small pieces. Slice the carrots and leeks (white and light green parts only), mince the garlic, and shred the cabbage.
3. Place the beans, peas, ham bone, bay leaves, cloves, and onion in a large soup pot. Add enough broth to cover all the ingredients by 3 inches. Bring to a boil, reduce to a simmer, and cook for 1 hour. Remove ham bone and allow it to cool slightly.
4. Add the turnips, potatoes, carrots, leeks, garlic, and thyme. Bring to a boil, reduce to a simmer, and cook for 15 minutes. Meanwhile, tear the meat off the ham bone, chop it, and set aside.
5. Add the cooked sausages, cabbage, and ham meat, simmering for 12 minutes. Discard bay leaves. Garnish with Swiss cheese and serve.

Pumpkin and Chili Soup

Serves 4–6

Can't find a 4-pound pumpkin? You can substitute one 29-ounce can of pumpkin, unseasoned—it won't affect the flavor.

1 (4-pound) pumpkin
¼ pound bacon (**or** ham)
2–3 Serrano chilies (**or** other medium-hot chilies)
2 onions
1 tablespoon butter
2 teaspoons cumin

9 cups Basic Chicken Broth (see recipe on page 5)
1½ cups grated Swiss, Havarti, **or** Muenster cheese
3 tablespoons chopped parsley

1. Cut the pumpkin in half and scrape out the seeds and slimy threads. Quarter it and remove all peel and stalk. Cut the pumpkin flesh into very small pieces. Chop the bacon (or ham). Remove the seeds from the chilies and mince the flesh. Chop the onions.
2. In a soup pot, warm the butter and sauté the chopped bacon on medium until almost crisp. Add the onions and sauté for about 5 minutes. Add the pumpkin, chilies, cumin, and broth. Bring to a boil; reduce to a simmer and cook for 20 minutes.
3. As it cooks, grate the cheese and chop the parsley. Make sure the soup is warmed through but not boiling when you add them.

Corn and Bacon Soup

5–6 medium ears corn
   (to make about 3½ cups
   kernels)
4 strips bacon
2 medium leeks
¾ pound red **or** Yukon gold
   potatoes
2 tablespoons chopped parsley

1 tablespoon oil
1½ cups milk
2 tablespoons pimentos **or** thin
   strips of red bell pepper

Serves 4–6

For a quicker version, use 3½ cups of frozen corn kernels boiled for several minutes in 3 cups of water. Then move on to step 2.

1. Using a large saucepan, place the husked ears of corn and enough cold water to cover them. Bring to a boil; then reduce to a simmer and cook for 20 minutes. Reserve 3 cups of the cooking liquid (and freeze the rest if you like). After the corn cools slightly, use a sharp knife to slice off the kernels. (Freeze the cobs, if you like, for making vegetable stock another day.)

2. Slice the bacon strips into small pieces. Slice the leeks thinly. Peel the potatoes and dice them into ½-inch cubes. Chop the parsley.

3. In a soup pot, heat the oil. Sauté the bacon over medium heat for 3 minutes. Add the leek slices and cook, stirring occasionally, for about 1 to 2 minutes.

4. Add the reserved corn broth and potatoes. Bring to a boil, then reduce to a simmer, and cook for 15 minutes.

5. Heat the milk slightly; add it to the soup pot, along with the corn kernels and pimentos. Simmer very gently for about 10 more minutes. Add the parsley.

Spring Mixed Greens Soup

3 russet potatoes
8 cups mixed greens (wild ones such as chicory, burdock, dandelion, etc., and others such as beet tops, spinach, chard, etc.)
1 yellow onion
10 scallions
½ cup chopped dill
¼ cup chopped flat-leaf parsley
2 ham hocks
2 bay leaves
½ cup light crea

1. Peel and dice the potatoes. Tear the greens into pieces. Chop the onion and the scallions (white and green parts). Chop the dill and parsley.
2. Place the ham hocks in a soup pot and cover with cold water. Bring to a boil, reduce to a simmer, and cook for 1 hour.
3. Make sure that you have 12 cups of cooking liquid from the ham hocks; if not, add more water. Discard the ham hocks.
4. Add the potatoes, mixed greens, onion, scallions, bay leaves, dill, and parsley to the soup pot with the ham hock broth. Bring to a boil, reduce to a simmer, and cook for 30 minutes, stirring occasionally. Discard the bay leaves. Garnish with a drizzle of cream and serve.

Midwestern Swedish Yellow Pea Soup

1 pound (16 ounces) dried
    whole Swedish yellow peas
    (split yellow peas can be
    substituted)
1 onion
4 medium russet potatoes
1½-pound pork loin (boneless)
12 cups Basic Chicken Broth
    (see recipe on page 5)

1 bay leaf
Salt and freshly ground black
    pepper

Serves 6–8

Split yellow peas can be substituted for the whole Swedish yellow peas.

---

1. Soak the dried peas overnight in cold water, then drain.
2. Chop the onion. Peel and quarter the potatoes.
3. Place the pork loin in a soup pot. Add the dried peas, onion, potatoes, chicken broth, and bay leaf. Bring to a boil, reduce to a simmer, and cook for 3½ to 4 hours. Skim off impurities as they form at the top.
4. Take the soup pot off the heat; remove the pork loin and potatoes using a slotted spoon. Once they have cooled slightly, shred the pork meat and chop the potatoes. Discard the bay leaf.
5. Add the meat and potatoes back to the soup pot and salt and pepper to taste. Reheat thoroughly, and serve.

White Bean and Ham Soup

Serves 6

Feel free to try this recipe with Beef or Vegetable Broth (pages 4 or 6).

¼ pound (4 ounces) ham
1 large carrot
1 onion
1 medium fennel bulb
6 cloves garlic
1 (14-ounce) can peeled
  tomatoes
2 tablespoons chopped sage
2 tablespoons olive oil

2 (16-ounce) cans cooked
  cannellini beans, drained
  and rinsed
4 cups Basic Chicken Broth
  (see recipe on page 5)
Pepper
Salt
Sage leaves (optional)

1. Slice the ham into thin strips, or dice it. Dice the carrot and onion. Chop the fennel and mince the garlic. Chop the canned tomato and the sage.
2. In a soup pot, heat the oil. Add the carrot, onion, fennel, and garlic, sautéing on medium for 5 minutes.
3. Stir in the beans, ham, chicken broth, tomato, sage, and pepper. Bring to a boil, reduce to a simmer, and cook for 20 minutes. Salt to taste and garnish with the extra sage leaves, if desired.

Puerto Rican White Bean and Sausage Soup

¾ pound (12 ounces) dried
   white beans
2 dry Spanish sausages
1 cup sliced banana squash
1 small yellow onion
3 scallions
2 tomatoes
2 teaspoons chopped oregano
½ of a red bell pepper
6 garlic cloves

10 cups water
⅛ teaspoon cayenne pepper
1 teaspoon white wine vinegar
Salt
1 teaspoon olive oil
⅓ cup Spanish sherry
5 cups Basic Chicken Broth,
   divided

Serves 4

Italian sweet sausage without fennel can be substituted for Spanish sausages.

1. Soak the beans overnight in cold water, then drain.
2. Slice the sausage into ¼-inch-thick pieces. Peel the squash and cut it into ¼-inch-thick pieces. Chop the yellow onion, scallions, tomatoes, and oregano. Mince the red bell pepper and 4 of the garlic cloves. Peel the remaining 2 garlic cloves, leaving them whole.
3. In a soup pot, combine the water, beans, whole garlic cloves, onion, cayenne, vinegar, and salt. Bring to a boil, reduce to a simmer, and cook for 30 minutes.
4. Meanwhile, heat the olive oil in a saucepan. Add the minced garlic and the sausage; sauté on medium for 4 minutes. Add the tomatoes, oregano, sherry, squash, and scallions. Pour in 1 cup of the ham broth, scraping up the brown bits from the bottom of the pan. When the bean mixture is done cooking, add this mixture to the soup pot.
5. Add the remaining 4 cups of ham broth to the soup pot. Bring to a boil, reduce to a simmer, and cook for 30 minutes.

Spanish Bean Soup with Sausage

Serves 8

Precook sausage in the microwave to reduce the fat content. If you like crispy sausage in recipes, brown it beforehand and add it to the recipe during the last half-hour.

1 cup (8 ounces) dried chickpeas (garbanzo beans)
1 beef bone
1 ham bone
8 cups water
1 chorizo (Spanish sausage)
1 pound potatoes
1 onion

4 tablespoons olive oil
1/4 pound (4 ounces) bacon
1 pinch of saffron threads
Salt

1. Soak the chickpeas overnight in cold water, then drain.
2. Place the two bones in a large soup pot; add the chickpeas and water. Bring to a boil, reduce to a simmer, and cook for 45 minutes.
3. Meanwhile, cut the chorizo into small pieces, and dice the potatoes and onion.
4. In a large saucepan or skillet, heat the oil. Sauté the bacon and onion on medium until the bacon is crisp. When the bone broth is done cooking, add the onion, bacon, potatoes, and saffron to the soup pot. Simmer for 15 minutes.
5. Remove the pot from the heat, stir in the sausage pieces, and salt to taste.

Texas Black-Eyed Pea Soup

2 cups dried black-eyed peas
1 pound ham
1 stalk celery
1 small onion
5 cloves garlic
2 serrano chilies
1 teaspoon minced thyme
2 tablespoons minced cilantro
¼ cup olive oil

12 cups Basic Chicken Broth
  (see recipe on page 5)
Salt and black pepper
Tabasco sauce
6 scallions (optional)

Serves 6

Black-eyed beans are actually legumes. You'll find them with the dried beans in your grocery store.

1. Soak the black-eyed peas overnight in cold water, then drain.
2. Dice the ham, celery, and onions. Chop the garlic, and seed the chilies, cutting them in half. Mince the thyme and cilantro.
3. Using a soup pot, heat the olive oil on medium. Add the ham, celery, onion, garlic, and chilies, sautéing for 4 minutes.
4. Pour in the chicken broth. Add the black-eyed peas and the thyme. Bring to a boil, reduce to a simmer, and cook for 1¼ hours.
5. Remove from the heat, add the cilantro, and cool slightly. Using a blender or food processor, purée until smooth. Add the salt, pepper, and Tabasco sauce to taste, and bring just to a simmer. Mince the scallions for garnish and serve.

Kielbasa and Bean Soup

1 pound (16 ounces) kielbasa
  sausage (low fat)
1 onion
1 stalk celery
2 (14½-ounce) cans whole
  tomatoes
2 teaspoons basil
1 teaspoon oregano
5 cloves garlic
½ chipotle pepper in adobo
  sauce

1 tablespoon olive oil
2 teaspoons thyme
5 cups Basic Chicken Broth
  (see recipe on page 5)
4 (15½-ounce) cans black
  beans, drained and rinsed
Salt and pepper

1. Thinly slice the sausage. Chop the onion and celery. Dice the canned tomatoes and mix with the basil and oregano. Mince the garlic. Drain and mince the chipotle.
2. Using a soup pot, heat the oil on medium. Add the onion, celery, and thyme, sautéing for 3 minutes. Add the garlic and cook for 1 additional minute.
3. Pour in the broth and scrape the bottom of the pan with a wooden spoon to loosen the cooked brown bits. Add the beans, tomatoes, kielbasa, and chipotle. Bring to a boil, reduce to a simmer, and cook for 20 minutes. Season with salt and pepper to taste, and serve.

CHAPTER 5
Beef, Veal, and Lamb Soups

Lamb and Barley Soup

2½ pounds lean lamb meat
3 tablespoons butter
2 onions
3 stalks celery
6 cups water

3 tablespoons fresh chopped parsley
1 cup pearl barley
1 bay leaf
Salt and pepper to taste

1. Cube the lamb meat. Slice the onion and coarsely chop the celery and parsley.
2. In a soup pot, heat the butter. Cook the lamb on medium–high heat for 3 minutes, turning the pieces to brown on all sides. Remove the lamb from the pot and set aside. Drain and discard all but 3 tablespoons of the fat.
3. Reheat the fat and sauté the onion on medium for 3 minutes. Add all of the ingredients, including the cooked lamb; bring to a boil, reduce to a simmer, and cook for 2 hours. Discard bay leaf.

Scotch Lamb Soup

2 cups cubed lean lamb meat
2 onions
2 tablespoons oil
8 cups water
1 bay leaf
2 stalks celery

4 medium potatoes
2 cups chopped cabbage
3 carrots
⅓ cup pearl barley
⅓ cup chopped parsley

1. Cube the lamb meat and chop the onions.
2. In a soup pot, heat the oil. Brown the lamb pieces on medium-high heat, turning them to brown on all sides. Add the water, bay leaf, and onion; bring to a boil, then reduce the heat to low and cook for 1½ hours.
3. Dice the celery and potatoes. Chop the cabbage and grate the carrots coarsely. Add the celery, potatoes, and barley, cover, and bring to a boil. Reduce to a simmer and cook for 15 minutes. Add the cabbage and cook for 10 to 15 minutes longer. Remove the bay leaf.

Lamb and Fennel Soup

2 pounds lamb ribs
4 cups Basic Chicken Broth
   (see recipe on page 5)
4 cups water
2/3 cup finely chopped fennel
   fronds
1/2 cup chopped flat-leaf parsley
1/2 an onion

2 1/4 pounds tomatoes
1/8 teaspoon red pepper
6 slices crusty Italian bread

Serves 6

If possible, try to get wild fennel fronds for this recipe. You'll notice that it adds flavor to the soup.

1. Trim off excess fat from the lamb ribs. Place the lamb in a soup pot and add the chicken broth and water; bring to a boil, then reduce to a simmer. For the first 30 minutes, regularly remove the impurities that rise to the top with a slotted spoon. Simmer for 1 1/2 hours.
2. Finely chop the fennel fronds. Coarsely chop the parsley, finely slice the onion, and chop the tomatoes. Add these ingredients to the pot, along with the red pepper.
3. Return to a boil, reduce to a simmer, and cook for an additional 30 minutes.
4. Remove the lamb, discarding the skin and bones. Cut the meat into bite-sized pieces and return them to the pot to rewarm. While it reheats, place a slice of the bread in the bottom of each individual soup bowl. Pour the soup over the bread and serve.

Irish Stew

4–6 cups Basic Chicken Broth **or** Scotch Broth (see recipes on pages 5 and 9)
2½ pounds lamb meat
2 onions
2½ pounds potatoes
Salt and pepper
2 tablespoons chopped parsley (optional)

1. Preheat the oven to 375 degrees. Trim off excess fat and cut the lamb into pieces, through the bones. Thinly slice the onions and potatoes.
2. Place these 3 ingredients in layers in an oven-ready casserole dish, sprinkling each layer with salt and pepper. A layer of potatoes should be on top.
3. Pour in enough broth to fill the casserole halfway up. Cover. Bake for 2 hours. Uncover and bake for an additional 30 minutes. Sprinkle with parsley and serve.

Apounduquerque Ground Beef and Pork Meatball Soup

¾ pound ground beef
¾ pound ground pork
⅓ cup uncooked rice
1 egg
1 teaspoon oregano
1 teaspoon pepper
2 tablespoons olive oil
1 medium onion, finely diced
1 clove garlic, crushed
½ cup tomato paste
10 cups Basic Beef Broth (see recipe on page 4)
½ cup chopped cilantro

1. In a bowl, combine the beef, pork, rice, egg, oregano, and pepper. Mold the mixture into meatballs about the size of golf balls.
2. In a soup pot, warm the oil. Sauté the onion on medium for 3 minutes. Add the garlic and sauté for an additional 2 minutes. Stir in the tomato paste. Pour in the broth. Bring to a boil, add the meatballs, and reduce to medium-low. Cook, covered, for 30 minutes. Stir in the cilantro and serve.

Beef Soup with Black Olives

4 pounds beef
3 yellow onions
3 carrots
2 cloves garlic
3 anchovy fillets
4 tablespoons olive oil, divided
1 tablespoon tomato paste
1 teaspoon black pepper
1 cup flour
1 cup dry red wine

4 cups Basic Beef Broth
  (see recipe on page 4)
1 tomato
8 black olives
2 tablespoons chopped parsley
1 teaspoon lemon juice

Serves 8

To serve, pour the soup into a bowl and then top each serving with a dollop of the olive mixture.

---

1. Cut the beef into 1½-inch cubes. Dice the onions and carrots. Mince the garlic and anchovies.

2. In a soup pot, warm 2 tablespoons of the oil on medium. Add the onions, carrots, and garlic, sautéing for 6 minutes. Add the anchovies, tomato paste, and pepper, cooking for 2 more minutes. Remove from heat.

3. Coat the beef with the flour. In a pan, heat the rest of the oil. On medium-high heat, brown the beef on all sides, turning several times. Drain the oil and discard.

4. Add the wine to the pan with the meat, stirring to loosen the cooked bits stuck to the bottom of the pan. Cook for 3 minutes. Add this and the beef broth to the soup pot with the vegetables. Simmer the mixture for 2 hours, checking to see if it needs more broth, wine, or water (or a combination of these) to keep the level of the liquid mostly covering the other ingredients.

5. Just before the soup is ready, coarsely chop the tomato, olives, and parsley; mix together, along with the lemon juice, and serve as a garnish.

New Mexican Beef Chili

Serves 8

Start out using about half the amount of chili powder listed, and add more to taste. Remember, too, that its strength will increase the longer the chili cooks.

3 pounds beef
2 onions
10 cloves garlic
7 fresh jalapeño peppers
¼ cup chili powder
2 tablespoons olive oil, divided
1 (28-ounce) can plum tomatoes
1 tablespoon red wine vinegar
  or red wine

6 cups water
4 cups cooked rice
Salt and pepper
Sour cream (optional)

1. Trim off the fat and cut the beef into ½-inch cubes; pat them dry with paper towels. Finely dice the onions and mince the garlic. Remove the stems and seeds, and mince the jalapeños.
2. In a dry saucepan, over medium heat, toast the chili powder for 1 minute or so, until the smell is heavenly. (Toast the entire ¼ cup of chili powder, or more, and reserve any that you don't use for guests to add as they like.)
3. In a large skillet, heat 1 tablespoon of the oil and brown the beef on all sides, turning several times. Drain off most of the fat and transfer the meat to a large stove-top ready casserole dish.
4. Warm the remaining tablespoon of oil in the skillet. Add the onions, garlic, and jalapeños. Cook them over medium heat for 3 minutes. Place them in the casserole dish with the meat. Stir in the chili powder and simmer everything for 2 minutes.
5. Pour in the plum tomatoes with their juice, the vinegar (or wine), and the water. Bring to a boil, reduce to a simmer, and cook, uncovered, for 1½ hours. About 15 minutes before the chili is done, add salt and pepper to taste.
6. Add some rice to each serving bowl and pour the chili over the top. Garnish with a dollop of sour cream if you like, and serve.

Beef and Onions in Red Wine Soup

1½ pounds beef
6 small yellow onions
2 tablespoons butter
2 teaspoons thyme
Pepper
2 tablespoons peanut oil
4 cups Red Wine Broth
(see recipe on page 15)

10 cremini **or** button mushrooms
2 tablespoons fresh chopped
chives

Serves 6

Don't be too impatient. The onions will take on a dark brown color when they're caramelized.

1. Cube the beef. Thinly slice the onions.
2. Heat the butter in a sauté pan. Add the onions and thyme. Over medium heat, cook for 3 minutes, stirring often. Continue cooking, stirring constantly, until the onions are caramelized. Add the pepper, cover, and set aside.
3. Preheat the oven to 500 degrees. In an oven-ready pan, warm the peanut oil. Over high heat on the stove top, brown the meat on all sides. Put the pan directly into the oven and roast for 20 minutes. Remove the pan from oven, cover loosely to keep warm, and set it aside.
4. Pour the red wine broth into a soup pot. While it is coming to a boil, cut the mushrooms into quarters and chop the chives. Add the mushrooms and simmer for 3 minutes. Add the chives and cook for another minute.
5. Rewarm the onions in the oven, then place them in a mound in the middle of each serving bowl. Place the meat pieces around one side of each bowl, along with the mushrooms. Pour the broth over the top.

Beef and Beer Stew with Dried Fruit

Serves 6–8

Coarsely chop the remaining parsley, sprinkle it over the top to garnish, and serve.

3 pounds beef
Salt and pepper
2 yellow onions
½ cup dried pineapple
½ cup dried apples
18 pearl onions
2 tablespoons butter
3 tablespoons peanut oil

1 cup Basic Beef Broth
   (see recipe on page 4)
10 sprigs flat-leaf parsley
2 sprigs thyme
3 cloves
1 bay leaf
2 bottles dark beer

1. Cut the beef into 1½-inch cubes; pat the beef dry with paper towels and lightly coat them with salt and pepper. Thinly slice the onions. Chop the dried fruits coarsely. Preheat the oven to 325 degrees.

2. Place the pearl onions in a small saucepan and add enough water to cover them. Bring to a boil; boil them for 1 minute. Drain the pan and rinse the onions under cold running water. Remove their skins and set them aside.

3. Heat the butter in a sauté pan. Add the yellow onions, stirring them almost constantly over medium heat until they are dark brown. Remove the pan from the heat, cover, and set aside.

4. Using a large oven-proof casserole dish, heat the oil over medium heat on the stove top. Brown the meat pieces on all sides, for about 8 minutes. Remove the pieces with a slotted spoon, reserving the cooking liquid in the pan. Set aside the meat.

5. Turn the heat to high and add the beef broth. With a wooden spoon, loosen the bits of cooked meat stuck to the bottom of the pan, incorporating them into the broth. Cook over medium heat for 3 minutes. Remove the pan from the heat.

6. Layer the beef, onions, dried fruits, and pearl onions into the pan, using about a third of each ingredient in each of three layers.

7. Make a bouquet garni (see "Bag o' Spices" on page 8) with half of the parsley, the thyme, cloves, and bay leaf. Slightly bury the spice bag in the center of the mixture.

8. Pour the beer over the mixture. Bring to a boil, then cover the pan and place it in the oven. Cook for 1 hour.

9. Remove the bouquet garni and the bay leaf.

White Bean and Lamb Soup

1 pound dried white beans
1 cup chopped onion
1 clove garlic
1½ cups diced tomatoes
6 sprigs parsley
2 tablespoons butter
1 pound lamb shanks
10 cups water
1 bay leaf

1 tablespoon thyme
2 whole cloves
20 black peppercorns
Dill (optional)

Serves 4–6

If substituting canned beans for dry beans, decrease the water by three cups per cup of beans. Add canned beans later; cook for about half the time you would dried beans.

1. Rinse the beans and soak them overnight; drain.
2. Coarsely chop the onion, mince the garlic, dice the tomatoes, and tie the parsley sprigs into a bundle.
3. In a soup pot, melt the butter. Add the onions, garlic, and the lamb. Sauté on medium heat for 5 minutes until the lamb is browned. Add the beans, water, tomatoes, bay leaf, parsley, thyme, cloves, and peppercorns. Bring to a boil, reduce to a simmer, and cook for 2 hours.
4. Remove the lamb from the pot, discarding the skin and the bones. Cut the meat into bite-sized pieces and return it to the pot. Discard the bay leaf and parsley sprigs. Reheat, then garnish with a bit of dill, if desired.

Beef and Vegetable Soup

1½ pounds beef short rib
1½ pounds stewing beef
¼ pound salt pork **or** uncut bacon
1 large yellow onion
1 large tomato
4 medium-sized sweet potatoes
3 scallions
1 large green pepper
½ pound fresh spinach
½ pound fresh kale

3 cloves garlic
2 tablespoons olive oil
12 cups water
½ teaspoon thyme
½ teaspoon pepper
1 (15½-ounce) can okra, drained

1. Cut the short rib into 3-inch pieces and the stewing beef into 2-inch cubes. Dice the onion and tomato, cube the sweet potatoes, and chop the scallions coarsely. Cut the green pepper into strips and trim the spinach and kale. Crush the garlic.
2. On medium-high heat, brown the pork and the short rib pieces on all sides. Add the stewing beef; brown it on all sides.
3. Add the water and bring it slowly to a boil. Add the thyme and pepper. Simmer it, covered, for 1 hour, frequently spooning off the impurities that rise to the top.
4. Meanwhile, heat the oil and sauté the onion, garlic, and scallions on medium for 3 to 5 minutes. Add the green pepper and cook for 1 additional minute. Set aside.
5. When the meat is ready, add the sautéed vegetables, along with the okra. Simmer for 30 minutes. Remove the short rib pieces and salt pork, and discard. Cool the soup to room temperature by placing the soup pot in a bath of ice water; then refrigerate for a few hours, or overnight. Remove the hardened fat layer that has formed on the top; reheat and serve.

Beef and Paprika Goulash

¾ pound sirloin
2 tablespoons peanut oil
2 cups finely chopped onion
2 cloves garlic, minced
1½ cups finely chopped red
   bell pepper

1 tablespoon paprika
   (any strength, to taste)
2 teaspoon caraway seeds
2 cups seeded and chopped
   tomatoes
Sour cream (optional)

Serves 4–6

You can substitute canned tomatoes for fresh ones. It can save you time, and won't affect the taste.

1. Trim the meat to cut off excess fat, then cube it into ½ -inch pieces.
2. In a soup pot, heat the oil. Add the beef, stirring often over medium heat, until it just begins to brown. Add the onion, garlic, and bell peppers. Sauté for 5 minutes, stirring often. Stir in the paprika and caraway seeds. Add the tomatoes, bring to a boil, and reduce to a simmer. Cook for 1 hour, stirring occasionally.
3. Ladle the soup into bowls and garnish with dollops of sour cream.

Minestrone with Meatballs

24 cooked meatballs
1 (15-ounce) can navy **or** other
   white beans, drained
1 tablespoon dried minced onion
1 teaspoon basil
1 bay leaf
2 cups Basic Beef Broth
   (see recipe on page 4)
2 cups water

1 cup ditali, orzo, **or** other
   pasta
1 (16-ounce) can diced tomatoes (liquid retained)
1 (10-ounce) package frozen
   mixed vegetables, thawed
1 teaspoon sugar

Serves 6

Frozen vegetables retain more natural nutrients than fresh vegetables due to the loss of nutrient value at room temperature once a vegetable is picked.

In a 4-quart saucepan, combine the meatballs, beans, onion, basil, bay leaf, broth, and water; bring to a boil. Add the pasta and cook for 15 minutes. Reduce to a simmer and add the tomatoes and their liquid, the vegetables, and sugar; heat through. Remove the bay leaf.

Moroccan Lamb and Garbanzo Bean Soup

¾ cup dried chickpeas (garbanzo beans)
4 (1-pound) lamb shanks (shoulder or neck can be substituted, as can 1¼ pounds lamb stew meat)
2 tablespoons ghee
2 onions, finely chopped
1 stalk celery, finely chopped
1 teaspoon turmeric
½ teaspoon (or to taste) cayenne pepper
1 teaspoon cinnamon

1 teaspoon finely chopped ginger root
1 pinch of saffron threads
8 cups any basic meat broth
¾ cup dried lentils, rinsed
6 tomatoes, seeded and coarsely chopped
2 tablespoons finely chopped parsley
½ cup finely chopped cilantro
1 cup plain yogurt
Salt and pepper

1. Soak the chickpeas overnight in cold water; drain.
2. In a soup pot, heat the ghee. On medium-high heat, lightly brown the lamb on all sides. Remove the lamb and set aside.
3. Add the onions and celery to the pot, sautéing for 3 minutes on medium heat. Add the turmeric, cayenne pepper, ginger, cinnamon, and saffron, stirring them in for another 3 minutes. Place the lamb back in the pot along with the chickpeas and the broth. Bring to a boil, reduce to a simmer, and cook for 1 hour. Regularly skim off and discard impurities that rise to the top.
4. Add the lentils and tomatoes and cook for another hour. Skim off any additional impurities as they form.
5. Using a slotted spoon, remove the bone if you are using one. Pull the meat off the bone, cube or shred it, and return it to the pot. Keep the soup pot on low heat. Stir in the parsley, cilantro, yogurt, and salt and black pepper to taste. Serve.

Italian Minestrone Cola Soup

2½-pound blade chuck roast
10 cups water
3 teaspoons salt, divided
1 small peeled onion, plus ¼
    cup diced onion
½ cup celery leaves
1 bay leaf
2 slices bacon, diced
½ cup chopped fresh green
    beans
½ cup green peas
½ cup thinly sliced zucchini
½ cup diced celery
½ cup thinly sliced carrots
¼ cup chopped parsley
1 clove garlic, minced
1 (6-ounce) can tomato paste
1 cup cola
1 tablespoon olive oil
1 tablespoon Worcestershire
    sauce
1½ cups (12 ounces) cooked
    kidney beans
½ cup dry elbow macaroni
1 tablespoon Italian seasoning
¼ teaspoon black pepper
Parmesan cheese, grated
    (optional)

Serves 12

While the parmesan cheese isn't a necessity for this soup, it will give it an added flavor—and flair!

1. In a large pan, combine the meat, water, 2 teaspoons of the salt, the whole onion, celery leaves, and bay leaf. Cover and simmer about 2½ hours until the meat is tender.
2. Remove the meat and finely dice it, discarding any fat and bones (should yield about 2 cups of meat). Strain the broth (should measure 8 cups). Add ice cubes to the broth to harden the fat; remove and discard the fat.
3. In a 5- to 6-quart kettle or Dutch oven, combine the beef broth and the meat; warm on low heat.
4. Pan-fry the bacon until crisp. Add the bacon and the drippings and all the remaining ingredients, *except* the parmesan cheese, to the broth. Cover and simmer for about 30 minutes, until the vegetables and macaroni are tender. Serve sprinkled with parmesan cheese, if desired.

Pepper Pot Soup

¼ pound salt pork

1½ pounds short rib of beef, cut into 3-inch pieces

1½ pounds stew beef, cut into 2-inch cubes

12 cups water

½ teaspoon dried thyme

1½ teaspoons salt

¼ teaspoon pepper

2 tablespoons olive oil

1 large onion, diced

2 cloves garlic, crushed

2 scallions, diced

1 large green pepper, cut into strips

1 (15½-ounce) can okra, drained

4 medium sweet potatoes, peeled and cubed

1 large tomato, peeled and cubed

½ pound fresh kale, washed and trimmed

½ pound fresh spinach, washed and trimmed

1. Place the salt pork and short rib pieces in a large kettle; brown the ribs on all sides. Add the stew beef and brown on all sides.
2. Add the water and slowly bring just to a boil. Using a spoon, skim off the fat that has risen to the top. Add the thyme, salt, and pepper; reduce to a simmer. Cook, covered, for 1 hour, occasionally skimming off any impurities.
3. While the meat is simmering, heat the oil in a skillet and sauté the onion, garlic, and scallions. Add the green pepper and sauté 1 minute more. Remove from heat and set aside.
4. After the meat is done cooking, add the sautéed vegetables and all the remaining ingredients, except the spinach, to the kettle. Continue to cook slowly, covered, for about 30 minutes, until the vegetables and meat are cooked. Remove from heat and cool slightly. Take out the short ribs and cut off and discard any fat. Cube the meat and return it to the kettle. Reheat the soup to serving temperature; then add the spinach and heat until the spinach has just wilted. Serve.

CHAPTER 6
Cheese, Cream, and Other Dairy Soups

Cream of Sorrel Soup

Serves 4

If you're looking for a nice change, replace the chicken broth with a vegetable broth in this soup.

2 cups sorrel leaves

2 tablespoons butter **or** vegetable oil

5 cups Basic Chicken Broth (see recipe on page 5)

½ cup whole milk **or** light cream

3 egg yolks

1 tablespoon of any fresh green herb, chopped

1. Tear the sorrel leaves away from the center rib and into a few larger pieces. Using an enamel or stainless steel soup pot, warm the oil, then add the sorrel, and stir until wilted down to about 3 tablespoons of leaves.

2. Add the stock and simmer for only about 2 minutes. Remove from heat and allow to cool very briefly. Using a wire whisk, lightly beat the egg yolks in a stainless steel bowl and mix in the cream. Temper this mixture by slowly adding about half of the hot broth to it, stirring constantly. Pour this mixture into the soup pot with the rest of the broth, making sure the mixture doesn't boil. Reheat on low. Garnish with a small amount of any green grass-style herb.

Cauliflower Cheese Soup

1 cup chopped onion
2 celery stalks
4 medium potatoes (russet or
    Yukon gold)
1 medium head cauliflower
2 cups shredded cheddar
    cheese
2 tablespoons butter
1 teaspoon curry powder
1 teaspoon mustard
1¼ cups skim milk

1½ cups peas
2 teaspoons dried dill
    (more if fresh)
¼ teaspoon dried rosemary
    (more if fresh)
Salt and pepper

Serves 8–10
If you can't find fresh peas, using frozen ones won't affect the taste in this recipe.

1. Chop the onion and dice the celery. Peel the potatoes and dice them into a ½-inch cubes. Finely chop the cauliflower. Grate the cheese.

2. In a soup pot, warm the butter on medium heat. Add the onion and celery, and sauté for 3 minutes. Add the potatoes and cauliflower. Pour enough water into the pot to cover all the ingredients. Add the curry and mustard. Bring the mixture to a boil, then reduce to a simmer and cook for 20 minutes.

3. Remove from heat and allow to cool slightly. Use a slotted spoon to remove the vegetables; working in batches, purée them. Add them back into the soup pot. With the pot still off the heat, stir in the milk gradually until the mixture is slightly thick.

4. Place the pot back onto low heat. Gradually sprinkle in the grated cheese, stirring until it just melts. Add the peas, dill, and rosemary, and cook for 5 to 10 minutes, until the peas are cooked.

5. Adjust the consistency with more milk, if necessary. Add salt and pepper to taste.

Cream of Asparagus Soup

1 pound asparagus
3 cups Basic Chicken Broth
  (see recipe on page 5)
2 cups water
3 tablespoons butter
3 tablespoons flour
¼ cup sherry **or** ⅓ cup
  white wine
1 small lemon

1 cup milk **or** half-and-half
Salt and pepper
Rye croutons (optional)

1. Trim off the woody ends of the asparagus. Chop the spears coarsely. (Discard the ends, or freeze them to use in making broth another day.)
2. In a soup pot, combine the broth, water, and asparagus. Bring to a boil, reduce to a simmer, and cook for 5 minutes. Keeping the liquids warm, carefully remove the asparagus using a slotted spoon. Once they have cooled, purée them in a blender or food processor. Return the puréed asparagus to the soup pot. Keep on very low heat.
3. In a saucepan, melt the butter. Sprinkle the flour over it, whisking the mixture constantly. Add the sherry (or wine), again whisking until it is smooth and bubbling slightly. Juice the lemon and mix it with about ½ cup of the asparagus liquid, then add this mixture to the saucepan. Slowly trickle the contents of the saucepan into the soup pot, stirring constantly. Simmer for 10 to 15 minutes.
4. Add the milk (or half-and-half) and salt and pepper to taste. Rewarm gently. Garnish with croutons and serve.

Cream of Onion Soup

2 cups milk
1 tablespoon oil **or** butter
5 cups minced yellow onion
2 teaspoons mustard (any kind)
2 tablespoons white **or** rye flour
3 cups water

1 teaspoon horseradish sauce
2 teaspoons total of pepper
(any kind), Worcestershire
sauce, **or** soy sauce
Salt to taste

> **Serves 6**
>
> A nut oil complements this soup recipe nicely. Or try a garnish of croutons and shredded cheese.

1. In a saucepan, warm the milk very slowly, up to just before the boiling point. Take the pan off the heat, keeping it covered.
2. In a soup pot, heat the oil. Stir in the onions and mustard. Cook on low heat for 15 minutes.
3. Sprinkle the flour over the onion mixture, whisking constantly. Add the water, hot milk, and the seasonings, and warm to serving temperature.

Cream of Carrot Soup

1 pound carrots
1 large onion
½ cup chopped celery
2 cups peeled and diced potato
1 clove garlic, minced
1 tablespoon olive oil

1 teaspoon sugar
4 cloves
Pepper
4 cups Basic Chicken Broth
(see recipe on page 5)
Salt

> **Serves 6**
>
> If you don't have a food processor handy, throw it all in a blender to purée.

1. Chop the carrots, onion, and celery. Peel and dice the potatoes.
2. In a soup pot, heat the oil. Add the carrots, onion, celery, potato, garlic, and sugar, and sauté on medium for 3 minutes. Reduce heat to low, cover the pot, and cook for 10 more minutes.
3. Uncover the pot and add the cloves, pepper, and chicken broth. Bring to a boil, reduce to a simmer, and cook 20 minutes.
4. Remove pot off the heat. Remove the cloves and allow the soup to cool slightly. Purée the soup in a food processor. Reheat and salt to taste.

Roasted Corn and Chipotle Chowder

Serves 12

Prepare the red bell peppers in advance. Store them covered with olive oil in a glass jar in your refrigerator.

5 ears fresh corn, husked
2 red bell peppers
7–8 small red new potatoes
2 small cans chipotle chilies, drained
2 tomatoes
1 medium-sized yellow onion
3 cloves garlic

6 slices bacon
3 tablespoons butter
8 cups Basic Chicken Broth
   (see recipe on page 5)
Salt and pepper
1½ cups crea

1. Using a heavy cast iron pan, roast the corn on the grill for 5 minutes, turning often. Cut the kernels off the cobs, setting the kernels and 3 of the cobs aside. Roast the red bell peppers on the grill or under the broiler, turning them a few times, until the skin is blackened, about 8 minutes. Put the peppers in a sealed plastic bag.

2. Quarter all but 3 of the potatoes. Cover the quartered potatoes with water in a pan and simmer for 15 minutes. Meanwhile, seed and dice the chipotle peppers, tomatoes, and the remaining potatoes. Chop the onion and mince the garlic. Remove the burnt skin from the bell peppers and cut the flesh into small pieces, discarding the core. When the potatoes are done, coarsely mash them; set aside.

3. In a soup pot, fry the bacon on medium heat until almost crunchy. Remove the bacon and set aside. Drain off and discard the grease.

4. In the pot, melt the butter. Add the onion and sauté for 3 minutes. Add the garlic, sautéing for 2 more minutes. Dice the bacon slices and add them to the pot.

5. Pour in the broth, the 3 reserved corn cobs (*not* the kernels), the diced potatoes, the mashed potatoes, the chilies, and the tomatoes. Bring to a boil, add salt and pepper to taste, reduce to a simmer, and cook for 20 minutes.

6. Remove the cobs from the soup and discard. Add the corn kernels, red pepper pieces, and cream. Heat thoroughly, and serve.

Cucumber and Buttermilk Soup

3 cucumbers
2 tablespoons fresh chopped
 dill
1 lemon
2 tablespoons butter

2 tablespoons flour
4 cups buttermilk
White pepper

Serves 4
To quickly seed the cucumber, cut it in half, lengthwise. Use a teaspoon to scoop out the seeds.

1. Peel the cucumbers and remove the heavily seeded core. Cut the flesh into slices. Chop the dill and juice the lemon.
2. In a soup pot, warm the butter and whisk in the flour, cooking for 3 minutes. Gradually whisk in the buttermilk. Bring almost to a boil. Add the cucumber slices and dill, simmering for 15 minutes.
3. Allow the soup to cool and then purée it in a food processor. Stir in the lemon juice and the white pepper. Reheat gently but thoroughly.

Italian Cheese Soup

3 eggs
3 tablespoons grated parmesan
 cheese

6 cups Basic Chicken Broth
 (see recipe on page 5)

Serves 4
When you pour the egg mixture into the hot broth, you'll see small pieces of cooked egg. In Italy, the pieces are called "rags."

In a soup pot, bring the broth to a boil, then reduce it to a simmer. In a small bowl, beat the eggs until they are frothy; stir in the cheese. Very gradually, stir the egg mixture into the broth and continue to stir for a couple of minutes, until the eggs have cooked. Serve.

Northwest Cream of Cauliflower Soup with Hazelnuts

1 pound (16 ounces) cauliflower
1 carrot
1 stalk celery
¼ of a small onion
Hazelnuts, shelled (to yield
* 1 tablespoon, chopped)*
2 tablespoons butter

4 cups Basic Chicken Broth
* (see recipe on page 5)*
1 cup milk
Salt and white pepper

1. Preheat oven to 275 degrees. Cut the cauliflower, carrots, and celery into 2-inch pieces. Chop the onion.
2. Roast the hazelnuts in the oven for 20 minutes. Rub them with a clean dishtowel to remove their skins. Chop them, along with the butter, in a food processor. Set aside.
3. In a soup pot, bring the chicken broth to a boil. Add the cauliflower, carrots, celery, and onion. Simmer for 12 minutes.
4. Remove from heat and allow to cool slightly. Transfer the vegetables and a small amount of the liquid to a blender or food processor; purée. Add the purée to the soup pot. Stir in the milk, salt, and white pepper, reheating gently but thoroughly.
5. Ladle the soup into bowls, garnish with some of the hazelnut butter, and serve.

Two Cheese Soup

½ cup finely chopped onion

½ cup finely chopped celery

½ cup finely chopped carrot

1 teaspoon fresh minced garlic

½ pound (8 ounces) Stilton cheese

½ pound (8 ounces) Monterey Jack cheese

2 tablespoons butter

1 bay leaf

⅓ cup flour

2 teaspoons cornstarch

3 cups Basic Chicken Broth (see recipe on page 5)

1 pinch of baking soda

1 cup whole milk

½ cup finely chopped broccoli florets

1 dash of cayenne pepper

¼ teaspoon black pepper

¼ cup chopped parsley (optional)

Serves 8

Stilton cheese is England's richest blue cheese. You'll find it in cheese shops and some supermarkets.

---

1. Finely chop the onion, celery, and carrot. Mince the garlic. Crumble both kinds of cheese.
2. Melt the butter on medium heat in a soup pot. Add the onion, celery, carrot, garlic, and the bay leaf. Sauté for 3 to 5 minutes.
3. Whisk in the flour and cornstarch, and cook for 2 minutes, stirring constantly. Pour in the broth. Add the cheese, baking soda, and milk. Stir well over low heat until the mixture thickens.
4. Add the broccoli and two types of pepper. Bring just to a boil, reduce to a simmer, and cook for 8 to 10 minutes. Chop the parsley for garnish. Remove the bay leaf and serve.

Tuscany Bread and Cheese Soup

1 large sourdough baguette
4 cloves garlic
3 tablespoons olive oil, divided
Salt
1 large Spanish onion
2 stalks celery
2 leeks
1 (28-ounce) can whole tomatoes, drained
2 teaspoons thyme
½ teaspoon black pepper

1 pinch of cayenne pepper
6 cups Roasted Vegetable Broth (see recipe on page 10)
2 tablespoons basil
½ cup parmesan cheese
½ cup flat-leaf parsley (optional)

1. Preheat the oven to 300 degrees. Cut the baguette into ½-inch-thick slices. Crush 1 clove of the garlic and rub the bread slices with it, then cut the bread into 1-inch cubes. In a bowl, toss the bread cubes with 1 tablespoon of the oil and a dash of salt. Place them, in a single layer, on a baking sheet; bake for 40 minutes. When they are done, take them out of the oven and set them aside.

2. Meanwhile, coarsely chop the remaining garlic, the onion, celery, and leek. Dice the tomatoes.

3. In a soup pot, heat the rest of the oil. Add the onion, celery, leeks, and garlic. Cook on low for 4 minutes. Stir in the thyme, black pepper, and cayenne pepper. Add the broth, tomatoes, and basil; bring to a boil, then reduce to a simmer and cook for 20 minutes.

4. Remove from heat and stir in the bread cubes. Let it sit, covered, for 5 minutes. Grate (or shave) the parmesan and chop the parsley for garnish.

Cheddar Cheese and Ale Soup

4 strips bacon
2 tablespoons butter
½ of a small yellow onion, diced
¼ cup white flour

4 cups Basic Chicken Broth (see recipe on page 5)
1 bottle ale
6 ounces cheddar cheese
White pepper

Serves 4

This soup is best made (and served!) with a light to amber ale.

1. In a saucepan, fry the bacon. Remove with a slotted spoon and allow to drain on paper towels. Discard half of the oil.
2. Add the butter and the onion to the pan, sautéing over medium heat for 5 minutes. Sprinkle in the flour and, stirring constantly, cook for 3 more minutes.
3. Add the broth, ale, cheese, and pepper, reheating gently but thoroughly. Ladle into bowls and garnish with the crumbled bacon.

Cream of Greens Soup

1 (10-ounce) package frozen spinach
1 green bell pepper
1 zucchini
2 tablespoons olive oil

4 cups Basic Chicken Broth (see recipe on page 5)
Pepper
½ cup whole milk
Salt

Serves 4

You can substitute 1 pound of fresh spinach or kale for this soup. To do so, simmer in the chicken broth for 10 minutes before starting to step 2 (in a separate pot).

1. Defrost the spinach, then squeeze out all excess moisture. Finely dice the green pepper and zucchini.
2. In a soup pot, heat the olive oil on medium. Add the bell pepper and sauté for 3 minutes. Add the spinach, chicken broth, and pepper. Bring to a boil, reduce to a simmer, and cook for 5 minutes. Drizzle in the milk, stirring constantly. Salt to taste and serve.

Creamy Turkey Soup

Serves 8

Two cups of cubed white meat chicken (cooked) works well in this recipe.

1 onion, chopped
2 cups cubed cooked turkey
1 bouquet garni (see "Bag o' Spices" on page 10)
3 tablespoons butter
3 tablespoons flour
½ cup sherry
4 cups Giblet Broth **or** Basic Chicken Broth (see recipes on pages 11 and 5)
1 cup milk
Salt and pepper

1. In a soup pot, melt the butter on medium heat. Sauté the onion for 3 minutes. Whisk in the flour and cook, stirring often, for 1 minute. Stir in the sherry and broth, and add the bouquet garni. Simmer the mixture for 30 minutes.
2. Take off heat. Remove and discard the herb bag. Allow the soup to cool slightly. Stir in the milk and the turkey, return to heat, and bring *almost* to a boil. Simmer for 1 minute. Salt and pepper to taste, and serve.

Rich Tomato Bisque

Serves 8

Garnish with your favorite croutons.

4 tablespoons butter
2 onions, chopped
2 cloves garlic, minced
1 (28-ounce) can whole tomatoes, liquid retained
1 (46-ounce) can tomato juice
2 bay leaves
1 (8-ounce) package cream cheese
2 cups half-and-half
Salt and pepper to taste

1. Melt the butter in a soup pot. Add the onions and garlic and sauté over medium heat until the onions are soft. Add the tomatoes and their liquid, the tomato juice, and bay leaves; simmer for 20 minutes, stirring constantly, chopping the tomatoes with the side of a spoon.
2. Remove from heat and let cool slightly. Discard the bay leaves. Purée the solids with some of the liquid in a blender or food processor, along with the cream cheese. Return to the soup pot. Add the half-and-half and salt and pepper to taste. May be served hot or cold.

Basque Squash and Chestnut Soup

2 medium-sized yellow onions
2 medium-sized butternut
   squashes
1 russet potato
7 cloves garlic
1 bouquet garni (see "Bag o'
   Spices" on page 10)
8 whole unshelled chestnuts
1 cup grated sheep's milk
   cheese (semisoft)
⅓ cup olive oil

8 cups Basic Chicken Broth
   (see recipe on page 5)
2 cups whole milk
1 teaspoon salt
White pepper

> **Serves 4–6**
>
> Let the cheese soften while preparing this soup. When the soup is finished, garnish with the softened, grated cheese and serve.

1. Cut the onions into thick slices. Peel and seed the squashes; then cut them into 1-inch chunks. Coarsely chop the potato and crush the garlic cloves. Prepare the bouquet garni using a variety of your choice of fresh herbs. Roast and shell the chestnuts, then slice them very thinly. Grate the sheep's milk cheese.
2. In a soup pot, heat the olive oil. Add the onions and sauté on medium heat for 2 minutes. Add the garlic, squash, and potatoes; sauté for 3 minutes.
3. Pour in the broth and milk and add the bouquet garni, salt, and white pepper. Bring to a boil, then reduce to a simmer and cook for 1 hour. Remove the herb bag.
4. Remove from heat and allow to cool slightly. Using a blender or food processor, purée the soup. Return it to the soup pot and bring to a boil, then add the chestnuts and heat thoroughly.

Blue Cheese Soup

Serves 8

For an elegant flair, add ⅓ cup of dry white wine.

2 tablespoons butter
½ cup finely chopped onion
½ cup finely chopped celery
½ cup finely chopped carrot
1 teaspoon minced garlic
⅓ cup flour
2 teaspoons cornstarch
3 cups Basic Chicken Broth
   (see recipe on page 5)
½ pound Stilton cheese,
   crumbled
½ pound cheddar cheese,
   crumbled

⅛ teaspoon baking soda
1 cup cream (heavy **or** light)
⅓ cup dry white wine
   (optional)
Salt
1 dash of cayenne pepper
¼ teaspoon freshly ground
   black pepper
1 bay leaf
¼ cup chopped fresh parsley
   (optional)

1. Melt the butter in a soup pot on medium heat, and add the onion, celery, carrot, and garlic. Cook until the vegetables are tender, about 8 minutes.
2. Whisk in the flour and cornstarch, stirring constantly; cook until it begins to bubble, about 2 minutes. Add the broth, the two cheeses, baking soda, cream, and wine (if using). Stir until smooth and thickened. Add the salt, cayenne, black pepper, and bay leaf. Bring to a slow boil and let simmer for 8 to 10 minutes.
3. Remove the bay leaf. Add milk or wine to thin if necessary. Garnish with the parsley and serve.

CHAPTER 7

Vegetable Soups

Oven-Roasted Butternut Squash Bisque

Serves 4

Toss the roasted squash seeds on top to garnish the soup. These seeds are edible.

3 pounds butternut squash
3 teaspoons sesame **or** olive oil
Black pepper
1 teaspoon cumin (curry
    powder can be substituted)
1 tablespoon orange zest
    (fresh is best)

4½ cups Basic Chicken **or**
    Vegetable Broth (see recipes
    on pages 5 and 6)
2 cloves garlic, sliced
½ teaspoon sugar
½ cup whole milk

1. Preheat the oven to 400 degrees. Cut the squash in half and scoop out the seeds and slimy threads. Rinse the seeds clean and dry them with a towel. Brush the exposed flesh of the squash halves with some of the oil and a bit of pepper. Put them on a foiled-lined baking sheet, cut side down; roast for 45 to 60 minutes, until tender.

2. While the squash roasts, coat the seeds with the rest of the oil and half of the cumin. Arrange the seeds on another foil-lined baking sheet in a single layer. Cover loosely with another piece of foil. Roast the seeds for about 10 minutes, turning them once.

3. Remove the squash from the oven and scoop the flesh into a soup pot. Add the chicken stock, orange zest, garlic, and the rest of the cumin. Bring to a boil, then reduce to a simmer and cook for 20 to 30 minutes.

4. Using a blender or food processor, blend the mixture. Return it to the pot and add the sugar and milk. Heat it thoroughly. Toss the squash seeds on top and serve.

Homemade Croutons

The weirder the bread, the better the crouton. Guests will "ooh" and "aah" when you announce that your squash bisque boasts a garnish of Irish soda bread croutons. Cornbread makes spectacular croutons, as do rye bread and pumpernickel. Toss with a few drops of oil, spread on a baking sheet, and bake at 325 degrees for 15 minutes, until crisp.

Cabbage and Tomato Soup

2 large onions
3 stalks celery
1 clove garlic
2 leeks (light green and white
    parts)
3 carrots
2 cups cubed new potatoes
1 cup shredded green cabbage
3 tablespoons olive oil
1 teaspoon rosemary

1 teaspoon parsley
1 teaspoon thyme
6 cups Basic Vegetable Broth
    (see recipe on page 6)
8 medium-sized whole tomatoes
    or 1 (16-ounce) can

Serves 6–8

Leeks tend to trap a lot of sand and grit in between their layers. It's important to wash leeks thoroughly before using them.

1. Chop the onions and celery, and thickly slice the garlic and leeks. Slice the carrots and cube the potatoes (skin on). Shred the cabbage.

2. In a soup pot, heat the oil on medium and sauté the onions, celery, garlic, and leeks for 5 minutes. Add the carrots and potatoes, along with the herbs, to the pot. Pour in the vegetable broth. Bring to a boil, then reduce to a simmer, cover, and simmer for 1 hour.

3. Add the tomatoes, whole, to the top of the broth, if they are fresh. Cover and heat until you can slip off the skins. If using canned tomatoes, just stir them in with liquid included. Crush the tomatoes with the back of a large spoon. Rewarm the soup briefly.

Corn Chowder

Serves 4

For an extra thick and creamy chowder, substitute 2 cups of half-and-half for the milk.

5 medium ears of corn
½ cup chopped celery
½ cup chopped carrot
½ cup chopped onion
2 tablespoon butter
4 cups Basic Chicken Broth
   (see recipe on page 5)
½ cup dry white wine
½ teaspoon roasted garlic paste
½ cup polenta (from a prepared
   roll or leftover homemade)

2 cups milk **or** half-and-half
2 tablespoons fresh chopped
   thyme
¼ cup sherry
Salt and pepper
Red pepper flakes (optional)

1. In a 350-degree oven, roast the corn in their husks for about 45 minutes. Cool. Remove the husks and cut the kernels off the cobs.
2. Coarsely chop the celery, carrots, and onion. Sauté them on medium heat in the butter until tender. Add the broth, wine, roasted garlic, and the fresh corn kernels. Bring to a boil and simmer for 30 minutes.
3. Add the polenta and simmer for another 20 minutes. Purée the mixture in a blender or food processor; return it to the soup pot.
4. Add the milk, thyme, and sherry. Salt and pepper to taste. Reheat gently, and serve, garnished with a few red pepper flakes.

Using Vinegar Instead of Wine

If you don't have wine handy for your recipe, substitute one to two tablespoons of wine vinegar or cider vinegar mixed with one cup of water.

Mulligatawny Soup

2 tablespoons oil **or** butter
1 clove garlic, coarsely
    chopped
1 tablespoon curry powder
2 tablespoons white flour
4 cups Basic Chicken Broth
    (see recipe on page 5) **or**
    any vegetable broth

1 stalk celery, shredded
1 carrot, shredded
1 apple, peeled and finely diced
2 tablespoons uncooked white
    rice **or** potato starch
1–2 cups milk
1 tablespoon lemon juice

Serves 6

Stir the soup before adding the lemon juice at the end. Otherwise, it can curdle.

Heat the oil in soup pot and sauté the garlic on medium for 2 to 3 minutes. Whisk in the curry and flour, stirring for 1 minute. Add the broth, mixing everything together. Add the celery, carrot, apple, rice (or potato starch), milk, and lemon juice. Simmer for 15 minutes and serve.

Cabbage Soup

1 small head green cabbage
1 onion
1 leek
1 carrot
1 tomato
2 tablespoons butter

5 cups Basic Beef Broth
    (see recipe on page 4)
½ cup sauerkraut
Salt and black pepper
Sour cream (optional)
Fresh chopped dill (optional)

Serves 4–6

Garnish with sour cream and dill, if desired.

1. Coarsely shred the cabbage. Chop the onion, thinly slice the leek (white part only) and carrot, and cut the tomato into chunks.
2. Using a soup pot, heat the butter. Add the onion, leek, and carrot; sauté on medium for 5 minutes. Add the beef broth and bring to a boil. Reduce to a simmer, add the cabbage, sauerkraut, and tomato chunks, and simmer for 45 minutes. Salt and pepper to taste.

Mushroom Soup

Serves 4–5

Want a fast and easy way to slice mushrooms? Use an egg-slicer; it gets the job done in a snap.

¾ pound fresh mushrooms
  (any kind, or a mix of types)
3 cups Potato and Vegetable
  Broth (see recipe on page 7)
3 tablespoon flour
3 tablespoon butter **or** oil

1 cup whole milk
Salt and black pepper
2 tablespoons sherry

1. Using caps and stems, slice all but 4 or 5 of the mushrooms; set the uncut mushrooms aside.
2. Pour the broth into a soup pot and add the sliced mushrooms. Simmer on medium heat for *about* 30 minutes, making sure the mushrooms do not overcook and begin to disintegrate.
3. Using a slotted spoon, remove the mushrooms and set them aside, covered. Allow the broth to cool.
4. In a small pan, make a roux by melting the butter over medium heat and whisking in the flour until the mixture is smooth and begins to bubble. Add the roux to the broth in the soup pot, whisking constantly as the broth rewarms. Cook gently for 10 minutes, whisking often.
5. Whisk the milk, salt, and black pepper into the soup pot, making sure that it does not boil. Stir in the sherry.
6. Slice the remaining raw mushrooms. Place the cooked mushrooms in serving bowls and pour the broth over them. Garnish with the raw mushroom slices.

Mill Your Own Pepper
If possible, use freshly ground black peppercorns when pepper is called for in a recipe. These retain their flavor better than pre-ground pepper and you'll need less of it to get the same flavor. (As a general rule, use about half to start, then taste—you can always add more later!)

Tomato Soup with Cream and Cognac

16 medium tomatoes
1 large onion
⅓ cup walnut oil **or** butter
2 cups Basic Vegetable Broth
    (see recipe on page 6)
Crushed basil **or** oregano leaves
1 pint heavy **or** medium cream

1 teaspoon brown sugar
4–5 tablespoons cognac
Salt and pepper

Serves 6

For a different flavor, you can substitute 4–5 tablespoons of brandy for the cognac.

---

1. Peel the tomatoes by bringing a large pan of water to a rolling boil. Drop the tomatoes in the water for about 15 seconds (the tomato peels should just begin to split open), then drain. Rinse the tomatoes with cold water; peel the tomatoes and discard the skins. Cut the tomatoes into chunks and crush them in a bowl with the back of a large spoon. Finely chop the onion.

2. In a large soup pot, heat the oil on medium; add the onions and sauté them for about 1 minute. Add the tomatoes, 1 cup of broth, and a few crushed basil (or oregano) leaves. Simmer for 30 minutes.

3. Force the mixture through a sieve, removing only the seeds and any tough onion pieces. Put the sieved mixture back on low heat.

4. In a saucepan, warm the cream and the brown sugar until it is almost to the boiling point (do not let it boil); using a whisk, quickly pour it into the soup pot with the tomato mixture. Add the cognac, and salt and pepper to taste. Keeps for up to 1 week in the fridge.

Pumpkin and Apple Soup

1 pound cooked pumpkin
1 large yellow onion
2 stalks celery
2 medium-sized tart apples
*1½ tablespoons butter **or** oil*
4 cups Basic Vegetable Broth
* (see recipe on page 6)*
1 teaspoon ginger
1 teaspoon curry powder

½ teaspoon nutmeg
½ teaspoon cinnamon
2 cups milk
Chopped nuts (any kind,
* toasted or raw), optional*

1. If using fresh pumpkin, preheat the oven to 350 degrees. Cut the pumpkin in half and remove seeds and slimy threads. Place each half cut-side down on foil-lined baking sheet; bake for 45 minutes.
2. Finely dice the onion. Dice the celery and apples.
3. In a soup pot, melt the butter. Sauté the onion on medium heat for about 2 minutes, until tender but not brown. Add all the vegetables, fruit, broth, and spices, including the flesh from the pumpkin (do not add the milk or nuts yet). Bring to a boil, then reduce to a simmer, and cook for 35 to 40 minutes.
4. Add the milk. Garnish with nuts, if desired.

Sunchoke Soup

8 cups Basic Chicken Broth
(see recipe on page 5)
1 pound sunchokes
1½ pounds potatoes (russets
are fine)
3 leeks (white and light green
parts)
2 cloves garlic
¼ teaspoon thyme

¼ teaspoon diced (**or** ground)
ginger
½ teaspoon marjoram
¼ cup half-and-half
Fresh chopped chives **or** green
onion (optional)

> **Serves 6**
>
> A sunchoke, also known as a Jerusalem artichoke, is neither related to the artichoke nor is it from Jerusalem.

1. In a soup pot, boil the broth. While it's coming to a boil, peel the sunchokes, potatoes, and leeks, and cut them into ½-inch-thick pieces. Peel and coarsely chop the garlic and ginger.

2. Put all the vegetables in the pot with the broth, along with the thyme. Bring back to a boil, then reduce to a simmer and cook for about 25 minutes. Add the marjoram and cool the mixture for 10 to 20 minutes.

3. Using a blender or food processor, purée the mixture; add the half-and-half. Return it to the stove and reheat on low heat. Thin the soup with a bit more broth or water, if desired. Garnish with chives or green onion.

Yellow Bell Pepper Soup

Serves 4

This soup looks great garnished with bread cubes, grated parmesan cheese, and chopped parsley.

3 tablespoons olive oil (**or** any nut oil), divided

2 medium onions, diced

1 medium carrot, peeled and diced

1 stalk celery, diced

4 yellow bell peppers, seeded and cut into chunks

2 large russet potatoes, peeled and cubed

1 bay leaf

2 sprigs thyme

3 cups water

1 small loaf Italian bread, cut into ½-inch cubes

Salt and pepper

4 teaspoons grated parmesan cheese

1 teaspoon chopped flat-leafed parsley

1. In a soup pot, heat 2 tablespoons of the oil on medium. Add the onion, carrot, and celery and sauté for 10 minutes.
2. Add the peppers, potatoes, bay leaf, thyme, and water to the pot. Bring to a boil, then reduce to a simmer and cook for 25 minutes.
3. Meanwhile, heat the remaining oil in a skillet and sauté the bread cubes for a few minutes, until they are lightly browned.
4. When the soup is done cooking, take it off the heat and let it cool slightly. Remove and discard the bay leaf and thyme sprigs. Using a blender or food processor, purée the soup. Season with salt and pepper to taste. Garnish with the bread cubes, parmesan, and parsley.

Acorn Squash Soup with Cider

3 acorn squash
2 tablespoons butter
1½ cups diced onion
3 cups hard cider **or**
   nonalcoholic cider
4 cups Basic Chicken Broth
   (see recipe on page 5)
1 teaspoon ground cardamom
½ teaspoon cinnamon

1 dash of nutmeg
Salt and pepper to taste
1 tablespoon orange juice
Popcorn, popped (optional)

Serves 8

For a nice flavor variation, use ¼ cup of fruit brandy in place of ¼ cup of the cider.

1. Preheat the oven to 400 degrees. Cut the squash in half and scoop out the seeds and slimy threads. Place the squash halves cut-side down on foil-lined baking sheets; bake for about 35 to 45 minutes, until tender.

2. In a soup pot, melt the butter on medium heat and sauté the onions until soft. Scoop out the cooked squash flesh and add it to the pot along with the cider and chicken broth. Bring to a boil, reduce to a simmer, and cook for about 20 minutes.

3. Remove from heat and let cool slightly. Using a blender or food processor, purée the mixture. Return it to the pot, adding the spices and orange juice. Garnish with popcorn, if desired, and serve.

Big Fresh Tomato Soup

Serves 6

Crushing the tomatoes with a wooden spoon will hasten the mingling of the flavors.

8–10 vine-ripened tomatoes, quartered
1 cup Basic Vegetable Broth (see recipe on page 4)
1 small onion, chopped
2 cloves garlic, chopped
3 tablespoons olive oil **or** butter, divided
2 tablespoons flour

4 cups whole milk **or** half-and-half
Salt and pepper
1 lemon
Diced green onions **or** fresh chopped chives (optional)

1. Put the tomatoes into a soup pot and crush them a bit with a wooden spoon. Add the broth and heat on medium.
2. In another pan, 1 tablespoon of the oil and sauté the onion for 2 minutes on medium heat. Add the garlic and sauté for 2 more minutes. Add this mixture to the soup pot; bring to a boil, reduce to a simmer, and cook until the volume is reduced by about a third.
3. In a medium-sized saucepan, heat the remaining oil on medium and whisk in the flour a bit at a time; cook, whisking constantly, until the mixture is smooth and light brown in color. Reduce the heat to low and gradually add the milk (or half-and-half) to the saucepan. Cook it until it thickens a little; do not let it boil. Add the dairy mixture to the soup pot and stir thoroughly; simmer for about 10 minutes.
4. Strain the soup through a sieve to remove the seeds. Allow it to cool slightly; then purée it in a food processor or blender.
5. Reheat on low. Season with salt and pepper to taste and a few squirts of lemon juice. Garnish with green onions or chives.

Escarole Soup

1 head escarole
1 large onion
1½ cups diced celery
3-4 cloves garlic
8 cups Basic Vegetable **or** Basic
   Chicken Broth (see recipes
   on pages 6 and 5)
2 bay leaves
2 tablespoons olive oil

1 teaspoon oregano
Salt and freshly ground black
   pepper
Parmesan cheese, grated
   (optional)

Serves 4

Grate the parmesan and add it as garnish along with an extra sprinkling of freshly ground black pepper.

1. Tear the escarole into small pieces. Dice the onion and celery. Mince the garlic.
2. In a soup pot, begin warming the broth, along with the bay leaves. In a large saucepan, heat the oil. Add the onion, garlic, celery, and oregano. Sauté for about 4 minutes on low heat. Add the escarole, stirring constantly, until it wilts. Transfer this mixture to the soup pot. Simmer gently for about 30 minutes. Remove the bay leaves.
3. Season with salt and pepper to taste.

Roasted Bell Pepper Soup

6 large red bell peppers
1 large green bell pepper
1 large yellow bell pepper
3 large red onions
2 cloves garlic
⅓ cup fresh chopped green herbs (almost any combination)
3 tablespoons olive oil
4 cups water

¼ cup red wine **or** red wine vinegar
1 teaspoon chili powder
2 tablespoons lemon **or** lime juice
Salt and pepper

1. Grill or broil the peppers, whole, turning them with oven tongs until they are charred and blistered. Put them into paper or plastic bags to cool; seal the bags tightly.
2. Meanwhile, chop the red onions and mince the garlic and herbs. In a soup pot, heat the oil. Sauté the onions on medium for about 3 minutes. Add the garlic and sauté for another minute. Set aside to cool slightly.
3. Remove the skins, seeds, and stems from the peppers. Chop the red peppers. Slice the yellow and green peppers into narrow strips about 1 inch long. Using a blender or food processor, purée the onion and garlic mixture with 1 cup of the water and the *red* bell peppers.
4. Return the mixture to the soup pot and add the remaining 3 cups of water. Add the wine and chili powder. Bring to a boil, then reduce to a simmer and cook for 15 minutes.
5. Remove the mixture from the heat and stir in the lemon juice and herbs, and salt and pepper to taste. Just before serving, add the yellow and green pepper strips and heat thoroughly.

Spinach and Dill Soup

2 (10-ounce) packages frozen
   spinach (**or** 2 pounds fresh
   spinach)
1 pound russet potatoes
2 cups chopped onion
1½ teaspoon minced garlic
½ cup fresh minced dill
¼ cup fresh minced basil leaves

2 teaspoons salt **and/or** mustard
6 cups water
Plain yogurt **or** sour cream
   (optional)

Serves 6–8

Garnish with a dollop
of yogurt or sour
cream, if you like.

1. Defrost the spinach (or, if using fresh, chop it). Cube the potatoes (peel on or off). Chop the onion. Mince the garlic, dill, and basil.
2. In a soup pot, combine the potatoes, onion, garlic, salt and/or mustard, and the water. Bring to a boil, reduce to a simmer, and cook for 20 minutes.
3. Remove from heat and allow to cool slightly. Using a blender or food processor, purée the potato mixture along with the spinach, dill, and basil. Return to the pot and heat slowly and thoroughly.

Squash and Chili Pepper Soup

1 squash (any fall-winter
   variety such as butternut)
2 yellow onions
1 chili pepper (any mild to
   medium-hot type, such as
   poblanos or serranos)
1 tablespoon cumin seeds
   (**or** ground cumin)
2 tablespoons butter

4 cups Basic Chicken Broth
   (see recipe on page 5)
1 cup cream, half-and-half,
   or milk
½ cup sliced almonds **or**
   pine nuts (optional)

1. Preheat oven to 375 degrees. Cut the squash in half and remove the seeds and slimy threads. Place the two halves cut-side down in a baking pan and add ½ inch of water to the pan; bake for 35 to 50 minutes (depending upon the thickness of the squash), until tender.
2. Meanwhile, chop the onions. Seed and mince the chili. If using cumin seeds, heat a heavy frying pan (preferably cast iron) on medium. Add the cumin seeds to the pan and toast them, stirring periodically, until they darken and emit a roasted aroma. Remove the seeds from the pan and set aside. Using the same pan, add enough oil to just coat the bottom of the pan, and toast the nuts (if using).
3. When the squash is done, allow it to cool slightly; save the water from the pan. Peel the squash and cut the flesh into chunks. In a soup pot, warm the butter. Sauté the onions and chilies on medium for about 3 minutes. Add the squash, broth, and the water from the squash pan. Bring to a boil, then reduce to a simmer. Add the cumin seeds (or ground cumin) and simmer for 40 minutes.
4. Remove from heat and allow to cool slightly. Purée the soup in a blender or food processor and return it to the soup pot. Stir in the dairy product and reheat; do not allow the soup to boil once the dairy has been added. Garnish with nuts and serve.

Belgian Watercress Soup

4 medium potatoes (Yukon
    gold **or** red)
2 medium-sized yellow onions
2 bunches watercress
3 tablespoons butter **or** oil
1 cup milk

¾ cup plain yogurt
Croutons (optional)

Serves 6

If you're looking to cut calories, use skim milk in this soup.

1. Place the potatoes, unpeeled, in a large saucepan with enough water to cover. Bring to a boil and cook for 20 to 30 minutes, depending upon their size. Reserve 2 cups of the water. Allow the potatoes to cool slightly.
2. Meanwhile, chop the onions. Cut off and discard the watercress stems and roughly tear the leaves. Dice the potatoes.
3. In a soup pot, melt the butter and sauté the onions on warm for 2 minutes. Add the potatoes, the reserved potato water, and the watercress; simmer for 4 minutes.
4. Add the milk and yogurt. Heat thoroughly, but do not boil. Garnish with croutons, if you like, and serve.

Spinach and Cider Soup

2 carrots
1 stalk celery
½ pound fresh spinach
1 clove garlic
1 tablespoon fresh chopped
  parsley
4 cups Basic Vegetable Broth
  (see recipe on page 6)
3 tablespoons olive **or** nut oil

2 tablespoons flour
1 teaspoon dill
½ cup apple cider
4 egg yolks
1 cup plain yogurt

1. Dice the carrots and celery. Remove the thickest stems from the spinach. Mince the garlic and chop the parsley.
2. In a soup pot, bring the broth to a boil. Add the carrots and celery, reduce to a simmer, and cook for 15 minutes. Remove from heat, cover, and set aside.
3. In a small saucepan, warm the oil. Sauté the onion on medium for 2 minutes. Add the garlic and cook for 1 minute more. Shake the flour over the mixture and whisk for about 2 minutes. Continuing to whisk constantly, add about ½ cup broth to the saucepan and cook for about 2 minutes.
4. Pour the onion mixture into the soup pot, stirring well. Add the spinach, parsley, dill, and cider to the pot. Bring to a boil, reduce to a simmer, and cook for 5 minutes.
5. Meanwhile, in a small bowl, beat together the egg yolks and yogurt until smooth. Pour this mixture into the soup pot, whisking it constantly. Heat thoroughly on low, making sure not to let the soup boil.

Multi-Mushroom Soup with Curry

1 ounce dried porcini and morel mushrooms (a combination)
1½ cups chopped leeks (white part only)
2 cups fresh chopped Portobello mushrooms
1 tablespoon fresh chopped chervil (optional)
*2 tablespoons oil **or** butter*

2 tablespoons flour
1 tablespoons curry powder
4 cups milk
1 cube chicken bouillon
1 tablespoon sherry (optional)

> **Serves 4**
>
> Soak the dried mushrooms for a few hours or overnight in room temperature water. Once soaked, they are ready to use just as you would fresh mushrooms.

1. Boil about 2 cups of water, remove from heat, and soak the dried mushrooms in it for 15 to 30 minutes.

2. Meanwhile, chop the leeks, Portobellos, and fresh chervil. In a soup pot, heat the oil on medium. Sauté the leeks, stirring constantly, for 3 minutes; shake the flour and curry on them, and stir until everything is coated. Add the milk and the bouillon cube. Bring *almost* to a boil, reduce heat to low heat, and whisk the mixture. Add the fresh mushrooms and cook for 5 minutes.

3. Drain the soaked dried mushrooms and squeeze out any excess moisture. (Freeze the cooking liquid for later use, if you like.) Chop them roughly and add them to the soup, cooking for 1 more minute. Stir in the sherry, if using. Ladle into soup bowls and top with the chopped chervil.

Pumpkin Soup

Serves 6–8

For a tasty snack, place your washed pumpkin seeds on a baking sheet and sprinkle with some seasoned salt. Bake them for 10–15 minutes.

1 small pumpkin (2½–3 pounds)
1 onion (yellow **or** red)
2 tablespoons olive oil **or** butter
½ teaspoon cinnamon
½ teaspoon ground cumin
¼ teaspoon curry powder
5 cups Basic Vegetable **or** Basic Chicken Broth (see recipes on pages 6 and 5)

¼ cup orange juice (**or** a combination of fresh orange zest and freshly squeezed orange juice)
2 teaspoons grated fresh ginger (optional)

1. Cut the pumpkin in half and scrape out the seeds and slimy threads. (Wash and save the seeds for later use, if you like.) Cut the pumpkin into chunks (this makes it easier to peel) and remove the peel. Cut the flesh into small chunks. Chop the onion.
2. In a soup pot, warm the oil. Add the onion and sauté on medium for 3 minutes. Add the pumpkin, along with the spices; cook briefly, stirring, until well mixed. Pour in the broth and the orange juice. Bring to a boil, reduce to simmer, and cook for 30 to 40 minutes.
3. Remove from heat and let cool slightly. Using a blender or food processor, purée the mixture. Return it to soup pot to rewarm, adding a bit more orange juice or a little milk to achieve the desired thickness. Garnish with the fresh ginger, if using.

Storing Fresh Ginger
Peel and store fresh ginger in a freezer bag so that you always have some on hand. Slice the ginger into disks about the thickness of a quarter. You'll still be able to grate it if necessary, and it is the perfect size to drop in a cup of boiling water to steep for ginger tea.

Asparagus Soup

1 pound fresh asparagus
1 onion
5 cups Basic Chicken Broth
    (see recipe on page 5)
¼ cup butter
¼ cup flour

White pepper
1 egg yolk
½ cup cream

(see recipe on page 5)

Serves 6

Freeze the tough ends from the asparagus to use for making broth another day.

---

1. Trim the tough ends from the asparagus and discard. Cut off the tips (do not discard) and slice the stalks. Chop the onion.
2. Put the asparagus tips in a saucepan with enough water to cover them. Bring to a boil, reduce to a simmer, and cook for 5 minutes. Drain and set the asparagus tips aside.
3. Pour 2 cups of the broth into a pot and add the asparagus stalks; bring to a boil, reduce to a simmer, and cook for 10 to 12 minutes. Remove from heat and allow to cool slightly. Force the stalks through a sieve, or purée them in a blender or food processor.
4. In a large soup pot, melt the butter. Sauté the onion on medium for 3 minutes. Whisk in the flour and cook for 1 more minute, stirring constantly. Drizzle in the rest of the broth, continuing to whisk until it thickens. Add the asparagus purée and white pepper. Reheat.
5. In a bowl, whisk together the egg yolk and the cream. Ladle some of the hot soup into this bowl, stirring well to incorporate. Add this mixture to the soup pot with the asparagus in it. Stir on low heat until it thickens. Add the asparagus tips, reheating thoroughly, but not allowing the soup to boil.

Green Peas for Color

The oldest trick in the book: Since asparagus, broad beans, and some other green veggies fade when cooked in a soup, chefs sometimes add a cup of frozen peas to the hot soup just before puréeing it. It revives the soup's color and adds a touch of sweetness.

Parsnip Soup with Pine Nuts

Serves 4

For a different flavor, substitute almonds for pine nuts as your garnish for this tasty soup.

1 onion
1 pound parsnips
2 tablespoons butter
6 cups Basic Chicken **or**
    Vegetable Broth (see recipes
    on pages 5 and 6)

¼–½ teaspoon cayenne pepper
½ cup cream
3 tablespoons pine nuts

1. Chop the onion and slice the parsnips. Melt the butter on medium heat in a soup pot. Add the onion and parsnips; cook for 10 minutes, stirring often.
2. Pour in the broth and add the cayenne. Bring to a boil, reduce to a simmer, and cook for 20 minutes.
3. Meanwhile, toast the pine nuts in a single layer under the broiler for 1 to 2 minutes.
4. When it is done cooking, remove the soup from the heat and allow it to cool slightly. Using a blender or food processor, purée the mixture. Reheat without boiling. Stir in the cream. (Be sure not to allow the soup to boil once the cream has been added.) Garnish with nuts and serve.

Differences in Onions

Onions vary in sweetness. Vidalia tend to be the sweetest, followed by red, then yellow. White onions are the least sweet and are better in meat dishes than in soups.

Tomato Soup
with Curry and Red Pepper

3 pounds tomatoes
1 large onion
2 cloves garlic
1 dried hot red pepper
¼ cup butter
3 tablespoons curry powder

3½ cups Basic Chicken Broth
 (see recipe on page 5)
1 bay leaf
½ cup sour cream

Serves 10

If you're looking for a cool, refreshing soup on a hot day, this soup can also be served chilled.

1. Chop the tomatoes into 2-inch chunks, removing the seeds. Dice the onions. Finely mince the garlic and red pepper.
2. In a soup pot, melt the butter. Sauté the onion and garlic on medium for 3 minutes, stirring constantly. Stir in the curry powder and cook for 5 more minutes.
3. Add the tomatoes, chicken broth, bay leaf, and red pepper. Bring to a boil, reduce to a simmer, and cook for 25 minutes.
4. Remove from heat and allow to cool slightly. Using a slotted spoon, remove and discard the bay leaf and the pepper pieces. In a blender or food processor, purée the mixture. Stir in the sour cream gradually. Heat gently but thoroughly; do not allow it to boil.

Which Tomatoes to Use

All tomatoes are not alike. Substitute plum tomatoes for a more robust flavor. Choose golden tomatoes for a more mellow taste. Reserve expensive varieties, such as hot-house, for recipes in which tomatoes are the main ingredient.

Mixed Vegetables and Herb Soup

2 tablespoons butter
3 cups mixed diced vegetables
1 tablespoons flour
5 cups Basic Beef Broth
   (see recipe on page 4)
2 cloves garlic, crushed
1 bay leaf
½ cup cream
White pepper

¼ cup grated cheese
   (such as pecorino Romano
   or Parmigiano Reggiano)
Salt
Nutmeg
3 tablespoons mixed chopped
   herbs (any combination)

1. In a soup pot, melt the butter on medium heat. Sauté the vegetables for 4 to 5 minutes. Whisk in the flour. Add the broth, stirring often as you bring it to a boil. Add the garlic and bay leaf. Reduce to a simmer and cook for 25 minutes.
2. When the mixture has cooked, discard the bay leaf and allow the soup to cool slightly. Drizzle in the cream and reheat the pot *almost* to a boil. Remove from heat and, again, allow to cool slightly.
3. Using a blender or food processor, purée the mixture along with the cheese. Return the mixture to the soup pot and reheat, but not boil. Add the pepper, salt, and nutmeg to taste. Garnish with the mixed herbs.

Texas Squash Blossom and Chili Soup

1 poblano chili
1 yellow summer squash
5 yellow cherry tomatoes
½ of a small onion
2 jalapeño **or** serrano chilies
2 cloves garlic
2 tablespoons olive oil
18 squash blossoms
6 cups Basic Chicken Broth
    (see recipe on page 5)

9 epazote leaves
1 teaspoon oregano
1 teaspoon basil
Salt and pepper
1 lime

Serves 6–8

If you can't find epazote leaves in your local store, look for Mexican tea. It's the same thing.

1. Place the whole poblano pepper on a baking sheet and broil it, turning it frequently, until the skin has blistered and darkened. Transfer the pepper to a plastic or paper bag and seal it tightly, setting it aside to steam (this makes it easier to peel).
2. Meanwhile, dice the squash and tomatoes. Finely chop the onion. Seed and dice the jalapeños (or serranos). Mince the garlic. Peel, seed, and dice the roasted poblano pepper.
3. In a soup pot, heat the oil. Add the squash, onion, garlic, and jalapeños; sauté for 4 minutes. Add the tomatoes, roasted poblano, and squash blossoms, and sauté for 1 minute.
4. Pour in the chicken broth and bring to a boil. Reduce to a simmer and add the epazote, oregano, and basil, and salt and pepper to taste. Garnish each serving with a thin curl of lime zest.

Tomato Bread Soup

1 tablespoon olive oil
1 leek, chopped (white part only)
4 cloves garlic, minced
2 cups peeled and chopped
   tomatoes
⅓ cup chopped fresh basil
½ teaspoon salt
1½ cups Basic Vegetable **or**
   Basic Chicken Broth, divided
   (see recipes on pages 6
   and 5)

½ teaspoon pepper
2 cups cubed day-old Italian
   bread
2 tablespoons grated parmesan
   cheese (optional)

1. In a heavy saucepan, heat the oil on medium. Sauté the leeks and garlic, stirring occasionally, for about 3 minutes until softened. Stir in the tomatoes and basil. Bring to a boil. Boil gently for 5 to 10 minutes, or until slightly thickened.

2. Add 1 cup of the broth, the salt, and pepper. Bring to a boil, stirring. Remove from the heat. Stir in the bread. If necessary, add the remaining broth to reach the desired consistency.

Beef Broth and Tomatoes Soup

1 pound yellow onions
3 shallots
6 cloves garlic
1 (14-ounce) can whole plum
    tomatoes
½ teaspoon sugar
Salt to taste
½ teaspoon black pepper
6 cups Basic Beef Broth
    (see recipe on page 4)

6 slices French bread
    (optional)
1 cup grated Gruyère cheese
    (optional)

Serves 6

This recipe, similar to French onion soup, is also good served with swiss cheese.

1. Thinly slice the onions, shallots, and garlic. Drain the tomatoes and slightly mash them.
2. In a soup pot, warm the olive oil. Add the onions, shallots, and garlic; sauté for 3 to 5 minutes, stirring often. Add the sugar and seasonings, stirring almost constantly until the onions are dark brown (caramelized).
3. Stir in the tomatoes and beef broth. Bring to a boil, reduce to a simmer, and cook for 30 minutes.
4. Toast the bread and grate the cheese. Place a bread slice and some cheese in each serving bowl, then ladle soup on top.

Curried Zucchini Soup

Serves 8

Five cups of chopped zucchini equals about 6 "baby" zucchinis, 2–3 medium sized ones, or 1 "jumbo" backyard garden variety.

1 tablespoon olive oil
5 cups chopped zucchini
2 onions, chopped
1 stalk celery, diced
1 clove garlic, minced
2 teaspoons curry powder
¾ teaspoon salt
½ teaspoon cinnamon
¼ teaspoon pepper
1 teaspoon packed brown sugar

6 cups Basic **or** Roasted Vegetable Broth (see recipes on pages 6 and 10)

1. In a soup pot, heat the oil over medium heat; sauté the zucchini, onions, celery, garlic, curry powder, salt, cinnamon, and pepper, stirring occasionally, for about 10 minutes until softened.
2. Sprinkle with the brown sugar and pour in the broth. Bring to a boil, then reduce to a simmer; cook, covered, for 20 minutes, or until the vegetables are very tender.
3. In blender or food processor, puree the soup, in batches, until smooth. Pour into a clean soup pot. Reheat, but do not boil. Season with more salt and pepper to taste.

Bean and Legume Soups

Peas in the Pod Soup

1 pound fresh peas pods
2 tablespoons chopped onion
3 tablespoons chopped parsley
8 cups Basic Vegetable Broth
  (see recipe on page 6)
4 tablespoons butter

4 tablespoons flour
Salt and pepper
Diced cooked bacon (optional)

1. Cut off the small stem ends of the pea pods and pull off the thin strings along their back. Shell the peas, reserving both peas and pods. Chop the onion and parsley.
2. Bring the broth to a boil in a soup pot. Add the peas and the pods, reduce heat, and simmer for 7 minutes. Remove from heat. Strain, reserving the liquid. Force the peas and pods through a sieve, discarding the tough residue.
3. In another large container, heat the butter. Sauté the onion and parsley on medium for 3 minutes. Whisk in the flour and cook on low for 2 to 3 minutes. Add 1 cup of the reserved broth. Stir in the strained peas and pods.
4. Add the rest of the broth, stirring constantly over low heat. Cover and simmer for 5 minutes. Garnish with bacon, if desired.

The Interchangeable Bean

Substitute beans at will. Go to your local food co-op and try those different-looking beans in your next chili or bean soup. All beans taste fairly mild so you can't make a drastic mistake and you may find a new favorite.

Black Bean Soup with Curry

1 cup uncooked black beans
1 yellow onion
1 carrot
3 cloves garlic
1 tablespoon butter
1 tablespoon olive oil
2 tablespoons curry powder
1½ teaspoons ground coriander

10 cups Basic Chicken Broth
   (see recipe on page 5)
½ teaspoon salt
½ teaspoon black pepper
1 tablespoon chopped cilantro
   (optional)

Serves 4–6

Garnish each serving with chopped cilantro. It adds color and flavor.

---

1. Soak the beans overnight in cold water, then drain. Cut the onion and carrot into a fine dice. Mince the garlic.
2. Using a soup pot or large saucepan, heat the butter and oil. Add the onion and carrot, sautéing for about 5 minutes on medium. Add the garlic and cook for 1 more minute. Add the curry and coriander and stir to combine for an additional 1 minute.
3. Pour in the chicken broth and beans, bringing the mixture to a boil. Reduce to a simmer and cook for 1½ hours.
4. Using a slotted spoon, remove about half of the beans and set aside. Cool the rest of the mixture slightly, then purée it in a blender or food processor. Combine with the whole beans back in the soup pot. Stir in the salt and pepper. Reheat if necessary. Chop the cilantro. Ladle the soup into bowls.

Thick Bean Broth

Any bean recipe gives you two options. Cook it longer and let the beans dissolve for a creamy texture. Serve it earlier in the cooking process, as soon as the beans are completely soft, for more distinct flavors in every bite.

Cuban Black Bean Soup

Serves 6

Plan in advance for the preparation of this soup. The black beans must be soaked overnight in cold water.

1 pound (16 ounces) dried
   black beans
4 cups cooked white rice
1 onion
1 red bell pepper
1 green bell pepper
1 tablespoon butter
4 cups Basic Beef Broth
   (see recipe on page 4)
2 bay leaves

½ teaspoon thyme
½ teaspoon oregano
½ cup rum (optional)

1. Soak the black beans overnight in cold water, then drain.
2. Cook the white rice if you do not have leftovers. Chop the onion and the red bell pepper coarsely. Dice the green bell pepper to a medium dice.
3. In a soup pot, heat the butter. Add the onion and sauté on medium for 3 minutes. Next add the beans, broth, bay leaves, thyme, oregano, and the red bell pepper (reserving the green one). Bring the mixture to a boil, reduce to a simmer, and cook for 1½ hours.
4. Remove about 1 cup of the beans with a slotted spoon and place them in a bowl. Mash them. Add them back into the soup pot, stirring a bit until the mixture thickens. Discard the bay leaves. Add the rum and green bell pepper dice. Cover and simmer for an additional 10 minutes.
5. Divide the rice among the serving bowls and pour the soup over the top.

Black Bean and Cumin Soup

1 cup dried black beans
1 onion
2 cloves garlic
1 stalk celery
1 carrot
7 cups broth
1 tablespoon oil
¾ teaspoon cumin
¾ teaspoon black pepper

Salt
Scallions (optional)
Plain yogurt (optional)

Serves 4–6

Any basic chicken, beef, or vegetable broth can be used for this soup.

1. Soak the beans overnight in cold water, then drain. Mince the onion and garlic. Finely dice the celery and carrot.
2. In a large saucepan or soup pot, bring the beans and the broth to a boil; reduce to a simmer and cook for 2 hours.
3. Using a smaller saucepan, heat the oil. Add the onion and garlic and cook for about 6 minutes over low heat. Add the celery and carrots and cook them for an additional 5 minutes.
4. Pour this vegetable mixture into the pan with the beans. Stir in the cumin and pepper. Simmer for 30 minutes. Remove from heat and let cool slightly. Purée the soup in a blender or food processor. Return the soup to the pot and reheat to serving temperature, adding salt to taste. Chop the scallions and use them as garnish for each individual serving, along with a dollop of plain yogurt.

Caribbean Black Bean Soup

Serves 4

Chop the cilantro and use as a garnish for each individual serving.

¾ pound (12 ounces) dried
    black beans
½ pound ham
1 yellow onion
2 tomatoes
4 scallions
1 teaspoon chopped oregano
6 cloves garlic
10 cups water
1 ham shank (ask the butcher
    to crack it)

1 bay leaf
¾ teaspoon black pepper
1 teaspoon red wine vinegar
Salt
1 tablespoon olive oil
⅓ cup Spanish sherry
Fresh cilantro (optional)

1. Soak the beans overnight in cold water, then drain. Cut the ham into ½-inch cubes. Quarter the onion. Chop the tomatoes, scallions, and oregano. Peel the garlic and mince 4 of the cloves, leaving the remaining 2 whole.

2. In a soup pot, combine the water, beans, ham shank, whole garlic cloves, bay leaf, onion, pepper, vinegar, and salt. Bring to a boil, reduce to a simmer, and cook for 45 minutes. Discard the ham bone and bay leaf.

3. Using a saucepan, heat the olive oil. Add the minced garlic, ham meat, tomatoes, oregano, sherry, and scallions. Sauté on medium for 6 minutes. Ladle out 1 cup of the cooked bean mixture and add it to the ham meat mixture. Stir, scraping up the brown bits from the bottom of the pan. Mix the contents of the saucepan into the soup pot with the bean mixture.

4. Bring to a boil, then reduce to a simmer and cook for 20 more minutes.

Lima Bean Soup

¼ cup cooked lima beans
⅓ cup cooked corn kernels
1 cup cooked peas
2 potatoes
4 carrots
2 stalks celery

1 onion
8 cups Basic Beef Broth
(see recipe on page 4)
2 cups tomato juice **or** V-8
Salt and pepper

> **Serves 8–10**
>
> Lima beans from a can will work just fine in this recipe.

1. Cook the lima beans, corn, and peas separately, if you don't have leftovers. Dice the potatoes, slice the carrots, and chop the celery. Slice the onion and separate it into rings.
2. Using a soup pot, bring the broth to a boil. Add the potatoes, carrots, celery, and onion rings. Bring to a boil again, reduce to a simmer, and cook for 15 minutes.
3. Stir in the lima beans, corn, and peas. Pour in the tomato juice. Salt and pepper to taste. Simmer for 10 more minutes.

Lentil Soup

1 cup dried lentils
1 onion
1 clove garlic
2 tablespoons butter **or** oil
1 tablespoon tarragon

1 teaspoon paprika
1 bay leaf
4 cups Basic **or** Roasted
Vegetable Broth (see recipes
on pages 6 and 10)

> **Serves 6**
>
> Save yourself some time with this soup. Lentils only need to be rinsed, not soaked.

1. Rinse the lentils very thoroughly. Dice the onion and mince the garlic.
2. In a large saucepan or soup pot, melt the butter. Sauté the onion for 5 minutes over low heat. Stir in the tarragon, paprika, and bay leaf; then add the lentils next. Pour in the vegetable broth, bring to a boil, reduce to a simmer, and cook for 30 minutes.
3. Remove from heat and allow to cool slightly. Discard the bay leaf. Using a blender or food processor, purée the mixture. Reheat for 5 minutes.

Kidney Bean Chili

Serves 4

Garnish each individual serving with a few cooked corn kernels, some grated cheddar cheese, and a sprinkling of chopped cashews, if desired.

1 green bell pepper
1 stalk celery
½ an onion
1 carrot
1 zucchini
1 clove garlic
2 tablespoons vegetable **or** nut oil
1 (18-ounce) can chopped tomatoes
1 (15- to 16-ounce) can cooked kidney beans
1 cup tomato sauce
¼ cup water
2 teaspoons chili powder
¼ teaspoon hot pepper sauce
1 teaspoon basil
1 teaspoon oregano
¾ teaspoon black pepper
Cooked corn kernels, shredded cheddar cheese, **and/or** chopped cashews for garnish (all optional)

1. Chop the green bell pepper, celery, and onion. Shred the carrot and zucchini. Mince the garlic.
2. In a large saucepan or soup pot, heat the oil. Sauté all the fresh vegetables on medium for 3 minutes. Add all the remaining ingredients, except the garnishes. Bring to a boil, reduce to a simmer, and cook for 5 more minutes.

Red Lentil and Sweet Potato Soup

¾ cup dried red lentils
2 sweet potatoes
½ of an onion
2 tablespoons vegetable oil
3 cups water
2 cups orange juice
2 tablespoons brown sugar
1 tablespoon ginger

¼ teaspoon nutmeg
¼ teaspoon cinnamon
Salt and pepper to taste
1 dash of red pepper flakes

Serves 4–6

Tangerine or carrot juice can be substituted for the orange juice in this recipe.

1. Rinse the lentils thoroughly. Cut the sweet potatoes into 1-inch chunks and chop the onion.
2. In a large soup pot, heat the oil. Add the onion and sauté for 3 minutes on medium heat. Add the water, juice, sugar, and ground seasonings, bringing everything to a boil. Add the sweet potatoes and lentils. Bring to a boil, reduce to a medium heat, and cook the mixture, uncovered, for 20 minutes.
3. Reduce to a simmer, stirring the soup frequently, for another 10 minutes.

Lentil and Beer Soup

Lentils cook quicker than other beans, and never require soaking. They are also rich in iron and protein.

2 cups dried lentils
2 onions
2 stalks celery
3 carrots
4 cups beer (a dark German
   beer is best here)
4 cups Basic Chicken Broth
   (see recipe on page 5)

1 meaty ham bone (diced
   ham can be substituted)
2 tablespoons butter
Salt and pepper

1. Rinse the lentils, then drain. Finely dice the onions and cut the celery and carrots into very thin slices.
2. In a soup pot or large kettle, combine the beer, broth, and lentils. If using the ham bone (as opposed to diced ham) add it now. Bring to a boil, then reduce to a simmer; cook, covered, for 2 hours with the bone, or 1½ hours without it.
3. Uncover and remove the bone, breaking the meat into small pieces. Add the meat back to the pot and discard the bone. Or add the separate ham dice now. Leaving the cover off, reduce heat to a very low simmer.
4. Using a small saucepan or skillet, melt the butter. Add the onions, celery, and carrots, sautéing them for 10 minutes, without browning them. Add them to the soup pot, along with salt and pepper to taste. Rewarm the soup, and serve.

Lentil and Spinach Soup

1 cup dried lentils
2 (10-ounce) packages frozen
  chopped spinach
½ of a yellow onion
3 tablespoons oil
1 teaspoon whole mustard
  seed
4 cups Basic Chicken Broth
  (see recipe on page 5)
4 teaspoons lemon juice

2 teaspoons black pepper
½ teaspoon coriander
Salt
Grated cheddar cheese
  (optional)

Serves 4–6

This soup goes well with thick slices of fresh, warm Italian bread.

1. Rinse the lentils thoroughly. Set the spinach out to thaw. Chop the onion.
2. Place the lentils in a large saucepan and add enough water to cover them by at least an inch. Bring to a boil, reduce to a simmer, and cook for 1½ hours.
3. In large soup pot, heat the oil on medium. Add the mustard seeds and cook 1–2 minutes, until they pop. Add the onion and cook for another 6 minutes.
4. Squeeze the spinach to remove excess moisture. Add the spinach to the soup pot containing the onions, along with the broth, lemon juice, pepper, and coriander. Stir in the lentils and salt to taste. Heat thoroughly. Garnish with grated cheddar cheese if desired.

Soybean Soup

1¼ cups uncooked soybeans
1 onion
1 small stalk celery
1 small carrot

2 cups seeded and diced
  tomatoes
3 cups water
2 tablespoons soy flour

1. Soak the soybeans overnight in cold water. Cover with fresh water in a saucepan, bring to a boil, reduce to a simmer, and cook for 1¼ hours. Drain and mash them.
2. Chop the onion and celery. Dice the carrot. Chop and seed the tomatoes.
3. In a soup pot, combine the water, onion, celery, and carrot. Bring to a boil, reduce to a simmer, and cook for 10 minutes.
4. Add the tomatoes and the mashed soybeans and simmer for 10 minutes. As soup is cooking, whisk the flour together with a bit of cold water. Drizzle in this thickener, stirring constantly, until you reach the desired consistency.

White Bean and Swiss Chard Soup

2 tablespoons olive oil
1 cup coarsely chopped onion
2 cups coarsely chopped Swiss
  chard (**or** bok choy)
1 tablespoon lemon juice

4 cups Basic Vegetable **or**
  Chicken Broth (see recipes
  on pages 6 and 5)
1 cup cooked cannellini beans

1. In a soup pot, warm the oil. Add the onion and sauté on medium for 2 minutes. Then add the Swiss chard and sauté for 3 minutes more.
2. Pour in the broth, the cooked beans, and the lemon juice. Bring to a boil, then reduce to a simmer. Cook for 10 minutes.

White Bean and Vegetable Soup

1 small zucchini

1 onion

2 tablespoons fresh chopped dill

3 tablespoon fresh chopped
  parsley

2 cloves garlic

1 lemon

4 tablespoons oil, divided

4 cups cooked Great Northern
  beans, divided

4 cups Potato and Vegetable
  Broth (see recipe on page 7)

²/₃ cup dry white wine

1 teaspoon curry powder **or**
  garam masala

1 tablespoon water

Salt and pepper

Serves 6–8

For the differences between curry powder and Garam Masala, see page 43.

1. Cut the zucchini into ¼-inch-thick slices. Chop the onion and herbs. Mince the garlic. Juice the lemon.

2. In a skillet, heat 2 tablespoons of the oil. Add the onion and sauté on medium for about 3 minutes. Add the garlic and sauté for 2 more minutes. Purée these ingredients in a blender or food processor, along with half of the beans.

3. Pour the purée into a soup pot and add the rest of the beans, the broth, wine, parsley, dill, and curry (or garam masala). Bring barely to a boil, reduce to a simmer, and cook for 20 minutes.

4. Using the skillet again, heat the remaining 2 tablespoons of oil. Add the zucchini pieces and the water. Sauté over medium heat, stirring frequently for about 7 minutes.

5. Add the zucchini to the soup pot, along with the lemon juice. Add water to thin the soup if necessary. Salt and pepper to taste, and simmer for 10 minutes. Serve.

White Bean and Parsley Soup

Serves 6

Compare the flavors of curly-leaf parsley and the Italian flat-leaf kind to find the one you prefer.

3 cups navy beans

2 onions

3 garlic cloves

1 teaspoon finely chopped rosemary

1 teaspoon finely chopped thyme

3 tablespoons olive oil, divided

12 cups Basic Chicken Broth (see recipe on page 5)

1 pound bacon slices

Italian flat-leaf parsley (optional)

Salt and pepper

1. Soak the beans in cold water overnight, then drain. Dice the onions, mince the garlic, and chop the rosemary and thyme.

2. In a large soup pot, heat 2 tablespoons of the oil. Add the garlic and onions and sauté for 3 minutes on medium heat. Pour in the broth and add the beans. Bring to a boil, reduce to a simmer, and cook for 1½ hours.

3. Meanwhile, heat the remaining tablespoon of oil in a skillet. Sauté the bacon on medium-high heat until crispy. Set the bacon aside on paper towels to cool.

4. When the soup is done cooking, use a slotted spoon to remove about 1½ cups of the cooked beans and allow them to cool slightly. Purée them in a blender or food processor with 2 cups of the liquid from the soup pot.

5. Stir the purée back into the soup pot. Add the rosemary and thyme, and salt and pepper to taste. Simmer for about 5 minutes to reheat. Chop the parsley and crumble the bacon; use as a garnish for each individual serving.

White Bean and Mushroom Soup

¾ pound fresh cremini
  (**or** button) mushrooms
¼–½ pound fresh shiitake
  mushrooms
1 large onion
2 medium potatoes
2 stalks celery
3 cloves garlic
4 tablespoons oil, divided
3 cups Mushroom Broth
  (see recipe on page 11)
3 cups Basic **or** Roasted
  Vegetable Broth (see recipes
  on pages 6 and 10)

2 cups canned, cooked navy
  (**or** cannellini) beans,
  drained
½ teaspoon dry mustard
½ teaspoon basil
½ teaspoon thyme
¼ cup dry white wine
Salt and pepper
Fresh parsley (optional)

Serves 8

If you don't have any fresh shiitake mushrooms, you can use 6–8 dried shiitakes, soaked in water overnight.

1. Slice the mushrooms. Chop the onion, dice the potatoes and celery, and mince the garlic.
2. In a soup pot, heat 2 tablespoons of the oil on medium. Add the garlic and onions, and sauté over medium heat for 3 minutes. Add the potatoes, celery, broths, and beans. Bring to a boil, then reduce to a simmer. Add the mustard, basil, thyme, and wine; cook, uncovered, for 15 minutes.
3. Add half of the cremini mushrooms to the soup pot and simmer for an additional 10 minutes. Remove the pot from the heat and let it stand for several minutes.
4. In a smaller saucepan, heat the remaining oil. Sauté the rest of the creminis and all the shiitakes. Cook, covered, for 10 minutes.
5. In a blender or food processor, purée the contents of the soup pot. Pour the purée back into the soup pot. Stir in the sautéed mushrooms. Add salt and pepper to taste. Simmer, covered, for 10 minutes, adding water if necessary to adjust the consistency. Chop the parsley and use as a garnish for each individual serving.

White Bean Minestrone

Serves 8

You can also use
1/3 pound of fresh
spinach in place of
the Swiss chard.

¾ cup dried Great Northern
    beans (**or** white pea beans)
6 cups water
⅛ pound (2 ounces) salt pork
1 onion
3 stalks celery (leaves
    included)
2 tomatoes
1 carrot
1 potato
2 cups coarsely chopped white
    cabbage
2 small zucchini

4 leaves Swiss chard
5 sprigs parsley
3 tablespoons olive oil
1 teaspoon thyme
6 cups Basic Beef Broth
    (see recipe on page 4)
1 teaspoon basil
1 cup cooked small-size pasta
    (optional)
Grated parmesan cheese
    (optional)

1. Soak the beans overnight in cold water, then drain. Place in a large soup pot with the water. Bring to a boil, reduce to a simmer, and cook for 1 to 1½ hours. Drain and set aside.

2. Shred the salt pork, chop the onion, celery leaves, and celery. Seed and coarsely chop the tomatoes. Dice the carrots and potato. Coarsely chop the cabbage and the zucchini. Tear the Swiss chard (or spinach) into pieces and discard the stems. Chop the parsley.

3. In a soup pot, heat the salt pork. Add the onion, celery leaves, celery, tomatoes, carrot, potato, parsley, and thyme, stirring everything together. Sauté for 5 minutes.

4. Pour in the beef broth, and add the cabbage, zucchini, and cooked beans. Bring the pot to a boil, reduce to a simmer, and cook for 15 minutes.

5. Stir in the chard, basil, and the pasta (if using). Simmer for 2 to 4 minutes until the leaves wilt. Ladle into bowls, garnish with the parmesan, and serve.

Bean Soup with Mushrooms

½ pound (8 ounces) uncooked
   chickpeas (garbanzo beans)
1 ounce dried shiitake
   mushrooms
1 cup broad beans
1 Spanish onion
1 (28-ounce) can whole tomatoes
3 garlic cloves
1 bunch rosemary
½ cup grated parmesan cheese

2 tablespoons olive oil
2 bay leaves
Salt and pepper to taste
6 cups Basic Vegetable Broth
   (see recipe on page 6)
1 cup spelt (also called farro)

Serves 6

Broad beans are also known as fava beans. If you can't find either of these, lima beans can also be substituted.

1. Separately, soak the chickpeas in cold water and the dried mushrooms in room temperature water for several hours or overnight.
2. Drain the chickpeas. Strain the mushrooms to remove any unwanted debris, reserving the liquid. Chop the mushrooms coarsely. Shell and cook the broad beans. Chop the onion. Drain and dice the tomatoes. Mince the garlic and chop the rosemary leaves (reserving the stems). Grate the cheese.
3. In a soup pot, heat the oil. Add the onions and garlic and sauté for 4 minutes on medium heat. Tie the stems of the rosemary together and drop into the pot with the bay leaves, salt, and pepper; stir.
4. Add the chickpeas, the mushrooms and their liquid, the broth, tomatoes, and spelt. Bring to a boil, reduce to a simmer, and cook for 1 hour.
5. Stir in the cooked broad beans, grated cheese, and rosemary leaves. Simmer for 2 minutes. Discard the rosemary stems and bay leaves, and serve.

Tuscan Chickpea and Chard Soup

Serves 6

This recipe also works very well with Basic Vegetable Broth (page 4), which will make it vegan-friendly as well.

1 pound (16 ounces) butternut
   squash
¾ pound (12 ounces) Swiss
   chard (**or** rainbow chard)
1 onion
4 cloves garlic
1 tablespoon olive oil
2 teaspoons oregano
1 teaspoon rosemary

6 cups Basic Chicken Broth
   (see recipe on page 5)
2 (15½-ounce) cans cooked
   chickpeas
Salt and pepper

1. Peel, seed, and dice the squash. Coarsely chop the chard. Chop the onion and mince the garlic.
2. Heat the olive oil in a soup pot. Add the onion, oregano, and rosemary; sauté on low for 4 minutes. Add the garlic and cook for 1 additional minute.
3. Add the broth, chickpeas, and squash; bring to a boil, then reduce to a simmer and cook for 10 minutes. Add the chard and simmer for 10 minutes more. Sprinkle in the salt and pepper to taste, and serve.

Three Bean Soup

¾ cup dried Anasazi beans
⅔ cup dried lima beans
⅓ cup dried cowpeas
1 cup sliced leek
2 cups sliced carrots
2 parsnips
1 cup chopped celery
½ cup fresh chopped parsley
3 cloves garlic
3 tablespoons olive oil
8 cups water

1 bay leaf
2 teaspoons lemon juice
1 teaspoon onion salt
½ teaspoon hot pepper sauce
Freshly ground black pepper

Serves 8

Having trouble finding cowpeas in your local market? Try looking for black-eyed peas— a more recognized name.

1. In 3 separate bowls, soak the 3 kinds of beans overnight in cold water, then drain.
2. Slice the leek, using only the white and light green parts. Cut the carrots into thin slices. Trim the tough core from the parsnips. Chop the celery and parsley. Mince the garlic.
3. In a large soup pot, heat the oil on medium. Add the leek and stir for 3 minutes. Add the water, beans, carrots, whole parsnips, and bay leaf. Bring to a boil, reduce to a simmer, and cook for 1 hour with the lid on.
4. Using a slotted spoon, remove the parsnips and allow them to cool slightly. Remove and discard the bay leaf. Ladle out 2 cups of the liquid from the soup pot into a food processor or blender, add the parsnips, and purée until smooth.
5. Return the purée to the soup pot along with the parsley, garlic, lemon juice, onion salt, hot sauce, and black pepper to taste. Simmer for 10 minutes, then serve.

Lentil and Soybean Soup

Serves 6

Plan in advance for preparing this soup. The soybeans must be soaked overnight in cold water.

1 cup soybeans
1 cup lentils
3 onions
3 carrots
3 stalks celery
5 cloves garlic
1 lemon
6 tablespoons olive oil
5 cups Roasted Vegetable Broth
   (see recipe on page 10)

Salt and pepper
Cinnamon
½ cup fresh chopped parsley

1. Soak the soybeans overnight in cold water, then drain. Rinse the lentils thoroughly.
2. Slice the onions and carrots. Coarsely chop the celery. Mince the garlic. Juice the lemon.
3. In a large saucepan or soup pot, combine the broth, soybeans, lentils, onions, garlic, and oil. Bring to a boil, reduce to a simmer, and cook for 45 minutes.
4. Add the celery, lemon juice, and salt, pepper, and cinnamon to taste. Bring back to a boil, adding extra cold water to cover all ingredients. Simmer for 45 minutes.
5. Chop the parsley and stir it into the soup pot; simmer for 2 more minutes and serve.

Brittany Bean Soup

1 pound (16 ounces) dried
   Great Northern beans
1 cup chopped tomatoes
2 cups sliced onions
2 leeks
3 cloves garlic
12 cups Potato and Vegetable
   Broth (see recipe on page 7)
1 bay leaf
2 sprigs thyme

Salt
½ cup cream
3 tablespoons butter
Freshly ground black pepper

Serves 6

When chopping the leeks, use only the white and light green parts.

---

1. Soak the beans overnight in cold water, then drain.
2. Chop the tomatoes. Thinly slice the onions and finely chop the leeks. Mince the garlic.
3. In a soup pot, combine the broth and beans. Add the tomatoes, onions, garlic, bay leaf, leeks, and thyme. Bring to a boil, reduce to a simmer, and cook for 1½ hours.
4. Remove from heat and allow to cool slightly. Discard the bay leaf and thyme stems. Using a blender or food processor, purée the entire contents of the soup pot. Return it to the soup pot and add salt to taste. Reheat it thoroughly on low.
5. Remove from heat. Stir in the cream and butter, mixing until the butter melts. Sprinkle with freshly ground black pepper and serve.

Black Lentil Soup

Serves 6–8

Out of vegetable broth? Water will work just as well for this recipe.

1 pound (16 ounces) dried
  black lentils
1 Spanish onion
1 (28-ounce) can whole
  tomatoes, drained
2 tablespoons fresh chopped
  ginger root
3 cloves garlic
2 tablespoons peanut oil
  or ghee (see page 82)
2 tablespoons sugar
1½ teaspoons ground coriander

1 teaspoon garam masala
  (see page 43)
1 teaspoon salt
½ teaspoon cayenne
12 cups Basic Vegetable Broth
  (see recipe on page 6)
1 cup plain yogurt
½ cup chopped scallions

1. Rinse the lentils thoroughly. Chop the onion and dice the tomatoes. Peel and finely chop the ginger root. Mince 2 of the garlic cloves.
2. Using a large soup pot, heat the oil on medium. Add the onion, minced garlic, ginger, and sugar. Sauté for 10 minutes, stirring occasionally, until the mixture caramelizes. Add the seasonings, stir, and sauté for 5 minutes.
3. Add the tomatoes and simmer for 10 minutes. (The sauce will be quite thick.) Pour in the vegetable broth and add the lentils. Bring to a boil, reduce to a simmer, and cook for 1½ hours.
4. Remove from heat. Mince the remaining garlic clove and add it to the soup. Stir in the yogurt, adding a bit at a time and mixing well. Coarsely chop the scallions and add them as garnish to the individual soup bowls.

Tunisian Bean Soup

1 cup uncooked chickpeas
1 cup dried lentils
3 large onions
3 cloves garlic
1 cinnamon stick
3 tablespoons olive oil
1 teaspoon turmeric
1½ teaspoon cumin seeds
2 teaspoons ground cumin
2 bay leaves
6 cups Potato and Vegetable
  Broth (see recipe on page 7)

1 (28-ounce) can of crushed
  tomatoes
Salt and black pepper
¼–½ teaspoon cayenne pepper
2 tablespoons lemon juice
Fresh mint (optional)
Currants (optional)

> **Serves 6**
>
> Garnish each serving with a few mint leaves and currants, if desired.

1. Soak the chickpeas overnight in cold water, then drain. Place the chickpeas in a large saucepan and add enough water to cover them by 3 inches. Bring to a boil, reduce to a simmer, and cook for 1 hour.

2. Meanwhile, rinse the lentils thoroughly. Finely dice the onion and mince the garlic.

3. When the chickpeas are ready, add the lentils and the cinnamon stick. Bring to a boil, reduce to a simmer, and cook for another 30 minutes.

4. While the chickpeas continue to cook, heat the oil in a soup pot. Add the onion, garlic, turmeric, cumin seeds, ground cumin, and bay leaves. Sauté on medium for 3 to 5 minutes. Add the broth and tomatoes to the soup pot. Bring to a boil, reduce to a simmer, and cook for another 15 minutes. Discard the bay leaves.

5. When the chickpeas and lentils are done, add them to the soup pot, discarding the cinnamon stick. Simmer for 5 minutes.

6. Season with salt, black pepper, and cayenne. Add the lemon juice.

Tuscan Bean Soup

½ cup dried black turtle beans
½ cup dried Great Northern
  beans
½ cup cranberry beans
½ cup dried chickpeas
½ cup dried lentils
1 Spanish onion
2 stalks celery
3 cloves garlic
1 (28-ounce) can whole tomatoes, drained
3 tablespoons olive oil

1 bay leaf
1 teaspoon rosemary
½ teaspoon black pepper
8 cups Basic Vegetable Broth
  (see recipe on page 6)
½ cup uncooked white rice
1 cup cooked and shelled
  broad beans (also called
  fava beans) **or** lima beans
Salt
Scallions (optional)

1. Soak the black turtle beans, Great Northern beans, cranberry beans, and chickpeas in cold water, in 4 separate containers, overnight, then drain.
2. Rinse the lentils thoroughly. Chop the onion and celery, mince 2 of the garlic cloves, and dice the tomatoes.
3. In a large soup pot, heat the oil on medium. Add the onion, celery, and minced garlic; Sauté for 4 minutes. Add the rosemary, bay leaf, and black pepper, stirring them in. Add the broth, black turtle beans, Great Northerns, cranberry beans, chickpeas, lentils, and the tomatoes. Bring to a boil, reduce to a simmer, and cook for 1½ hours.
4. Add the rice and simmer for 20 minutes.
5. Add the broad beans and salt to taste ; simmer for an additional 2 minutes. Mince the remaining garlic clove and stir it into the soup. Remove and discard the bay leaf. Chop the scallions to add as garnish.

Italian Bean Soup

3 cups mixed dried beans
½ bunch spinach
1 small onion
1¼ cup tomatoes
1 large carrot
1 small stalk celery
2 cloves garlic
1 tablespoon olive oil
8 cups Basic Beef Broth
   (see recipe on page 4)

1 teaspoon oregano
½ cup cooked leftover pasta
   (small shells or similar)
Romano cheese (optional)

Serves 8
You can use any combination of dried beans for this recipe; it is a great way to clear your pantry of those partially used bags of beans.

1. Soak the beans overnight in cold water, then drain.
2. Tear the spinach leaves, discarding the stems. Chop the onion and crush the tomatoes. Julienne the carrot and celery, and mince the garlic.
3. In a large saucepan or soup pot, heat the oil to medium. Add the onion and garlic, and sauté for 3 minutes. Add the beans, broth, and oregano; bring to a boil, reduce to a simmer, and cook for 45 minutes.
4. Add the tomatoes, carrots, and celery. Simmer for 15 minutes. Stir in the spinach and the pasta and simmer for 5 minutes. Grate the Romano to use as a garnish for each individual serving.

Easy Slicing with the Mandolin

A slim metal or plastic board with a planelike blade, known as a mandolin, makes cutting delicate julienne strips and paper-thin slices into child's play. These once-rare tools have become widely available. Compact, inexpensive Japanese models, like the Benriner, are a great choice. They usually sell for about $25 and slip into a knife drawer easily.

Garlic Soup

Serves 4

Fear not: Though this soup contains a lot of garlic, the taste is not strong.

20 cloves garlic
2 cups diced onions
1 cup diced green pepper
3 cups chopped tomatoes, fresh or canned
3–4 slices dark bread
4 cups broth (beef is best)

Salt
Freshly ground black pepper
Grated cheese (your favorite), optional

1. Separate the garlic cloves and boil them in water in their skins for 30 second. Rinse in cold water, drain, and slip off the peels. Slice the cloves thinly. Dice the onions and the green pepper. Roughly chop the tomatoes. Cut the bread into small cubes.
2. Using a soup pot, heat the olive oil at medium to medium high, then add the onions and green peppers. Sauté for 4 to 8 minutes. Add the garlic and tomatoes. Simmer for 15 minutes.
3. Add the broth and bring the mixture to a boil. Reduce heat, salt to taste, and add enough of the bread cubes to reach the consistency desired. Garnish with black pepper and grated cheese.

Storing Potatoes and Other Root Vegetables

Tubers and roots contain lots of starch, which turns to sugar in the cold. Many people enjoy the resulting sweeter flavor, and keep these foods for long periods in unheated "root cellars," or refrigerator drawers. Whatever your taste preference, store root vegetables in a dark place, away from heat sources. They should not be stored in plastic bags, as they are living things and need to breathe.

Carrot and Apricot Soup

1 small white onion
1 clove garlic
²⁄₃ cup dried apricots
3 large carrots
1 bay leaf

2 cups orange **or** tangerine juice
⅓ cup whole milk **or**
  half-and-half
⅓ cup cottage cheese (small
  curd best) **or** plain yogurt

Serves 6

Unsulfured apricots work best with this recipe. They don't have any orange color added to them.

1. Slice the onion and the garlic clove, thinly. Chop the apricots and carrots. Put all of them into a soup pot with the bay leaf and citrus juice. Bring to a boil, then reduce to a simmer; cook for about 45 minutes, covered.
2. Remove from heat and allow to cool slightly. Using a blender or food processor, mix the two dairy products. Pour the contents of the soup pot into the blender with the dairy mixture and purée. Return the purée to the soup pot and heat thoroughly, but do not allow it to boil. Serve.

Slow-Cooker French Onion Soup

4 large yellow onions, thinly
  sliced
¼ cup butter
3 cups Basic Beef Broth
  (see recipe on page 4)
1 cup dry white wine

¼ cup medium dry sherry
1 teaspoon Worcestershire sauce
1 clove garlic, minced
6 slices French bread, buttered
¼ cup Romano **or** parmesan
  cheese

Serves 6

To convert this to a stovetop method, simmer in a covered pot at a low temperature for 1 hour, adding water when necessary.

1. In a large frying pan, melt the butter on medium heat and sauté the onions until limp. Transfer to a slow cooker. Add the broth, wine, sherry, Worcestershire, and garlic. Cover. Cook on low for 6 to 8 hours.
2. Place buttered French bread on a baking sheet. Sprinkle with the cheese. Place under a preheated boiler until lightly toasted. To serve, ladle soup into bowl. Float a slice of toasted French bread on top.

Onion Soup

Serves 6–8

If you're looking for a change in flavor, use Basic Chicken Broth or Basic Vegetable Broth for this recipe (see recipes on pages 5 and 6).

1½ pounds yellow onions
3 tablespoons butter
1 tablespoon olive oil
8 cups Basic Beef Broth
   (see recipe on page 4)
1 teaspoon salt
¼ teaspoon sugar
3 tablespoons white flour
½ cup dry white wine

Salt and pepper
3 tablespoons cognac
6–8 pieces of toast
1–2 cups grated Swiss cheese
   (optional)

1. Thinly slice the onions. In a soup pot, heat the butter and olive oil on low. Add the onions and sauté, covered, for 10 to 15 minutes.

2. Meanwhile, pour the broth into a saucepan and slowly bring it to a boil. Reduce the heat and leave the broth at a rolling boil.

3. Increase the heat to medium and stir in the sugar and salt. Cover and cook for about 10 minutes, stirring frequently, until the onions turn golden brown. Sprinkle the flour over the onions and stir for a few minutes. Add the wine and the broth that has been boiling. Simmer 30–40 minutes, adding salt and pepper to taste.

4. Grate the cheese. Trim the bread slices into rounds and place 1 in the bottom of each serving bowl. Sprinkle the toasted bread rounds with the cognac. Ladle the warm soup over the bread and garnish with cheese.

Celery Root and Mushroom Soup

3½ cups celery root (about 2
    medium ones)
2 russet potatoes
2 tablespoons olive oil, divided
5 Portobello mushrooms
Freshly ground black pepper

25 morel **or** shiitake mushrooms
4 cups Basic Chicken **or**
    Vegetable Broth (see recipes
    on pages 5 and 6)
3 teaspoons chopped celery
    leaves **or** flat-leaf parsley

Serves 4–6

If you'd like, the
mushroom stems can
be frozen to use for a
broth another day.

1. Preheat the oven to 375 degrees. Trim and peel the celery roots and peel
   the potatoes. Cut them into small cubes. Toss with 1 tablespoon of olive
   oil (you can add a bit of salt and pepper, too, if you like), spread out
   evenly on a baking sheet, and roast for 35 to 40 minutes.
2. Meanwhile, remove the stems from all the mushrooms. Thinly slice
   the mushroom caps.
3. Pour the broth into a saucepan and bring it to a simmer over medium
   heat. Chop the celery leaves (or parsley). When the vegetables are
   just about done roasting, warm the remaining olive oil in a large pot.
   Sauté the mushrooms on medium-high heat for 3 to 4 minutes.
4. Place a mound of mushrooms into each serving bowl. Add the
   roasted celery roots and potatoes on top. Ladle the broth over the
   vegetables. Sprinkle lightly with freshly ground black pepper. Garnish
   with the celery leaves and serve.

Using Different Mushrooms

*Don't hesitate to substitute exotic dried mushrooms such as
wood ear, enoki, and porcini in any recipe calling for fresh mushrooms. However, you might have to alter the amount used,
depending on the type. Some mushrooms have very little flavor
(such as buttons) and absorb the flavors of other ingredients.
Others (such as shiitakes and dried morels) have a distinct taste
and are best used in a recipe that does not have a lot of other
intense, competing flavors.*

Roots Soup

1 small onion
2 medium carrots
1 medium parsnip
1 small celery root (**or** jicama)
1 medium-sized sweet potato
2 cloves garlic
4 cups Basic Vegetable **or**
    Mushroom Broth (see recipes
    on pages 6 and 11)
1½ teaspoons oil (**or** butter)

1½ teaspoons curry powder
3 tablespoons white flour
Salt and pepper
Cilantro sprigs (optional)

1. Peel all the vegetables. Chop the onion. Slice the carrots, parsnip, and celery root into ¼-inch-thick pieces. Cut the potato into ½-inch-thick slices and finely chop the garlic. In a saucepan, bring the broth to a boil.

2. In a soup pot, heat the oil. Add the onion and sauté on medium heat for 3 minutes. Add the garlic and curry powder, and sauté for 30 seconds. Sprinkle the flour over the top and whisk for 3 to 5 minutes. Add the boiling broth and the parsnip and carrots. In a small bowl, whisk the flour and water together until smooth; add this mixture to the soup pot. Bring to a boil, then reduce to a simmer, and cook for 15 minutes.

3. Add the potato and celery root, and salt and pepper to taste. Simmer for 10 to 20 minutes, until the vegetables are tender. Garnish each serving with a sprig of cilantro.

Borscht

4 large beets
⅓ cup barley flakes **or** rolled
 oats
1 teaspoon brown sugar
½ tablespoon lime **or** lemon juice

2 cups buttermilk **or** plain yogurt
Salt and pepper
2 scallions
Sour cream (optional)

> **Serves 2–4**
>
> To cut some calories, substitute plain yogurt for both the buttermilk and the sour cream in this recipe.

1. Remove the stems from the beets, but don't peel. Cover them with water in a large saucepan. Bring to a boil, then reduce to a simmer and cook for 30 to 40 minutes.
2. Remove from heat. Spoon out the beets and set them aside to cool. Transfer 1 cup of the beet cooking liquid to a smaller saucepan. (Reserve the remaining liquid.) Add the barley (or oats) and cook over medium heat for about 20 minutes, until all the liquid is absorbed. Remove from heat and let cool.
3. Peel the cooked beets and cut them into quarters. Using a blender or food processor, purée the beets with the barley, brown sugar, and lime (or lemon) juice. Add enough of the reserved beet liquid to thin slightly.
4. Pour the purée into a saucepan or soup pot. Add the buttermilk (or yogurt). Heat the soup thoroughly, but do not allow it to boil. Add salt and pepper to taste. Thinly slice the white parts of the scallions. Garnish each serving with a dollop of the sour cream (or yogurt) and a sprinkling of the scallions.

Peeling Cooked Beets with a Towel

To remove the skins of cooked beets or potatoes, wrap them in a clean, dry kitchen towel or paper towel, and rub off the thin outer skin. This is best done while they are warm from cooking. This is healthier and less wasteful than using a paring knife or vegetable peeler because most of the nutrients are in the skin and the layers directly beneath it. The beets will color your towel red, but most of the color will wash out.

Potato Pumpkin Soup

1½ pounds raw pumpkin
2 potatoes
2 tablespoons butter
2½ cups Basic Chicken Broth
   (see recipe on page 5)
Salt and pepper

⅔ cup milk
Croutons (optional)
Fresh chopped parsley
   (optional)

1. Peel the pumpkin and cut the flesh into cubes. Peel the potatoes and cut them into 1-inch slices. Place both in a large bowl and add enough water to cover the vegetables by 2 inches. Let stand for 1 hour.
2. Drain and dry the vegetables with a clean dishtowel. In a soup pot, melt the butter and sauté the pumpkin and potatoes on medium-low for 12 minutes, stirring occasionally.
3. In a saucepan, bring the broth to a boil. Add it to the soup pot with the pumpkin and potatoes. Cover and simmer for 20 minutes.
4. Drain, reserving the cooking liquid. Allow the vegetables to cool slightly. In a blender or food processor, purée the vegetables. Return the reserved liquid and the vegetables to the pot. Simmer, uncovered, for 5 more minutes, adding salt and pepper to taste.
5. Thicken, if necessary, by boiling briefly with the cover off. Reduce heat to low and drizzle in the milk, stirring constantly. Garnish with croutons and parsley.

Turnip and Caraway Seed Soup

½ cup butter **or** oil (avocado oil is a good choice)

2 pounds small round turnips, peeled and sliced

2 onions, finely chopped

1 pinch of pepper

1 pinch of sugar

1 teaspoon caraway seeds

8 cups Basic Chicken Broth (see recipe on page 5)

¼ cup sour cream **or** plain yogurt

¾ cup cream

Goat cheese **or** blue cheese crumbles (optional)

1 tablespoon chopped dill (optional)

Serves 6–8

Thoroughly chilled in the refrigerator, goat cheese crumbles easily between the fingers, or by flaking it with the tines of a fork.

1. In a soup pot, melt the butter on low heat and sauté the onion for 5 to 6 minutes. Add the turnips, tossing them with the buttery onion. Sprinkle with the pepper, cover, and cook on medium until the vegetables are bathed in their own juices.

2. Uncover, add the sugar, and cook until the juices have mostly evaporated and the turnips are caramelized, tossing every few minutes. Add the caraway seeds and broth, and salt and pepper to taste. Bring to a boil, then reduce to a simmer and cook until the turnips begin to fall apart.

3. Remove from heat and allow to cool slightly. Using a food processor or a blender, purée the mixture. In a separate bowl, whisk the dairy products together. Pour the purée and the dairy mixture into the soup pot. Reheat slowly and thoroughly, but don't allow it to boil. Garnish each serving with the cheese crumbles and dill.

Autumn Roots Soup

Garnish with a dollop of yogurt (or sour cream) just before serving.

2 cups Basic Beef Broth
  (see recipe on page 4)
2 cups water
1 carrot
3 beets
1 parsnip
1 celery root
1 onion

2 potatoes (red, russet,
  or Yukon gold)
2 tablespoons butter **or** oil
  (avocado is a good choice)
2 tablespoons white flour
Plain yogurt **or** sour cream
  (optional)

1. In a saucepan, combine the broth and water and bring to a boil. Peel and grate all the vegetables.
2. In a soup pot, heat the oil. Sauté the onion on medium for 3 minutes. Sprinkle the flour over the onion and whisk for 3 to 5 minutes. Pour the boiling broth into the soup pot and mix well. Add the vegetables. Bring to a boil, then reduce to a simmer and cook for 20 minutes.

Salsify Soup

Serves 4

The salsify root has a faint oyster taste and looks a bit like an elongated turnip.

5 medium salsify roots
½ of a lemon
4 cups whole milk

Salt and white pepper
Fresh chives

1. Peel and thinly slice the salsify. Place it in a soup pot and cover with cold water. Squeeze the lemon and add the juice to the pot. Bring to a boil, reduce to a simmer, and cook for 10 minutes.
2. Remove from heat and allow to cool slightly. Purée the mixture in a blender or food processor. Transfer the purée to the soup pot and add the milk gradually, until the desired consistency is achieved. Bring almost to a boil, then stir in the salt and white pepper to taste. Reheat thoroughly, but gently. Chop the chives to use as a garnish for each individual serving.

Four Potato Soup

4 purple potatoes
3 Yukon gold potatoes
3 red bliss potatoes
1 Idaho **or** russet potato
1 Spanish onion
2 stalks celery
2 red bell peppers
½ of a habanero chili
4 cloves garlic

4 pounds chicken pieces
5 tablespoons peanut oil
8 cups water
2 teaspoon ground cumin
2 teaspoon paprika
¼ teaspoon cayenne
½ cup cream
Salt and pepper
4 tablespoons chopped cilantro

Serves 8
You can use virtually any variety or combination of potatoes in this recipe. Shoot for 3 to 4 pounds of total spud weight.

1. Peel all the potatoes and cut them into 1-inch cubes. Chop the onion and celery. Seed and chop the bell peppers and chili. Mince 3 of the garlic cloves.

2. Using a soup pot, heat 3 tablespoons of the oil. Add the chicken pieces and brown them on all sides. Pour in the water. Bring to a boil, reduce to a simmer, and cook for 10 minutes.

3. Using a slotted spoon, remove the chicken pieces, reserving the cooking liquid. Set the chicken aside to cool. Strain the cooking liquid, discarding the solids, and set aside.

4. Meanwhile, using a blender or food processor, purée the uncooked onion, celery, red peppers, the minced garlic, and the chili. Once the chicken has cooled, pull the meat off the bones, discarding the skin and bones. Chop the meat into chunks.

5. Using a soup pot, heat the remaining oil. Pour in the puréed vegetable mixture and simmer for 4 minutes. Add the cumin, paprika, and cayenne, stirring to coat well. Add 4 cups of the reserved cooking liquid from the chicken, the meat, and all the potatoes. Bring to a boil, reduce to a simmer, and cook for 20 minutes, adding more of the chicken cooking liquid if necessary.

6. Remove from heat and add salt and pepper to taste. Mince the remaining garlic clove and chop the cilantro. Stir in the cream, garlic, and cilantro, and serve.

Potato and Salmon Chowder

1 pound salmon fillet
1 large onion
2 stalks celery
1 fennel bulb
6 red bliss potatoes
2 teaspoons thyme
1 teaspoon whole fennel seeds
2 bay leaves
4 cups Basic Vegetable Broth
   (see recipe on page 6)
1 cup tomato juice

2 tablespoons fresh chopped
   tarragon
4 tablespoons fresh chopped
   Italian flat-leaf parsley
   (optional)
1½ cups whole milk
Salt and pepper

1. Remove the skin from the salmon and cut the meat into 1-inch cubes. Chop the onion, celery, and fennel bulb. Cut the potatoes into 1-inch cubes.
2. Using a soup pot, melt the butter. Add the onion, celery, and fennel, cooking for 4 minutes on medium heat. Add the thyme, fennel seeds, and bay leaves, stirring to coat. Pour in the broth and tomato juice. Add the potatoes. Bring to a boil, reduce to a simmer, and cook for 20 minutes.
3. Add the salmon and simmer for another 5 minutes. Remove from heat and discard the bay leaves. Chop the tarragon and parsley. Stir the milk and the tarragon into the soup. Add salt and pepper to taste. Garnish with the parsley and serve.

Potato Soup with Roasted Garlic

1 large head garlic
1½ pounds russet potatoes
3 yellow onions
1 carrot
9 cloves garlic
6 cups water **or** Potato and
    Vegetable Broth (see recipe
    on page 7)

5 sprigs rosemary
1 (10-ounce) box tofu (silken
    kind)
Salt and white pepper

Serves 4–6
Use the leftover roasted garlic from this recipe as a spread on slices of warm sourdough or French bread.

1. Preheat oven to 350 degrees. Cut off and discard the very top of the whole garlic head. Place the garlic (top up) in a small baking dish with a lid, and drizzle some olive oil over the garlic. Cover and bake for 35 to 45 minutes, until tender. Set aside to cool.
2. Meanwhile, cut the potatoes into medium-sized chunks and chop the onion. Slice the carrot and peel the garlic cloves.
3. Using a soup pot, combine the potatoes, garlic, water (or broth), onion, carrot, and 4 of the rosemary sprigs. Bring to a boil, reduce to a simmer, and cook 25 minutes.
4. Take off heat and allow to cool slightly, discarding the rosemary sprigs. Break the tofu into pieces. Remove the pulp from the roasted garlic head by squeezing it from the bottom. (It will yield about 4 tablespoons of pulp.) Add the tofu and 2 tablespoons of the roasted garlic to the soup pot and mix well.
5. Purée the mixture in a blender or food processor. Return the pot to the heat and warm on low, adding salt and white pepper to taste. Garnish with the remaining rosemary sprig and serve.

Georgian Potato Soup

6 cups diced potatoes
1 small onion
3 scallions
3 carrots
2 cloves garlic
1 tablespoon chopped parsley
2 small tart apples
1/3 cup chopped dried apricots
1 1/4 cups cream
1/2 cup cottage cheese
2 1/2 tablespoons flour

1/4 teaspoon cumin
2 teaspoon mustard
1/2 teaspoon white pepper
1 tablespoon hot pepper flakes
1 teaspoon dill
1 tablespoon oil
3 cups Basic Chicken **or**
    Vegetable Broth (see recipes
    on pages 5 and 6)
1/3 cup currants

1. Cut the potatoes into 1/2-inch dice. Finely chop the onion and scallions. Julienne the carrots. Mince the garlic and chop the parsley. Peel the apples and cut them into 1/2-inch dice. Chop the dried apricots.
2. In a mixing bowl, combine 1 cup of the cream, the cottage cheese, and the flour. Beat until smooth. Then whisk in the rest of the cream. Set aside in the refrigerator. In a small bowl, stir together all the spices and the parsley. Divide into 2 equal portions and set aside.
3. Using a soup pot, heat the oil. Add 4 cups of the potatoes, the onions, scallions, garlic, carrots, apples and half of the spice mixture. Stirring constantly, cook over medium heat for 4 minutes, scraping the bottom of the pan often. Pour in the broth and add the apple pieces and the other half of the spice mixture. Bring to a boil, reduce to a simmer and cook for 12 minutes, stirring often.
4. Remove from heat and allow to cool slightly. Using a blender or food processor, purée the mixture. Return it to the pot, add the remaining diced potatoes, and bring to a boil. Reduce to a simmer and cook for 15 minutes, adding a bit more broth or water as necessary.
5. Remove from heat. Stir in the refrigerated dairy mixture, the currants, and the apricots. Return to heat and simmer gently for 4 minutes, making sure not to let it boil. Serve.

Spicy Onion and Apple Soup

5 cups chopped tart apple
2 cups chopped onion
3–4 cloves garlic
2 tablespoons fresh minced
  ginger
2 tablespoons lemon juice
2 tablespoons oil
2 teaspoons dry mustard
1 teaspoon cumin
½ teaspoon cardamom
½ teaspoon allspice

¼ teaspoon cayenne pepper
Salt and pepper to taste
4 cups Basic Vegetable Broth
  (see recipe on page 6)
2 cinnamon sticks
Brown sugar (optional)
Raisins (optional)

Serves 4–6

Garnish with a sprinkling of brown sugar and raisins, and serve.

1. Peel and chop the apples. Chop the onions and mince the garlic and ginger. Juice the lemon.
2. In a soup pot, heat the oil on medium. Add the onion, garlic, and ginger, sautéing for about 2 minutes. Add all the spices and sauté for another 3 to 4 minutes.
3. Add the apples, broth, cinnamon sticks, and lemon juice. Bring to a boil, reduce to a simmer, and cook for 10 minutes.
4. Remove from heat and allow to cool slightly. Take out the cinnamon sticks and purée the soup in a food processor or blender. Return to the pot and warm to serving temperature on medium heat.

Potato Purslane Soup

2 leeks
1 onion
2 large russet potatoes
1¼ cups purslane
1 cup watercress
1 tablespoon olive oil

3 cups water
1½ cups milk
Salt and pepper

1. Preheat the oven to 300 degrees. Cut the leeks into thin rings, using only the white and the light green parts. Dice the onion. Peel and cut the potatoes into a ½-inch dice. Remove the stems from the purslane and the heavy stems from the watercress. Place the leek pieces in a single layer on a foil-lined baking sheet. Bake for 35 minutes. Set aside.

2. While the leeks are cooking, heat the olive oil in a soup pot. Add the onion, sautéing for 8 minutes. Add the potatoes and the water, bringing the mixture to a boil. Reduce to a simmer and cook for 20 minutes.

3. Stir in 1 cup of the purslane and all the watercress, simmering for 2 minutes. Remove from heat and allow to cool slightly. Using a blender or food processor, purée the contents of the soup pot. Return it to the pot, stir in the milk and salt and pepper to taste, and reheat. Serve garnished with the remaining ¼ cup of purslane and the crisp leeks.

Potato and Vegetable Chowder

1 green bell pepper
1 red bell pepper
4 scallions
¾ pound baby potatoes
2–3 ears corn
2 tablespoon butter
1 teaspoon thyme

1 cup whole milk
Salt and pepper
3 cups Potato and Vegetable
 Broth (see recipe on page 7)

Serves 4–6

Substitute 1½ cups of frozen corn kernels if you're having trouble finding 2–3 fresh ears of corn.

1. Coarsely chop the green and red bell peppers. Cut the scallion into thick slices and cut the potatoes into chunks. Shuck the corn. Using a sharp knife, cut the kernels from the cobs, and discard the cobs (or defrost frozen corn).

2. Using a soup pot, heat the butter on medium. Add the bell peppers and scallions, sautéing for 3 minutes. Pour in the broth and add the potatoes and the thyme, bringing the mixture to a boil. Reduce to a simmer and cook for 15 minutes.

3. Add the corn and salt and pepper to taste, then drizzle in the milk, stirring constantly. Reheat gently and serve.

Potato Soup with Capers

1 pound baby potatoes
1 pound Yukon gold **or** russet
    potatoes
2 yellow onions
3 cloves garlic
1 tablespoon finely chopped
    ginger root
4 tomatoes
2 ears corn

4 tablespoons oil
4 pounds chicken pieces
2 teaspoons cumin seeds
6 cups Basic Chicken Broth
    (see recipe on page 5)
1 cup cream
2 tablespoons fresh chopped
    cilantro
3 tablespoons capers

1. Place the baby potatoes in a pot, cover with water, and bring to a boil; reduce to a simmer and cook for 12 to 18 minutes, until tender.
2. Meanwhile, peel the other potatoes and submerge them in a bowl filled with cold water. Finely chop the onions, garlic, and ginger root. Coarsely chop the tomatoes. Shuck (or defrost) the corn. Using a sharp knife, cut the kernels of the cobs, and discard the cobs.
3. Heat the oil in a large skillet. Place the chicken pieces, in a single layer, and brown for 7 minutes on each side. Using a slotted spoon, remove the pieces and set aside, reserving 1–2 tablespoons of the fat.
4. In a soup pot, combine the reserved fat, the onions, garlic, cumin seeds, and ginger, stirring for 10 minutes. Add the chicken broth. While it is coming to a boil, slice the big potatoes as thin as possible (as thin as potato chips if you can). Add them to the pan, along with the tomatoes and the chicken pieces. Reduce to a simmer and cook for 15 minutes, frequently skimming off any fat that rises to the top.
5. Remove from heat and allow to cool slightly. Take out the chicken pieces and set aside. Using a blender or food processor, purée the soup. Return the mixture to the soup pot and heat thoroughly on medium.

(continued)

6. Remove the skin and bones from the chicken pieces, cubing the meat and discarding the rest. Add the meat and the corn kernels to the pot. Cut the cooked baby potatoes into halves and add them to the soup pot.

7. Remove from heat. Chop the cilantro and add it to the pot, along with the capers. Drizzle in the cream, stirring constantly. Return the pot to the heat and bring the mixture to a gentle simmer; cook for 5 minutes, making sure not to let it boil.

Potato Soup with Watercress

2 leeks
3 medium russet potatoes
1 bunch watercress
3 tablespoons butter
6 cups Basic Chicken Broth
  (see recipe on page 5)

1 cup whole milk
Salt and white pepper
8 watercress leaves

Serves 4–6
If you'd like to spice up this recipe a bit, add 2 medium-sized onions for additional flavor.

1. Slice the leeks thinly, using only the white parts. Dice the potatoes and chop the watercress, reserving 8 whole leaves.

2. Using a soup pot, heat the butter. Add the leeks and sauté for 5 minutes on low heat. Pour in the broth and add the potatoes and watercress. Bring to a boil, reduce to a simmer, and cook for 5 minutes.

3. Remove from heat and allow to cool slightly. Using a blender or food processor, purée the mixture. Return it to the pot, adding the milk and salt and white pepper to taste. Reheat gently, but thoroughly. Garnish with the whole watercress leaves, and serve.

German Potato Soup with Marjora

2 pounds russet potatoes
1 carrot
1 stalk celery
1 leek
1 onion
5 cups Basic Beef Broth
   (see recipe on page 4)
Salt to taste
¼ teaspoon white pepper
¼ teaspoon thyme

¼ teaspoon marjoram, plus
   extra for garnish
1 bay leaf
2 tablespoons butter
3 tablespoons flour

1. Cut the potatoes into ¼-inch-thick slices. Chop the carrot and celery. Thinly slice the leek (white part only) and the onion.
2. Using a soup pot, combine the potatoes and broth. Bring to a boil, then reduce to a simmer and add the carrot, leek, celery, onion, salt, pepper, thyme, marjoram, and bay leaf. Cook for 25 minutes.
3. Remove from heat. Pour the mixture through a strainer, reserving only the liquid and the potatoes. Discard all the other vegetables. Purée the potato mixture, return it to the soup pot, and set aside.
4. In a small sauce pan, melt the butter and whisk in the flour. Heat until it begins to bubble. Pour in 1 cup of the potato purée, whisking constantly to incorporate. Pour this butter-flour mixture into the soup pot with the rest of the potato mixture. Reheat gently but thoroughly. Garnish with marjoram and serve.

Potato-Leek Soup

4 large potatoes
3 leeks
1 stalk celery
1 yellow onion
1 cup water

*1½ cups Basic Chicken **or** Beef*
Broth (see recipes on pages
5 and 4)
1 cup whole milk
Fresh chives (optional)

1. Thinly slice the potatoes, leeks (white parts only), celery, and onion. Place them in a soup pot and cover with water. Bring to a boil, reduce to a simmer, and cook for 30 minutes.
2. Pour in the broth, and bring to a boil. Strain the soup, pressing all the liquids out of the vegetables and discarding the solids.
3. Chop the chives. Stir in the milk and reheat gently, but thoroughly. Garnish with the chives, and serve.

Serves 2–4

For this soup, make sure that you use only the white part of the leeks.

Potato and Arugula Soup

1¼ pounds Yukon gold
5 cups arugula leaves
5 cloves garlic
3 slices multigrain bread

6 cups water
1 dash of red pepper flakes
Salt and pepper
Olive oil

1. Cut the potatoes into thick slices. Remove the stems from the arugula and tear the leaves. Thinly slice the garlic and cut the bread into cubes.
2. In a soup pot, combine the water and potatoes. Bring to a boil, reduce to a simmer, and cook for 15 minutes. Add the arugula and the garlic, and simmer for 5 more minutes.
3. Stir in the red pepper and bread pieces. Cover the pot, remove from the heat, and let stand for 10 minutes.
4. Reheat very gently. Ladle the soup into serving bowls and drizzle some olive oil over the top, then serve.

Serves 4–6

Yellow Finn potatoes can be substituted for Yukon gold potatoes in this recipe.

Potato-Bean Soup

½ pound potatoes
1 cup sliced carrots
½ pound tomatoes
½ cup sliced leeks
½ pound zucchini
1 cup chopped green beans
4 cloves garlic
6½ cups Basic Vegetable Broth
    (see recipe on page 6)
½ cups uncooked macaroni

6 cups cooked white beans
Freshly ground black pepper
14 fresh basil leaves
½ cup parmesan cheese
⅓ cup olive oil
Salt

1. Dice the potatoes and slice the carrots into rounds. Chop the tomatoes and slice the leeks into thin rings. Dice the zucchini and coarsely chop the green beans. Peel the garlic.
2. In a soup pot, bring the broth to a boil. Add the potatoes, carrots, and green beans. Reduce heat and simmer for 20 minutes.
3. Add the leeks, zucchini, and macaroni, simmering for an additional 10 minutes. Add the white beans and the tomatoes, and simmer for 5 more minutes. Pour in a little water if the soup needs to be thinned. Reduce to a *very* low heat.
4. Grate the parmesan. Using a food processor, combine the garlic, black pepper, and basil leaves. Add some of the cheese and olive oil to the mixture, creating a paste. Gradually add the rest of the cheese and oil.
5. Ladle the soup into individual bowls and add a dollop of the oil and cheese paste.

CHAPTER 10

Grain and Nut Soups

Brussels Sprouts Soup with Nuts

½ cup whole almonds **or** walnuts, plus extra for garnish
1 large onion
1 large stalk of celery
1 large potato
1 large tomato
1 clove garlic
1½ pounds Brussels sprouts
1 tablespoon olive oil

⅓ cup dry white wine
1 bay leaf
2½ teaspoons mixed herbs and spices (such as dill and caraway)
1–2 tablespoon lemon juice
Salt and black pepper
Fresh parsley

1. Preheat oven to 275 degrees. Place the nuts in a single layer on a baking sheet. Bake for about 20 minutes, until you can smell the roasted aroma. Set them aside to cool.
2. Meanwhile, coarsely chop all the vegetables, making sure to trim off the bottoms of the Brussels sprouts and pull off the toughest leaves. When the nuts are cool, rub them with a dry dishtowel to remove the skins. In a food processor, grind the nuts until they are nearly the consistency of a nut butter.
3. In a soup pot, heat the oil. Sauté the onion over medium heat until golden. Add the celery, potato, tomato, garlic, about 1 pound of the Brussels sprouts, and the wine. Pour in enough water to cover all the vegetables. Bring to a boil, then reduce heat and add the ground nuts, the bay leaf, and the spice mix. Simmer for 35 to 40 minutes. Remove the bay leaf.
4. With a slotted spoon, remove the solid ingredients and allow them to cool slightly. Purée them in a blender or food processor (in batches, if necessary), and return them to the soup pot. Thin the soup with a bit of water if desired. Turn the heat to low and cover the pot.
5. In a saucepan or steamer, steam the rest of the Brussels sprouts in water for about 10 minutes, making sure they are still bright green. Add them to the soup pot, along with the lemon juice and salt and pepper to taste. Chop the reserved nuts and the parsley. Garnish each serving with a sprinkling of nuts and parsley.

Tomato and Hearty Grains Soup

2 medium onions
2 celery stalks
2 carrots
2 potatoes
2 tablespoons oil
1 (28-ounce) can crushed **or**
   puréed tomatoes
½ cup raw brown rice (**or**
   wild rice; don't use white)
¼ cup raw pearl barley
¼ cup raw millet (**or** quinoa)

2 bay leaves
2 teaspoons mixed herbs
   (whatever you like), plus
   extra for garnish (optional)
6 cups Roasted Vegetable Broth
   (see recipe on page 7)
Salt and pepper
Mustard (optional)
Chopped green onions
   (optional)

Serves 8

Garnish with green onions or a bit more of the mixed herbs.

1. Cut the onions into thin slices. Finely dice the celery, carrots, and potatoes (peels on or off potatoes).

2. In a soup pot, heat the oil and sauté the onions on medium for 2 to 3 minutes. Add all the rest of the ingredients. Bring to boil, reduce to a simmer, and cover. Cook for 1 hour, stirring every so often, since the grains tend to sink to the bottom of the pot. Discard the bay leaves.

3. Add salt and black pepper to taste, and a bit of mustard, if you like. If the soup is too chunky, add water to thin to the desired consistency. Simmer for another 15 minutes. Garnish with green onions or a bit more of the mixed herbs.

Tofu Soup with Rice

6 cups Basic Chicken, Beef, or
  Vegetable Broth (see recipes
  on pages 5, 4, and 6)
6 cups mung bean sprouts
1 bunch scallions
1 bunch coriander
1 bunch mint

1 bunch basil
1 tablespoon chili oil **or** hot
  pepper sauce
2 lemons
4 cups cooked white rice
1 pound (16 ounces) firm tofu

1. Pour the broth into a large saucepan and heat on medium. Mince the sprouts, scallions, coriander, mint, and basil. In a bowl, toss them well with the chili oil and set aside to let the flavors mingle. Juice the lemons and cut the tofu into 1-inch cubes.
2. Stir the lemon into the hot broth. Place 1 cup of rice in the bottom of each serving bowl. Spoon the sprout and herb mixture on top of the rice and ladle the broth over the top.

Greek Rice and Lemon Soup

3 cups Basic Chicken Broth
  (see recipe on page 5)
½ cup uncooked long-grain rice
2 eggs

¼ cup lemon juice
Black pepper
Parsley **or** dill

1. In a medium saucepan, bring the broth to a boil. Add the rice, reduce to a simmer, and cook, covered, for about 20 minutes. Remove from heat and set aside, leaving the cover on.
2. In a medium bowl, whisk together the eggs and the lemon juice. Whisk in about 2 tablespoons of the hot rice broth. Drizzle this mixture into the rice mixture, stirring constantly, until it thickens.

Almond and Zucchini Soup

1 cup whole almonds
2 medium zucchini
4 cloves garlic
2 tablespoons butter
4 cups Basic Chicken **or**
　Vegetable Broth (see recipes
　on pages 5 and 6)
½ cup dry white wine

½ cup cream
Salt
Freshly ground black pepper
3–4 slices bacon (optional)

Serves 4

If you're looking to cut some calories, the bacon garnish is optional for this soup. It's tasty with or without.

1. Preheat oven to 275 degrees. Place the almonds in a single layer on a baking sheet. Bake them for about 20 minutes, until you can smell the roasted aroma. Set them aside to cool.

2. Meanwhile, cook the bacon and set it aside to drain on paper towels. Grate the zucchini and mince the garlic. Rub the almonds in a dry dishtowel to remove the skins; then grind the almonds in a food processor.

3. In a soup pot, melt the butter on medium. Stir in the zucchini and garlic and cook for 5 minutes, stirring almost constantly. Pour in the broth and the wine and simmer, uncovered, for 15 minutes. Stir in the almonds and remove from heat.

4. Allow the soup to cool slightly. In a blender or food processor, purée the mixture and then strain it back into the soup pot. Stir in the cream and add salt to taste. Reheat gently but thoroughly; do not allow it to boil. Crumble the bacon. Garnish each serving with a sprinkling of freshly ground black pepper and the crumbled bacon.

Storing Nuts

Squirrels freeze their nuts under the cold ground in winter. Maybe they're not so stupid after all. Nuts go rancid within a couple of months at room temperature. Store them in the freezer, in airtight containers.

Malaysian Peanut Soup

Serves 6

If you can't find Napa cabbage at your local store, try asking for Chinese cabbage. It's the same thing.

2 heads Napa cabbage
1 large onion
1 russet potato
2 sweet potatoes
1 (28-ounce) can whole tomatoes
1 tablespoon minced ginger
3 cloves garlic
5 tablespoons soy sauce (reduced sodium is best), divided
2 tablespoons lemon juice, divided
1/4 teaspoon black pepper

1 pound dry roasted peanuts (no salt or additives)
2 tablespoons peanut oil
1 tablespoon sugar
2 teaspoons cumin
2 teaspoons coriander
1 teaspoon turmeric
1/4–1/2 teaspoon cayenne
6 cups Basic Vegetable Broth
2 tablespoons Thai fish sauce
1 teaspoon hot pepper sauce

1. Trim and quarter the cabbages and chop the onion. Cut both kinds of potatoes into 1-inch cubes. Drain and dice the tomatoes. Mince the ginger and peel the garlic.
2. In a shallow dish, toss the cabbage with 2½ tablespoons of the soy sauce, 1 tablespoon of the lemon juice, and the pepper. Marinate in the refrigerator for 30 minutes.
3. Preheat the grill or broiler. Cook the marinated cabbage for about 6 minutes, turning them several times. Cut into 1-inch pieces and set aside.
4. Chop ½ cup of the peanuts. Set aside for the garnish. In a blender or food processor, purée the remaining peanuts into a thick paste. Set aside. Purée the garlic cloves and the ginger (together), and set aside.
5. In a large soup pot, heat the oil on medium. Add the garlic mixture, the onion, and the sugar; sauté for 3 minutes. Add the cumin, coriander, turmeric, and cayenne, stirring well. Add the tomatoes, increase the heat to medium-high, and cook until the mixture begins to bubble. Reduce to a simmer and cook for 5 minutes. Add the broth, both kinds of potatoes, the remaining soy sauce, and the fish sauce. Bring to a boil, reduce to a simmer, and cook for 20 minutes.
6. Add the cabbages, peanut paste, the remaining lemon juice, and the hot sauce. Simmer for 2 minutes. Garnish with the chopped peanuts.

Millet and Spinach Soup

1 (10-ounce) package frozen
   spinach
3 cups uncooked millet
1 large onion
3 cloves garlic
2 potatoes
1 carrot
1 teaspoon grated ginger
½ of a lemon
2 tablespoons nut oil
1 (14- to 16-ounce) can diced
   tomatoes

2 teaspoons curry **or** garam
   masala (see page 41)
8 cups Roasted Vegetable Broth
   (see recipe on page 10)
1 tablespoon chopped parsley
Salt and pepper
Plain nonfat yogurt (optional)

Serves 8

For added flavor, gar-
nish each serving with
a dollop of yogurt.

1. Defrost the spinach. Rinse the millet thoroughly. Chop the onion and
   mince the garlic. Dice the potatoes. Chop the carrot and grate the
   ginger. Squeeze the excess water from the spinach, and chop it
   coarsely. Juice the lemon.
2. In a large soup pot, combine the oil, millet, onion, garlic, potatoes,
   carrot, diced tomatoes in their juice, ginger, curry (if using garam
   masala instead, do *not* add it yet), and broth. Bring to a boil, reduce
   to a simmer, and cook for 1½ hours.
3. Chop the parsley and stir it into the soup, along with the spinach and
   lemon juice (if using garam masala, add it now). Add a bit more
   water if necessary to adjust the consistency. Simmer for another
   10 to 15 minutes. Add salt and pepper to taste.

Yucatan Rice and Chicken Soup

3 white onions
2 green bell peppers
1 dried chipotle chili
1 chipotle chili in adobo
    sauce, with 1 teaspoon of
    the sauce
3 cloves garlic
5 tablespoons peanut oil,
    divided
4 pounds chicken pieces
½ avocado leaf

10 cups water **or** Basic
    Chicken Broth (see recipe
    on page 5)
1 teaspoon epazote
½ cup uncooked white rice
3 scallions
½ cup chopped cilantro
¼ cup lime juice
2 cups yellow corn tortilla
    chips (optional)

1. Chop the onions and seed and chop the bell peppers. Mince both chipotle chilies and the garlic.
2. In a large saucepan, heat 3 tablespoons of the oil. Add the chicken pieces and brown them on both sides. Pour in the water (or broth); bring to a boil, reduce to a simmer, and cook for 15 minutes.
3. Using a slotted spoon, remove the chicken pieces, reserving the liquid. Strain the liquid and set aside 8 cups of it, discarding the rest. Tear the meat from the bones in chunks and set it aside, discarding the bones and skin.
4. Heat the remaining oil in a large soup pot. Add the onions, bell peppers, and garlic, and cook over medium heat for about 4 minutes. Add the avocado leaf, epazote, both chipotle chilies with their sauce; mix well. Add the chicken pieces and the 8 cups of reserved liquid. Bring to a boil, then reduce to a simmer; cook for 20 minutes, covered.
5. Add the rice and simmer for 20 more minutes.
6. Remove from heat, keeping it covered. Chop the scallions and cilantro, and stir them into the pot along with the lime juice. Cover the pot again and let the flavors mingle for 1 minute. Remove the avocado leaf. Garnish with the tortilla chips, and serve.

Barley and Wild Mushroom Soup

2½ pounds fresh mushrooms
   (a mix of any types)
1 large Spanish onion
1 stalk celery
2 carrots
5 tablespoons oil, divided
10 cups Mushroom Broth
   or Wild Mushroom Broth
   (see recipes on pages
   11 and 14)
½ dry white wine

2 teaspoons thyme
1 bay leaf
½ teaspoon black pepper
1 cup uncooked pearled barley
½ cup chopped Italian flat-leaf
   parsley
2 cloves garlic
1 tablespoon balsamic vinegar

Serves 6–8

For a heartier taste, you can use a dry red wine in place of a bottle of the white wine.

1. Slice the mushrooms, removing the stems and reserving them. Chop the onion, celery, and carrots.
2. In a large soup pot, heat 2 tablespoons of the oil. Add all the mushroom stems and a few of the sliced mushroom caps. Cover on low heat and cook for 5 minutes, until they begin to release juice. Add the broth and wine. Bring to a boil, reduce to a simmer, and cook for 20 minutes.
3. Strain the liquid from the soup pot into another container, reserving 8 cups and discarding the rest. Set aside. Heat the remaining oil in the soup pot on medium heat. Add the onions, celery, and carrots, and cook for 4 minutes. Stir in the thyme, bay leaf, and pepper, coating the vegetables. Add the remaining mushroom caps and sauté for 5 minutes. Pour in the reserved broth and add the barley. Bring to a boil, then reduce to a simmer; cook for 1 hour, covered.
4. Chop the parsley and mince the garlic. Remove the pot from the heat and stir in the balsamic vinegar, parsley, and garlic. Remove the bay leaf, and serve.

Wild Rice Soup

2 stalks celery
1 carrot
1 onion
½ green bell pepper
3 tablespoons fresh chopped parsley
1 tablespoon butter
3 tablespoons flour
¼ teaspoon black pepper
1½ cups cooked wild rice
1 cup water

1 cup whole milk
2 cups Basic Chicken Broth **or** Wild Mushroom Broth (see recipes on pages 5 and 14)
⅓ cup slivered almonds
Salt

1. Slice the celery, coarsely shred the carrot, and chop the onion, bell pepper, and parsley.
2. In a soup pot, heat the butter. Add the vegetables and sauté on medium for 4 minutes.
3. Shake on the flour and pepper. Stir in the cooked wild rice, water, and broth. Bring to a boil, reduce to a simmer, and cook for 15 minutes.
4. Remove from heat. Drizzle in the milk, stirring constantly. Add the almonds and parsley, and salt to taste. Reheat thoroughly, but do not boil.

Rice and Coriander Soup

¼ cup fresh minced ginger root
3 scallions
1¼ coriander leaves
5 cups Basic Vegetable Broth
   (see recipe on page 6)
1½ cups uncooked white rice
1 pound whole ginger root
   (in addition to the minced
   ginger above)
2 tablespoons salt, divided

1 tablespoon Chinese grain
   vinegar
½ cup sugar
½ teaspoon fresh chopped hot
   red pepper

Serves 6–8

You will have quite a bit of pickled ginger left over. Refrigerate whatever you don't use, and use it for other Chinese dishes.

1. Mince enough ginger root to make ¼ cup. Finely chop the scallions and the coriander leaves.
2. Pour the broth into a soup pot and add the rice; bring to a boil, reduce to a simmer, and cook for 1 hour.
3. Meanwhile, prepare the pickled ginger: Peel the whole ginger root and slice it very thinly. Boil water in a saucepan and add the ginger slices; boil for 20 seconds, then drain. Place the ginger slices in a bowl and sprinkle with 1 tablespoon of the salt. Let it sit at room temperature for 30 minutes. Drain and discard the liquid. Toss the ginger with the vinegar and the sugar, coating it well. Chop the hot red pepper and stir it in. Set aside.
4. When the rice mixture is done cooking, stir the remaining salt, the ¼ cup of minced ginger, the scallions, and 1 cup of the coriander leaves into the rice mixture. Remove from heat. Ladle the soup into serving bowls. Garnish each serving with the ¼ cup of coriander leaves and some of the pickled ginger.

Mushroom and Barley Soup

6 cup water, divided
1 ounce dried shiitake mush-
    rooms
2 cups sliced fresh mushrooms
    (any kind)
2 onions
2 carrots
2 stalks celery
2 tablespoons oil
3 tablespoons pearl barley
1 bay leaf

⅛ teaspoon thyme
⅛ teaspoon pepper
Salt
2 cups Basic Vegetable **or** Beef
    Broth (see recipes on pages
    6 and 4)

1. Boil 1 cup of the water, remove from heat, and soak the dried shi-itakes in it for 15 to 30 minutes. Meanwhile, slice the fresh mush-rooms and chop the onions, carrots, and celery; then chop the soaked mushrooms, reserving the soaking liquid.
2. In a soup pot, heat the oil. Add the fresh mushrooms and the onion, sautéing on medium for 8 minutes.
3. Add the broth, the remaining water, carrots, celery, soaked mush-rooms, and their soaking liquid. Bring to a boil, reduce to a simmer, and cook for 45 minutes.
4. Add the barley, bay leaf, thyme, and pepper, simmering for another 40 minutes. Discard the bay leaf, salt to taste, and serve.

Rice and Egg Soup

6 cups Potato Vegetable Broth
   (see recipe on page 7)
1 cup Basic Vegetable Broth
   (see recipe on page 6)
3 eggs
1 lemon

1½ cups cooked long-grain rice
Black bread cubes **or** croutons
   (optional)

Serves 6
Garnish with a few bread cubes (or croutons), and serve.

Place the broths in a soup pot on medium-high heat. Juice the lemon and whisk it into the eggs in a small bowl. Whisk in a few tablespoons of the hot broth, stirring constantly to incorporate. Drizzle this mixture into the soup pot, stirring and heating to combine. Stir in the cooked rice and heat for a few minutes.

Tortilla Soup

4 whole green chilies
2 medium-sized tomatoes
1 onion
2 cloves garlic
3 corn tortillas
¼ cup shredded cheddar
   cheese
2 tablespoons olive oil
1½ cups Basic Beef Broth
   (see recipe on page 4)
1½ cups water

1½ cups Basic Chicken Broth
   (see recipe on page 5)
1½ cups tomato juice
1 teaspoon ground cumin
1 teaspoon chili powder
Freshly ground black pepper
4 teaspoons Worcestershire
   sauce

1. Roast the chilies on the grill or under the broiler, turning them a few times, until the skin is blackened. Transfer the peppers to a paper or plastic bag, seal it tightly, and set aside to steam (this makes them easier to peel).
2. Meanwhile, drop the tomatoes into a pan of boiling water for about 15 seconds, until the peels just begin to split open; drain and rinse the tomatoes under cold water. Peel, seed, and dice the tomatoes. Chop the onion and mince the garlic. Cut the tortillas into ½-inch-wide strips and shred the cheese. Peel, seed, and dice the roasted chilies.
3. Using a soup pot, heat the oil. Add the onion, chilies, and garlic, sautéing on medium heat for 5 minutes. Add the tomatoes, both kinds of broth, water, tomato juice, cumin, chili powder, pepper, and Worcestershire sauce. Bring to a boil, reduce to a simmer, and cook for 45 minutes.
4. Add the tortillas and cheese; mix well and simmer for 10 minutes.

CHAPTER 11

Pasta Soups

Spaghetti Soup

1 pound (16 ounces) dried red kidney beans

1 Spanish onion

3 cloves garlic

3 tablespoons peanut oil

1 pound hamburger meat

2 tablespoons chili powder

1 tablespoon oregano

1½ teaspoon ground coriander

1 dash of cinnamon

1 dash of allspice

1 dash of ground cloves

1 dash of cayenne pepper

2 bay leaves

1 (28-ounce) can diced tomatoes

8 cups water

3 cups cooked spaghetti

1 cup grated cheddar

1. Soak the beans overnight in cold water to cover, then drain. Chop the onion and mince the garlic.
2. Place the beans in a large saucepan with enough water to cover them. Bring to a boil, reduce to a simmer, and cook for 1½ hours. Drain, reserving 1 cup of the cooking liquid, and set aside both.
3. Using a soup pot, heat the oil. Add the ground beef and brown it, breaking it up with a wooden spoon as it cooks. With a slotted spoon, remove the meat and set it aside to drain on paper towels, reserving the oil in the pan.
4. Add the onion and garlic to the soup pot, and sauté them for 3 minutes. Add the chili powder, oregano, coriander, cinnamon, allspice, cloves, cayenne, and bay leaves. Stir for 5 minutes.
5. Add the tomatoes and their liquid and simmer for 2 minutes. Place the beef back in the pot, add the water, and bring to a boil. Reduce to a simmer and cook, uncovered, for 10 minutes. Stir in the beans and some of the reserved cooking liquid. Simmer for 2 minutes.
6. Remove the bay leaves. Grate the cheese. Put some of the cooked spaghetti in each bowl, ladle the chili mixture over the spaghetti. Garnish with the grated cheese.

Macaroni and Cheese Soup

1 small carrot
1 small stalk celery
1 small onion
¼–½ pound (4–8 ounces)
   cheddar cheese
1 cup uncooked elbow macaroni
¼ cup butter
4 cups Basic Chicken Broth
   (see recipe on page 5)

½ teaspoon white pepper
2 tablespoons cornstarch
2 tablespoons water
1 (8-ounce) can corn kernels,
   drained
½ cup peas (optional)

Serves 6

Out of corn starch? Potato starch can be substituted for corn starch in this soup.

1. Finely chop the carrot, celery, and onion. Cube the cheese.
2. In a pot, cook the macaroni in unsalted water, according to the directions on the package. Rinse it in cold water, and set aside.
3. In a large skillet, melt the butter. Add the carrots, celery, and onion, sautéing for 3 minutes on medium heat. Remove the pan from the heat and set aside.
4. In a soup pot, combine the milk and cheese. Stirring constantly, cook on medium-low heat until the cheese melts. Add the chicken broth and pepper; mix well.
5. In a small glass, whisk the cornstarch into the water until smooth; add it to the soup pot. Simmer, stirring constantly, for 1 minute. Add the macaroni, the sautéed vegetables, the corn, and peas (if using). Reheat on low.

Chicken Tortellini Soup

Serves 6

Save your leftovers for a day before making this soup. Any kind of leftover cooked vegetables can be used in this recipe.

1 onion
2 cloves garlic
2 cups cubed cooked chicken
1 tablespoon oil
6 cups Basic Chicken Broth
   (see recipe on page 5)

1 teaspoon dill
9 ounces tortellini (fresh **or** dried)
2 cups leftover cooked vegetables
¼ teaspoon pepper
Romano cheese (optional)

1. Chop the onion, mince the garlic, and cube the chicken.
2. In a soup pot, heat the oil. Sauté the onion and garlic for 3 minutes on medium heat. Add the chicken broth, tortellini, vegetable mix, chicken cubes, dill, and pepper. Bring to a boil, reduce to a simmer and cook for 7 minutes for fresh tortellini and 15 minutes for dried tortellini.
3. Grate the cheese as a garnish, and serve.

Armenian Noodle Soup

Serves 6–8

If you'd like to add a personal touch to your cooking, try growing fresh mint in a small pot on your windowsill.

1 onion
6 tablespoons butter
8 cups Scotch Broth
   (see recipe on page 9)
½ cup tomato sauce

2 cups uncooked egg noodles
   (¼-inch wide)
1 tablespoon fresh chopped mint (optional)

1. Finely chop the onion. In a saucepan, heat the butter. Sauté the onion for 3 minutes on medium heat.
2. In a soup pot, combine the broth and tomato sauce, and bring to a boil. Stir in the noodles. Simmer for 4 minutes.
3. Add the onions to the soup pot. Chop the mint. Ladle the soup into the individual bowls, garnish with the mint, and serve.

Minestrone with Penne

2 large Spanish onions
6 cloves garlic
3 carrots
3 stalks celery
1 medium head green cabbage
10 large kale leaves
1 (28-ounce) can plum tomatoes
1 (16-ounce) can chickpeas
   (also called garbanzo beans)
½ cup olive oil

½ teaspoon thyme
2 bay leaves
12 cups water
1 cup (8 ounces) penne pasta
Salt and pepper

> **Serves 10**
>
> Experiment with vegetable pastas such as tomato or spinach. They frequently have a more substantial consistency and more nutrients than regular pasta.

1. Chop the onions, garlic, carrots, celery, cabbage, and kale. Cut the plum tomatoes in pieces, reserving their liquid. Drain and rinse the chickpeas.

2. Using a soup pot, heat the oil. Add the onions, garlic, carrots, and celery, and cook for 6 minutes. Add the cabbage, kale, thyme, and bay leaves, stirring well for 1 minute. Add the water, tomatoes, and chickpeas, bringing to a boil. Reduce to a simmer and cook for 45 minutes. Discard the bay leaves.

3. Add the penne and simmer for 15 minutes. Add salt and pepper to taste, and serve.

Pasta e Fagioli

1 tablespoon olive oil
1 medium onion, chopped
1 cloves garlic, finely chopped
1 large carrot, sliced in ¼-inch rounds
1 small zucchini, chopped
1 tablespoon fresh basil, chopped
2 tablespoons (tightly packed) fresh chopped parsley leaves
½ cup (tightly packed) fresh spinach, stems removed
*1–2 cups coarsely chopped fresh **or** canned tomatoes*
*1 cup canned kidney beans (**or** your favorite bean), including the liquid*

*4 cups Basic Chicken Broth (see recipe on page 5) **or** water*
2 tablespoons lemon juice
½ tablespoon white wine vinegar
1 teaspoon dried oregano
Salt and freshly ground black pepper to taste
1 cup (8 ounces) cooked short pasta (such as spirals, bow-ties, elbows)
*Grated Swiss **or** parmesan cheese (optional)*

1. Heat the olive oil in a heavy saucepan or Dutch oven. Add the onion, garlic, and carrot, and cook until the onions begin to turn brown and caramelize. Add the zucchini, basil, parsley, and spinach. Cook until the basil and spinach are wilted. Add all the remaining ingredients except the pasta and cheese, and stir to combine. Bring the mixture to a boil, then simmer gently for 20 to 30 minutes.
2. Divide the pasta among the serving bowls, ladle the soup over the top, and sprinkle with grated cheese.

Artichoke and Orzo Soup

8 baby artichokes
2 cups water
2 tablespoons lemon juice
1 yellow onion
2 tablespoons olive oil
6 cups Basic Chicken Broth
   (see recipe on page 5)
2 large eggs

¼ pound (4 ounces) uncooked
   orzo pasta
¼ cup grated Parmigiano
   Reggiano cheese

Serves 6
"Large" eggs connotes an actual measurement, not a rough estimate. Buy eggs labeled "large" when they're specified in a recipe.

1. Trim the artichokes to remove the outer leaves. Mix the water and lemon juice, and dip the artichokes into it. Cut the top inch off the artichokes and trim the stem, then dip them again. Discard the dipping liquid and dry off the artichokes. Cut them in half, lengthwise. Cut each in half again, into ⅛-inch pieces. Very finely dice the onion.

2. In a large saucepan, heat the oil and add the onion. Sauté on medium for 3 minutes, stirring often. Stir in the artichoke slices and cook for an additional 5 minutes. Remove from heat, cover, and set aside.

3. In a soup pot, bring the chicken broth to a simmer. Add the orzo and simmer for 6 minutes. Place the serving bowls (or tureen) in the oven to warm. Add the artichoke mixture to the broth mixture and stir well. Reduce heat to lowest setting.

4. Grate the cheese. In a medium bowl, whisk the eggs slightly, then whisk in the cheese. Ladle the soup into the warmed serving bowls, drizzle with the egg and cheese mixture, and serve.

Pasta and Tofu Soup with Roasted Garlic

Serves 6–8

You can store the left-over roasted garlic in the refrigerator to use another day.

1 whole head garlic, plus 8
   cloves
8 cups garlic broth
¼ pound (4 ounces) firm tofu
1 tablespoon peanut oil
2 teaspoons low-sodium soy
   sauce
2 tablespoons sesame oil
3 tablespoons balsamic vinegar

Salt and black pepper
2 cups cooked pasta shells
2 large eggs
Scallions

1. Roast the whole garlic head: Preheat oven to 350 degrees. Cut off and discard the very top of the whole garlic head. Place the garlic (top up) in a small baking dish with a lid, and drizzle some olive oil over the garlic. Cover and bake for 35 to 45 minutes, until tender. Allow to cool. Squeeze out the roasted garlic pulp and discard the rest.

2. In a blender or food processor, purée 1 cup of the broth with 2½ tablespoons of the roasted garlic. Set aside. Mince the 8 fresh garlic cloves and cut the tofu into small cubes.

3. Using a soup pot, heat the oil. Add the minced garlic and sauté on low heat for 6 minutes. Add the roasted garlic purée and the remaining broth. Bring to a boil, reduce to a simmer, and cook for 5 minutes.

4. Add the soy sauce, sesame oil, balsamic vinegar, tofu, and salt and pepper to taste, stirring on low heat until thoroughly warmed. Cover and leave on low heat while you whisk the eggs in a small bowl. Uncover and drizzle the eggs on top of the soup. Simmer for 5 minutes.

5. Chop the scallions. Divide the cooked pasta among the serving bowls. Ladle the soup over the top, and garnish with the scallions, and serve.

Pork and Escarole Soup with Ditalini

2 tablespoons olive oil
2 cloves garlic, minced
1½ cups sliced pork (½-inch pieces)
3 cups (tightly packed) thinly sliced escarole
6 cups Basic Chicken Broth (see recipe on page 5)
½ cup ditalini pasta
1 tablespoon chopped fresh oregano

½ teaspoon dried thyme
3 tablespoons grated parmesan cheese, plus extra for garnish
Salt and freshly ground black pepper

Serves 4

1½ teaspoons of dried oregano can be substituted for the 1 tablespoon of fresh oregano called for in this soup.

1. In a soup pot, heat the olive oil on medium-low. Add the garlic and sauté until soft. Add the pork, increase heat to medium-high, and brown quickly. Reduce heat back to medium-low. Add the escarole and cook until it just begins to wilt. Add the broth, increase heat to high, and bring to a boil. Reduce to a simmer and add the oregano, thyme, and parmesan; simmer for 5 minutes. Add salt and pepper to taste.
2. Cook the pasta until al dente, according to package directions. Drain and stir it into the soup. Ladle into warm soup bowls and sprinkle with parmesan.

Using Pork Elsewhere
Although pork is not really "the other white meat," today's pigs are not fat. In fact, pork tends to be leaner than beef. Substitute pork for beef in any recipe, but remember to remove the fat from around the edges.

Quadretti and Chickpea Soup

4 plum tomatoes
3 cloves garlic
3 tablespoons olive oil
1 teaspoon dried rosemary
   (**or** 2 teaspoons fresh)
2 cups canned chickpeas
   (garbanzo beans), drained
   and rinsed
Salt and freshly ground pepper

4 cups Basic Beef Broth
   (see recipe on page 4)
½ cup quadretti pasta
¼ cup grated parmesan cheese

1. Drop the tomatoes into a pot of boiling water for about 15 seconds (until the peels just begin to split); drain and rinse under cold water. Peel, seed, and roughly chop the tomatoes. Mince the garlic cloves.

2. In a large soup pot, heat the oil on medium. Add the garlic and sauté for 3 minutes. Stir in the tomatoes and rosemary. Reduce heat to medium-low and cook until the tomatoes have reduced, about 15 minutes.

3. Add the chickpeas and salt and pepper to taste; cook for about 5 minutes. Pour in the broth, cover, and cook another 15 minutes.

4. Using a slotted spoon, remove about ½ cup of the chickpeas. Mash them with a fork or purée them in a blender; return the purée to the soup and heat thoroughly.

5. Cook the pasta until al dente, according to package directions. Drain, stir into soup, and heat through. Remove from heat, stir in the parmesan, and serve.

Curry-Style Tomato Noodle Soup

1 tablespoon peanut oil **or** ghee (see page 82)
1 onion, finely chopped
2 cloves garlic, finely minced
1 tablespoon curry powder
2 (28-ounce) cans chopped plum tomatoes, including liquid
4 cups Basic Chicken Broth, divided (see recipe on page 5)
¼ teaspoon cinnamon
Salt and pepper
4 cups cooked egg noodles

Serves 8

After cooking the egg noodles, sprinkle a few drops of olive oil on the drained pasta to keep it from sticking together.

1. In a large saucepan or soup pot, warm the oil on medium-low heat. Add the onion and sauté for 5 minutes. Add the garlic and curry powder, and sauté for a 3–4 minutes, stirring constantly. Add the tomatoes, along with their liquid, to the pot. Add 2 cups of the broth, the cinnamon, and a sprinkling of salt and pepper. Simmer over medium-low heat, partially covered, for 25 minutes.

2. Remove from heat and allow to cool slightly. Purée the soup in a blender, in small batches, and return it to the pot. Add the remaining broth and salt and pepper to taste; heat to serving temperature. Divide the cooked noodles among the serving bowls and ladle the soup over the top.

Linguine with Beef and Black Bean Chili

2 tablespoons vegetable oil
1 pound ground beef
¾ cup finely diced onion
1 jalapeño chili pepper, seeded
 and thinly sliced
2 tablespoons chili powder
1 tablespoon ground cumin
2 cloves garlic, finely chopped
1 (15-ounce) can black beans,
 rinsed well and drained

1 (16-ounce) can crushed
 tomatoes
2 tablespoons chopped fresh
 cilantro
1 cup water
1 cup Basic Beef Broth
 (see recipe on page 4)
Salt and freshly ground pepper
1 pound (16 ounces) linguine

1. In a soup pot, heat the oil on medium and brown the meat, stirring with a wooden spoon to break it up. Add the onion, jalapeño, chili powder, cumin, and garlic, and cook until the onion is golden brown. Add the beans, tomatoes, cilantro, water, and broth. Bring to a boil, reduce to a simmer, and cover; simmer for 15 minutes.
2. Cook the linguine until al dente, according to package directions; drain.
3. Skim off any fat that has accumulated on the top of the soup. Add the cooked linguine and salt and pepper to taste. Stir over medium heat until the pasta is well coated with sauce and the mixture begins to simmer. Serve.

Orzo and Egg Soup

8 cups Basic Chicken Broth
(see recipe on page 5)
½ cup uncooked orzo pasta

3 eggs
½ cup lemon juice

1. In a soup pot, bring the broth to a boil. Stir in the orzo, reduce to a simmer, and cover; cook for 10 minutes. Remove from heat, keeping covered to allow the pasta to cook further.
2. In a medium bowl, beat the eggs until they are frothy. Drizzle in the lemon juice, beating until it thickens. Place the soup pot with the orzo on low heat. Drizzle about 2 cups of the hot pasta broth into the egg mixture, beating constantly; then stir all the egg mixture into the soup pot. Serve immediately.

Serves 6–8

Orzo is actually rice shaped pasta. In fact, you can substitute ½ cup of rice if you'd like. (See page 182 for Greek Rice and Lemon Soup.)

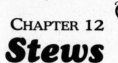

CHAPTER 12
Stews

Gone-All-Day Stew

1 (10¾-ounce) can condensed tomato soup
1 cup water
¼ cup flour
2 pounds beef chuck, cut into 1-inch cubes
3 medium carrots, cut diagonally into 1-inch pieces
½ cup diced celery
6 medium-sized yellow onions, quartered
4 medium potatoes, peeled and cut into 1½-inch cubes
2 beef bouillon cubes
1 tablespoon Italian herb seasoning
1 bay leaf
Salt and pepper

Preheat the oven to 275 degrees. In a bowl, mix together the soup, water, and flour until smooth. In a roasting pan with a cover, combine this mixture with all the remaining ingredients; bake for 4 to 5 hours. Remove from the oven and discard the bay leaf. Add salt and pepper to taste, and serve.

Sloppy Joe Stew

1 tablespoon olive oil
1 pound ground beef
½ cup chopped onions
½ teaspoon salt
1 dash of pepper
1 (14-ounce) can diced tomatoes
2 large potatoes, peeled and sliced
1 cup sliced carrots
½ cup chopped celery

Warm the oil in a large, heavy skillet over low heat and brown the hamburger, stirring it with a wooden spoon to break it up. Drain off the fat. Stir in the onions, salt, and pepper. Add all the remaining ingredients, mixing well. Bring to a boil, reduce to a simmer, and cook until the potatoes are tender, about 20 minutes.

Carolyn's Southwestern Chicken Stew

3 pounds chicken pieces
(breasts, thighs, legs), skin
and fat removed
¼ cup flour, plus 1 tablespoon
¼ cup olive oil
2 tablespoons minced garlic
5 cups Basic Chicken Broth
(see recipe on page 3)
1 (14-ounce) can whole tomatoes, roughly chopped
1 (6-ounce) can tomato paste
16 pearl onions
1½ teaspoons seasoned salt
1½ teaspoons ground cumin
4 sprigs oregano
4 sprigs thyme

1 bay leaf
¼ teaspoon crushed red
pepper flakes
½ pound (8 ounces) kielbasa
2 cups cubed new potatoes
2 cups coarsely chopped
zucchini
2 cups coarsely chopped
carrots
2 cups coarsely chopped
yellow squash
1 (8-ounce) can whole kernel
corn
Fresh chopped cilantro
(optional)

Serves 6
To cut down on the fat, you can substitute smoked turkey sausage for the kielbasa.

1. In a bag, coat the chicken pieces with the ¼ cup of flour. Heat the oil in a soup pot or Dutch oven and brown the chicken. Using a slotted spoon, remove the chicken and set aside. Drain off all but 1 teaspoon of the drippings.

2. Whisk the remaining flour and the garlic into the drippings, mixing for 30 seconds. Stir in next 10 ingredients starting with chicken broth and ending with red pepper flakes. Bring to a boil; reduce to a simmer and cook, uncovered, for 20 minutes.

3. Add the chicken pieces and the kielbasa; cover and simmer 20 minutes longer.

4. Skim off any fat that has accumulated on the top. Add all the vegetables. Simmer, covered, for 30 minutes. Discard the bay leaf. Garnish with the cilantro, and serve.

Brunswick Stew

2 (2½-pound) whole chickens
8 cups (2 quarts) water
1 tablespoon salt
1½ cups ketchup, divided
2 tablespoons light brown sugar
1½ teaspoons dry mustard
1½ teaspoons fresh grated
  ginger
½ of a lemon, sliced
1 clove garlic, minced
1 tablespoon butter
¼ cup white vinegar
3 tablespoons vegetable oil

1 tablespoon Worcestershire
  sauce
¾ teaspoon hot sauce
½ teaspoon pepper
2 (28-ounce) cans diced tomatoes
2 (15-ounce) cans whole kernel
  corn, including liquid
2 (15-ounce) cans creamed-style
  corn
1 large onion, chopped
¼ cup (firmly packed) light
  brown sugar
Salt and pepper to taste

1. Place the chickens in large soup pot or Dutch oven. Add the water and salt, and bring to a boil; cover, reduce heat, and simmer for 45 minutes, or until the chicken is tender. Drain off all but 4 cups of the cooking liquid.
2. Remove and discard the skin and bone from the chickens. Shred the meat and add it to the pot with the reserved cooking liquid.
3. In a small saucepan, combine ½ cup of the ketchup, the sugar, mustard, ginger, lemon, garlic, butter, vinegar, oil, Worcestershire, hot sauce, and pepper; cook on medium heat, stirring occasionally, for 10 minutes.
4. Stir the ketchup mixture into the soup pot with the chicken and broth. Add the remaining 1 cup ketchup and all other remaining ingredients; simmer, stirring often, for 4 hours or until thickened.

Montana Stew

2 tablespoons all-purpose flour
1 tablespoon paprika
4 teaspoons chili powder,
   divided
2 teaspoons salt
2½ pounds beef, cubed
3 tablespoons oil
2 medium onions, sliced
1 clove garlic, minced
1 (28-ounce) can diced tomatoes

1 tablespoon cinnamon
1 teaspoon ground cloves
½ teaspoon crushed red pepper
2 large potatoes, cubed
2 cups roughly chopped carrots
Salt and pepper

Serves 8
Hearty stews are just right for family reunions and tailgate picnics.

1. In a small bowl, mix together the flour, paprika, 1 teaspoon chili powder, and salt; coat the beef in this mixture. Heat the oil in a large soup pot or Dutch oven and brown the beef.
2. Add the onion and garlic, and cook until soft; then add the tomatoes, the remaining chili powder, cinnamon, cloves, and peppers. Cover and simmer for 2 hours.
3. Add the potatoes and carrots. Simmer for about 45 minutes, until the vegetables are tender. Add salt and pepper to taste, and serve.

🌶 A Bowl You Don't Have to Wash!

Use squash as a soup bowl. Many small squashes make excellent complements to soups and stews. Cut them in half, remove the seeds and prebake in the microwave or oven. Ladle your soup or stew into the squash for a festive look.

Tomato-Seafood Stew

½ pound shrimp, shelled and deveined
1 tablespoon olive oil
1 cup chopped onion
2 garlic cloves, minced
1 (16-ounce) can diced tomatoes, including liquid
1 (8-ounce) can tomato sauce
1 potato, peeled and chopped
1 medium green pepper, chopped
1 celery stalk, chopped

1 medium carrot, shredded
1 teaspoon dried thyme, crushed
¼ teaspoon black pepper
4 dashes hot sauce
1 (20-ounce) can whole baby clams, drained
2 tablespoons fresh chopped parsley

1. Cut the shrimp in half lengthwise. Heat the oil on medium in a soup pot and sauté the onion and garlic for about 3 minutes, until the onion softens. Stir in the tomatoes and their liquid, the tomato sauce, potato, green pepper, celery, carrot, thyme, black pepper, and hot pepper sauce. Bring to a boil, then reduce to a simmer. Cover and simmer for about 20 minutes, until the vegetables are tender.
2. Add the shrimp, clams, and parsley. Bring to boiling, reduce to a simmer, and cover; cook about 2 or 3 minutes, until the shrimp turns pink.

Scandinavian Beef and Vegetable Stew

3 pounds stewing beef
3 pounds beef marrow bones
12 cups (3 quarts) water
2 bay leaves
3 whole cloves
1 teaspoon rosemary
2 teaspoons salt
½ teaspoon freshly ground
 black pepper
6 carrots, peeled and sliced

1 medium-sized cabbage,
 cut into eighths
1 onion, chopped
¼ cup cider vinegar
1 tablespoon brown sugar
1 tablespoon flour
3 tablespoons cold water

Serves 8
This hearty stew will soon become a winter favorite!

1. Cut the stewing beef into bite-size pieces, trimming off any excess fat. In a soup pot, boil the beef bones in the water for 1½ hours. Remove and discard the bones, reserving the marrow. Strain the broth through a sieve or cheesecloth to remove any impurities. Return the broth to the soup pot.

2. Add the stewing beef, bay leaves, cloves, rosemary, salt, and pepper to the broth. Simmer, covered, for 2 hours, or until the beef is tender. Periodically skim off any fat as it rises to the top.

3. Add the reserved marrow to the soup pot. Bring the mixture to a boil, reduce to a simmer, and add the carrots and cabbage; cook, covered, for 20 minutes, or until the vegetables are just tender. Remove the bay leaves.

4. Using a slotted spoon, remove the meat and vegetables from the broth. Arrange in a serving dish and cover to keep warm. Simmer the onion in the broth for 5 minutes. Add the vinegar and sugar. Whisk together the flour and water; add it to the broth, stirring constantly until the mixture is thickened and smooth. Add salt and pepper to taste. Pour the sauce over the meat and vegetables, and serve.

French Chicken and Pork Stew

1 (⅓-pound) boneless pork shoulder chop
1 (3- to 4-pound) whole chicken
8–10 small white onions, peeled
½ pound small mushrooms
4 cups Basic Beef Broth (see recipe on page 4)
¼ cup dry white wine
2 tablespoons Dijon mustard
2 tablespoons fresh chopped parsley
1 teaspoon cornstarch
1 teaspoon water

1. Cut the pork into ¾-inch cubes. Cut the chicken into serving pieces (breasts, thighs, wings, etc.).
2. In a large, deep skillet, cook the pork in its own fat on medium heat until browned. Remove the pork with a slotted spoon and set aside.
3. Add the chicken and onions to the pan with the pork drippings. Cook on medium heat for about 20 minutes, turning the chicken pieces occasionally, until the chicken and onions are well browned. Using a slotted spoon, remove the meat and vegetables from pan and set aside.
4. Add the mushrooms to the pan and sauté them in the drippings until soft; remove from pan and set aside.
5. Add the broth to the pan and bring to a boil, scraping the bottom of the pan with a wooden spoon to loosen any cooked bits; continue to boil until the liquid has reduced by about half. Return the chicken, onions, and mushrooms to pan. Add the wine and mustard; bring to a boil. Cover, reduce heat, and simmer for about 30 minutes, until the chicken is cooked through. Stir in the reserved pork and the parsley; bring to simmer again.
6. With a slotted spoon, remove all the meat and vegetables from the pan and transfer to a warm serving platter. Whisk together the cornstarch and water until smooth; add this mixture to the pan juices and quickly bring to a boil, whisking constantly until it thickens. Pour the broth over the chicken and vegetables, and serve.

Hearty Quick (or Slow) Tomato Stew

4 cups (1 quart) tomato juice

1 (14½-ounce) can Italian
　　stewed tomatoes

2 cups water

2 medium potatoes, unpeeled,
　　chopped

1 (15-ounce) can chickpeas
　　(garbanzo beans), drained
　　and rinsed

1 (15-ounce) can kidney beans,
　　drained

1 cup uncooked lentils, rinsed

1 large onion, chopped

1 cup diced red pepper, seeded

1 cup diced green pepper,
　　seeded

1 (10-ounce) package chopped
　　frozen spinach

2 carrots, julienned

2 tablespoons dried parsley

2 tablespoons chili powder

2 teaspoons dried basil

2 teaspoons garlic powder

1 teaspoon ground cumin

Topping:

½ cup sour cream

½ cup yogurt

¼ cup fresh chopped chives

Serves 6

Garnish each serving with a dollop of the sour cream, yogurt and chives mixture.

1. Quick method: Combine all the ingredients except the toppings in a large Dutch oven. Bring to a boil, reduce heat, and simmer for 30 minutes, or until lentils are tender.
2. Slow method: Combine all the ingredients except the toppings in a slow cooker. Set on low and cook for about 6 hours.
3. Mix the topping ingredients together in a small bowl.

African Pork and Peanut Stew

2 tablespoons peanut oil, divided
2 pounds boneless pork butt, cut into 1-inch cubes
1 onion, chopped
2 cloves garlic, minced
½ teaspoon curry powder
½ teaspoon ground coriander
½ teaspoon ground cumin
½–1 teaspoon crushed red pepper flakes
½ teaspoon ground ginger
¼ teaspoon cinnamon
1 bay leaf

1 teaspoon salt
2 cups Basic Chicken Broth (see recipe on page 3)
1 tablespoon tomato paste
½ cup chunky peanut butter
2 plum tomatoes, seeded and chopped
1 green bell pepper, seeded and cut into 1-inch pieces
½ teaspoon lemon juice
¼ cup chopped cilantro
½ cup chopped unsalted peanuts

1. In a large heavy pot, heat 1 tablespoon of the oil on high. When hot, add the pork cubes and brown on all sides. Add the onion and cook until soft. Stir in the garlic, curry powder, coriander, cumin, and crushed red pepper. Cook 1 minute. Add the ginger, cinnamon, bay leaf, salt, chicken broth, and tomato paste. Bring to a boil, then cover and simmer on low for 45 minutes.
2. Add the peanut butter and stir well to blend. Cook the stew another 3 minutes, uncovered, for the flavors to blend. Stir in the chopped tomato and bell pepper. Simmer for 2 or 3 more minutes, until the vegetables just begin to soften.
3. Add the lemon juice. Garnish with the chopped cilantro and peanuts, and serve.

Polish Stew

1 pound Polish sausage, cut in
  ½-inch pieces
3 tablespoons oil
1½ pounds beef, cubed
2 onions, sliced
2 cups sliced mushrooms
1 (1-pound) can sauerkraut
1 cup dry white wine

1 (8-ounce) can tomato sauce
2 teaspoons soy sauce
1 teaspoon caraway seeds
¼ teaspoon vegetable sea-
  soning

Serves 8

Start your preparation for this stew early in the day. It requires a baking time of 2–2½ hours.

1. In a heavy ovenproof skillet, sauté the sausage over medium heat for 15 minutes. Using a slotted spoon, remove the sausage and set aside. Add the oil to sausage drippings and brown the beef for 15 minutes. Remove the beef with a slotted spoon and set aside. Preheat the oven to 375 degrees.

2. Add the onion to the skillet with the drippings and sauté for about 3 minutes, until the onion softens; using a slotted spoon, remove and set aside.

3. Add the mushrooms to the skillet with the drippings and sauté, along with the sauerkraut and wine, for about 3 minutes. Add all the remaining ingredients, along with the sausage, beef, and onion, mixing well. Cover and bake for 2 to 2½ hours; stir the mixture every 30 minutes.

New Hampshire Goulash

Serves 6

For a nice variation to this recipe, try substituting cooked rice for the noodles.

3 tablespoons oil
3 pounds beef stew meat, cut
  in 1-inch cubes
3 cups chopped onions
1 cup chopped green peppers
1 clove garlic, minced
1 (16-ounce) can tomato sauce
1 tablespoon chili powder

½ teaspoon soy sauce
2 (5-ounce) cans mushrooms
1 tablespoon paprika
3 tablespoons brown sugar
¼ teaspoon pepper
1½ cups sour cream (optional)
Cooked egg noodles, buttered

1. Heat the oil in a large, heavy skillet on medium heat, and brown the meat well on all sides. Add all the remaining ingredients except the sour cream and noodles; mix well. Cover and cook at a low simmer for about 2½ to 3 hours, until beef cubes are tender.
2. Stir in the sour cream just before serving (if using). Serve over hot buttered noodles.

Hearty Smoked Sausage Stew

Serves 8

Prepare this stew the night before. You can leave it to cook in your slow cooker during the day and come home to a finished meal.

1 pound dried red kidney beans
6 cups Basic Chicken Broth
  (see recipe on page 5)
2 cups water
1 pound smoked sausage, sliced
1 cup barley
2 bay leaves

½ teaspoon garlic powder
1 teaspoon thyme
Salt and pepper

1. Rinse the beans and soak them overnight in a bowl with enough cold water to cover. Drain and rinse again.
2. Mix together all the ingredients, except the salt and pepper, in a large slow cooker; cover and cook on low for 8 hours. Discard the bay leaves. Add salt and pepper to taste, and serve.

Grandma's Beef Stew

⅓ cup flour
1 teaspoon salt
¼ teaspoon freshly ground
    black pepper
2 pounds stewing beef, cut
    into cubes
¼ cup shortening
4 cups water
1 tablespoon lemon juice
1 tablespoon Worcestershire
    sauce

1 teaspoon sugar
1 large onion, sliced
2 bay leaves
¼ teaspoon allspice
12 small carrots, trimmed and
    scraped
12 small white onions, trimmed
8 small new potatoes, peeled

Serves 8

This recipe may bring back memories of your grandmother's warm and cozy kitchen.

1. Mix together the flour, salt, and pepper. Toss the beef cubes in the mixture; shake off excess.
2. In a soup pot, melt the shortening on high heat. When the fat is very hot, add as many of the beef cubes to the pan as you can without crowding them, and brown on all sides; remove with a slotted spoon and set aside; repeat this process until all the beef is browned.
3. In a saucepan, bring the water to a boil. Return all the meat to the pot and add the boiling water. Stir in the lemon juice, Worcestershire sauce, sugar, onion, bay leaves, and allspice. Reduce the heat, cover, and simmer for about 1½ to 2 hours, until the meat is tender.
4. Add the carrots, onions, and potatoes; cover and cook for about 20 to 25 minutes, until the vegetables can be pierced easily with a fork. Discard the bay leaves before serving.

Oniony Beef Stew

Serves 4

To maintain a smooth, creamy sauce, make sure the sour cream mixture doesn't boil.

1 (2½-pound) boneless beef
   chuck roast
1 tablespoon vegetable oil
3 cups chopped onion
1 clove garlic, crushed
1 (8-ounce) can tomato sauce
1½ teaspoons caraway seeds
1½ teaspoons salt
1 teaspoon dill seeds
¼ teaspoon pepper
1½ teaspoons Worcestershire
   sauce

2 tablespoons brown sugar
   (optional)
1 cup sour cream
1 pound (16 ounces) cooked
   noodles

1. Trim off the excess fat from the roast and cut the meat into 1-inch cubes. In a soup pot or Dutch oven, heat the oil on medium heat and sauté the beef cubes, onion, and garlic until the beef is browned.
2. Add all the remaining ingredients except the sour cream and noodles. Simmer, stirring occasionally, for about 1½ hours, until the meat is tender.
3. Stir in the sour cream and cook, stirring often, until heated thoroughly, but do not let the mixture boil. Serve over hot cooked noodles.

Coastal Oyster Stew

*1 pound (16 ounces) shucked
  oysters, with their liquid*
2 cups water
½ cup diced onions
½ cup diced celery
6 tablespoons sweet butter
1½ cups heavy cream
*2 tablespoons fresh chopped
  parsley*

*1 tablespoon fresh chopped
  chervil*
*Salt and freshly ground black
  pepper*

Serves 4
For an authentic flair, serve oyster crackers with this stew. You'll definitely impress your guests.

1. Pick through the oysters, removing any bits of shell. Place them in a small saucepan with their liquid and the water. Heat slowly until the oysters begin to curl, about 5 minutes. Remove the oysters and set aside. Strain the liquid and set aside.

2. In a soup pot, melt the butter on medium-low heat and sauté the onion and celery about 6 minutes, until tender. Add the reserved oyster liquid and the heavy cream. Heat *almost* to the boiling point, reduce heat, and simmer for 10 minutes. Add the oysters, parsley, chervil, and salt and pepper to taste; simmer for 1 minute. Serve with crackers.

Cuban Chicken Stew

Serves 4

To collect the lime juice, cut the lime into quarters over a bowl. Squeeze the juice out one quarter at a time.

2 tablespoons butter
3 pounds boneless, skinless
    chicken, cut into bite-size
    pieces
1 cup finely diced onions
1 clove garlic, minced
1 teaspoon cayenne pepper
2 teaspoons paprika
1 cup Basic Chicken Broth
    (see recipe on page 5)

3 cups milk
2 large yuccas, peeled and
    diced into 1-inch-thick cubes
4 ears yellow corn, shucked,
    cut into 1-inch-thick slices
Juice of 1 lime

1. Melt the butter in a soup pot over medium heat and cook the chicken pieces until no longer pink. Remove the chicken with a slotted spoon and set aside.
2. Add the onion, garlic, cayenne, and paprika to the chicken drippings in the soup pot and cook, stirring constantly, until the onion is translucent. Add the stock, milk, yucca, corn, and chicken to the pot. Bring *almost* to a boil, reduce heat to a simmer, and cover. Cook, stirring occasionally, for about 1 hour, until the yucca is tender.
3. Remove from heat, stir in lime juice, and serve.

Potato and Garbanzo Stew

1 tablespoon olive oil
1 Spanish onion, chopped
2 cloves garlic, minced
3 fresh tomatoes, coarsely
    chopped, divided
1 teaspoon paprika
⅓ cup chopped fresh basil
1 teaspoon oregano
2 large russet potatoes, diced
1 cup Basic Chicken Broth
    (see recipe on page 5)
    or water

1 (15-ounce) can garbanzo
    beans (chickpeas), drained
¼ cup basil, chopped
Salt and pepper
½ cup fresh chopped parsley
    (optional)

Serves 4
For added color, garnish each individual serving with fresh chopped parsley before serving.

1. In a soup pot, heat the oil on medium. Add the onion, garlic, 2 of the tomatoes, the paprika, and oregano. Sauté, stirring occasionally, for 5 minutes. Add the potatoes and broth. Cover and bring to a boil; boil for 5 minutes, stirring occasionally.
2. Add the chickpeas. Reduce heat to a simmer and cook for about 5 minutes, until the potatoes are done. Add the remaining tomato, basil, and salt and pepper to taste; heat for 3 minutes.

Chicken Fennel Stew

Serves 6

Fennel looks somewhat like celery, but it has a mild licorice flavor. It can be eaten raw or cooked.

1 cup dried white beans
8 cups water
1 large yellow onion, chopped
2 large cloves garlic, minced
2 celery ribs, chopped
1 small fennel bulb, diced
2 cups Basic Chicken Broth
　(see recipe on page 5)
2 (2-ounce) turkey sausages,
　casings removed
1 teaspoon salt

1 large boneless, skinless
　chicken breast, cut into
　½-inch pieces
4–5 small new red potatoes,
　scrubbed and diced
½ teaspoon dried thyme
1 cup green beans, trimmed
　and cut into ½-inch pieces

1. Rinse the beans and soak them overnight in enough cold water to cover. Drain and rinse them again.
2. Put the beans in a soup pot with the water. Bring to a boil and add the onion, garlic, celery, fennel, and broth. Reduce to a simmer and cook for 1½ hours.
3. Brown the sausage in a skillet on medium heat, using a wooden spoon to break them up. Add the chicken to the skillet and cook until brown around the edges, about 5 minutes. Add the sausage and chicken to the soup pot with the bean mixture. Add the potatoes, salt, thyme, and green beans. Return to a simmer and cook, covered, for 45 minutes.

Chicken Stew with Garlic

1 whole head garlic
2 tablespoons olive oil, plus 1 teaspoon
1 (3-pound) whole chicken, cut into serving pieces (breasts, thighs)
⅛ teaspoon garlic salt
⅛ teaspoon oregano
½ teaspoon freshly ground black pepper, divided
1 red bell pepper, coarsely chopped
1 yellow bell pepper, coarsely chopped

1 orange bell pepper, coarsely chopped
2 fresh tomatoes, chopped
1 cups Basic Chicken Broth (see recipe on page 5)
24 pearl onions, peeled
3 medium white potatoes, peeled and cut into 1-inch cubes
2 ears of corn, cut into 2-inch chunks
1 small yellow squash, sliced
1 tablespoon fresh chopped sage
¼ teaspoon salt

> **Serves 4 to 5**
>
> Look in your pantry. One (14-ounce) can of whole tomatoes with the juice can be substituted for the 2 fresh tomatoes.

1. Preheat the oven to 400 degrees. Slice off and discard the very top of the garlic head. Place the garlic on a piece of foil large enough to wrap it in. Drizzle the garlic with the 1 teaspoon of olive oil, wrap it in the foil, and bake for 40 minutes, until soft. Remove and set aside to cool.

2. Season the chicken parts with garlic salt, oregano, and ¼ teaspoon of the pepper. In a large soup pot heat the remaining olive oil on medium-high heat. Add the chicken and sauté until browned, about 5 minutes per side. Using a slotted spoon, remove the chicken and set aside.

3. Pour off all but 1 tablespoon of the drippings in the pot. Add the bell peppers and sauté on medium heat for 2 minutes. Squeeze the roasted garlic pulp out of its skin and add it to the pot. Stir in the tomatoes with their juice, the broth, and the chicken. Bring to simmer over high heat. Reduce to low and simmer for 15 minutes.

4. Stir the onions, potatoes, corn, squash, and sage into the stew. Simmer for 15 more minutes. Season with salt and the remaining ¼ teaspoon pepper. Serve immediately in shallow bowls.

CHAPTER 13
Healthy Choices

Chilled Cucumber-Mint Soup

Serves 4

This is a refreshing summertime soup—and there's no cooking!

1 cucumber, halved, peeled, and seeded
¼ cup chopped scallions
¼ cup chopped fresh mint

2 cups low-fat milk
1 cup plain low-fat yogurt
Salt and pepper to taste

Purée the cucumber, scallions, and mint in a food processor or blender. Add the milk and yogurt and process until smooth. Transfer to a large bowl and stir in the yogurt. Season with salt and pepper. Cover and chill for 1 to 2 hours before serving.

Light and Lean Chowder

Serves 2–4

If you don't have fresh broccoli handy, substitute green beans. They hold up well while slow cooking and offer similar nutritional value as broccoli.

1 (14½-ounce) can reduced-sodium, fat-free chicken broth
1 cup small broccoli florets
1 cup sliced mushrooms
½ cup chopped onion
1 tablespoon margarine
2 tablespoons flour

¼ teaspoon salt
⅛ teaspoon pepper
1 (13½-ounce) can evaporated skim milk
1 (8-ounce) can corn kernels, drained
1 tablespoon chopped pimiento

1. In a small saucepan, combine the broth and broccoli and bring to a boil. Reduce the heat to low, cover, and simmer for 5 minutes. Set aside.
2. In a large saucepan on medium heat, sauté the mushrooms and onions in the margarine until tender. Stir in the flour, salt, and pepper. Add the milk all at once and heat, stirring continuously, until it begins to bubble; continue to stir, letting the mixture bubble, for 1 minute more. Stir in the broccoli and broth mixture, the corn, and pimiento. Heat thoroughly and serve.

Broccoli-Leek Soup

2 tablespoons olive oil
2 medium leeks, finely chopped
   (white parts only)
1 pound red potatoes, peeled
   and finely chopped
1½ pounds broccoli florets and
   stalks, cut into 1-inch pieces
5 cups reduced-sodium, fat-free
   chicken broth

Salt and white pepper
2 tablespoons fresh chopped
   chives (optional)

Parmesan Topping:

½ cup plain nonfat yogurt
¼ cup grated parmesan cheese
1 pinch of white pepper

Serves 8

For added color and flavor, garnish each individual serving with chives before serving.

1. In a large soup pot, heat the olive oil on medium. Add the leeks and sauté for 3 to 5 minutes, until softened. Add the potatoes and broccoli, and sauté for 2 minutes, stirring frequently. Add the broth and bring to a simmer. Cover partially and simmer for 15 to 20 minutes, until the vegetables are tender when pierced with a knife.

2. Remove from heat and allow to cool slightly. In a blender or food processor, purée the soup. Add salt and pepper to taste. Reheat to serving temperature.

3. Make the parmesan topping: Combine the yogurt, cheese, and pepper in a small bowl and whisk until combined.

4. Ladle the soup into bowls and spoon the parmesan topping on top.

Any Squash Soup with Apples and Potato

3 pounds of squash (butternut, Hubbard, Delicata, or buttercup—**or** a combination)
1 tablespoon olive oil
3 carrots
2 medium-sized yellow onions
1½ pounds apples (any variety)
1 pound potatoes (white **or** red)

5 cloves garlic
2 thyme sprigs
8 cups of reduced-sodium, fat-free broth (chicken **or** vegetable)

1. Preheat the oven to 400 degrees. Cut squash(es) in half, scoop out and discard all the seeds and slimy threads. Brush the exposed flesh with half of the olive oil. Peel and chop the carrots and onions into large chunks; toss them with the rest of the olive oil.
2. Place the squash, carrots, and onions on a foil-lined baking sheet along with the squash, cut-side down. Roast the carrots and onions for 45 minutes and remove. Roast the squash for 15 more minutes after that.
3. Cut the apples into large chunks. Peel and cut the potatoes into medium-sized chunks. Cut the garlic into small pieces. Place all of them in the soup pot, along with the broth and thyme. Add the scooped-out flesh of the squash and the carrots and onion. Bring to a boil, then reduce to a simmer and cook for 30 minutes.
4. Remove from heat and allow to cool slightly. Remove the thyme stems. Using a blender or food processor, purée the soup. Return it to the pot and reheat gently. Serve.

Chili Bean Soup

1 pound dried pink beans
6–8 cups water
1 teaspoon garlic salt
1 teaspoon onion salt
¼ teaspoon dried thyme
¼ teaspoon dried marjoram
1¼ cups reduced-sodium, fat-
    free beef **or** chicken broth

1 (16-ounce) can chopped
    tomatoes
1 packet chili seasoning mix
1 cup hot water

Serves 6

This soup requires some advanced planning. The dried pink beans must be soaked overnight in cold water.

1. Rinse the beans and soak them overnight in cold water to cover. Drain.
2. Place the beans in a large pot and add the water, garlic salt, onion salt, thyme, and marjoram. Bring to a boil, reduce the heat to low, and cover; simmer for 2½ to 3 hours until tender. Add hot water if necessary to keep the beans from boiling dry.
3. Spoon out 1 cup of the beans and about ½ cup of liquid from the pot; using a potato masher, mash them thoroughly. Return them to the pot, along with the broth, tomatoes, chili mix, and the 1 cup hot water. Stir well and heat for at least 10 minutes to blend the flavors. Ladle into soup bowls and serve.

Pumpkin Cheese Soup

1 (5–6 pound) whole pumpkin
2 teaspoons reduced-fat margarine, melted
2 tablespoons water
1 large onion, chopped
2 large carrots, shredded
2 celery stalks, chopped
4½ cups reduced-sodium, fat-free vegetable broth
1 clove garlic, minced
½ teaspoon salt

½ teaspoon pepper
½ teaspoon nutmeg
¾ cup plus 2 tablespoons 1 percent milk
1 cup low-fat cheddar cheese, grated
6 tablespoons dry white wine
⅓ cup minced fresh parsley

1. Preheat the oven to 350 degrees. Cut off the top of the pumpkin (reserving it) and scoop out and discard the seeds. Brush the inside with the melted margarine. Replace the top and place the pumpkin on a foil-lined baking sheet. Bake for about 45 minutes, until tender when pierced with a fork. (The pumpkin should be a bit droopy but still hold its shape well.)

2. Meanwhile, heat 2 tablespoons of water in a soup pot. Add the onion, carrots, and celery and cook for about 10 minutes, until soft. Add the broth, garlic, salt, pepper, and nutmeg. Cover and simmer for 20 minutes.

3. Remove from the heat and let cool slightly. Working in 2 or 3 batches, purée the vegetable mixture in a blender or food processor. Pour back into the soup pot and stir in all the milk. Reheat gently. Add the cheese and wine, and heat until the cheese melts, stirring frequently to avoid scorching.

4. Place the hot pumpkin on a serving platter and ladle in the soup. Sprinkle with the parsley. To serve, ladle out soup at the table, scooping a little bit of pumpkin into each serving.

Autumn Soup

4 cups fat-free chicken broth
1 cup chopped onion
2 slices bread, cut into cubes
2 tart apples, cored and
   coarsely chopped
1 (1-pound) butternut squash,
   halved lengthwise and
   seeded

1 teaspoon salt
1 teaspoon diced marjoram
1 teaspoon diced rosemary
1 teaspoon pepper
2 eggs
½ cup buttermilk

Serves 6

Use powdered buttermilk for cooking, and reconstitute only what you need for this recipe.

1. Combine the broth, onion, bread cubes, apples, squash, salt, marjoram, rosemary, and pepper in a large, heavy saucepan. Bring to a boil, reduce the heat to low, and simmer, covered, for 45 minutes.
2. Remove from heat. Take out the squash halves and let cool slightly. Scoop out the squash flesh from the skins and return the flesh to the saucepan; discard the skin. Working in batches, purée the soup in a blender or food processor. Return the purée to the pan.
3. In a small bowl, beat together the eggs and buttermilk. Stir a little of the hot soup into the egg mixture, and then add it to the soup. Reheat gently for 5 minutes to blend the flavors; do not boil. Ladle into bowls and serve.

Sweet Potato–Ginger Soup

1 tablespoon olive oil
1 onion, chopped
2 tablespoons fresh minced ginger
1 (1½-pound) butternut squash, peeled, seeded, and diced
4 large sweet potatoes, (about 1½ pounds total), peeled and diced
1 large russet potato, peeled and diced
8 cups (2 quarts) reduced-sodium, fat-free chicken broth
½ cup plain low-fat yogurt

1. Heat the oil over medium heat in a soup pot for 30 seconds. Add the onion and sauté until translucent, about 5 minutes. Add the ginger and cook for about 1 minute. Add the squash, sweet potatoes, russet potato, and broth. Bring to a boil, reduce the heat to low, cover, and cook until the vegetables are tender, about 30 minutes.
2. Remove from heat and allow to cool slightly. Working in 1-cup batches, purée in a food processor or blender until smooth. Pour into a clean saucepan, stir in the yogurt, and reheat gently. Ladle into bowls and serve.

When Are Onions "Translucent," and When Are They "Caramelized?"

After a few minutes of sizzling gently in oil or butter, onions wilt as their cell walls collapse, giving up their juices. This gives the once-opaque raw onion a watery, "translucent" appearance. The edges, once rough and sharp, are then "soft." As the water evaporates from the juices, the onions' natural sugars concentrate on the exterior of the pieces, and brown in the heat. The first stages of this transformation give onions a golden appearance. Since browned sugar is known as caramel, the browning of onions is often referred to as "caramelizing."

Artichoke Hearts Soup

*4 large artichokes (**or** 6 smaller ones), cleaned*
Juice of 2 small lemons, divided
16 cups (1 gallon) water
1 tablespoon salt
3 medium-large taro roots

1 medium leek
3 stems of celery leaves
1 tablespoon garlic powder
1 teaspoon marjoram
3 tablespoons yogurt

> **Serves 8**
>
> Use a knife to cut off the leaves and trim around the solid core attached to the stem of the artichoke. Remove the fibrous, inedible material to expose the "heart."

1. Trim the *uncooked* artichokes to hearts (see the sidebar on this page for instructions). Cut each heart into a few small, bite-sized pieces. Place them in a bowl of water with the juice of 1 of the lemons to prevent the artichokes from becoming black.
2. Bring the 1 gallon of water in a soup pot to a boil. Add the salt and the artichoke pieces, after rinsing them off. Simmer for 20 minutes or until all the artichoke hearts are well cooked.
3. While the artichokes are cooking, peel, clean, and cut the taro roots into ½-inch cubes. Soak in fresh water and set aside. Chop up the leek and the celery leaves. When the artichokes are cooked, remove them from the cooking water and set aside.
4. Add the taro root, celery, and leeks to the water in the soup pot. Bring to a boil, reduce to a simmer, and cook for another 15 to 20 minutes until the taro roots are soft. With a hand-held blender, blend the root vegetables with the cooking water until puréed. Adjust the flavor; add water if the soup is too salty, or add salt if needed.
5. Return the artichoke hearts to the pot. Add the garlic powder, marjoram, and the juice of the remaining lemon. Bring to a light boil, then reduce to a simmer and cook for 3 minutes. Add the yogurt to the soup just before turning off the heat. Mix well and serve.

Low-Salt Pepper Soup

Serves 4

Using green peppers will give this soup a strong "peppery" taste. Red or yellow bell peppers will result in a mild, sweet taste.

4 bell peppers, cut in half and seeded

½ tablespoon olive oil, plus 1 teaspoon

2 cloves garlic, minced

1 medium-sized yellow onion, chopped

1 medium potato, peeled and cut into 1-inch pieces

1 cup low-sodium, fat-free chicken broth

½ cup low-fat milk

1. Preheat the oven to 350 degrees. Place the peppers open-side down on a baking sheet and brush with the teaspoon of olive oil. Bake until tender (about 30 minutes).

2. Meanwhile, sauté the garlic and onion in the ½ tablespoon of olive oil for a few minutes. Add the potato and chicken broth. Bring to a boil, then cover and reduce the heat. Simmer for 15 minutes, or until the potato is tender. Add a little water if it starts to dry out.

3. When both the peppers and the potato mixture have cooked, place them in a food processor or blender and purée until smooth. Return the mixture to the saucepan, stir in the milk, and warm over low heat to serving temperature.

Navy Bean Soup

3 tablespoons olive oil, divided
1 leek, chopped (about ½ cup)
1 cup tomato sauce or purée
2 (12-ounce) cans navy beans,
  drained
2 cloves garlic, minced
5 cups reduced-sodium, fat-free
  chicken broth
1 teaspoon chili powder
Juice of ½ of a lemon

2 tablespoons fresh chopped
  sage
6 small slices white or wheat
  bread, toasted

Serves 6

Two tablespoons of
fresh rosemary can be
substituted for the 2
tablespoons of fresh
sage called for.

1. Heat 2 tablespoons of oil in a large soup pot or Dutch oven; add the
   leek and cook until golden brown. Add the tomato sauce, beans, and
   garlic, stirring to combine. Add the chicken broth, chili powder, and
   lemon juice, and stir to blend. Heat to a simmer and cook for about
   20 minutes.

2. Remove from heat and allow to cool slightly. Purée the soup in a
   blender or food processor and return it to the pot. Heat the rest of
   the olive oil in a skillet, add the sage, and sauté for a few minutes.
   Add this mixture to the soup pot; bring it to a simmer and cook for
   another 20 minutes. To serve, place a slice of bread in each serving
   bowl and ladle the soup over the top.

Pumpkin and Coconut Cream Soup

6 cups (1¾ pounds) peeled and cubed fresh pumpkin

2 cups water **or** reduced-sodium, fat-free vegetable broth

1 (½-inch) piece fresh ginger, peeled

1 tablespoon chopped lemongrass

2 scallions, finely sliced (white parts only)

2 cups coconut cream, divided

1 teaspoons salt

¼ teaspoon white pepper

Freshly squeezed lime **or** lemon juice

Zest of 1 small lime (very finely shredded)

1. In a large saucepan, combine the pumpkin, water (**or** broth), ginger, and lemongrass. Cover and bring to a boil; reduce the heat to medium-low and simmer until the pumpkin is very tender, about 12 minutes. Add the scallions and cook briefly.

2. Transfer the contents of the saucepan to a blender or food processor and process until the soup is partially puréed. Pour in 1 cup of the coconut cream and process until smooth.

3. Return the purée to the saucepan. Add ½ cup of the remaining coconut cream. Season with salt and pepper, and heat through without allowing the soup to boil. Taste and adjust the seasoning; squeeze in lime or lemon juice to taste.

4. Ladle the soup into bowls. Add the remaining coconut cream to each bowl, forming a swirl on each serving, and garnish with the lime zest.

Baked Fish Chowder

3 large potatoes, peeled and
*   thinly sliced*
4 large onions, thinly sliced
2 tablespoons unsalted butter
*   plus extra for greasing*
Salt and pepper to taste
½ teaspoon celery seed

6 cups low-fat milk
*2 pounds cod **or** haddock*
*   fillers, cut into bite-sized*
*   pieces*
¼ cup fresh chopped parsley

Serves 8
To cut back on calories, substitute reduced-fat margarine for the unsalted butter.

1. Preheat the oven to 350 degrees. Grease a large casserole or baking dish with butter. Arrange half of the potatoes in the dish; then add half of the onions. Dot the onion layer with butter and season with salt, pepper, and celery seed.
2. Arrange the fish on top of the onions in a single layer, and season with salt and pepper. Add the remaining potato, then onion. Dot the onion layer with butter and season with salt and pepper. Pour the milk over the fish and vegetable mixture.
3. Bake, uncovered, for 1 hour, or until the fish flakes easily and the potatoes are tender. Garnish with the parsley, and serve.

Meatless Chili

1 tablespoon olive oil
2 Spanish onions, chopped
1 teaspoon cumin
½ teaspoon cinnamon
4 cloves garlic, minced
1 (35-ounce) can whole
   tomatoes with purée,
   drained and liquid reserved

⅓ cup water
1 tablespoon Tabasco sauce
Salt to taste
1 cup bulgur wheat
1 (19-ounce) can kidney beans,
   drained

1. Heat the oil in a skillet over medium heat for 20 seconds. Add the onions and cook until translucent. Add the cumin, cinnamon, and garlic. Stir, then add the reserved tomato liquid, water, Tabasco, and salt. Cook for 5 minutes.
2. Add the bulgur, stir, and cook for 5 minutes. Chop the tomatoes and add to the skillet. Reduce the heat and simmer for 10 minutes.

Butternut Squash Soup with Apple

1 shallot
1 clove garlic
¼ cup water
3 cups cored, peeled, and
   cubed butternut squash

3 cups reduced-sodium, fat-free
   chicken broth
¾ cup apple cider
¼ cup plain nonfat yogurt
½ of an apple

1. Mince the shallot and garlic. Pour the water into a soup pot, and cook them until soft, about 2 minutes. Add the squash and the broth. Bring to a boil, then reduce to a simmer and cook for about 20 minutes.
2. In a blender or food processor, blend the mixture. Add the cider and yogurt and continue blending. Put the soup back into the pot. Dice the apple, leaving the skin on. Reheat on low.

Carrot and Parsnip Soup with Ginger

3 cups shredded carrots
3 cups shredded parsnips
1 (1-inch) piece ginger root
2 cups reduced-sodium, fat-free
   vegetable broth

¾ cup 2 percent milk
1 teaspoon lemon juice
Salt and white pepper

1. Shred the carrots, parsnips, and the peeled ginger root.
2. Using a soup pot, add the carrots, parsnips, ginger, and broth. Bring to a boil, reduce to a simmer, and cook for 25 minutes.
3. Remove from heat and allow to cool slightly. Using a blender or food processor, purée the soup. Add the milk and reheat *almost* to a boil. Add the lemon juice and salt and white pepper to taste.

Serves 4

Chop some fresh chives and add as a garnish to each serving of this soup.

Fennel-Tomato Soup

2 fennel bulbs
4 tomatoes
1 yellow onion
1 tablespoon olive oil

6 cups reduced-sodium, fat-free
   chicken broth
Salt and pepper

1. Cut off the feathery parts of the fennel to use as a garnish. Slice the bulbs into fourths, removing and discarding the cores. Coarsely chop the rest of the fennel. Chop the tomatoes and cut the onion into a fine dice.
2. In a soup pot, heat the oil. Sauté the onion on medium for 3 minutes. Add the chopped fennel and simmer for 10 minutes, stirring often.
3. Add the broth, tomatoes, and salt and pepper to taste if desired. Bring to a boil, reduce to a simmer, and cook for 15 minutes. Garnish with the fennel fronds, and serve.

Serves 6

Whenever possible, prepare vegetables just before using them in a recipe; as soon as they are cut or peeled (exposed to air), vegetables begin to lose their nutrients and flavor.

Eggplant and Carrot Soup

1 eggplant
8 large carrots
2 potatoes
1 stalk celery
4 yellow onions
3 cloves garlic
2 tablespoons parsley
2 tablespoons olive oil

8 cups reduced-sodium, fat-free
   vegetable broth
Salt and pepper
2 teaspoons fresh chopped
   mint (optional)

1. Peel and dice the eggplant. Peel and chop the carrots and the potatoes. Chop the celery and onions. Mince the garlic. Chop the parsley.
2. In a soup pot, heat the oil. Add the onions and garlic, and sauté on medium heat for 5 minutes. Add the eggplant and cook for 10 minutes.
3. Add the remaining vegetables and parsley to the pot, along with the broth. Bring to a boil, then reduce to a simmer and cook for 40 to 45 minutes, adding salt and pepper to taste if desired.
4. Using a blender or food processor, purée the soup. Reheat gently. Chop the mint for garnish, and serve.

Black Bean Vegetarian Chili

2½ cups dried black beans
1 yellow onion
2 stalks celery
1 green bell pepper
1 cup chopped tomatoes
4 cloves garlic
1 tablespoon chopped cilantro
7½ cups water
1 cup (8 ounces) tomato sauce

6 tablespoons tomato paste
2 tablespoons lime juice
2 tablespoons red wine vinegar
1½ teaspoons cumin
1½ teaspoons chili powder

Serves 4
For a different flavor, substitute 2 tablespoons of balsamic vinegar for the 2 tablespoons of red wine vinegar.

1. Soak the beans overnight in cold water to cover, then drain.
2. Chop the onion, celery, green bell pepper, and tomatoes. Finely chop the garlic and cilantro.
3. In a large soup pot, add the beans and the water. Bring to a boil, reduce to a simmer, and cook for 1½ hours.
4. Stir in all the remaining ingredients. Bring the mixture back to a boil, reduce to a simmer, and cook for an additional 30 minutes.

Lentil Soup with Apples

Serves 8–10

Read the label on the apple juice carefully. This recipe calls for a juice with no added sugar.

1½ cups lentils
2 medium leeks
3 stalks celery
1 onion
6 whole cloves
1 tablespoon vegetable oil
6 cups water

2 cups apple juice (with no added sugar)
1 bay leaf
1½ cups diced tart apple

1. Rinse the lentils. Slice the leeks thinly, using only the white and the light green parts. Chop the celery coarsely. Stud the onion with the cloves.
2. In a large saucepan or soup pot, heat the oil on medium. Add the leeks and sauté, stirring often for 3 minutes. Add the water and the apple juice, bringing the mixture to a boil. Add the lentils, celery, whole onion, and bay leaf. Bring the mixture back to a boil, reduce to a simmer, and cook, uncovered, for 45 minutes.
3. Toward the end of the above cooking period, peel and chop the apple. Add it to the mixture and simmer, again uncovered, for 15 more minutes. Discard the celery pieces, whole onion, and bay leaf. Serve.

Quick Soups

Miso Soup

Yields 4 cups

Miso is a paste that is mainly made up of fermented soybeans and salt. All varieties of miso can be used in making miso soup.

6 tablespoons miso paste (any kind)

4 cups water **or** Dashi (see recipe on page 6)

½ cup (4 ounces) tofu, cut into ¼-inch cubes

1 scallion, sliced diagonally into ½-inch-long pieces

Bring the water (or dashi) *almost* to a boil in a saucepan; do not let it boil. Add the miso paste and tofu pieces. Garnish with slices of scallion.

✳ Prep time: 5 minutes; cooking time: 5 minutes

Chinese Chicken Corn Soup

Serves 4

If all you have on hand is regular canned corn, simply pour the can (including the liquid) into a food processor and chop it up for a few seconds.

3 cups Basic Chicken Broth (see recipe on page 5)

1 (8¼-ounce) can creamed corn

1 cup skinned, diced, and cooked chicken

1 tablespoon cornstarch

2 tablespoons cold water

2 egg whites

2 tablespoons finely minced fresh parsley

1. Combine the broth, corn, and chicken pieces in a large saucepan. Bring mixture to a boil over medium heat, stirring occasionally. Whisk together the cornstarch and the cold water, then add it to the soup. Continue cooking, uncovered, for 3 minutes.
2. Beat the egg whites until foamy; stir into soup. Reduce heat to a simmer and cook until foamy. Ladle soup into individual bowls and garnish with parsley. Serve hot.

✳ Prep time: 15 minutes; cooking time: 15 minutes

Mushroom and Onion Chowder

2 tablespoons mild nut oil
  or butter
½ pound (8 ounces) mushrooms
  (any variety), coarsely
  chopped
1 medium onion, diced
1 cup diced potatoes
1 cup Basic Vegetable Broth
  (see recipe on pages 6)
¼ cup sherry
¼ teaspoon thyme

¼ teaspoon dill
¼ teaspoon ground cloves
2 cups plain yogurt
  (nonfat is fine)
Caraway seeds **or** parsley
  (optional)

Serves 4
If you're running low on vegetable broth, substitute it with either a cup of mushroom broth or a cup of water.

1. In a soup pot, heat the oil (or butter). Add the mushrooms and onions and sauté for 3 to 4 minutes. Add the potatoes and broth (or water). Bring to a boil, then simmer for 10 to 15 minutes until the potatoes are cooked.
2. Add all the remaining ingredients and heat thoroughly, but do not boil. Garnish with caraway seeds or parsley.

✳ Prep time: 15 minutes; cooking time: 25 minutes

Cauliflower Soup with Coriander

Serves 6

Using half-and-half or whole milk instead of cream will reduce the fat in this recipe without losing the flavor.

2 cups cauliflower florets
2 potatoes
2 onions
4 cloves garlic
1-inch piece fresh ginger root
3 tablespoons oil **or** ghee
  (see page 82)
1 teaspoon ground cumin
2 teaspoon ground coriander
$\frac{1}{4}$ teaspoon ground turmeric

$\frac{1}{3}$ teaspoon (or more) cayenne
  pepper
8 cups Basic Chicken Broth
  (see recipe on page 5)
1 teaspoon salt
1 cup cream
Salt and pepper to taste

1. Cut the cauliflower into florets. Peel and dice the potatoes into a $\frac{1}{2}$-inch dice. Chop the onions and garlic. Peel and thinly slice the ginger root.
2. In a soup pot, heat the oil. Add the onions, ginger, and garlic, and sauté on medium heat until the onions are golden brown. Add all the spices, stirring for 1 minute longer. Add the potatoes, cauliflower, broth, and salt. Cook for 10 minutes.
3. Remove from heat and allow to cool slightly. Purée the mixture in a blender or food processor. Stir in the cream and add salt and pepper to taste, reheating gently just before serving.

✱ Prep time: 15 minutes; cooking time: 20–25 minutes

Hearty Ground Turkey and Vegetable Soup

1 pound ground turkey
1 small onion, chopped
1 small green pepper, chopped
1 (16-ounce) can green beans
1 (16-ounce) can diced potatoes
1 (16-ounce) can stewed
  tomatoes
1 can tomato soup
Salt and pepper to taste

Brown the turkey in a Dutch oven until cooked through. Add the onion and green pepper. Mix in the green beans, diced potatoes, stewed tomatoes, and the tomato soup. Heat until warmed through, about 15 minutes. Add salt and pepper to taste.

✳ Prep time: 15 minutes; cooking time: 25 minutes

Serves 4

A Dutch oven is a cast iron pot that is useful for slow cooking in an oven. You can pick one up at your nearest kitchen store.

Peanut Butter Soup

3 tablespoons butter
2 tablespoons minced onion
1 tablespoon flour
1 cup peanut butter
Salt and pepper
4 cups Basic Chicken Broth
  (see recipe on page 5)
1 cup heavy whipping cream
1 tablespoon Madeira wine

In a large saucepan, melt the butter over medium-low heat and sauté the onion until soft. Whisk in the flour and cook, stirring constantly, until smooth. Stir in the peanut butter and add the broth. Season to taste with salt and pepper. Cook, stirring, over low heat until thickened and smooth. Add the cream. Just before serving, stir in the Madeira.

✳ Prep time: 15 minutes; cook time: 10 minutes

Serves 4

No need to be choosy with this soup. Plain or crunchy peanut butter can be used.

Pinto Bean Soup

4 tablespoons butter
¼ cup finely chopped onions
2 tablespoons finely chopped and seeded green bell pepper
2 tomatoes, finely chopped
1 teaspoon finely chopped garlic
1 teaspoon finely chopped fresh cilantro
1 teaspoon red chili powder
1 pinch cayenne pepper

1 tablespoon tomato paste
1 (10-ounce) can cooked pinto beans
4 cups Basic Chicken **or** Beef Broth (see recipes on pages 5 and 4)
Salt and pepper to taste
4 teaspoons sour cream (optional)

1. Melt the butter in a large saucepan over medium heat. Add the onions, green bell peppers, tomatoes, and garlic. Cover the pan with a lid and simmer for 4 minutes.
2. Add the cilantro, red chili powder, cayenne pepper, and tomato paste. Stir the ingredients together and simmer for 3 minutes.
3. Add the pinto beans, broth, and salt and pepper to taste. Bring to a boil and cook vigorously for 4 minutes, or until the beans are heated through.

✱ Prep time: 15 minutes; cooking time: 15 minutes

Tuna Chowder

2 tablespoons butter
3 stalks celery, chopped
1 large onion, chopped
1 large potato, diced
3 tablespoons flour
3 cups milk
2 (6½-ounce) cans water-
    packed tuna

¼ pound (4 ounces) cheddar
    cheese, grated
1 teaspoon thyme
1 teaspoon dill
Salt and pepper
¼ cup fresh chopped parsley
    (optional)

> **Serves 6**
>
> For added color and flavor, garnish each serving with chopped fresh parsley.

1. In a large soup pot, melt the butter; sauté the celery, onion, and potato until the potato is tender. Whisk in the flour until smooth. Add the milk and blend thoroughly. Cook for 5 minutes, stirring, until the mixture thickens.
2. Add the tuna, cheese, thyme, and dill. Season with salt and pepper to taste. Heat over medium-low for 5 to 10 minutes.

✱ Prep time: 15 minutes; cooking time: 20 minutes

Very Quick Sausage and Vegetable Soup

2 cups Basic Beef Broth
    (see recipe on page 4)
1 (14½-ounce) can Italian stewed
    tomatoes, including liquid
1½ cups water
2 cups frozen hash brown
    potatoes

1 (10-ounce) package frozen
    mixed vegetables
½ pound (8 ounces) smoked
    sausage, sliced
⅛ teaspoon pepper
Salt to taste
2 tablespoons grated parmesan
    cheese (optional)

> **Serves 4**
>
> While the grated parmesan cheese is considered optional for this recipe, it is highly recommended.

Combine the broth, undrained tomatoes, and water in a large saucepan. Bring to a boil. Stir in the potatoes, vegetables, sausage, pepper, and salt to taste. Return to boiling. Reduce heat and simmer, covered, for 5 to 10 minutes. Sprinkle with cheese when in bowls.

✱ Prep time: 15 minutes; cooking time: 20 minutes

Nigerian Peanut Soup

2 cups water
2 (2-ounce) packets instant chicken broth and seasoning mix
1½ small dried green chili peppers, finely chopped

¼ cup diced and seeded green bell pepper
¼ cup diced onion
3 tablespoons chunky-style peanut butter

1. Heat the water in saucepan; dissolve the broth mix in the water. Add the chili peppers and bring mixture to a boil. Stir in the bell pepper and onion and return to a boil. Reduce heat to low, cover, and simmer until vegetables are tender, about 10 minutes.
2. Reduce heat to lowest setting; add the peanut butter and cook, stirring constantly, until the peanut butter is melted and mixture is well blended.

✱ Prep time: 15 minutes; cooking time: 15 minutes

Spring Asparagus Soup

1 bunch thin spring asparagus
4 cups shrimp broth

Raw peas (optional)
Sour cream (optional)

Chop the asparagus into 1-inch lengths, keeping the tips separate. Bring the broth to a simmer and add all the asparagus *except* for the tips; simmer for 4 minutes. Add the tips and cook 1 additional minute. Pour into bowls and toss in a few raw peas. Top each bowl with a dollop of sour cream.

✱ Prep time: 5 minutes; cooking time: 10 minutes

Cauliflower and Mushroom Soup

1¼ pounds cauliflower
½ pound (8 ounces) cremini
   mushrooms
2 cloves garlic
2 tablespoons olive oil
5 cups water

⅓ cup whole milk
Salt and pepper
4 tablespoons walnut, almond,
   or avocado oil

Serves 6
If you're fresh out of walnut oil, you can substitute it with either almond oil or avocado oil.

1. Cut the cauliflower into florets. Cut the mushrooms into ½-inch slices and mince the garlic.
2. In a soup pot, heat the olive oil on medium. Add the mushrooms and sauté for 5 minutes. Add the garlic and sauté for 1 more minute. Pour in the water and add the cauliflower. Bring to a boil, then reduce to a simmer and cook for 6 more minutes.
3. Remove from heat and allow to cool slightly. In a blender or food processor, purée the mixture. Pour it back into the soup pot over medium heat. Drizzle in the milk and add salt and pepper to taste. Just before serving, garnish each serving bowl with 1–2 teaspoons of the flavored oil.

✳ Prep time: 10 minutes; cooking time: 15 minutes

Flavored Oils

To infuse oil with flavor and complexity, stuff herbs, spices, and garlic cloves into a bottle of it, and steep for at least three days, or up to two weeks or more. Fine olive oil is transformed into a heavenly condiment when perfumed by rosemary, thyme, savory, garlic, peppercorns, dried mushrooms, or truffles. You can also buy infused oils at gourmet stores.

Quick Pea Soup

2 stalks celery
1 medium onion (yellow **or** white)
2 tablespoons butter **or** oil
2 cups Basic Vegetable Broth (see recipe on page 6)
1 (16-ounce) bag frozen baby peas
½ teaspoon garlic powder **or** 2 cloves garlic, minced
White pepper
½ cup milk (any type)
½ teaspoon nutmeg, plus extra for garnish (both optional)
Lemon peel (optional)

1. Chop the celery and onion. In a soup pot, melt the butter on medium heat. Add the celery and onion, sautéing for 2 to 3 minutes. Pour in the broth, peas, garlic, and pepper. Bring to a boil, reduce to a simmer, and cook for 5 minutes.
2. Remove from heat and allow to cool slightly. Using a food processor or blender, purée the mixture. Rewarm it in the soup pot with the milk and nutmeg (if using), stirring constantly for 3 to 5 minutes; do not allow it to boil. Garnish with grated lemon peel and a sprinkling of nutmeg.

✱ Prep time: 10 minutes; cooking time: 15 minutes

Chickpea Soup with Cumin

3 (15½-ounce) cans chickpeas
(also called garbanzo
beans)
1 tablespoon olive oil
½ teaspoon garlic powder **or**
2 cloves garlic, minced
2½ cups Basic Chicken Broth
(see recipe on page 5)

1 tablespoon cumin
Freshly ground black pepper
2 teaspoons lemon juice

Serves 4

You can substitute 2
cloves of minced garlic
for ½ teaspoon of
garlic powder. Sauté
the garlic for about 3
minutes on a lightly
oiled skillet.

1. Drain and rinse the chickpeas In a saucepan or soup pot, heat the
   oil. Slowly add the garlic, chickpeas, broth, cumin, and pepper to
   taste, stirring. Heat to *near* boiling, then remove from heat and allow
   to cool slightly.
2. Using a blender or food processor, purée the mixture. Reheat, stirring
   in the lemon juice just before removing from the heat.

✱ Prep time: 5 minutes; cooking time: 5 minutes

CHAPTER 15
Ethnic Soups

Thai Shrimp Soup

Serves 6–8

Rmember, you can freeze the shrimp shells to make broth for another time.

5 lime leaves
2 tablespoons dried lemongrass
40 raw shrimp in their shells
10 cups water
1 onion
½ pound (8 ounces) small
  button mushrooms
2 tablespoons shrimp paste
2 tablespoons Thai chili

6 tablespoons lemon juice
1 tablespoon Thai fish sauce
  (nam pla)
6 sprigs coriander leaves

1. Soak the lime leaves and the lemongrass in water overnight, or for at least several hours.
2. Peel and devein the shrimp (leave their tails on). Set the shrimp aside. Place the shells, the water, and the onion (cut in half, peel on) in a large saucepan. Bring to a boil and cook over medium-high heat, uncovered, for 15 minutes.
3. Strain the liquid into a soup pot and discard the solids. Drain the lime leaves and lemongrass, discarding the liquid; then add them to the pot. Bring to a boil, reduce to a simmer, and cook for 15 minutes. Add the whole mushrooms and simmer for 1 more minute.
4. In a small bowl, combine the shrimp paste, chili, and lemon juice; add it to the soup pot. Add the fish sauce and the uncooked shrimp. Bring to a boil, reduce to a simmer, and cook for 1 minute. Add the coriander leaves and simmer for 1 additional minute.

Spanish Mussel Soup

1 cup onion
2 cloves garlic
2 cups chopped spinach
1 tomato
½ cup olive oil
½ teaspoon rosemary
½ teaspoon black pepper

½ teaspoon ground coriander
3 pounds of mussels
6½ cups Fish Broth
   (see recipe on page 8)

Serves 6–8

This recipe is equally good with virtually any of your favorite shellfish.

1. Chop the onions, garlic, and spinach. Seed and dice the tomato.
2. In a soup pot, heat the olive oil. Sauté the onion and garlic on medium for 3 minutes, then add the spinach, tomato, and rosemary, and stir for 3 more minutes. Stir in the pepper and coriander and take the pot off the heat.
3. Scrub the mussels and remove their beards. In a large pan, bring the fish broth to a boil; add the mussels, cover tightly, and turn off the heat. Check in a few minutes to see if they have been steamed open. Once they have, remove the meat from the mussel shells. Discard the shells. Strain the broth and discard all solids.
4. Add the mussel meat and the strained broth to the vegetables. Bring to a boil, reduce to a simmer, and cook for 5 minute. Remove from heat and allow to cool slightly. Using a blender or food processor, purée the mixture. Reheat and serve.

Vietnamese Crab and Pineapple Soup

Serves 8

Be sure that you use fresh pineapple with this recipe. Canned pineapple will adversely affect the taste.

1 cooked Dungeness Crab
15 medium-sized raw shrimp
15 medium-sized steamer clams
1 cup cubed fresh pineapple
½ of an onion
4 cloves garlic
½ pound (8 ounces) ripe
    tomatoes
2 scallions
4 sprigs cilantro
5 basil leaves
3 sprigs dill
6 mint leaves
3 tablespoons olive oil

10 cups water
1 stalk lemongrass
3 tablespoons Vietnamese
    fish sauce
2 tablespoons sugar
½ teaspoon chili garlic sauce
    (if you can find it)
Salt
2 tablespoons lime juice
1 pinch of saffron
1 bay leaf

1. Remove the meat from the crab, peel and devein the shrimp (leaving their tails on), and scrub the clamshells. Cut the pineapple into bite-sized chunks. Chop the onion, crush the garlic cloves, and seed and chop the tomatoes. Chop the scallions, cilantro, basil leaves, dill, and mint.
2. Using a soup pot, heat the oil. Add the onion and sauté on medium for 3 minutes. Add the garlic and tomatoes, cooking for 3 more minutes. Add the pineapple, water, and lemongrass, bringing everything to a boil. Reduce to a simmer and cook for 20 minutes.
3. Add the fish sauce, sugar, chili garlic sauce, salt, and lime juice. Bring to a boil. Add the clams in their shells and the crab, cooking for about 5 minutes, until the clams open.
4. Add the shrimp, saffron, cilantro, bay leaf, basil, dill, mint, and scallions. Simmer for 2 to 3 more minutes, until the shrimp turn pink. Discard the bay leaf and lemongrass stalk and serve.

Crab Cioppino Soup

2 cooked Dungeness crab

1 cup onion

1 (28-ounce) can peeled tomatoes, including liquid

3 cloves garlic

3 teaspoons fresh chopped
   basil leaves

2 tablespoons olive oil

¼ teaspoon oregano

1 bay leaf

1 cup dry white wine

1 cup Fish Broth (see recipe
   on page 8)

Salt

Serves 4
For an alternate flavor in this soup, substitute 1 cup of Chicken Broth (page 5) for the 1 cup of Fish Broth.

1. Remove the crabmeat from the shells and discard the shells (or freeze them for making broth another day). Chop the onion and the tomatoes, reserving the juice. Mince the garlic and chop the basil leaves.

2. In a soup pot, heat the olive oil. Add the onion, sautéing on medium for 3 minutes. Add the tomatoes and their liquid, oregano, basil, bay leaf, wine, broth, and half of the minced garlic. Bring to a boil, reduce to a simmer, and cook for 30 minutes.

3. Add the rest of the garlic, the crab, and the salt, simmering for 1 to 2 minutes. Discard the bay leaf and serve.

Asian Salmon in the Oven Soup

Serves 6

Garnish each bowl with some of the chopped cilantro, scallions, and sesame seeds.

4 cloves garlic
2 tablespoons ginger root
4 cups shredded cabbage and
  carrots
⅓ cup cilantro
3 scallions
8 cups (2 quarts) clam juice
2 tablespoons tamari **or**
  soy sauce

½ teaspoon ground coriander
1½ pounds salmon fillets
  (about 1 inch thick)
2 teaspoons sesame seeds
  (optional)

1. Preheat oven to 375 degrees. Mince the garlic, peel the ginger, and grate the cabbage and carrots together. Chop the cilantro and scallions.
2. Using a saucepan, stir together the clam juice, tamari (or soy sauce), garlic, ginger, and coriander. Bring to a boil, reduce to a simmer, and cook for 5 minutes. Set aside, covered to keep the mixture warm.
3. In deep baking dish large enough to hold all the ingredients, spread the grated cabbage and carrot mixture in a layer. Place the salmon fillets on top, skin side down. Pour the clam juice broth over the salmon. Loosely cover the baking dish with foil and cook for 18 minutes.
4. With a spatula, transfer the salmon fillets to the centers of the individual serving bowls. Divide the cooked vegetables among the bowls, then the cooking liquid.

German Frankfurter and Lentil Soup

1 ham bone
2 stalks celery
2 carrots
*1½ cups green **or** brown dried*
*   lentils*
8 cups Basic Beef Broth
*   (see recipe on page 4)*

1 tablespoon black peppercorns
2 medium onions
6 frankfurters
2 tablespoon butter

1. Crack the ham bone. Chop the celery and carrots.
2. In a soup pot, combine the lentils, beef broth, ham bone, celery, carrots, and peppercorns. Bring to a boil, reduce to a simmer, and cook for 1½ hours. Skim off the impurities every few minutes until no more rises to the top.
3. Remove from heat, discarding the ham bone. Force the mixture through a coarse sieve and discard the solids. Return the strained soup to the pot. Slice the onions thinly. Cut the frankfurters diagonally into ½-inch slices.
4. In a small saucepan, heat the butter. Sauté the onions for 3 minutes on medium, then add the frankfurter slices and cook for another 3 minutes.
5. Add the onion and frankfurter mixture to the soup pot. Return it to heat and simmer for 5 minutes.

Chinese Pork and Pickle Soup

Serves 4

For better flavor, use a good quality dry sherry wine instead of so-called "cooking sherry."

2 pork chops
1 tablespoon sesame oil
1 tablespoon sherry
1 tablespoon dark soy sauce
Pepper
¼ pound (4 ounces) Chinese
    preserved vegetable*

4 cups Basic Chicken Broth
    (see recipe on page 5)
2 scallions

1. Debone the pork chops and trim off the fat (discard the bones and fat). Using a sharp knife, cut the meat into the thinnest slices. In a bowl, toss the meat with the oil, sherry, soy sauce, and pepper, coating all the pieces. Refrigerate for 45 minutes.
2. Pour the sauce off the preserved vegetable, discarding the sauce. Thinly slice the vegetable.
3. Pour the broth in a soup pot. Bring to a boil, reduce to a simmer, and add the meat and the vegetable. Stir to separate the meat slices. Cook for 10 minutes.
4. Finely chop the scallions, including the green parts. Stir in and cook for 1 more minute.

    * Look for a jar of any such Chinese version; similar to the hot Korean *Kim Chi*, these are like pickles.

Hungarian Goulash with Sour Crea

1½ pounds beef (chuck or
    blade steak)
2 onions
1 pound tomatoes
1 bouquet garni (see "Bag o'
    Spices" on page 10)
¼ cup oil (**or** lard)
2 tablespoons flour

1 cup dry red wine
1 cup Basic Beef Broth
    (see recipe on page 4)
2 tablespoons Hungarian
    paprika
1 pound potatoes
½ cup sour crea

Serves 6

The word goulash refers to a random mixture. This Hungarian-born dish consists of some sort of meat in a thick, gravylike sauce, seasoned with paprika.

1. Trim off the excess fat from the meat and cut it into ¾-inch cubes. Slice the onions and seed and dice the tomatoes. Prepare the bouquet garni using your choice of fresh herbs.
2. Preheat oven to 325 degrees. In an oven-ready casserole dish or soup pot, heat the fat. Sauté the meat on medium high until browned on all sides. Remove the meat, setting it aside but reserving the fat in the pot.
3. Add the onions and sauté on medium for 3 minutes. Whisk in the flour and simmer for 2 minutes more. Whisk in ¼ cup of the broth and stir well. Add the rest of the broth, the wine, tomatoes, paprika, and bouquet garni; Bring to a boil. Transfer it to the oven and bake for 1½ hours.
4. Meanwhile, peel and cube the potatoes. Stir them into the oven mixture when the 1½ hours are up. Cook for another 30 minutes. Remove and discard the bouquet garni, stir in the sour cream, and serve.

German Beef and Cabbage Soup

3 pounds beef
1 cup shredded white cabbage
1 onion
2 carrots
1 small turnip
1 medium parsley root
½ of a small celery root
2 tomatoes
3 pounds beef bones

12 cups (3 quarts) beef broth
⅛ pound (2 ounces) beef liver
   (optional)
5 black peppercorns
Salt and black pepper

1. Wipe the beef off with a damp cloth and leave it whole. Shred the cabbage. Slice the onion, carrots, turnip, and parsley root. Peel and dice the celery root. Cut the tomatoes into quarters.
2. Rinse the beef bones in cold water. Bring a large pot of water to a boil and plunge the bones into it. Once it returns to a boil, drain immediately and rinse the bones in cold water again.
3. In a soup pot, combine the broth, the beef, the beef bones, and all remaining ingredients. Bring to a boil, reduce to a simmer, and cook for 2 hours.
4. Strain and reserve all solid ingredients except for the bones. Chill the broth until the fat layer solidifies and can be removed (several hours or overnight). Remove and discard the fat, then reheat the broth with all the cooked ingredients. Add salt and pepper to taste and serve.

Vietnamese Beef and Red Curry Soup

2 pounds flank steak
16 cups (4 quarts) water
4 star anise
1-inch section of cinnamon stick
8 ounces rice sticks (dried
    noodles, ¼-inch wide)
2 tablespoons peanut oil
2 tablespoons red curry paste
Salt

1 teaspoon sugar
Bean sprouts
1 lime
Fish sauce

Serves 6–8

Garnish by drizzling in small amount of fish sauce and adding some bean sprouts and lime wedges to each bowl.

1. Cut the meat into thin, 1½-inch long slices.
2. Place the beef pieces in a large pot with enough water to cover. Bring just to a boil, then drain. Rinse the meat. Place the meat back into the pot with the 4 quarts of fresh water. Add the star anise and the cinnamon stick. Bring to a boil, reduce to a simmer, and cook for 3½ hours.
3. Meanwhile, place the dried noodles in a bowl, covering them with hot water. Set aside.
4. When the meat is ready, heat the oil in a small saucepan. Stir in the curry paste, cooking for a couple of minutes. Add this mixture to the meat mixture. Add salt and the sugar, simmering everything for 20 minutes. Meanwhile, coarsely chop the bean sprouts and cut the lime into thin wedges.
5. Drain the noodles and divide them among individual serving bowls. Pour in the soup.

Caribbean Beef Soup

1½ pounds beef
½ an onion
½ green bell pepper
1 stalk celery
1 teaspoon ginger root
5 cloves garlic
1 chili pepper (any kind)
4 sprigs cilantro
4 tomatoes
3 plantains
1 sweet potato
½ pound butternut squash

3 new potatoes
1 chayote squash
3 ears corn (white if available)
3 tablespoons oil
1 dash cumin
Salt
¼ teaspoon white pepper
⅓ cup dry red wine
16 cups (4 quarts) Basic Beef Broth, divided (see recipe on page 4)

1. Cut the beef into 1½-inch cubes. Chop the onion, green bell pepper, and celery. Mince the ginger and garlic. Seed and mince the chili. Chop the cilantro and tomatoes. Slice the plantains into ¾-inch pieces. Cut the sweet potato and the butternut squash into 1-inch pieces. Quarter the new potatoes. Core the chayote and dice it into 1-inch pieces. Slice each of the corn ears into 6 pieces.

2. In a soup pot, heat the oil. Add the garlic, beef, and onions, and sauté on medium for 8 minutes. Add the green pepper, celery, ginger, chili pepper, cilantro, cumin, salt, white pepper, wine, tomatoes, and 4 cups of the beef broth. Bring to a boil, reduce to a simmer, and cook for 40 minutes. Add the squashes, potatoes, remaining beef broth, and corn; simmer for 30 to 45 minutes more.

German Beef and Sauerkraut Soup

2 cups diced potato
1 cup chopped yellow onion
½ cup carrots
1 stalk celery
1 clove garlic
2 tablespoons fresh chopped
    flat-leaf parsley
2 tablespoons olive oil
1 pound (16 ounces) beef
    stew meat
1½ cups Basic Beef Broth
    (see recipe on page 4)

1 (14-ounce) can peeled, diced
    tomatoes, including liquid
¾ cup (6 ounces) beer
¼ cup dry red wine
½ cup sauerkraut in juice
1 bay leaf
⅛ teaspoon thyme
¼ teaspoon pepper
1 tablespoon butter
1 tablespoon flour

Serves 4

Look for a dark German beer at your local liquor store. It adds just the right touch in this recipe.

1. Dice the potatoes. Chop the onion, shred the carrot, and chop the celery. Mince the garlic and chop the parsley.

2. In a soup pot, heat the oil. Add the beef, browning it on all sides on medium–high heat. Pour in the broth. Add all the remaining ingredients *except* the butter and flour. Bring to a boil, reduce to a simmer, and skim off any impurities that rise to the surface. Cover the pot and simmer for 2 hours.

3. Heat the butter in a small pan, then whisk in the flour. Stir it constantly for 3 minutes. Take off heat. Spoon in a little of the soup broth and whisk to a paste; whisk the paste into the soup pot. Simmer, uncovered, for 10 more minutes. Remove bay leaf before serving.

Japanese Chicken Soup

1 large chicken breast
2 large mushroom caps, sliced
1 scallion, sliced
1 teaspoon sake (dry sherry can be substituted)
¾ teaspoon cornstarch
½ teaspoon peanut oil

4 cups Fish Broth (see recipe on page 8)
1 teaspoon soy sauce
½ teaspoon sesame oil

1. Remove the skin and bones from the chicken breast, discarding them. Cut the meat diagonally into 8 strips. Slice the mushroom caps into thin strips. Cut the scallion into thin slices.
2. In a bowl, toss the chicken pieces with the sake and the cornstarch. In a soup pot, quick sauté (on high heat) the chicken strips in the olive oil. Remove the chicken with a slotted spoon and add the broth to the pot; bring to a boil, scraping up any cooked-on bits from the bottom of the pan. Reduce to a simmer and return the chicken strips to the pot; cook for 10 minutes. Add the scallions and mushrooms, simmering for an additional 5 minutes. Stir in the soy sauce and sesame oil, and serve.

Matzo Ball Soup

4 eggs
4 tablespoons olive oil
16½ cups Basic Chicken Broth,
    divided (see recipe on
    page 5)

1 cup matzo meal
Salt and black pepper

Serves 6–8

Moisten your hands with cold water before shaping the chilled matzo mixture into balls.

1. In a bowl, mix together the eggs, olive oil, ½ cup of the chicken broth, and the matzo meal. Refrigerate for at least 1 hour.
2. In a large pot, bring salted water to boil. Form 28 small matzo balls from the chilled dough. Add them to the boiling water, and simmer for 35 minutes.
3. In a soup pot, bring the remaining broth to a boil. Place several matzo balls in each individual soup bowl. Pour the hot chicken broth over the matzo balls and serve.

What Does "Lightly Salted Water" Really Mean?

Lightly salted water tastes like tears. Thoroughly salted water tastes like seawater. For foods that absorb a lot of water as they cook, like beans or pasta, lightly salted is the way to go, since your aim is to draw out the natural flavors of the food, not to make them "salty." For foods that don't absorb water, such as green vegetables, the point is to use salt's properties of sealing in nutrients, color, and flavor. For that reason, you would salt the water more assertively. Excess salt can easily be washed from those vegetables. Make no mistake, though: Salt is an important part of coaxing the best flavors from your good ingredients.

German Lentil and Bacon Soup

1 pound (16 ounces) dried lentils
12 cups water
1 meaty ham bone
3 onions
4 stalks celery, with leaves
1 bay leaf

½ teaspoon thyme
1 potato
3 carrots
6 strips bacon (commercial soy bits can be substituted)
Salt and pepper

1. Rinse the lentils. Put the lentils and water in a large soup pot with the ham bone, 2 of the whole onions, 3 of the whole stalks of celery with their leaves, the bay leaf, and the thyme. As this mixture is coming to a boil, peel and grate the potato and add it to the pot. Bring the mixture completely to a boil, reduce to a simmer, and cook for 3 hours, stirring regularly.

2. When the soup has only about 30 minutes left to cook, thinly slice the carrots. In a small saucepan, cover them with water and simmer them for 15 minutes. Drain and set aside.

3. In a skillet, sauté the bacon on medium heat. Leaving the bacon grease in the pan, transfer the bacon to paper towels to absorb the grease. Coarsely chop the remaining onion and slice the remaining celery. Sauté them in the bacon fat on low heat for 5 minutes, without allowing them to brown. Using a slotted spoon, transfer them to paper towels to drain. Discard the bacon fat.

4. When the mixture in the soup pot is done cooking, reduce the heat to the lowest setting. Remove the whole onion, whole celery, bay leaf, and ham bone from the soup pot; discard everything *except* the ham bone. Cut the meat from the bone and add the meat back into the pot. Stir in the sautéed carrots and celery. Add salt and pepper to taste. Crumble the bacon on top of the soup in a tureen or individual bowls.

French Lentils and Rice Soup

¼ pound uncooked long-grained rice

4 carrots

2 onions

1 small head lettuce

¼ pound (4 ounces) dried red lentils

2 tablespoons butter

6 cups Basic Chicken Broth (see recipe on page 5)

⅔ cup white bread crumbs

Salt and pepper

Serves 8

About ½ pound of kale or spinach can be used in place of the lettuce. Be aware, however, that this will add a lot more flavor to the final soup.

1. Cook the rice according to the package directions. Drain, rinse under cold water, and drain again. Set aside.
2. Cut the carrots and onions into thin slices. Shred the lettuce. Rinse the lentils.
3. Using a large saucepan or soup pot, heat the butter. Add the carrot and onion pieces and sauté for 3 to 5 minutes on medium heat. Add the lentils and the broth, stirring well. Bring to a boil, reduce to a simmer and cook for 20 minutes.
4. Add the lettuce, bread crumbs, and salt and pepper to taste. Bring to a boil, reduce to a simmer, and cook for 10 minutes.
5. Remove from heat and allow to cool slightly. In a blender or food processor, purée the soup. Reheat it the serving temperature, along with the rice.

Madras Curried Tomato and Lentil Soup

Serves 6–8

If you're having problems finding curry leaves, try substituting 2 tablespoons of ground coriander.

1 pound Italian plum tomatoes
1 tablespoon minced onion
2 teaspoons fresh minced garlic
3 cups cooked lentils
1 cup water
1 teaspoon cumin
¼ teaspoon cayenne
Coarse salt
1 tablespoon lemon juice

1 tablespoon ghee (see page 80) **or** nut oil
1 teaspoon black mustard seeds
8 fresh **or** dried curry leaves (kari)

1. Peel and halve the tomatoes. Scoop the pulp and seeds into a blender or food processor and purée. Set aside the purée and the rest of the tomato parts. Mince the onion and garlic.
2. Pour the water into a soup pot. Add the lentils and whisk, to crush some of the cooked lentils. Add the puréed tomato, the cumin, cayenne, onion, garlic, and salt. Bring to a boil, reduce to a simmer, and cook for 10 minutes.
3. Add the lemon juice and the tomato halves. Simmer for 1 more minute. Cover and remove from heat.
4. Using a small saucepan that has a lid, heat the ghee until very hot. Add the mustard seeds gradually (you may need to put the lid on since the seeds may jump out of the pan). Once they stop spattering, add the curry leaves. Turn the heat off. Shake the pan back and forth a few times. Ladle the soup into serving bowls and garnish with the mustard seed mixture.

Indian Kohlrabi, Green Tomato, and Lentil Soup

1⅓ cups tomatoes
1 pound (16 ounces) kohlrabi
½ pound (8 ounces) hard,
   green unripe tomatoes
1 onion
3 tablespoons fresh chopped
   coriander
4½ cups cooked yellow lentils
1 tablespoon crushed dry
   fenugreek leaves

8 dried **or** fresh curry leaves
1 tablespoon sambaar powder
1 tablespoon ground coriander
4 tablespoons light sesame oil
1 teaspoon black mustard seeds
1 teaspoon coarse salt

Serves 8
Curry powder can be substituted for the sanbaar powder but it is milder and less authentic.

1. Purée the 1⅓ cups of tomatoes. Peel and slice the kohlrabi. Slice the green tomatoes and the onion. Chop the fresh coriander.
2. Combine the cooked lentils with cold water to make a total of 6 cups. Using a soup pot, combine the lentils, the puréed tomatoes, fenugreek leaves, sambaar, and the *ground* coriander. Bring to a boil, reduce to a simmer, and cover; cook for 10 minutes.
3. Add the kohlrabi and simmer for an additional 10 minutes. Add the green tomatoes and onion and simmer for 5 more minutes. Remove from heat.
4. Using a small saucepan with a lid, heat the sesame oil to a high temperature. Add the mustard seeds, using the lid to keep them from popping out, if necessary. When the seeds stop spattering, remove from heat. Stir in the salt and *fresh* chopped coriander. Pour this mixture into the soup pot. Stir well and serve.

Hot and Sour Chinese Soup

Serves 6

This traditional Chinese soup can also be made with chicken or beef.

3 cups Basic Chicken Broth
    (see recipe on page 5)
1 tablespoon soy sauce
4 dried Chinese mushrooms,
    boiled for 15 minutes, then
    cut into strips
1 (6-ounce) can bamboo
    shoots, drained
¼ pound lean pork, cut into
    strips

1 cake tofu, cut into strips
1 teaspoon white pepper
2 tablespoons lemon juice
3 tablespoons cornstarch
3 tablespoons cold water
1 egg, lightly beaten
1 tablespoon sesame oil
2 stalks scallions, chopped

1. In a soup pot, mix together the broth, soy sauce, mushrooms, bamboo shoots, and pork. Bring to a boil; reduce the heat and simmer for 5 minutes. Add the tofu, pepper, and lemon juice; bring to a boil.
2. Whisk together the cornstarch and water until smooth; add it to the soup and boil, stirring constantly, until it thickens slightly. Reduce heat and stir the egg into the broth. Remove the pot from the heat; stir in the sesame oil and sprinkle with scallions.

Beef Bourguignon

¼–½ pound (4–8 ounces)
   bacon chunk with rind
2 tablespoons olive oil
3 pounds raw beef
1 onion
1 carrot
Salt and pepper
2 tablespoons flour
3 cups dry red wine
3–4 cloves garlic

3 cups Basic Beef Broth
   (see recipe on page 4)
2 tablespoons tomato paste
1 pinch of thyme
1 bay leaf
20 pearl onions
1 pound (16 ounces) fresh
   cremini, Portobello, **or** button
   mushrooms

Serves 6

This is as classic a French dish as bouillabaisse. Considered a stew, it can easily incorporate a bit more liquid and become a soup.

1. Preheat the oven to 450 degrees. Cut the rind off the bacon, reserving the rind. Slice the bacon meat into strips. Bring 6–8 cups of water to a boil; add the rind and the bacon meat, and simmer for 10 minutes. Drain, discard the liquid and rind, and pat the bacon meat dry.
2. In a large saucepan, warm the olive oil on medium heat. Sauté the bacon meat for 2 minutes to brown it slightly. With a fork, remove the bacon from pan and set it aside.
3. Cut the beef into 2-inch cubes and pat them dry with paper towels. Heat the bacon drippings on medium and sauté the beef, turning it several times to brown it on all sides. Remove the beef and set it aside with the bacon.
4. Slice the onion and carrot. Add them to the same oil to sauté for 4 minutes. Discard the oil, leaving the vegetables in the pan.
5. Using a large stove top- and ovenproof container with a lid, place the bacon and beef in the bottom. Sprinkle on salt, pepper, and the flour, rubbing them into the meats. Without its lid, place the dish in the oven for 4 minutes. Remove, toss the meats slightly and cook for 4 more minutes. Take out of the oven. Reduce oven temperature to 325 degrees.

(continued)

6. Pour the wine and 2 cups of the broth over the meats. Mash the garlic and add it to the mixture, along with the tomato paste and herbs. Place the dish on the top of the stove, bringing it to a boil. Reduce to a simmer. Put the lid on the dish and place it back in the oven for 2½ hours, making sure it simmers very gently.

7. Meanwhile, heat the remaining broth in a saucepan. Simmer the pearl onions gently for 5 minutes. Quarter the mushrooms and add them, cooking the mixture for another 7 minutes. When the meat is ready, strain the casserole and discard most of the liquid, leaving just enough to create the thickness of soup. Skim off any fat. Place the onions and mushrooms on top, rewarm in the oven for 5 minutes, and serve. Discard the bay leaf.

Hungarian Beef Soup

Serves 6

Use leftover beef, cutting it into cubes. If you have raw beef, cut it up more finely, and cook it quite thoroughly before adding it to the other ingredients.

2 onions
4 small potatoes
4 carrots
2 stalks celery
2 small turnips
3 small tomatoes (but not cherry or cocktail ones)
3 tablespoons nut oil

1 teaspoon paprika (Hungarian is best)
1 tablespoon caraway seeds
4 cups Veal Broth (see recipe on page 13)
2 cups cubed cooked beef
1 cup plain yogurt

1. Finely dice the onions, potatoes, carrots, celery, turnips, and tomatoes.
2. In a soup pot, heat the oil. Sauté the onions on medium for 3 minutes, then add all the vegetables, the paprika, and the caraway seeds. Add the broth. Bring to a boil, reduce to a simmer, and cook for 10 minutes. Add the meat and simmer for another 5 minutes. Take it off the heat. Gradually whisk in the yogurt, and serve.

CHAPTER 16

Chilled Soups and Desserts

Chilled Tomato Soup with Guacamole

1 leek
1 stalk celery
1 bulb fennel (small)
1 red bell pepper
½ a Spanish onion
15 large beefsteak tomatoes
5 cloves garlic
1 sprig thyme
1 sprig rosemary
3 sprigs parsley
2 sprigs basil
4 dried fennel sticks

1 tablespoon anise seeds
2 teaspoons fennel seeds
1 teaspoon coriander seeds
3 tablespoons olive oil
3 cups water
White pepper
Tabasco sauce
Celery salt (**or** onion salt)
4–6 tablespoons guacamole
4–6 nasturtium flowers
   (optional)

1. Coarsely chop the leek (white part only). Coarsely chop the celery, fennel bulb, red bell pepper (discarding seeds and membranes), and the Spanish onion. Cut each of the tomatoes into 8 pieces. Crush the garlic cloves gently.
2. Prepare 2 bouquet garnis (see "Bag o' Spices" on page 8): In the first bag, combine the thyme, rosemary, parsley, basil, and fennel sticks. In the second one, combine the anise, fennel, and coriander seeds.
3. In a soup pot, heat the olive oil. Add the leek, celery, fennel bulb, red bell pepper, onion, and garlic. Cover, turn the heat very low, and allow to soften for 10 minutes.
4. Add the 2 bouquet garnis, the tomato pieces, and the water. Bring to a boil, reduce to a simmer, and cook for 15 minutes.
5. Remove from heat and allow to cool slightly. Discard the bouquet garnis. Using a blender or food processor, purée the mixture. Season with salt, white pepper, Tabasco sauce, and celery salt to taste. Refrigerate to chill thoroughly.
6. Ladle the soup into individual serving bowls. Garnish each with 1 tablespoon of guacamole and a nasturtium flower.

Avocado Vichyssoise

1¼ pounds new potatoes
4 cups light vegetable broth
   or Basic Chicken Broth
   (see recipe on page 5)
1 lemon
2 avocados

¼ teaspoon cumin **or** curry
   powder
Fresh cilantro (optional)

Serves 6
Two varieties of avocado are available. One type has smooth green skin; the other has darker pebbled-textured skin.

1. Quarter the potatoes. Place them in a large saucepan covered with water. Bring to a boil, reduce to a simmer, and cook for 15 minutes.
2. Meanwhile, chill the chicken broth and peel and coarsely chop the avocados. Juice the lemon and chop the cilantro, reserving some leaves.
3. When the potatoes are cooked, drain them and put the potatoes into a large bowl or soup pot; discard the cooking liquid. Add the avocados, broth, lemon juice, and cumin (or curry). Using a blender or food processor, purée the mixture. Refrigerate to chill thoroughly. Garnish with a few cilantro leaves and serve.

Pitting an Avocado

For both types of avocado, start by cutting through the skin, down to the pit, and scoring the fruit lengthwise. Gripping both halves, give a quick twist to separate one half from the pit, leaving the other half holding that large nut. If you plan to use only half of the avocado, it's best to leave the pit in the unused portion, since it prevents the fruit from turning brown overnight. To remove the pit, hack into the middle of it with the blade of your knife, gripping the fruit in the palm of your other hand; twist the knife clockwise to loosen the pit. It should fall right out of a ripe avocado.

Melon Soup with Almonds

Serves 4

Garnish with the toasted almonds and chopped mint.

1 small, ripe honeydew melon
½ of a jalapeño chili
½ cup lime juice
½ cup plain yogurt
Salt and pepper
½ cup sliced almonds
2 teaspoons water
¼ cup fresh chopped mint

1. Cut the flesh of the melon into ½-inch cubes. Seed and mince the jalapeño.
2. Using a blender or food processor, purée the melon cubes, lime juice, yogurt, and salt and pepper to taste. Refrigerate until thoroughly chilled.
3. Preheat the oven to 325 degrees. Using a baking dish with low sides, combine the sliced almonds with the water and additional salt to taste. Cook for 15 minutes. Allow them to cool. Meanwhile, chop the mint.
4. Ladle the soup into 4 individual soup bowls.

Fruit Soup with Sesame

Serves 6

Garnish with the reserved fruit and the toasted sesame seeds and serve.

2 teaspoons sesame seeds
½ pound (8 ounces) cherries
  (Queen Anne **or** bing)
1 pint strawberries
½ pint blackberries
4 plums
¼ cup minced candied ginger
Cinnamon

1. Preheat the oven to 350 degrees. Place the sesame seeds in a single layer in a small baking dish. Toast for 3 to 4 minutes. Remove from heat.
2. Reserve 6 cherries, 3 strawberries (cut in half) and 3 blackberries (cut in half) for a garnish. Pit the plums and cherries and slice into bite-sized pieces. Remove the stems from the strawberries and quarter them. Mince the candied ginger. Purée together all of the fruit (*except* the fruit reserved for garnish).
3. Divide the fruit mixture into the individual soup bowls. Add a faint dash of cinnamon to each bowl.

Swedish Rhubarb Soup

2 pounds fresh rhubarb
2 teaspoons potato starch **or**
   cornstarch
1 cup sugar

6 cups water
Cinnamon (optional)
Raspberries (optional)

1. Trim the rhubarb, peeling some of the stalks if necessary. Cut them into ½-inch pieces.
2. Using a large saucepan, combine the rhubarb pieces, water, and sugar. Simmer for 6 minutes, or until tender, stirring several times. Allow to cool slightly.
3. Whisk in the potato starch (or cornstarch), stirring well until the soup thickens slightly. Chill thoroughly.
4. Ladle into individual soup bowls.

> **Serves 6**
>
> Garnish with a couple of shakes of cinnamon and a few raspberries.

Strawberry Soup

4 cups sliced strawberries
1 banana
1½ cups cubed toasted pound
   cake
1 cup orange juice

1 cup light sour cream
1 tablespoon raspberry **or**
   cherry liqueur
1 ice cube
6 mint sprigs (optional)

1. Preheat oven to 325 degrees. Stem and slice the strawberries. Cut the banana into fourths. Cut the cake into ½-inch cubes and toast.
2. Using a food processor or blender, purée the strawberries, banana, orange juice, sour cream, and liqueur. Pour the mixture into a bowl. Add the ice cube and stir until it melts, chilling the fruit mixture.
3. Ladle the soup into the individual bowls. Garnish with the cake croutons and a sprig of mint.

> **Serves 6**
>
> It's simple to make "cake croutons." Place a single layer of cubed pound cake in the toaster oven. Toast for 5 minutes, turn and toast again briefly.

Cherry Tomato Gazpacho

Serves 2

Top with walnuts and the fresh chopped dill as a garnish.

1 cup diced cucumber
¼ teaspoon pepper
2 tablespoons walnut oil
1 clove garlic, minced
¾ cup cherry tomatoes

1 cup plain yogurt
2 tablespoons fresh chopped
    dill (optional)
Walnuts (optional)

1. Begin ahead of time by peeling and dicing the cucumber and marinating it in the refrigerator (for at least 2 hours) in the pepper, walnut oil, and minced garlic cloves.
2. When the cucumber is done marinating, drain the cucumbers. Add the cherry tomatoes and the yogurt, stirring well. Chop the dill. Pour the soup into serving bowls.

Parade of Summer Vegetables Gazpacho

Serves 6–8

For this summer soup, be sure that you visit your local vegetable stand and buy only the freshest vegetables available.

4 large tomatoes
4 ears corn
1 cup peas
1 cup green beans
4 zucchini

3 summer squash
1 cup broccoli florets
½ cups cooked pasta shells
10 cups V-8 (low-sodium)

1. Chop and seed the tomatoes, husk the corn, shell the peas, and trim the green beans. Cut the zucchini and the summer squash into bite-size chunks. Cut the smallest florets off the broccoli.
2. Steam the broccoli florets for 8 minutes. Steam or roast the corn separately, for about 8 minutes. With a sharp knife, cut the kernels off the cobs.
3. In individual soup bowls, pour the V-8. Divide the raw vegetables equally among the bowls; then divide the corn and pasta. Top each bowl with a few of the florets. Serve.

Scandinavian Fruit Soup

¼ cup tapioca
1 cup dried peaches
1 cup prunes
1 cup dried cherries

2 cups raisins **or** currants
2 small tart apples
1 cup dried apricots
½ cup sugar

1. Using a large soup pot, combine the tapioca, peaches, prunes, cherries, and raisins. Cover with cold water. Bring to a boil.
2. Meanwhile, dice the apples. Add them to the pot, reduce to a simmer, and cook for 20 minutes, stirring often.
3. Add the apricots and the sugar, simmering and stirring often until the tapioca is transparent but not mushy. Add water to reach the desired consistency.

> **Serves 8–10**
>
> Serve hot in mugs or as a cold soup. It keeps well refrigerated or frozen.

Cucumber Soup

1 large cucumber
2 cups plain yogurt
½ cup tomato paste
½ teaspoon coriander
1 clove garlic, minced

Black pepper to taste
Fresh mint (optional)

Peel and dice the cucumber and put it in a blender or food processor. Add the rest of the ingredients (*except* the mint) and blend until smooth. Chill in the refrigerator until ready to serve, garnished with fresh mint.

> **Serves 4**
>
> For an added color and flavor, drop a few fresh, cherry tomatoes in each individual bowl before serving.

Chilled Shrimp and Cucumber Soup

Serves 4–6

Garnish with additional chopped dill and serve in chilled bowls.

8 large cucumbers
   (about 2 pounds)
¼ cup red wine vinegar
1 tablespoon sugar
1 teaspoon salt
1 pound raw shrimp (the
   smallest you can find)
2 tablespoons sweet butter
½ cup dry white vermouth
Salt and freshly ground black
   pepper

1½ cups cold buttermilk
¾ cup chopped fresh dill
   (or more to taste), plus
   additional for garnish

1. Peel and coarsely chop the cucumbers. Toss them with the vinegar, sugar and salt; let stand for 30 minutes.
2. Meanwhile, peel and devein the shrimp. Rinse them and pat them dry. Melt the butter in a small skillet. Add the shrimp, raise the heat, and toss them until they turn pink, 2 to 3 minutes. Remove the shrimp with a slotted spoon and set aside. Add the vermouth to the skillet and boil until it is reduced to a few teaspoonfuls; pour over the shrimp and season with salt and pepper.
3. Drain the cucumbers and transfer them to a food processor fitted with a steel blade. Process briefly, then add the buttermilk and continue to process until smooth. Add the fresh dill to taste and process briefly, about 1 second.
4. Pour the cucumber mixture into a bowl and stir in the shrimp and their liquid; refrigerate, covered, until very cold.

Fresh Cantaloupe and Raspberry Soup

1 ripe cantaloupe
1 cup fresh raspberries, plus 4
   raspberries for garnish
½ cup orange juice
Juice of ½ a lemon
Juice of ½ a lime
4 large fresh mint leaves

Serves 4

Garnish each serving with a mint leaf and a whole raspberry.

1. Cut the cantaloupe in half, clean out the seeds, peel the halves, and cut the flesh into 1-inch pieces. Put the cantaloupe in a blender to create a smooth purée. Pour into a large bowl. Blend the raspberries into a smooth purée. Pour this into a strainer and push the juice and pulp through the strainer into a small bowl in order to remove the seeds. This should yield about ½ cup (repeat with more raspberries if it comes up short).
2. Stir the purées together, then add the juices and stir to blend.

Roasted Vegetable Gazpacho

4 beefsteak tomatoes
2 medium zucchini
1 medium eggplant
2 medium onions
10 cloves garlic
6 tablespoons olive oil
4 cups Roasted Vegetable Broth
   (see recipe on page 10)
¼ cup sherry vinegar
Black pepper
4 slices stale bread
Fresh cilantro (optional)

Serves 6–8

Garnish with the freshly chopped cilantro before serving.

1. Preheat the oven to 400 degrees. Cut the tomatoes and zucchini into large chunks. Peel the eggplant and the onions; cut them into chunks. Peel the garlic cloves, leaving them whole. Toss the vegetables in a bowl with olive oil; place them in a single layer on a roasting pan. Cook for 25 minutes, turning the vegetables over halfway through.
2. Purée the vegetables with the broth and place in a large bowl. Add the sherry vinegar and pepper. Tear the bread into pieces (discard the crusts) and stir them into the mixture. Refrigerate for several hours (or overnight).

Summer Borscht

4 medium-sized beets, cleaned
5 cups water
1 pinch of salt
1 tablespoon white vinegar
2 hard-boiled eggs, chopped
2 medium-sized pickling cucumbers, chopped
1 bunch scallions, chopped
4 tablespoons sour crea

1. Boil the beets in the water, unpeeled, for 20 to 25 minutes; remove the beets with a slotted spoon, leaving the water to boil. When the beets are cool enough to handle, peel and grate them; return them to the boiling water. Cook for another 10 to 15 minutes, adding the salt and vinegar. Remove from heat and allow to cool. Refrigerate until thoroughly chilled.
2. Pour the soup into large serving bowls. Add some egg, cucumbers, scallions, and a tablespoon of sour cream to each; mix well and serve.

Cooking Beets—Preserving Nutrition
The flavorful, nutrient-rich juices in beets are water soluble. To lock in the sweetness, color, and food value of these wonderful vegetables, consider cooking them in their skins. When boiling them, put a few drops of red wine vinegar in the water, which also helps seal in the juices. Beets can also be baked whole, like potatoes, then peeled and sliced.

Introduction to One-Pot Slow Cooker Recipies

Cooking should be fun. It's a simple enough thought, but too many people turn it into drudgery. Perhaps they find a handful of recipes they like and keep repeating them, never savoring the chance to experiment with new spices or new combinations of flavors. In this increasingly hectic world some people simply resent the time it takes to prepare a good meal. Others just see food as fuel for the body and ignore its impact on the soul and its role in bonding family and friends.

Slow cooking can bring the joy back into food. Not only does the slow cooker offer limitless opportunities for experimentation, it is a surprisingly versatile appliance. Most people think of slow cookers as best suited to soups and stews, which they certainly excel at, but slow cookers also can bake breads and cakes as well as serve as a romantic fondue pot. They can roast meat, steam vegetables, and even keep hot apple cider at the perfect temperature for a holiday gathering.

And we really shouldn't be surprised. Virtually every culture on the planet has some sort of slow-cooked repertoire. In part, this is because people throughout history have been busy ensuring their survival—they couldn't spare time to stand over a fire. In part, it's because every culture has a "leftover" dish. From goulash and chili to shepherd's pie, soups, and spaghetti sauces, people have developed ways to recombine yesterday's meals into new, flavorful creations.

In fact, throughout history, slow cooking has had a prominent place. When people first discovered fire, they also discovered that burying the animal carcass and vegetables below a bed of coals helped it cook more evenly and thoroughly. Clay pots brought the opportunity to keep the food clean while providing an efficient way to heat it even in hot climates.

So now we are coming full circle in our experiences with food. Instead of looking for ever-faster ways to prepare tasteless meals that keep our bodies running, we are looking for ways to regain the advantages our ancestors found in slow cooking. The meals in this cookbook offer the chance to combine old foods in new, exciting ways. They take you beyond the slow-cooker box to tempt you to experiment with flavors you may never have dreamed of. And most important, they rekindle the spirit of food preparation, the fact that it should be a constant part of our daily existence instead of a too-quick interruption.

In that spirit, many of these recipes are downright fun. They provide the chance to experiment with ingredients many people pass by in the grocery store. Many also provide the opportunity to get a whole group of family and friends involved chopping, cleaning, and mixing ingredients. And, who can resist the fun of seeing a dish cook through the clear cover?

Also note that these recipes are extremely healthy. Most avoid high-fat, high-sugar contents while replacing salt with flavors derived directly from the meats, vegetables, and plant spices. The slow-cooking process also retains more nutrients than many other methods of cooking.

Even more exciting is the fact that these recipes are easy. They require only a few simple utensils, an occasional unique ingredient, and an extremely basic knowledge of cooking terms. The rest of the magic is achieved through the science of slow cooking—the fact that food is cooked evenly through indirect heat and doesn't dry out. Flavors meld, meats and vegetables blend, spices release their hidden aromas, and everyday ingredients become exciting adventures.

CHAPTER 17
The Slow Cooker

Although slow cooking was common throughout history, the invention of the cast-iron stove changed all that. Sure, people still put the occasional stew or soup "on the back burner," but they more often baked their bread and main dishes quickly in a hot oven. What they lost in flavor and control they made up for with convenience.

The Resurgence of the Slow Cooker

It wasn't until the 1960s that Americans and Europeans began to see the advantages of slow cooking again. One important factor was the women's movement. Suddenly meals had to be planned the evening before they would be eaten because Mom wasn't there to hover over the stove. If you wanted anything that took longer than a half-hour, it needed to be cooked during the day.

Enter the Crock-Pot®. The Rival Corporation, an appliance manufacturer, saw the need for a new appliance that would create healthy, home-cooked meals without infringing on free time. They went back to an earlier time in history and revisited the clay pot. By putting an electric plug in the pot and heating elements around the crock to substitute for hot coals, they created the first modern-day slow cooker.

> The slow cooker we know was first introduced in the 1960s as a response to women working outside the home in large numbers. It became more popular as an energy-saving device during the energy crisis of the 1970s.

How the Slow Cooker Works

Of course, the electric slow cooker also provided a few other advantages over the clay pot and hot coals. Today's slow cookers usually have two settings—high and low. The low setting is equivalent to about 200 degrees Fahrenheit, while the high setting is about 300 degrees. However, the reason they are listed as high and low is because the actual degrees don't matter. Because the food heats indirectly, absorbing the heat from the crockery, it will cook the same within a 50-degree temperature range.

The cover also is an important component of the slow cooker. It usually is a heavy glass or plastic cover that fits securely, creating a seal that holds the steam in the slow cooker. This is an important factor in creating those marvelous flavors—foods are cooked in their own steam, literally infusing the flavor back in through the cooking process. This keeps the food moist and works to tenderize the toughest cuts of meat and the most stubborn vegetables.

Slow cookers heat up slowly, usually taking two to three hours to get up to their highest temperature. This ensures that the food retains its nutrients while also preventing scorching or burning. It's also the reason you don't need to be home while the meal cooks.

The temperature of the cooked food on the low setting is about 200 degrees. This is hot enough to inhibit bacterial growth, yet it is low enough that stirring isn't necessary. Stirring is usually done to eliminate hot spots in a dish. Since the slow cooker never gets hot enough to burn the food, there are no hot spots to eliminate.

Because the food cooks slowly, the same dish can take a different amount of time on different days. The reason is that the size of the food pieces, the fat content, and the liquid content all conduct heat differently. The lean three-pound pork roast that took eight hours last week could take nine hours this week if it has more fat and you've added a few more vegetables to the pot this time.

> **How often should I stir the food in the slow cooker?**
> Because it cooks by indirect heat, you never need to stir the food to make sure it's evenly cooked. However, you may want to stir it at first to make sure the ingredients are well mingled.

What Is a Real Slow Cooker?

Note that some companies have tried to pass off their "hot plate" appliances as slow cookers. While these imposters do allow slow cooking, they do not have the same effect as a true slow cooker. A real slow cooker has a crockery insert that warms up evenly, thus spreading the heat evenly throughout the food. A device that provides heat only from the bottom to a metal container is no different than putting a pot on the stove, no matter how low the temperature setting goes.

Since the early days of Crock-Pots®, many variations have developed. Today they come in all shapes and sizes. Some include separate compartments so vegetables and meat can be cooked at the same time without blending. Most even include special-purchase options such as bread bakers and meat roasters. And virtually all of them come in pleasing colors to fit in any kitchen décor.

Slow-cooker recipes need very little water because they "recycle" the water in the vegetables and meats via steam. If you're converting an oven recipe for the slow cooker, use about one-fourth the water.

How to Choose the Right Slow Cooker

With so many different styles from which to choose, how do you pick the one that's right for you? Well, if you're like most people, you probably got your first slow cooker as a housewarming or wedding present.

Relax, it will be just fine. Sure, there are small one-quart versions that are perfect for hot-dip appetizers and there are massive eight-quart models designed to make enough stew for a small army. There are versions with automatic timers and warming settings. Some have removable crockery inserts, while others have the crock built into the device. But a slow cooker remains a slow cooker. It's a relatively simple device that's hard to use incorrectly.

If you are lucky enough to plan your purchase of a slow cooker, define what you will be using it for. Do you have more than four people in your family? If so, you might want to go with a six-quart or even eight-quart version. Someone who does a lot of entertaining might want the larger version. And, if you like to freeze leftovers, by all means go for a bigger one.

If you're a small family, you might want to start with the midsize and most versatile type of slow cooker. The 2½-quart version—the one first introduced by the Rival Corporation—is still the most popular for first-time buyers. It is large enough to make meals for groups of up to eight people while small enough to remain energy efficient and to correctly cook small quantities of food.

Also take a look at how you plan to use your slow cooker. Are you routinely gone for more than nine hours during the day? If so, you might want to consider the automatic timer and warming function because even a slow cooker can overcook some food. Do you want to make entire meals? The two-compartment model would provide more options.

If you don't like to spend a lot of time washing pots and pans, consider a slow cooker with a removable crockery insert. These can be cleaned in the dishwasher while self-contained units must be sponge cleaned.

If this is your first slow cooker and you aren't sure how you will be using it, choose a reasonable middle ground. That removable crock is a real time saver. Likewise, 3½ to 4 quarts adds enough flexibility to cook large meals without being too large to store in your cupboard or to properly cook a small meal.

Note that most of the recipes in this book are well suited to slow cookers in the three- to six-quart size range. However, that is simply the optimal size for the dish mentioned. Most can also go into slightly smaller or larger slow cookers without severely affecting the food quality.

> Because a slow cooker uses indirect heat to cook food, it needs to be filled at least halfway and no more than three-quarters full. Any more or less will cause food to cook unevenly.

Why the Prices Vary

As a general rule, the pricing on slow cookers is relatively easy to decipher. The more options they offer and the larger the capacity, the more expensive they run. A basic 2½-quart model with a built-in crock and two temperature settings will sell for under $10 at a discount store. Add a quart more space, a warming setting, and removable crock, and it will sell for $30 to $40.

When you start getting larger and fancier, the prices go up quickly. The eight-quart slow cooker with removable crock, automatic timer, digital readout, warming function, and two compartments will sell for about $80.

Many slow cookers also offer special utensils such as bread baking inserts, vegetable steamers, meat roasters, and insulated carrying cases. As a rule, you need to special order these directly from the manufacturer. However, if you do find them at the store, resist the urge to purchase them until you are sure you need them. These inserts can cost as much as a basic slow cooker, yet they can easily be re-created using aluminum cans and simple utensils you already own.

The good news is that it's hard to go wrong when buying a slow cooker. If you buy an inexpensive slow cooker and find you need a bigger one with more options, you likely will find plenty of times you can use them both at once. And, since they're an extremely durable appliance, you can always pass your smaller, simpler slow cooker on to your oldest child when he rents his first apartment!

What You Can Do with a Slow Cooker

Slow cookers are extremely versatile. They gained their reputation as the perfect appliance for cooking soups and stews, but they also do an excellent job with pot roasts and whole chickens. They are a natural choice for long-cooking vegetables such as squash and potatoes and are an absolute necessity for potluck events and entertaining because they keep food warm for long periods without overcooking.

But those uses are just the beginning. Think of your slow cooker as both a pot and an oven that never goes above 350 degrees Fahrenheit. It can be used to melt cheeses for fondue or candy coatings for special desserts. It is a convenient way to cook rice or beans without having to worry about the bottom scorching. It also does a superb job baking cookies, cakes, and breads. It even does a good job on dishes requiring a little more attention, such as fresh fish.

Just think of your slow cooker as something other than the appliance you use when you'll be gone all day, and suddenly you will find all sorts of uses for it.

> One hour on high equals about two hours on low. Most recipes respond well to either temperature setting, although flavors tend to meld better when cooked on the low setting.

What You Shouldn't Do with a Slow Cooker

Still, there are a few things that a slow cooker can't do. Because it cooks foods over several hours, it won't brown meats and vegetables. For that reason, some recipes ask you to brown the meat, garlic, and onions, for example, in a skillet before putting them into the slow cooker. Others use spices and vegetables as a substitute for that browned taste.

In fact, any recipe that requires quick cooking or high heat isn't well suited to a slow cooker. You can't deep-fry or parboil anything.

Milk products also offer special challenges for slow cookers. Some cheeses will separate when cooked over the long term and most milk products will turn brown. There's a reason many slow-cooker recipes call for condensed cream soups instead of "real" cream or whole milk—the cooking process in canned soups stabilizes the milk so it doesn't react to lengthy cooking times.

Rice and pastas also add special challenges when slow cooking, because they tend to absorb too much water when cooked over long periods. As a result, many recipes ask you to add these items later in the cooking process. If you put them in for a full eight-hour cooking period, you may find them a little mushy.

Basic Techniques for Slow Cooking

Even the most inexperienced cook can quickly master slow-cooker recipes. Just keep the following things in mind:

- Cut meat and vegetables to the same size to ensure even cooking in soups and stews.
- Place slow-cooking items such as hard vegetables—rutabagas, turnips, potatoes—on the bottom of the slow cooker.
- Don't peek. Every time you lift the cover of the slow cooker, valuable steam escapes, reducing the internal temperature several degrees. Every time you lift the cover, plan to add at least twenty minutes to your cooking time.

- Slow-cooker recipes don't like water. Because the food is infused with steam, very little water escapes. When converting a recipe from a regular cookbook, use about half the water and add more during the last hour of the cooking cycle if necessary.

- Don't preheat the slow cooker. A few recipes ask you to preheat the slow cooker, usually because you will be melting cheese or chocolate in it. However, most are designed to start with both the crock and the food at room temperature. This ensures even heating of the food and prevents thermal shock from adding cold food to a warm crock. (The result could be a cracked crock.)

- Most traditional slow-cooker recipes take seven to nine hours on the low setting. The high setting takes about half that time but doesn't tenderize the meat as much.

- Spices and aromatic vegetables have different characteristics when slow cooked. Some, such as green peppers and bay leaves, increase in intensity when slow cooked. Others, such as onions and cinnamon, tend to lose flavor over the long cooking process. Most slow-cooker recipes reflect this difference, although you may have to adjust for your own tastes.

- When cooking traditional slow-cooker meals such as soups, stews, and meats, make sure the slow cooker is at least half full and the food does not extend beyond one-inch below the top. This ensures even cooking.

- Don't bother stirring. Remember, the steam from the food permeates the other foods in the slow cooker, so there is no need to stir. The flavors will blend anyway. Some recipes call for stirring at the beginning or the end of the process to accentuate this blending, but very few recipes require stirring midprocess.

- Throw away the timer. In our harried lives, we look for exact measurements in everything, yet slow cookers are very forgiving appliances. Dishes usually taste about the same within a two-hour window. If a recipe calls for eight hours, rest assured that seven to nine hours of cooking time is probably fine. Even breads and cakes will have fifteen- to thirty-minute windows because of the slow cooking process.

- Don't thaw food in the slow cooker. While it may seem a natural use, frozen food actually heats up too slowly to effectively prevent bacterial growth when in a slow cooker. It's better to thaw food overnight in a refrigerator or use the microwave.

How to Clean and Care for Your Slow Cooker

Slow cookers are very simple appliances. However, they do need some special care. If you follow these rules your slow cooker will produce healthy meals for many years:

- Never, never, never immerse the slow cooker in water. If it's plugged in at the time, you could receive a shock. If it isn't plugged in, you could damage the heating element.
- Always check for nicks or cuts in the electrical cord before plugging it into the outlet. This is especially important because you may be leaving the slow cooker on for several hours with no one in the house.
- If the crockery container is removable, it can be washed in the dishwasher. If not, use a soft cloth or sponge to wash it out. Always use a damp cloth to wash the metal housing.
- Remove baked-on food from the crockery container with a nonabrasive cleaner and a damp sponge. Do not scrub with abrasives, as these can scratch the crock, creating areas for bacteria to reside.

> Parts of the slow cooker can be cleaned in a dishwasher. If you have a removable crockery core, place it on the bottom rack. If you have a plastic cover, be sure to place it in the top rack of the dishwasher so it doesn't warp.

Appetizers

Broccoli Dip

Cooking time: 3–4 hours
Preparation time: 15 minutes
Attention: Minimal
Pot size: 1–2 quart
Serves 12 as an appetizer

1 small yellow onion
2 celery ribs
8 ounces (1 cup) fresh mushrooms,
    sliced
2 garlic cloves

2 cups fresh broccoli, chopped
¼ cup butter
1 (10¾-ounce) can cream of
    mushroom condensed soup

1. Peel the onion and chop into ¼-inch pieces. Chop the celery into ¼-inch pieces. Clean the mushrooms by wiping with a damp cloth, then slice paper-thin. Peel the garlic and chop into ⅛-inch pieces. Chop the broccoli florets into ¼-inch pieces.
2. Combine all the ingredients in the slow cooker. Cover and cook on low setting for 3 to 4 hours.

Serve with premium gourmet crackers.

Roasted Garlic

Cooking time: 4–5 hours
Preparation time: 15 minutes
Attention: Minimal
Pot size: 1–2 quart
Serves 8

3 bulbs of premium garlic

3 tablespoons olive oil

Cut off the tops of the garlic bulbs and discard tops. Spread olive oil on the bottom of the slow cooker. Place the garlic bulbs (right side up) in the slow cooker. Drizzle remaining olive oil on top of the garlic. Cover and cook on low setting for 4 to 5 hours. Ready when tender and golden. Squeeze cloves to remove softened garlic; discard skins

Use roasted garlic as a spread for French bread. Because the garlic sweetens as it roasts, there is no need for butter.

Honey-Pineapple Chicken Wings

Cooking time: 6–7 hours	
Preparation time: 15 minutes	
Attention: Minimal	
Pot size: 5–6 quarts	
Serves 12 as an appetizer	

3 pounds chicken wings
1 garlic clove
1 cup fresh or canned pineapple, cubed
½ teaspoon salt
½ teaspoon ground black pepper
1 cup honey
½ cup soy sauce
2 tablespoons vegetable oil

1. Cut the wing tip off each chicken wing and discard tips. Mince the garlic with a sharp kitchen knife. Cut the pineapple into 1 inch cubes.
2. Combine the salt, pepper, honey, soy sauce, pineapple, vegetable oil, and garlic in a bowl and mix well. Place the wings in the slow cooker. Pour the sauce over the wings and cook covered on low setting for 6 to 7 hours.

To keep the wings from drying out during a party, mix in a half cup of water every hour.

Handling Raw Chicken

Chicken is perhaps the most dangerous raw meat. To prevent salmonella and other bacteria from being transmitted, thoroughly wash your hands and all utensils before and after handling it.

Li'l Baby Reubens

Cooking time: 2 hours

Preparation time: 10 minutes

Attention: Medium

Pot size: 2–4 quarts

Serves 12–24 as an appetizer

½ pound corned beef
1 medium onion
1 (16-ounce) can sauerkraut
2 cups Swiss cheese, shredded
1 cup Cheddar cheese, shredded
1 cup mayonnaise (do not substitute low-fat mayonnaise)
Thousand Island dressing
Rye crackers

1. Shred the corned beef with a fork. Peel and chop the onion into ¼-inch pieces. Drain and rinse the sauerkraut. Combine the corned beef, sauerkraut, Swiss cheese, onion, Cheddar cheese, and mayonnaise in the slow cooker. Cook covered on low setting for 2 hours, stirring every 15 minutes.
2. Serve each appetizer with rye crackers and a small dollop of Thousand Island dressing.

Spicy dill pickles are a perfect complement to this full-bodied appetizer.

Preventing Food from Sticking

Because it uses slow, indirect heat, food will not burn in a slow cooker. However, some dishes will stick a little bit. Simply spray the container with vegetable oil cooking spray before adding ingredients.

Artichoke Dip

Cooking time: 1 hour

Preparation time: 10 minutes

Attention: Constant

Pot size: 1–3 quarts

Serves 6 as an appetizer

6 ounces (1½ cups) marinated artichoke hearts
1 clove fresh garlic
⅓ cup light mayonnaise
½ cup Parmesan cheese, grated
⅓ cup light sour cream

1. Drain the artichoke hearts and chop into pieces about the size of a penny. Finely mince the garlic with a sharp kitchen knife.
2. Combine the mayonnaise, grated Parmesan, sour cream, and garlic. Mix in the chopped artichoke hearts. Put mixture in the slow cooker, cover, and cook on low setting for 1 hour. Mix periodically while it is cooking.

For a truly unique appetizer, spread a thin layer of olive oil on pocket bread and bake in a conventional oven for 10 minutes. Cut each half circle of pocket bread into eight triangles and let guests scoop the dip with the bread.

Storage Tip

Store the slow cooker with the lid alongside instead of on top to prevent the chance that mold will grow if you don't use it for several weeks.

Barbecued Turkey Meatballs

1 egg
1 clove garlic
3 tablespoons fresh onion, chopped
1 slice bread
1 medium-sized apple
1 pound ground turkey
¼ teaspoon salt
2 small cans tomato sauce
¼ cup brown sugar
1 tablespoon vinegar

1. Beat the egg lightly with a fork. Peel the garlic and chop finely. Peel the onion and chop finely. Toast the bread in a toaster and break into pieces no larger than ¼ of a penny to make crumbs. Mince the apple with a sharp kitchen knife.
2. Use your hands to mix the ground turkey with the egg, garlic, onion, salt, and bread crumbs. Make sure all the ingredients are mixed well. The mixture should be sticky. Form the mixture into meatballs about the size of a golf ball. Place them on a cookie sheet and brown in a 350-degree oven for 20 minutes.
3. Transfer all the meatballs into the slow cooker. Combine the tomato sauce, brown sugar, minced apple, and vinegar in a bowl and stir until mixed well. Pour this sauce over the meatballs and cook covered on low setting for 4 to 6 hours.

Prepare several servings of the meatballs and store them in the freezer. Then simply put them in the slow cooker frozen and pour the sauce on top for a quick, no-attention appetizer.

Cooking time: 8 hours
Preparation time: 20 minutes
Attention: Minimal
Pot size: 3–6 quarts
Serves about 30

Green Apple Salsa

6 large tomatoes
3 large, tart green apples
1 large Vidalia onion
1 large green bell pepper
1 large red bell pepper
1 small green jalapeño pepper
1 (5-ounce) can tomato paste
1½ cups packed brown sugar

1½ cups cider vinegar
½ teaspoon lime juice
2 tablespoons chili powder
2 teaspoons mustard seeds
½ teaspoon cayenne pepper
1 teaspoon salt
1 tablespoon vegetable oil

1. Crush the tomatoes in the bottom of the slow cooker with a wooden spoon. Peel and chop the apples into ¼-inch pieces. Peel and chop the onion into ¼-inch pieces. Remove the stems and seeds from the green, red, and jalapeño peppers; chop into ¼-inch pieces.
2. Combine all the ingredients in the slow cooker and cook covered on low heat for 8 hours. If the sauce seems too runny, remove the cover for the last hour.

This tasty salsa is wonderful served with baked tortilla chips. It also makes an excellent addition to meat loaf or hamburgers.

Preparing a Day Ahead
If you're preparing the food the evening before you will be cooking it, add the dry ingredients to the slow cooker that evening. Add the water or other liquid right before turning it on.

Mock Stuffed Grape Leaves

Cooking time: 2–4 hours

Preparation time: 30 minutes

Attention: Minimal

Pot size: 2–4 quart

Serves 12–24 as an appetizer

1 cup cooked white rice
½ cup golden raisins, plus extra for garnish
¼ cup apple jelly, plus extra for garnish
⅛ teaspoon saffron
½ teaspoon salt
1 bunch fresh Swiss chard leaves

1. Combine the cooked white rice, raisins, apple jelly, saffron, and salt. Mix with a spoon until all ingredients are evenly distributed.
2. Wash the Swish chard leaves in cold water. Using a large melon scoop, place one scoop of rice mixture in the center of each leaf. Fold ends in and roll up tightly, as you would an egg roll. Place them in layers in the slow cooker. Cook covered on low setting for 2 to 4 hours.

Add a small dollop of apple jelly and a raisin on the top of each appetizer for a sweeter taste.

Heat Retention

Because slow cookers use porous stoneware "crocks" to cook the food, the heat is absorbed and retained. You will notice that the crock stays warm for an hour or more after you unplug it.

Spicy Shrimp and Cheese Dip

Cooking time: 1–2 hours

Preparation time: 20 minutes

Attention: Minimal

Pot size: 1–3 quarts

Serves 12–24 as an appetizer

1 slice bacon
1 cup popcorn shrimp, cooked
3 medium-sized yellow onions
2 garlic cloves
1 medium tomato
3 cups Monterey jack cheese, shredded
¼ teaspoon Tabasco sauce
¼ teaspoon cayenne pepper
¼ teaspoon ground black pepper

1. Cook the bacon in a frying pan until crisp; keep grease in pan. Lay bacon on a paper towel to cool. When cool, crumble it with your fingers. If the shrimp is not precooked, boil it in water for 10 minutes.
2. Peel and chop the onions into ¼-inch squares. Peel the garlic and mince with a sharp kitchen knife. Peel and chop the tomato into ¼-inch squares. Add the onion and garlic to the bacon drippings in the frying pan and sauté on medium-low heat until they are limp.
3. Combine all the ingredients in the slow cooker; stir well. Cook covered on low setting for 1 to 2 hours, or until the cheese is fully melted.

Cooking tip: If the dip is too thick, add milk in half-cup increments until it's the consistency you like.

Cleaning

Use a rough sponge to remove any dried-on food from the slow cooker when cleaning it. A scouring pad could scratch the surface, creating a place for bacteria to grow.

Creamy Refried Bean Dip

Cooking time: 2 hours
Preparation time: 10 minutes
Attention: Medium
Pot size: 2–4 quarts
Serves 12–24 as an appetizer

1 cup shredded Monterey jack cheese
1 cup shredded Cheddar cheese
1 (12-ounce) can refried beans
1 cup picante sauce
⅓ cup sour cream
3 ounces cream cheese
1 tablespoon chili powder
¼ teaspoon ground cumin
tortilla chips

1. Combine the refried beans, picante sauce, shredded cheeses, sour cream, cream cheese, chili powder, and cumin in a medium-sized bowl; mix well with a large spoon.
2. Place the mixture in the slow cooker and cook on low setting for 2 hours, stirring every 15 minutes.

Serve with tortilla chips and a bowl of Green Apple Salsa (page 307) for additional flavor.

Converting Recipes

Don't translate quick recipes. The best recipes for slow cookers are those that take about an hour of time or more in the oven or simmering on a stove top. Others likely contain ingredients that need to be cooked fast.

Baked Brie with Strawberry Chutney

Cooking time: 4–5 hours
Preparation time: 10 minutes
Attention: Medium
Pot size: 1–3 quarts
Serves 8–12 as an appetizer

1 cup strawberries
½ cup brown sugar
⅓ cup cider vinegar
⅛ teaspoon nutmeg
2 tablespoons grapefruit juice
1 (8-ounce) piece of Brie cheese
1 tablespoon sliced almonds, toasted

1. Remove the green tops from the strawberries and slice berries in quarters. Combine the strawberries, brown sugar, vinegar, nutmeg, and grapefruit juice in slow cooker. Cover and cook on low setting for 4 hours. Remove top, turn heat to high and cook 30 minutes, stirring every few minutes. Put mixture in refrigerator to cool.
2. Place the Brie on an ovenproof plate and cover with sliced almonds; bake uncovered in 350-degree oven for about 10 minutes. Cheese should be partially melted but not fully melted. Remove from the oven and top with room-temperature chutney.

Serve with raw celery sticks and a dry white wine.

Add a Little Vino

A half cup of wine adds an elegant taste to many dishes without adding many calories. And, since the alcohol evaporates in the cooking process, you get all the flavor without the hangover!

Southwestern Apricot Salsa

Cooking time: 1–2 hours

Preparation time: 15 minutes

Attention: Minimal

Pot size: 1–3 quarts

Serves 12–24 as an appetizer

2 tablespoons red onion, chopped

½ teaspoon fresh jalapeño pepper, minced

2 cups canned apricots in light syrup, chopped

½ tablespoon olive oil

1 tablespoon fresh cilantro

½ teaspoon white vinegar

½ tablespoon lime juice

¼ teaspoon lime peel, grated

¼ teaspoon ground cumin

½ teaspoon garlic salt

½ teaspoon ground white pepper

1. Peel and chop the onion into ¼-inch pieces.
2. Remove the stem from jalapeño pepper and mince.
3. Drain and rinse the apricots and cut into ¼-inch pieces.
4. Combine all the ingredients in the slow cooker. Cook uncovered on low setting for 1 to 2 hours.

This salsa is excellent served hot or cold with baked taco chips.

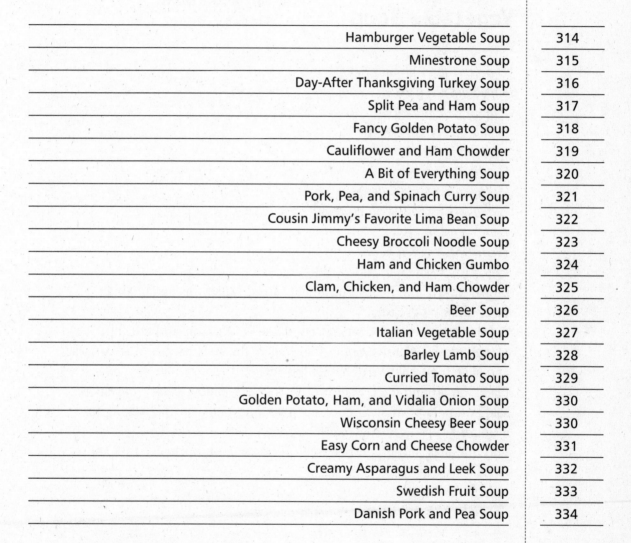

Hamburger Vegetable Soup

Cooking time: 7–8 hours

Preparation time: 15 minutes

Attention: Minimal

Pot size: 3–6 quarts

Serves 6

½ pound lean ground beef
4 medium-sized fresh tomatoes
1 large yellow onion
½ cup celery, sliced
3 medium carrots
6 cups beef broth
½ teaspoon table salt
½ teaspoon ground black pepper
1 cup fresh peas
1 cup fresh green beans

1. Brown the ground beef in a medium-sized skillet on medium-high heat; drain off grease.
2. Cut the tomatoes into ½-inch cubes. Peel the onion and cut into ¼-inch pieces. Cut the celery into ¼-inch-thick slices. Peel the carrots and slice them into ¼-inch-thick pieces.
3. Place the ground beef, beef broth, tomatoes, onion, celery, carrots, salt, and pepper in slow cooker. Cover and cook on low setting for 6 hours.
4. Add the peas and green beans. Cover and cook on low 1 to 2 more hours.

Garnish with fresh parsley before serving.

Hold the Cream, Please

To create a dairy-free cream soup, remove some of the cooked vegetables from the broth and puree them in a blender. Stir them back into the soup.

Minestrone Soup

Cooking time: 9–11 hours

Preparation time: 30 minutes

Attention: Medium

Pot size: 3–6 quarts

Serves 8

1 pound beef stewing meat

1 (28-ounce) can tomatoes

1 medium onion

6 cups water

1 beef bouillon cube

2 tablespoons dried parsley

1½ teaspoon table salt

1½ teaspoon dried thyme

½ teaspoon ground black pepper

1 medium zucchini

2 cups cabbage, chopped

1 (16-ounce) can garbanzo beans, drained

1 cup uncooked shell macaroni

1. Cut the meat into 1-inch cubes. Cut the tomatoes into ½-inch cubes; reserve liquid. Peel the onion and cut into ¼-inch pieces. Combine the beef, water, tomatoes with their liquid, bouillon cube, onion, parsley, salt, thyme, and pepper in slow cooker. Cover and cook on low for 8 to 10 hours.

2. Cut the zucchini into ¼-inch thick slices. Chop the cabbage into ¼-inch pieces. Add the zucchini, cabbage, beans, and macaroni to soup. Cover and cook on high for 1 hour.

Sprinkle with Parmesan cheese right before serving.

De-Meating Your Dish

Substitute vegetable bouillon or broth for a meat broth in any soup recipe. It adds a cleaner, lighter flavor with none of the fat. Add beans in place of meat to create a vegetarian dish.

Day-After Thanksgiving Turkey Soup

Cooking time: 6–8 hours
Preparation time: 20 minutes
Attention: Minimal
Pot size: 3–8 quarts
Serves 6

1 large yellow onion
1 fresh green pepper
1 cup carrots, sliced
1 cup celery, diced
1 cup fresh mushrooms, sliced
1 pound leftover turkey, shredded
¼ teaspoon pepper
¼ teaspoon oregano
¼ teaspoon basil
1 tablespoon chicken bouillon
3 cups boiling water
1 cup tomato sauce
1 tablespoon soy sauce

1. Peel the onion and carrots, and remove the seeds and stem from the green pepper. Cut the celery, carrots, onion, and green pepper into ¼-inch pieces. Wash the mushrooms by wiping with a damp cloth; slice paper-thin with a sharp paring knife.
2. Add all ingredients to the slow cooker. Cover and cook on low setting 6 to 8 hours.

What else but Halloween Is Here Pumpkin Bread (page 368) as a complement to this soup?

Bell Peppers

Bell peppers have different flavors depending on their color. Green is the most acidic and sour tasting. Red has the most peppery flavor. Yellow and orange have a gentle flavor. Combine them to create unique flavors and a beautiful dish.

Cheesy Broccoli Noodle Soup

Cooking time: 4–5 hours

Preparation time: 30 minutes

Attention: Minimal

Pot size: 3–6 quarts

Serves 6

2 cups noodles
2 cups fresh broccoli, chopped
1 medium-sized white onion
2 cups processed cheese, cubed
2 tablespoons butter
1 tablespoon flour
½ teaspoon table salt
5½ cups skim milk

1. Cook the noodles in boiling water in a saucepan until they are limp but still crunchy in the middle. Chop the broccoli into 1-inch pieces. Peel and chop the onion into ¼-inch pieces. Cut the cheese into ½-inch cubes.
2. Combine all ingredients in the slow cooker. Cover and cook on low setting for 4 to 5 hours.

Serve as a first course for Beef Roast with Dried Fruit (page 392).

Slow-Cooker Buffet

Don't forget the slow cooker at your next large buffet. Add a soup or hot hors d'oeuvre to the menu for a fast and easy way to serve a crowd.

Ham and Chicken Gumbo

1½ pounds chicken breasts
½ pound smoked ham
1 tablespoon oil
1 cup fresh okra, sliced
2 medium-sized white onions
1 medium-sized green bell pepper
4 large red tomatoes
¼ cup canned or fresh green
   chilies, diced

2 tablespoons fresh cilantro,
   chopped
6 cups chicken broth
3 (16-ounce) cans navy beans **or**
   3½–4 cups dry navy beans,
   cooked
½ cup dry white rice
¾ teaspoon table salt
½ teaspoon ground black pepper

1. Remove the bones and skin from the chicken and discard. Cut the
   chicken and ham into 1-inch pieces. Place the oil, ham, and chicken
   in medium-sized skillet and cook on medium heat until chicken is no
   longer pink inside. Cut the okra into ¼-inch pieces. Peel the onions
   and cut into ¼-inch pieces. Remove the stem and seeds from the
   green pepper and chop into ¼-inch pieces. Cut the tomatoes into
   ½-inch pieces. Dice the green chilies with a sharp paring knife.
   Chop the cilantro into ¼-inch pieces.
2. Combine all the ingredients except the cilantro in the slow cooker.
   Cover and cook on low setting for 7 to 9 hours. Stir in cilantro right
   before serving.

Serve with Slightly Seedy White Bread (page 374) and an assort-
ment of cheeses.

Cooking rice

Processed white rice typically needs less water added than long-grain
brown rice or wild rice, which can take up to six cups of water per
cup of dry rice. If in doubt, read the package directions.

Clam, Chicken, and Ham Chowder

Cooking time: 8–10 hours

Preparation time: 30 minutes

Attention: Minimal

Pot size: 3–8 quarts

Serves 8

4 chicken breasts
1 pound bacon
½ pound ham
2 large yellow onions
4 medium carrots
4 celery ribs
4 medium potatoes
1 cup clams, with juice
2 cups whole kernel corn,
 with liquid

4 cups chicken broth
½ teaspoon table salt
½ teaspoon ground black pepper
1 bunch green onions
¾ cup flour
4 cups milk
4 cups Cheddar cheese, shredded
½ cup whipping cream

1. Remove the skin and bones from the chicken breasts and cut meat into 1-inch pieces. Cut the bacon into 1-inch pieces. Cut the ham into ½-inch cubes. Peel the yellow onions and chop into ¼-inch pieces. Peel the carrots and chop into ¼-inch rounds. Chop the celery into ¼-inch pieces. Peel the potatoes and cut into ½-inch cubes.

2. Put the bacon, ham, and chicken meat in a large skillet with the celery and yellow onions; sauté on medium heat until the bacon is crisp. Drain grease off and put the mixture in the slow cooker. Add the carrots, potatoes, clams, corn, salt, pepper, and chicken broth. Cover and cook on low setting for 7 to 9 hours.

3. Remove the roots and first layer of peel from the green onions and chop the onions, including the green stems, into ¼-inch pieces. In a medium mixing bowl combine the flour, milk, cheese, and cream. Whisk quickly until slightly frothy; stir into soup. Cover and cook on low setting for 1 hour. Stir in the green onions right before serving.

Serve with an assortment of pickled vegetables and cheeses.

Beer Soup

Cooking time: 4 hours

Preparation time: 15 minutes

Attention: Minimal

Pot size: 3–8 quarts

Serves 6

2½ tablespoons butter
1½ tablespoons flour
2 cups pilsner beer
½ cinnamon stick
½ teaspoon sugar
2 egg yolks
½ cup milk

1. Melt the butter in a medium-sized skillet on medium heat. Add the flour and cook until the flour browns; transfer the flour mixture to the slow cooker. Add the beer, cinnamon, and sugar. Cover and cook on high setting for 4 hours.
2. Turn slow cooker down to low setting. Whisk together the egg yolks and milk; stir into the soup. Cook 15 minutes uncovered on high setting. Strain before serving.

Serve as a first course for Sparkling Beef Tips (page 399)

Problems with Cinnamon

While it tastes wonderful, cinnamon is a tricky spice. It can kill yeast, causing bread not to rise. It also does not permeate a soup or stew but tends to remain on top of the liquid.

Italian Vegetable Soup

Cooking time: 6–8 hours

Preparation time: 20 minutes

Attention: Minimal

Pot size: 3–6 quarts

Serves 6

2 pounds hamburger
1 small zucchini
3 medium potatoes
1 can corn
1 (16-ounce) can tomato sauce
2 tablespoons ground oregano
1/8 teaspoon basil
1/2 teaspoon garlic salt
3 bay leaves

1. Brown the hamburger in a medium-sized skillet on medium-high heat on the stove; drain off the grease.
2. Cut the zucchini into 1/2-inch pieces. Peel and cut the potatoes into 1/2-inch squares.
3. Add all ingredients to the slow cooker. Cook covered on low setting for 6 to 8 hours.

Serve with a side of garlic buttered linguine.

Removing Bay Leaves
Bay leaves add flavor to a dish, but be sure to remove them before serving food. The leaves can be sharp.

Barley Lamb Soup

Cooking time: 7–9 hours
Preparation time: 20 minutes
Attention: Minimal
Pot size: 3–8 quarts
Serves 8

2½ pounds lamb
2 medium-sized white onions
3 celery ribs
3 cups parsley, chopped
3 tablespoons butter
1 cup medium-sized barley
½ teaspoon table salt
½ teaspoon ground black pepper
1 bay leaf
6 cups water

1. Cut the lamb into 1-inch cubes, trimming off the fat as you cut. Peel and chop the onions into ¼-inch pieces. Chop the celery, including leaves, into ¼-inch pieces. Chop the parsley into ½-inch pieces.
2. Heat the butter in a large skillet on medium heat until brown; add the lamb and sauté for about 10 minutes. Using a slotted spoon, remove the meat from the skillet and put it into the slow cooker. Add the onion to the skillet and sauté until translucent. Drain off the grease and add the onion to the slow cooker. Add the celery, parsley, barley, salt, pepper, bay leaf, and water to the slow cooker. Cover and cook on low setting for 7 to 9 hours.

Serve with a fresh green salad and hard-boiled eggs.

How to Sauté

When a recipe calls for sautéing, cook the food on medium-high to high heat in a frying pan. Oil is the most common ingredient in which to sauté although water and flavored vinegar are good, low-fat alternatives.

Curried Tomato Soup

Cooking time: 8–10 hours
Preparation time: 30 minutes
Attention: Minimal
Pot size: 3–8 quarts
Serves 8

1 medium-sized white onion
2 garlic cloves
12 plum tomatoes
4 cups chicken broth
1 tablespoon curry powder
¼ teaspoon cinnamon
½ teaspoon table salt
4 cups dry egg noodles

1. Peel the onion and chop into ¼-inch pieces. Peel the garlic and mince with a sharp kitchen knife. Chop the tomatoes into ¼-inch pieces.
2. Combine all the ingredients except the egg noodles in the slow cooker. Cover and cook on low setting for 7 to 9 hours.
3. Add the egg noodles. Cover and cook on low setting 1 additional hour.

Use as a first course for East Indian Green Curried Chicken (page 502).

Cooking with Tomatoes

When using fresh tomatoes in a recipe, be sure to cook them for at least four hours on the low setting. This will release the acid and the dish will taste much more mellow. It also will prevent your guests from getting heartburn.

Golden Potato, Ham, and Vidalia Onion Soup

Cooking time: 8–10 hours

Preparation time: 15 minutes

Attention: Minimal

Pot size: 3–8 quarts

Serves 8

1 cup ham
2 large Vidalia onions
½ small red bell pepper
4 large golden potatoes

2 cups chicken broth
½ teaspoon ground black pepper
1 cup skim milk
1 cup ricotta cheese

1. Cut the ham into ½-inch pieces. Peel and cut the onions into ¼-inch pieces. Remove the stem and seeds from the red pepper and cut into ¼-inch pieces. Peel the potatoes and cut into ½-inch pieces.
2. Add the ham, onions, bell pepper, potatoes, chicken broth, and black pepper to the slow cooker. Cover and cook on low setting for 8 to 10 hours. A half-hour before serving, add skim milk and ricotta cheese; mix in. Cover and continue to cook on low setting.

Serve with gourmet crackers and fresh vegetables such as red pepper, carrot and celery sticks.

Wisconsin Cheesy Beer Soup

Cooking time: 1–2 hours

Preparation time: 10 minutes

Attention: Frequent

Pot size: 3–8 quarts

Serves 8

1 large onion
1 cup sharp Cheddar cheese
½ cup vegetable broth
1 cup pilsner beer

2 cups 1 percent milk
½ teaspoon garlic powder
½ teaspoon ground black pepper

Peel the onion and chop into ¼-inch pieces. Shred the cheese with a vegetable grater. Combine all ingredients in the slow cooker. Cover and cook on low setting for 1 to 2 hours, stirring every 10 minutes. Do not overcook, as the cheese will begin to separate.

Serve sprinkled with freshly made white popcorn.

Easy Corn and Cheese Chowder

Cooking time: 8–9 hours	
Preparation time: 15 minutes	
Attention: Minimal	
Pot size: 3–6 quarts	
Serves 6	

1 medium-sized yellow onion
4 medium carrots
4 celery ribs
1½ cups shredded Cheddar cheese
¾ cup water
1 teaspoon table salt
1 teaspoon ground black pepper
2 cups whole kernel corn, canned or fresh
2 cups canned creamed corn
3 cups milk

1. Remove peel and chop the onion into ¼-inch pieces. Peel the carrots and chop into ¼-inch slices. Chop the celery into ¼-inch slices.
2. Combine the water, onions, carrots, celery, salt, and pepper in slow cooker. Cover and cook on low setting for 8 to 9 hours. One hour before serving, add the corn, milk, and cheese. Cover and cook on low setting for 1 more hour.

Using Frozen Corn

Substitute canned or frozen corn in any recipe calling for fresh corn. It holds up well even over several hours of cooking. And because the kernels are small, even frozen corn heats up quickly.

Creamy Asparagus and Leek Soup

Cooking time: 8–10 hours

Preparation time: 20 minutes

Attention: Medium

Pot size: 3–8 quarts

Serves 6

2 medium potatoes
2 large leeks
3 medium carrots
2 celery ribs
2 pounds asparagus
2 teaspoons thyme
4 cups chicken broth
2 cups 1 percent milk

1. Peel and chop the potatoes and leeks into ¼-inch pieces. Chop the carrots and celery into ¼-inch pieces. Remove the tips from the asparagus and set aside. Chop the green part of the stalks into ¼-inch pieces.
2. Put the carrots, celery, potatoes, leek, thyme, asparagus stalks, and chicken broth in slow cooker. Cover and cook on low setting for 7 to 9 hours.
3. Put the mixture into a blender and purée until creamy. Stir in the milk and add the asparagus tips. Cover and cook on low setting for 1 additional hour.

Serve with Zucchini Bread (page 369) for a nice blend of flavors.

Too-Thin Soups

Try adding half the recommended water. If it's still runny, remove the cover from the slow cooker for an hour or two before serving.

Cooking time:	8–10 hours
Preparation time:	30 minutes
Attention:	Minimal
Pot size:	3–8 quarts
Serves 8	

Swedish Fruit Soup

1 cup dried apricots
1 cup dried apples
1 cup dried prunes
1 cup dried pears
1 cup dried peaches
1 cup canned dark, sweet cherries, pitted
½ cup sweet red wine
1 cup orange juice
¼ cup lemon juice
½ cup brown sugar
½ cup quick-cooking tapioca

1. Cut dried fruit into 1-inch pieces.
2. Add all the ingredients to the slow cooker; stir well. Cover and cook on low setting for 8 to 10 hours.
3. Check after 5 hours to determine if water needs to be added (it should have the consistency of a light syrup—if it is thicker than that, add ½ cup water).

This is excellent served warm over a traditional white cake with vanilla ice cream.

Low-Fat Sautéing

For a fat-free alternative, add flavored vinegars when sautéing meats and vegetables. They will add a light flavor to the dish and tend to blend well with almost any recipe.

Danish Pork and Pea Soup

Cooking time: 8–10 hours

Preparation time: 30 minutes

Attention: Minimal

Pot size: 3–8 quarts

Serves 8

1 pound yellow split peas
2 pounds lean bacon
1 pound pork sausage links
4 medium leeks
3 medium carrots
2 celery ribs
1 teaspoon salt
1 teaspoon ground black pepper
6 cups vegetable stock

1. Rinse the split peas. Chop the bacon and sausage into 1-inch pieces. Peel the leeks and chop into ¼-inch pieces. Cut the celery and carrots into ¼-inch pieces.
2. Put the bacon and sausage into a large skillet and cook on medium-high heat until meat is brown on all sides; drain off the grease. Spread out the meat on paper towels to absorb more grease.
3. Add all ingredients to the slow cooker. Cover and cook on low setting for 8 to 10 hours.

Serve with open-faced cucumber and cream cheese sandwiches on rye toast.

De-Fatting Meat

To remove most of the fat from ground beef or bacon, cook it in the microwave, then lay it on several paper towels to drain. Lay a paper towel on top of the meat and pat it lightly before adding to the slow cooker.

CHAPTER 20
All-In-One Meals

Hamburger Potato Casserole

Cooking time: 7–9 hours

Preparation time: 20 minutes

Attention: Minimal

Pot size: 4–6 quarts

Serves 4

1 pound lean ground beef
3 medium potatoes
4 medium carrots
1 medium-sized yellow onion
1 cup fresh peas
2 tablespoons dry white rice
1 teaspoon table salt
½ teaspoon ground black pepper
1 cup tomato juice

1. Brown the beef in a medium skillet on medium-high heat; drain off the grease. Peel the potatoes and cut into ¼-inch slices. Peel the carrots and slice into ¼-inch rounds. Peel the onion and cut into ¼-inch pieces.
2. Combine all ingredients except peas in the slow cooker; stir well. Cover and cook on low setting for 5 to 7 hours. Add peas and cook for 2 hours.

Serve with Hot Fruit Medley (page 592) for dessert.

Save the Veggies for Last

Add quick-cooking vegetables no more than two hours before serving. Peas especially can become too mushy if added early, so if you don't want them like that, add them later.

Spinach, Cheese, and Egg Casserole

Cooking time: 5–6 hours

Preparation time: 20 minutes

Attention: Medium

Pot size: 3–6 quart

Serves 8

2 bunches fresh spinach
2 cups cottage cheese
1½ cups Cheddar cheese, grated
3 eggs
¼ cup flour
1 teaspoon table salt
½ cup butter, melted

1. Clean the spinach in cold water and remove the stems. Tear the leaves into 1-inch pieces. Place the spinach leaves, cottage cheese, and Cheddar cheese in a large mixing bowl.
2. In a small bowl, combine the eggs, flour, table salt, and butter, mixing well until all the ingredients are melded; pour over the spinach mixture. Mix well with a wooden spoon.
3. Pour mixture into the slow cooker and cook covered on high setting for 1 hour. Stir well after the hour is up and reduce heat to low setting.
4. Cover and cook 4 to 5 additional hours.

Try this for an elegant Sunday brunch. Complement it with champagne and buttery croissants. Your guests will never believe you made it in the slow cooker!

Hold the Yolk

Egg yolks contain all of the fat and cholesterol in an egg. Use egg whites instead of whole eggs when making pasta, cakes and other dishes. Usually two egg whites can be substituted for one whole egg.

Corned Beef Dinner

Cooking time: 8–9 hours

Preparation time: 20 minutes

Attention: Minimal

Pot size: 4–6 quarts

Serves 6

2 yellow onions

6 small potatoes

12 carrots

1 rutabaga, peeled and
quartered

6 ribs celery

1 head cabbage

3 pounds corned beef brisket

2 bay leaves

20 black peppercorns

2 cups water

1. Peel the onions and slice into quarters. Peel the potatoes and slice in halves. Peel the carrots and cut into quarters. Peel the rutabaga and slice into eight pieces. Cut the celery ribs into quarters. Cut the cabbage into eight pieces.
2. Place the corned beef brisket in the bottom of the slow cooker. Put the bay leaves and peppercorns on top. Layer the vegetables in the following order: onions, potatoes, celery, carrots, cabbage, and rutabaga. Add water. Cook covered on low setting for 8 to 9 hours, or until the rutabaga is soft.
3. Remove the bay leaves before serving. Cut the meat into thin slices across the grain.

Arrange the meat and vegetables on a large platter. Use the juice left in the bottom of the slow cooker as you would gravy.

Hard Potatoes

Try cooking them for less time; add them later in the cooking process. Or, if you're making a pot roast, put them into the slow cooker whole.

Sausage and Fall Vegetable Harvest

Cooking time: 6–8 hours

Preparation time: 20 minutes

Attention: Minimal

Pot size: 3–6 quarts

Serves 4

1 pound acorn squash
2 medium potatoes
4 carrots
4 ribs celery
¼ cup green bell pepper, chopped
2 yellow onions
1 cup zucchini, sliced
1 cup fresh or frozen peas
1 cup fresh or frozen green beans

2 cups fresh or canned beef broth
2 tablespoons red wine
¼ teaspoon ground black pepper
1 teaspoon dried, crushed rosemary
½ pound sausage in large round
    links **or** patties
2 tablespoons flour
½ cup warm water

1. Peel the squash and cut into ½-inch cubes. (Squash has a very tough skin so use a large, sharp knife and work on a hard surface.) Peel the potatoes and cut into ½-inch cubes. Peel the carrots and cut into 1-inch lengths. Cut the celery ribs into 1-inch lengths. Core the green pepper and chop with a medium-sized knife into pieces about ¼-inch square. Peel the onions and quarter. Cut the zucchini into slices about ¼-inch thick.

2. Combine the squash, potatoes, carrots, celery, zucchini, green beans, broth, wine, black pepper, and rosemary in slow cooker.

3. Cut the sausage into ½-inch slices. If using sausage patties, break them into marble-sized chunks. Combine the sausage, green peppers, and onions in a frying pan and cook on medium-high heat until the sausage and onions are browned. Drain off the grease and lay the mixture on paper towels for 2 minutes to soak up additional grease. Add the sausage, onions, and green peppers to the vegetables in the slow cooker. Cook covered on low heat for 6 to 8 hours.

4. One hour before serving, add the peas, and use a fork to mix 2 tablespoons flour and ½ cup water in a small bowl until the mixture is smooth; add this to the vegetables and sausage, stirring until it is well mixed. Cook covered for 1 additional hour.

Serve with Heavy Brown Bread (page 375) and cream cheese.

339

Mixed Meat Tetrazzini

Cooking time: 6–8 hours
Preparation time: 30 minutes
Attention: Minimal
Pot size: 4–6 quarts
Serves 8

1 bunch small green onions
1 cup celery
½ cup pimiento-stuffed green
   olives, chopped
1 green bell pepper
½ pound fresh mushrooms

1 cup chicken, precooked and cubed
1 cup turkey, precooked and cubed
1 cup ham, precooked and cubed
1 pound package spaghetti
1 tablespoon dried parsley
3 cups chicken broth

1. Peel and chop the green onions into ¼-inch pieces. Chop the celery and olives into ¼-inch pieces. Remove the stem and seeds from the green pepper and chop pepper into ¼-inch pieces. Clean the mushrooms by wiping them with a damp cloth, then slice paper-thin. Precook meat in the microwave or use leftover meats; cut into 1-inch cubes. Break the spaghetti noodles into approximately 1-inch lengths.

2. Layer ingredients in the slow cooker in the following order:
   1. Spaghetti
   2. Meats
   3. Onions
   4. Olives
   5. Celery and parsley
   6. Pepper
   7. Mushrooms

3. Pour the chicken broth over the top. Cover and cook on low setting for 6 to 8 hours.

Scoop out of the slow cooker with a large serving spoon and sprinkle with Parmesan cheese before serving.

Pasta Twist

For a different taste in your next pasta dish, experiment with vegetable pastas such as tomato or spinach. They frequently have a more substantial consistency and more nutrients than regular pasta.

Smoky Beef and Beans Dinner

Cooking time: 4–6 hours

Preparation time: 15 minutes

Attention: Minimal

Pot size: 3–6 quarts

Serves 4

1 pound lean ground beef
1 large yellow onion
¾ pound bacon
2 cans pork and beans
1 can lima beans
1 can kidney beans
1 cup ketchup
¼ cup brown sugar
1 tablespoon liquid smoke flavoring
3 tablespoons white vinegar
1 teaspoon salt
½ teaspoon ground black pepper

1. Place the ground beef in a medium-sized skillet on the stove; cook on medium-high heat, stirring until the meat is brown. Drain off grease and place the meat in the slow cooker.
2. Peel and chop the onion into ¼-inch pieces. Slice the bacon into 1-inch pieces. Place the bacon and onion in skillet and cook on medium-high heat, stirring until the bacon is crisp.
3. Put all ingredients in the slow cooker; stir well. Cook covered on low setting 4 to 6 hours.

Serve with Raisin Bread Pudding (page 600) for dessert.

The Interchangeable Bean

Substitute beans at will. Go to your local food co-op and try those different-looking beans in your next chili or bean soup. All beans taste fairly mild so you can't make a drastic mistake and you may find a new favorite.

New Orleans–Style Jambalaya

Cooking time: 7–8 hours

Preparation time: 45 minutes

Attention: Medium

Pot size: 4–8 quarts

Serves 8

1 (3-pound) chicken

1 pound hot smoked sausage

3 tablespoons olive oil

1 cup celery, chopped

¾ cup fresh parsley, chopped

1 large yellow onion

⅔ cup green pepper, chopped

2 garlic cloves

8 whole tomatoes

1 cup green onions, chopped

2 cups chicken broth

1 (6-ounce) can tomato paste

1½ teaspoons thyme

2 bay leaves

2 teaspoons oregano

1 teaspoon chili powder

1 teaspoon salt

½ teaspoon cayenne pepper

1 teaspoon ground black pepper

1 teaspoon garlic powder

2 cups uncooked long grain rice, washed and rinsed

3 pounds raw shrimp

Cooking time: 7–9 hours
Preparation time: 15 minutes
Attention: Minimal
Pot size: 3–6 quarts
Serves 6

New England Dinner

6 medium carrots
2 medium-sized yellow onions
4 celery ribs
1 small head cabbage
3-pound boneless chuck roast
½ teaspoon table salt
½ teaspoon ground black pepper
1 envelope dry onion soup mix
2 cups water
1 tablespoon vinegar
1 bay leaf

1. Clean the carrots and cut in half. Peel the onions and slice into quarters. Cut the celery ribs in half. Remove outer leaves from the cabbage, then cut the head into eighths.
2. Place the carrots, onion, and celery in the slow cooker. Put the roast on top. Sprinkle with salt and pepper, then add the soup mix, water, vinegar, and bay leaf on top. Add the cabbage. Do not mix ingredients. Cover and cook on low setting for 7 to 9 hours.

Serve with a dip made of half horseradish and half sour cream.

Spicing It Up

Instead of a marinade, rub meat with dry seasonings before placing in the slow cooker. You can buy prepared mixes or experiment with some of your favorites. Dried garlic, onion, and parsley are a good place to start.

Ten-Story Casserole

Cooking time: 4 hours

Preparation time: 20 minutes

Attention: Minimal

Pot size: 3–6 quarts

Serves 6

1½ pounds ground turkey

6 medium potatoes

2 medium-sized white onions

½ teaspoon table salt

½ teaspoon ground black pepper

1 (15-ounce) can corn

1 (15-ounce) can peas

1 (10¾-ounce) can cream of celery condensed soup

¼ cup water

1. Brown the turkey in a medium-sized skillet on medium-high heat. Drain off grease and spread the turkey on paper towels to cool. Peel the potatoes and cut into ¼-inch slices. Peel the onions and slice into ¼-inch rings.
2. Place ingredients in the slow cooker in the following layers:
   1. One-fourth of potatoes, half of onions, sprinkle of salt, sprinkle of pepper
   2. Half can of corn
   3. One-fourth of potatoes
   4. Half can peas
   5. One-fourth of potatoes, remaining half of onions, sprinkle of salt, sprinkle of pepper
   6. Half can corn
   7. One-fourth of potatoes
   8. Half can peas
   9. Turkey
   10. Cream of celery soup and water
3. Cover and cook on high setting for 4 hours.

Serve with a dessert of Strawberry Rhubarb Sauce (page 603) over vanilla ice cream.

Kielbasa and Cabbage Dinner

Cooking time: 7–8 hours

Preparation time: 15 minutes

Attention: Minimal

Pot size: 4–6 quarts

Serves 6

1½ pounds kielbasa
2 medium yellow onions
4 medium potatoes
1 red bell pepper
4 large ripe tomatoes
2 garlic cloves
1½ heads green cabbage
1 cup dry white wine
1 tablespoon Dijon mustard
¾ teaspoon caraway seeds
½ teaspoon ground black pepper
¾ teaspoon table salt

1. Cut the kielbasa into 3-inch pieces. Peel the onions and chop into ¼-inch pieces. Peel the potatoes and cut into 1-inch cubes. Remove the stem and seeds from the red pepper and chop into ¼-inch pieces. Chop the tomatoes into ½-inch pieces. Peel the garlic and mince with a sharp paring knife. Shred the cabbage into ¼-inch strips with a sharp kitchen knife.
2. Combine all ingredients in the slow cooker. Cover and cook on low setting for 7 to 8 hours.

Serve with Rice Pudding (page 596) for dessert.

Slicing Meat
To slice thin strips of meat, position a cleaver or large knife at a 45-degree angle to the meat and slice it across the grain into strips.

Smoky Little Sausage Hot Dish

Cooking time: 6–7 hours

Preparation time: 15 minutes

Attention: Minimal

Pot size: 3–6 quarts

Serves 4

1 pound smoky wieners
2 cups cooked macaroni
1 medium-sized yellow onion
¾ cup American cheese
3 tablespoons pimientos, chopped
3 tablespoons flour
¾ teaspoon table salt
¼ teaspoon ground black pepper
1 cup milk
1 cup water
½ tablespoon vinegar
1 cup fresh peas
1 teaspoon dry parsley

1. Cut the wieners into 1-inch lengths. Cook the macaroni in boiling water until soft but not mushy. Peel the onion and chop into ¼-inch pieces. Grate the cheese using a vegetable grater. Chop the pimientos into ¼-inch pieces.
2. Combine the cheese, flour, salt, pepper, milk, water, and vinegar in a medium-sized saucepan on the stove; cook on medium heat, stirring frequently, until the mixture is smooth and thick. Pour into the slow cooker. Add the wieners, macaroni, peas, onions, parsley, and pimientos; stir well. Cover and cook on low setting for 6 to 7 hours.

Serve with Grandma's Apples and Rice (page 595) for dessert.

CHAPTER 21
Vegetarian

Mexican-Style Stuffed Red Peppers

Cooking time: 4–6 hours

Preparation time: 30 minutes

Attention: Minimal

Pot size: 4–6 quarts

Serves 4

4 large red bell peppers
2 cloves garlic
½ cup green chives, chopped
1 large tomato
2 sprigs fresh cilantro
½ cup cooked rice
½ cup cooked black beans
   (fresh or canned)
½ cup fresh, canned, or
   frozen corn
½ teaspoon dried crushed basil
¼ teaspoon ground black pepper
½ teaspoon chili powder
½ cup tomato sauce
2 cups water
¼ cup Cheddar cheese, shredded

1. Remove the stem and seeds from the red peppers. Peel the garlic and mince with a sharp kitchen knife. Chop the chives into ¼-inch pieces. Chop the tomato into ¼-inch pieces. Crush the cilantro or mince with a sharp knife.
2. Combine the rice, beans, chives, corn, diced tomatoes, garlic, cilantro, basil, black pepper, and chili powder in a bowl; mix well with a large spoon. Use an ice cream scoop to spoon a portion of the mixture into each red pepper. The mixture should come to the top of the peppers but should not overflow.
3. Pour the tomato sauce and water into the slow cooker. Place the stuffed red peppers in the slow cooker so they stand upright. Cook covered on low setting for 4 to 6 hours. Five minutes before serving, sprinkle Cheddar cheese on the top of each red pepper. Cover and cook on low setting until cheese melts.

Spread butter on flour tortillas, sprinkle on garlic salt, and bake in a 350-degree oven for 10 minutes to create a crunchy complement to this meal.

Mushrooms for Meat

To turn any meat dish into an instant vegetarian entrée, substitute Morel mushrooms for the meat. Be sure to substitute by volume, not weight because even these heavier mushrooms weigh less than meat.

Cooking time: 8–10 hours	
Preparation time: 20 minutes	
Attention: Medium	
Pot size: 5–6 quarts	
Serves 8	

Garlicky Red Beans

1 pound red beans
3 cups water
1 medium-sized yellow onion
1 bunch green onions
7 cloves garlic
1 celery rib
1 green bell pepper
½ cup fresh parsley

½ cup ketchup
1 tablespoon Worcestershire sauce
2 tablespoons Tabasco sauce
2 bay leaves
1 teaspoon thyme
½ teaspoon table salt
½ teaspoon ground black pepper

1. Soak the beans overnight in six cups water. Drain and rinse the beans. Place them in slow cooker and add 3 cups of fresh water. Cook covered on low setting for 3 hours.

2. Peel and chop the yellow onion into ¼-inch pieces. Clean and cut the green onions into ½-inch lengths. Be sure to use all of the green stems. Peel and slice the garlic paper-thin, using a sharp paring knife. Chop the celery into ¼-inch pieces. Remove the seeds from the bell pepper and cut the pepper into ¼-inch pieces.

3. Add the yellow onion, green onion, garlic, celery, bell pepper, parsley, ketchup, Worcestershire, Tabasco, bay leaves, thyme, salt, and pepper to slow cooker; stir until ingredients are well mingled with beans. Cook covered on low setting for 5 to 7 hours.

Serve over brown rice with a side of fresh-steamed broccoli for a complete, healthy meal.

Garlic in Jars?

Beware of prepared garlic. While preminced garlic looks like a good buy and certainly sounds easier, after being chopped it releases an oil while stored. This affects both the taste and consistency in your recipes. Fresh garlic is always best.

Caribbean Black Beans and Rice

Cooking time: 7–9 hours

Preparation time: 30 minutes

Attention: Medium

Pot size: 3–6 quarts

Serves 6

1 large red bell pepper
Olive oil for basting red pepper,
   plus 1½ teaspoons more
½ green bell pepper
2 cloves garlic
1 cup raw white rice (yields 3
   cups cooked)

2 (16-ounce) cans of black beans
2 tablespoons white vinegar
2 teaspoons Tabasco or other
   hot sauce
3 tablespoons cilantro, chopped
1 teaspoon table salt
½ teaspoon ground black pepper

1. Remove the stems and seeds from the red bell pepper and cut into quarters. Lightly cover the inside "meat" of the pepper with olive oil. Bake in 350-degree oven for 1 hour; remove and cut into ¼-inch-long strips. Remove the seeds from the green bell pepper and cut into ¼-inch-long strips. Peel and slice the garlic paper-thin with a sharp paring knife. Prepare the rice according to package directions to yield 3 cups of cooked rice.

2. Sauté the red pepper, green pepper, and garlic in 1½ teaspoons olive oil for 2 minutes on medium-high heat in a large skillet on the stove. Drain off the oil; combine with cilantro, salt, and black pepper and place mixture in the slow cooker. Drain and rinse the black beans; add them to the slow cooker. Add vinegar, Tabasco, and rice to slow cooker. Stir until all ingredients are well mingled. Cook covered on low setting for 6 to 8 hours. Because this meal does not have a great deal of liquid, you may need to add ¼ to ½ cup water about halfway through the cooking process.

Serve with Slightly Seedy White Bread (page 374).

Spinach, Rice, and Vegetable Casserole

Cooking time: 6–8 hours	
Preparation time: 20 minutes	
Attention: Medium	
Pot size: 3–6 quarts	
Serves 8	

1 large yellow onion
3 cloves of garlic
1 bunch parsley
2 bunches spinach
1 cup fresh tomatoes, chopped
2 tablespoons olive oil

3 cups water
2 tablespoons tomatopaste
⅛ teaspoon table salt
⅛ teaspoon ground black pepper
1 cup uncooked white rice

1. Peel and chop the onion into ¼-inch pieces. Peel and slice the garlic paper-thin with a sharp paring knife. Chop the parsley into ¼-inch lengths. Wash the spinach and remove the stems. Chop the tomatoes into ¼-inch pieces.

2. Heat the oil over medium-high heat in a medium-sized skillet. Add the onions, parsley, and garlic; sauté for 3 to 5 minutes, until the onions are translucent. Drain off oil and transfer the mixture to the slow cooker. Add the water, tomato paste, chopped tomatoes, salt, and pepper. Mix well so ingredients are well mingled. Add spinach and rice; stir. Cook covered on low setting for 6 to 8 hours, or until rice is done.

Pair this meal with fresh cantaloupe and honeydew melon cubes to offset the robust tomato flavor.

Sautéing with Water

For a healthy alternative, sauté onions and garlic in a few tablespoons of water instead of oil or butter. They tend to get a little crisper this way but this cooking method saves many grams of fat.

Creamy Roasted Corn with Rice

Cooking time: 7–9 hours

Preparation time: 20 minutes

Attention: Medium

Pot size: 3–6 quarts

Serves 6

3 tablespoons olive oil

1 cup uncooked white rice

4 cups chicken broth

½ cup skim milk

½ cup dry white wine

½ teaspoon table salt

½ teaspoon ground black pepper

½ teaspoon nutmeg

2 cups fresh or frozen corn, cooked

⅓ pound cream cheese

4 fresh scallions

1. Heat the olive oil on medium-high in a medium-sized skillet. Sauté the rice, stirring constantly for 3 to 5 minutes, until slightly browned. Drain and place in the slow cooker.
2. Add the chicken broth, milk, white wine, salt, pepper, and nutmeg to the slow cooker. Cook covered on low setting for 6 to 8 hours, or until rice is soft.
3. Cut the cream cheese into ½-inch cubes. Peel and slice the scallions paper-thin, using a sharp paring knife.
4. Add the corn, scallions, and cream cheese to the slow cooker; stir well. Cook covered 30 to 60 minutes, stirring every 10 minutes. The cheese should be fully melted and integrated into the sauce.

Preparing Frozen Veggies

Thaw frozen vegetables in the refrigerator the night before you will use them. If you have more than 2 cups of frozen vegetables in your recipe, it could cause the food to heat too slowly at the beginning of the cooking process.

Lemony Bulgur Garbanzo Pilaf

Cooking time: 6–9 hours

Preparation time: 30 minutes

Attention: Medium

Pot size: 3–6 quarts

Serves 6

1 cup medium-grind bulgur

2 cups cooked chickpeas, **or** 1 cup dried

½ teaspoon table salt

½ teaspoon ground black pepper

2 cups vegetable stock or bouillon

1 small yellow onion

1 small green bell pepper

3 cloves garlic

1 tablespoon olive oil

½ teaspoon cumin

⅓ cup fresh lemon juice

1 cup fresh parsley, chopped

1. Wash the bulgur and chickpeas, then place them in the slow cooker along with the salt, pepper, and vegetable stock. Cook covered on low setting for 2 to 3 hours.

2. Peel and chop the onion into ¼-inch pieces. Remove the seeds from the green pepper and chop into ¼-inch pieces. Peel and mince the garlic, using a sharp kitchen knife.

3. Heat the olive oil to medium-high heat in a medium-sized skillet. Add the onion, green pepper, and garlic; sauté for 3 to 5 minutes, stirring constantly, until the onions are translucent. Drain off oil. Add the onions, green pepper, garlic, and cumin to the slow cooker; mix well. Cook covered on low setting for 4 to 6 additional hours.

4. Add the lemon juice and parsley to the slow cooker; mix well. Cook uncovered for 30 minutes more on low setting.

For a creamy alternative, add half a cup of grated mild Cheddar cheese and eliminate the parsley and lemon juice.

Eggplant and Tomatoes with Pasta

Cooking time: 3½–5 hours
Preparation time: 45 minutes
Attention: Frequent
Pot size: 3–6 quarts
Serves 4

¾ cup yellow onion, chopped

3 cloves garlic

¾ pound of eggplant, cubed

2 tablespoons fresh basil, chopped

1 (16-ounce) can Italian plum tomatoes with juice

2 tablespoons olive oil

2 tablespoons balsamic vinegar

½ cup chicken broth

1 tablespoon tomato paste

½ teaspoon dried oregano

⅛ teaspoon hot red pepper flakes

½ teaspoon table salt

12 ounces pasta shells or pieces (rotini, wagon wheels, bow ties, etc.)

1. Peel and chop the onion into ¼-inch pieces. Peel and mince the garlic. Peel and cut the eggplant into 1-inch cubes. Chop the fresh basil into ¼-inch lengths. Pour the canned tomatoes into a medium-sized bowl and break into approximate quarters, using a wooden spoon.

2. In a small skillet, heat the olive oil on a medium-high heat; sauté the onions and garlic for 3 to 5 minutes, stirring constantly, until the onions are translucent. Drain and place in the slow cooker.

3. Add the eggplant, balsamic vinegar, chicken broth, tomato paste, and oregano to the slow cooker; stir well so that all the ingredients are well mingled. Cook uncovered on high setting for 3 to 4 hours, or until the sauce is slightly thickened.

4. Reduce the temperature setting to low. Add the basil and red pepper flakes to the sauce in the slow cooker; stir to incorporate. Boil the pasta in water with the ½ teaspoon of salt in a pot on the stove for 10 minutes. Drain off the water and add the pasta to the slow cooker; stir well so that all of the pasta is covered with sauce. Cover and cook on low setting for 30 to 60 minutes, or until the pasta is soft but not overcooked.

Complement this meal with tomato slices topped with goat cheese and fresh basil.

Minted Lentil and Tofu Stew

Cooking time:	8–9 hours
Preparation time:	10 minutes
Attention:	Minimal
Pot size:	3–6 quarts
Serves 6	

2 cups dry yellow lentils
6 cups salted water (add 1 tablespoon table salt to water and
   stir until dissolved)
¼ cup fresh spearmint, chopped
1 tablespoon fresh peppermint, chopped
2 cups firm tofu, cubed
½ teaspoon soybean oil
1 teaspoon lemon juice
1 cup water
1 teaspoon table salt

1. Soak the lentils overnight in 6 cups salted water. Wash and drain. Cut the spearmint and peppermint into ¼-inch pieces. Cut the tofu into 1-inch cubes.
2. Add all ingredients except tofu to the slow cooker; stir until ingredients are well mixed. Cook covered on low setting 7 to 8 hours. Add tofu and cook 1 to 2 more hours.

Substitute 2 tablespoons of Italian seasoning for the spearmint and peppermint to create an herbed version of this lentil stew.

Fresh vs. Dry Pasta

Fresh pastas typically contain more egg than dried pastas. This accounts for the creamier flavor but also adds cholesterol and fat to your diet. Make up for the flavor by adding more spices to your sauce.

Creamy Vegetarian Chili

Cooking time: 8–9 hours

Preparation time: 15 minutes

Attention: Minimal

Pot size: 3–6 quarts

Serves 6

2 cups dried red kidney beans
2 cups firm tofu, cubed
2 large carrots
2 large yellow onions
1 tablespoon chili powder
1 teaspoon garlic salt
1 teaspoon ground black pepper
1 cup fresh or frozen corn
½ cup low-fat sour cream

1. Soak the beans overnight in 6 cups water. Cut the tofu into 1-inch cubes. Peel and slice the carrots into ¼-inch rounds. Peel and slice the onions into ¼-inch squares.
2. Drain and wash the beans. Add all ingredients except tofu to the slow cooker; mix with a wooden spoon until all the ingredients are well mingled. Cook covered on low setting 7 to 8 hours. Add tofu cook 1 to 1½ hours. Approximately 30 minutes before serving, stir the chili, then add the sour cream; stir well. Cook uncovered on low setting for the remaining half-hour.

Serve this chili with Corn Bread in the Round (page 366) to create an almost-authentic Tex-Mex treat.

Cooking time: 6 hours	
Preparation time: 20 minutes	
Attention: Medium	
Pot size: 3–6 quarts	
Serves 4	

Nutty Barley Pilaf

1¾ cup pearl barley
½ cup butter, divided
2 medium-sized yellow onions
8 ounces (1 cup) fresh
  mushrooms, sliced

4 cups vegetable broth
¼ cup toasted macadamia nuts,
  chopped
¼ cup toasted pecans, chopped
½ cup fresh parsley, chopped

1. On the stove, sauté the barley in four tablespoons of the butter in a medium-sized skillet on medium heat until the barley is golden; stir often. Pour the mixture into the slow cooker.
2. Peel and chop the onions into ¼-inch pieces. Clean the mushrooms by wiping with a damp cloth; slice paper-thin with a sharp paring knife. Put the onions and mushrooms in the skillet and sauté, stirring often, in the remaining butter on medium heat for about 5 minutes. Add this to the slow cooker and stir well. Pour 2 cups of vegetable broth over the mixture. Cover and cook on low setting for 4 hours.
3. Add the remaining broth and cook uncovered for 2 hours, stirring occasionally.
4. Chop the nuts finely with a sharp paring knife. Place on a cookie sheet in the oven and heat for 15 minutes at 350 degrees. Roughly chop the parsley. Fifteen minutes before serving, stir the nuts and parsley into the mixture.

Serve with fresh apple and orange slices to complement the nutty flavors in this dish.

Keeping Cut Fruit from Browning

Apples and bananas won't get brown if you cover them with a thin layer of half lemon juice and half water. The acidic lemon juice also will add a slight tang to blander fruit.

Preparation time: 40 minutes	
Attention: Medium	
Pot size: 3–6 quarts	

Buddhist Monk's Soup Serves 6

1 pound butternut squash
1 large sweet potato
1 quart water
½ cup raw peanuts, shelled and skinned
⅓ cup dried mung beans
3 tablespoons vegetable oil
1 square of tofu
1 quart unsweetened coconut milk
1 teaspoon table salt
1 (12-ounce) package cellophane noodles

1. Peel the squash and sweet potato and cut into 3-inch pieces. Put them into the slow cooker with 1 quart of water and salt. Cook covered on high setting for 6 to 8 hours or until soft.
2. Soak the mung beans and peanuts in water until soft, about 30 minutes. Sauté the tofu in the vegetable oil on medium-high heat until brown; drain off grease and cut the tofu into ¼-inch strips. Add beans, peanuts, tofu, coconut milk, salt, and cellophane noodles. Cover and cook on low setting for 1 hour.

Serve with Heavy Brown Bread (page 375) and three-year-old Cheddar cheese for an authentic monastery meal.

Making Your Own Pasta

Use semolina flour to make homemade noodles. It is made from high gluten wheat and is more finely ground. The pasta is slightly stiffer than that made with regular flour so it holds up better to slow cooking.

Vidalia Onion and Lentil Casserole

Cooking time: 6 hours

Preparation time: 15 minutes

Attention: Minimal

Pot size: 3–6 quarts

Serves 4

1 large Vidalia onion, chopped
2 cups dried lentils
1 teaspoon table salt
3 cups water

2 cups tomato sauce
¼ cup brown sugar
2 tablespoons Dijon mustard
⅓ cup dark molasses

Peel the onion and chop into ¼-inch pieces. Rinse the lentils and place in the slow cooker. Add the onion, salt, water, tomato sauce, brown sugar, mustard, and molasses; stir well. Cover and cook on low setting for 6 hours.

Peel and slice another onion into ¼-inch rings. Sauté rings until crisp and place them on top of the casserole before serving.

Root Vegetable Soup

Cooking time: 6–8 hours

Preparation time: 15 minutes

Attention: Minimal

Pot size: 3–8 quarts

Serves 6

2 medium-sized yellow onions
3 medium carrots
1 medium rutabaga
1 large beet
1 medium turnip

3 medium potatoes
¼ teaspoon ground black pepper
1 teaspoon ground nutmeg
3 cups vegetable broth

Peel all the vegetables and chop into ¼-inch cubes. Combine all ingredients in the slow cooker. Cover and cook on low setting for 6 to 8 hours.

This is an excellent complement to hot beef sandwiches.

Cooking time: 7–9 hours

Preparation time: 30 minutes

Attention: Minimal

Pot size: 3–8 quarts

Serves 4

Portobello-Stuffed Artichokes

4 large artichokes
4 large portobello mushrooms
3 garlic cloves
2 tablespoons grated Parmesan cheese
½ teaspoon ground black pepper
1 tablespoon olive oil
1 teaspoon salt

1. Remove the stems from the artichokes and discard the outer 2 to 3 layers of leaves. Trim the base so that the artichokes stand flat. Cut off the top of the artichoke and hollow out the center, removing all purple-tinged leaves and fuzzy material.
2. Chop the mushrooms into ¼-inch pieces. Peel the garlic and mince with a sharp kitchen knife. Combine the mushrooms, garlic, Parmesan cheese, black pepper, and olive oil in a medium-sized mixing bowl. Stuff the mixture into the artichoke centers.
3. Pour water into the slow cooker (so it is about 1½ inches deep) and stir in the salt. Set the artichokes in the water. Cover and cook on low setting for 7 to 9 hours. The leaves should be tender when done.

Sweet Potato and Apple Bake (page 274) makes a nice complement to this meal.

Releasing Garlic's Potential

Get the most out of garlic by "popping" the clove before adding it to a dish. Hold a large knife on its side and place the peeled clove under it. Push down until you hear the clove pop. You'll release all the wonderful oils without having to chop.

CHAPTER 22
Breads

Corn Bread in the Round

Cooking time: 2 hours

Preparation time: 10 minutes

Attention: Minimal

Pot size: 4–8 quarts

Serves 12–16

1¼ cups bread flour

¾ cup yellow cornmeal

¼ cup sugar

4½ teaspoons baking powder

1 teaspoon salt

1 egg

1 cup skim milk

⅓ cup melted butter

3 empty aluminum cans, approximately 12 ounces each

½ teaspoon vegetable oil

1. Mix together the flour, cornmeal, sugar, baking powder, and salt; set aside. Lightly beat the egg and combine with milk and butter. Add this mixture to the dry mixture and stir until all the dry ingredients are moistened; do not mix too much. Batter should remain lumpy.

2. Grease the insides of three empty cans using the ½ teaspoon vegetable oil. Pour ⅓ of the mixture into each can. Cover each can with aluminum foil that has been greased on the inside. Place the cans on a trivet in the bottom of the slow cooker. Cook on high for 2 hours or until a long wooden skewer inserted into the bread comes out clean. Let stand for 5 minutes before removing from the cans.

Serve corn bread, ham steaks, and Northwestern Baked Beans (page 543) for a traditional farm-style meal.

Bread Baking Inserts

Many slow cookers have bread baking inserts available. You can use these or use metal vegetable and coffee cans instead. Three soup cans will make the equivalent of a loaf and give you fun, individual little loaves of bread.

Traditional Dressing for Poultry or Red Meat

Cooking time: 6 hours

Preparation time: 20 minutes

Attention: Medium

Pot size: 3–6 quarts

Serves 8

1 loaf of corn bread
8 slices dry white bread
1 medium-sized yellow onion
2 stalks celery
4 eggs, beaten
2 cups chicken broth
2 (10 ¾-ounce) cans cream of chicken condensed soup
1 teaspoon sage
½ teaspoon black pepper
2 tablespoons butter

1. Tear the bread into pieces about the size of a quarter.
2. Peel and chop the onion into ¼-inch pieces. Chop the celery into ¼-inch pieces.
3. Mix together all the ingredients except the butter. Place in the slow cooker. Dot the butter on top. Cover and cook on high setting for 2 hours.
4. Keep covered and cook on low setting for 4 additional hours.

This makes an excellent complement to Dilled Turkey Breast (page 408).

Halloween Is Here Pumpkin Bread

Cooking time: 3–4 hours

Preparation time: 15 minutes

Attention: Minimal

Pot size: 4–6 quarts

Serves 12

1 cup vegetable oil
1 cup white sugar
1 cup brown sugar
4 eggs
2 cups canned pumpkin
3 cups flour
2 teaspoons salt

1 teaspoon cinnamon
1 teaspoon nutmeg
2 teaspoons baking soda
2 cups chopped walnuts

1. Blend the oil and white and brown sugars in a medium-sized mixing bowl using a wooden spoon. Beat the eggs with a fork until they are frothy. Stir the eggs and pumpkin into the oil and sugar mixture. Combine the flour, salt, cinnamon, nutmeg, and soda in a medium-sized bowl and mix well. Add this mixture to the batter and stir well. Chop the walnuts into ⅛-inch pieces with a sharp paring knife, then stir them into the batter.

2. Grease the inside of a 2-pound coffee can, then sprinkle the greased area lightly with flour. Add the batter to the can and cover with aluminum foil. Poke 3 sets of holes into the aluminum foil with a fork. Place the coffee can into the slow cooker. Cook covered on high setting for 3 hours. Test the bread before removing it by inserting a long wooden skewer. If it comes out clean, the bread is done. If there is batter on it, cook for an additional half-hour.

Serve this instead of rolls at your next fall holiday gathering.

Testing Bread

To test bread or cake to see if it's done, insert a toothpick into the center. If it comes out clean, it's done. If crumbs or batter stick to it, it needs to bake longer.

Cooking time:	3–4 hours
Preparation time:	20 minutes
Attention:	Minimal
Pot size:	4–6 quarts
Serves 12	

Zucchini Bread

2 eggs
⅔ cup vegetable oil
2 tablespoons sugar
1½ cups zucchini, peeled and grated
2 teaspoons vanilla
2 cups flour
¼ teaspoon salt
½ teaspoon baking powder
1 teaspoon cinnamon
½ teaspoon nutmeg
1 cup chopped walnuts

1. Beat the eggs in a medium-sized mixing bowl with a fork until foamy. Add oil, sugar, grated zucchini, and vanilla; mix well with a wooden spoon. Stir remaining ingredients into the batter; mix well.
2. Grease the inside of a 2-pound coffee can and lightly sprinkle with flour. Pour the mixture into the coffee can. Cover with a piece of aluminum foil. Poke 3 sets of holes in the aluminum foil with a fork. Put the coffee can in the slow cooker. Cover and cook on high setting 3 to 4 hours. Test after 3 hours by inserting a long wooden skewer into the bread. If it comes out clean, the bread is done.

Cooking tip: Avoid the temptation to peak at your bread before the minimum cooking time is up. Even breads that don't contain yeast can be affected by sudden changes in humidity or temperature.

Banana Nut Bread

Cooking time: 4–5 hours
Preparation time: 20 minutes
Attention: Minimal
Pot size: 4–6 quarts
Serves 12

3 very ripe bananas
½ cup walnuts, chopped
2 large eggs, beaten
1 cup sugar
½ teaspoon salt
1 teaspoon baking soda
½ cup melted shortening
2 cups flour

1. Grease a 2-pound coffee can by putting a small amount of shortening on a paper towel and rubbing it inside the can. Sprinkle the inside of the can with a small amount of flour.
2. Mash the bananas. Cut the walnuts into $\frac{1}{16}$-inch pieces. Add the eggs, sugar, salt, baking soda, shortening, flour, and walnuts to mashed bananas. Mix well by stirring with a wooden spoon. Place the mixture in the coffee can. Cover the can with aluminum foil. Poke 3 sets of holes in the aluminum foil with a fork. Put the coffee can in the slow cooker. Cover and cook on low setting 4 to 5 hours.

Serve with Earl Grey teal as a dessert after a heavy meal.

Cheddar and Onion Bread

Cooking time: 4–6 hours	
Preparation time: 15 minutes	
Attention: Medium	
Pot size: 4–6 quarts	
Serves 12	

2 tablespoons white onion, grated
½ cup Cheddar cheese, grated
2 teaspoons active dry yeast

1 cup warm water
3 cups bread flour
1 teaspoon salt

1. Grate the onion using the finest side of a vegetable grater. Grate the cheese using the coarser side of the grater. Grease a 2-pound coffee can by putting shortening on a paper towel and rubbing the inside of the coffee can.
2. Dissolve the yeast in half a cup of warm water. In a large bowl, combine the flour, yeast, salt, and remaining warm water. If the dough is too dry, add more water. Stir in the Cheddar cheese and onions. Roll the dough into a ball and place in the coffee can. Cover lightly with a paper towel and place in a warm place for 1 to 2 hours. Dough should rise to twice its original size.
2. Cover the coffee can with aluminum foil. Poke 3 sets of holes in the aluminum foil with a fork. Place the coffee can in the slow cooker. Cook, covered, on low setting for 4 to 6 hours. Bread is fully cooked when it bounces back when lightly touched.

This is an excellent complement to Beef Roast with Dried Fruit (page 392).

Yeast

Yeast is a live entity that grows when it gets warm. However, if it's added to boiling water, you can kill it. You can make a heavy, dense bread by leaving out the yeast and substituting baking soda.

Honey Oatmeal Bread

Cooking time: 4–6 hours

Preparation time: 15 minutes

Attention: Medium

Pot size: 4–6 quarts

Serves 12

2 teaspoons dry active yeast
1¼ cups warm water
½ cup honey
2 tablespoons vegetable oil
1 cup quick-cooking oats
1½ teaspoons salt
3 cups bread flour

1. Grease a 2-pound coffee can by putting shortening on a paper towel and rubbing it on the inside of the coffee can.
2. Dissolve the yeast in half a cup of the warm water. In a large bowl, combine all ingredients. If the dough is too dry, add more water. Roll the dough into a ball and place in the coffee can. Cover lightly with a paper towel and place in a warm place for 1 to 2 hours. Dough should rise to twice its original size.
3. Cover the coffee can with aluminum foil. Poke 3 sets of holes in the aluminum foil with a fork. Place the coffee can in the slow cooker. Place the lid on the slow cooker and cook on low setting for 4 to 6 hours. Bread is fully cooked when it bounces back when lightly touched.

Serve with Congo Stew (page 490) for a unique juxtaposition of flavors.

Grandma Margaret's Summer Dill Bread

2 tablespoons grated onion
2 teaspoons dry active yeast
¼ cup warm water
3 cups flour
½ teaspoon baking soda
1 teaspoon salt
2 tablespoons dill weed
1 cup cottage cheese
1 tablespoon milk, if needed

1. Grate the onion using the finest side of a vegetable grater. Grease a 2-pound coffee can by putting shortening on a paper towel and rubbing it on the inside of the coffee can.
2. Dissolve the yeast in warm water. In a large bowl, combine all the ingredients **except** the onion. If the dough is too dry, add 1 tablespoon of milk. Stir in the onions. Roll the dough into a ball and place it in the coffee can. Cover lightly with a paper towel and put in a warm place for 1 to 2 hours. Dough should rise to twice its original size.
3. Cover the coffee can with aluminum foil. Poke 3 sets of holes in the aluminum foil with a fork. Place the coffee can in the slow cooker. Cover the slow cooker and cook on low setting for 4 to 6 hours. Bread is fully cooked when it bounces back when lightly touched.

This is excellent served with Spicy Pot Roast (page 396).

Slightly Seedy White Bread

Cooking time: 4–6 hours

Preparation time: 15 minutes

Attention: Medium

Pot size: 4–6 quarts

Serves 12

2 teaspoons dry active yeast

1½ cups warm water

3 cups bread flour

1 tablespoon nonfat dry milk

2 tablespoons olive oil

1½ teaspoons salt

¼ cup poppy seeds

¼ cup sesame seeds

½ cup sunflower seeds

1. Grease a 2-pound coffee can by putting shortening on a paper towel and rubbing it on the inside of the coffee can.
2. Dissolve the yeast in half a cup of warm water. In a large bowl, combine the flour, dry milk, oil, remaining water, salt, and yeast. If the dough is too dry, add more water 1 tablespoon at a time. Stir in the seeds. Roll the dough into a ball and place it in the coffee can. Cover lightly with a paper towel and place in a warm place for 1 to 2 hours. The dough should rise to twice its original size.
3. Cover the coffee can with aluminum foil. Poke 3 sets of holes in the aluminum foil with a fork. Place the coffee can in the slow cooker. Cover the slow cooker and cook on low setting for 4 to 6 hours. Bread is fully cooked when it bounces back when lightly touched.

Serve as a complement to Wild Duck Gumbo (page 434).

Cooking time: 4–6 hours
Preparation time: 15 minutes
Attention: Medium
Pot size: 4–6 quarts
Serves 12

Heavy Brown Bread

1 cup stone-ground rye flour
1 cup stone-ground whole wheat
    flour
1 cup stone-ground cornmeal
½ teaspoon baking soda
4 teaspoons baking powder

1 teaspoon salt
¾ cup molasses
1¾ cups milk
1 cup raisins
3 cups water

1. Grease a 2-pound coffee can by putting shortening on a paper towel and rubbing it on the inside of the coffee can.
2. In a large bowl, combine the flours, cornmeal, baking soda, baking powder, and salt; mix well. Add the molasses and milk. Mix until all ingredients are well combined. Stir in the raisins. Place the batter in the coffee can. Cover the coffee can with aluminum foil. Poke 3 sets of holes in the aluminum foil with a fork. Put 3 cups of water in the slow cooker. Place the coffee can in the slow cooker. Cover the slow cooker and cook on low setting for 4 to 6 hours. Bread is fully cooked when it bounces back when lightly touched.
3. Empty the water from the slow cooker and remove the foil from the coffee can. Put the coffee can back in slow cooker with the cover slightly ajar, so that steam can escape. Cook on low setting for 15 additional minutes.

This is perfect served with Beef Roast (page 392).

Baking Bread

When baking bread in soup, vegetable, or coffee cans, cover the can with aluminum foil and poke a few holes in it with a fork. Also use the slow cooker cover.

Almond and Chocolate Chip Bread

Cooking time: 4–6 hours

Preparation time: 15 minutes

Attention: Medium

Pot size: 4–6 quarts

Serves 12

1½ teaspoons dry active yeast
1 cup water, plus extra as needed
3 cups bread flour
1 tablespoon nonfat dry milk
¾ teaspoon salt
3 tablespoons sugar
½ teaspoon vanilla
2 tablespoons butter, softened
¾ cup semisweet chocolate chips
⅓ cup almond slivers

1. Grease a 2-pound coffee can by putting shortening on a paper towel and rubbing it on the inside of the coffee can.
2. Dissolve the yeast in half a cup of the warm water. In a large bowl, combine the flour, dry milk, yeast, remaining water, salt, sugar, vanilla, and butter. If the dough is too dry, add more water 1 tablespoon at a time. Stir in the chocolate chips and almonds. Roll the dough into a ball and place it in the coffee can. Cover lightly with a paper towel and place in a warm place for 1 to 2 hours. Dough should rise to twice its original size.
3. Cover the coffee can with aluminum foil. Poke 3 sets of holes in the aluminum foil with a fork. Place the coffee can in the slow cooker. Cover the slow cooker and cook on low setting for 4 to 6 hours. Bread is fully cooked when it bounces back when lightly touched.

Toast the bread and spread with peanut butter for a nutritious, tasty breakfast treat.

CHAPTER 23
Stews

Tomato and Bean Stew

Cooking time: 8–10 hours

Preparation time: 20 minutes

Attention: Minimal

Pot size: 4–8 quarts

Serves 6

2 medium potatoes

1 large white onion

1 medium-sized red bell pepper

1 medium-sized green bell pepper

2 medium carrots

1 (15-ounce) can garbanzo beans

1 (15-ounce) can kidney beans

1 cup dry lentils

1 (10-ounce) package chopped frozen spinach

1 (14½-ounce) can Italian stewed tomatoes

4 cups tomato juice

2 cups water

2 tablespoons dried parsley

2 tablespoons chili powder

2 teaspoons dried basil

2 teaspoons garlic powder

1 teaspoon ground cumin

1. Wash the potatoes but do not peel them; cut into 1-inch cubes. Peel the onion and cut into ¼-inch pieces. Remove the stem and seeds from the red and green peppers and cut into ¼-inch pieces. Wash the carrots and chop them into ¼-inch rounds. Drain and rinse the beans. Rinse the lentils.
2. Add all ingredients to the slow cooker; mix lightly. Cover and cook on low setting for 8 to 10 hours.

Serve with Italian Beets (page 575) to add some sharp flavors to the mellowness of this dish.

Hold the Foil When Freezing

When freezing soups and stews remember not to wrap tomato-based dishes in aluminum foil. The acid in the tomatoes will react with the aluminum.

Cooking time: 8–10 hours	
Preparation time: 15 minutes	
Attention: Minimal	
Pot size: 6 quarts	
Serves 8	

Cuban Black Bean Stew

1 large yellow onion
1 green bell pepper
4 garlic cloves
8 ounces (1 cup) peeled baby
   carrots
2 celery stalks
4 fresh tomatoes
2 tablespoons olive oil
1 teaspoon ground black pepper

1 teaspoon cayenne pepper
1 teaspoon dried thyme
1 bay leaf
2 cups dried black beans, rinsed
2 chicken bouillon cubes
4 cups water
4 tablespoons balsamic vinegar

1. Peel and chop the onion into ½-inch pieces. Remove the stem and seeds from the green pepper; chop the pepper into ½-inch pieces. Peel the garlic cloves and mince with a sharp kitchen knife. Cut the baby carrots in half. Chop the celery into ¼-inch pieces. Chop the tomatoes into ½-inch pieces.
2. Heat the olive oil in a large skillet on medium-high heat on the stove. Add the onion, green pepper, garlic, and ground spices. Sauté, stirring constantly, until the onions are soft, about 5 minutes. Drain off the oil and place the mixture in the slow cooker.
3. Add the carrots, celery, black beans, bay leaf, tomatoes, and crumbled bouillon cubes to the slow cooker. Add the water; stir until all ingredients are mixed. Cook covered on low setting for 8 to 10 hours.
4. 10 minutes before serving, stir in the balsamic vinegar.

Serve pan-fried plantain slices for an authentic Cuban meal.

Moravian Ham, Tomato, and Green Bean Stew

Cooking time: 5–6 hours

Preparation time: 10 minutes

Attention: Minimal

Pot size: 3–6 quarts

Serves 6

2 cups precooked ham, chopped

4 medium-sized yellow onions

4 cups diced fresh tomatoes

6 cups fresh green beans

¾ teaspoon table salt

½ teaspoon ground black pepper

1. Chop the ham into 1-inch cubes. Peel and chop the onions into ½-inch pieces. Peel the tomatoes with a sharp paring knife, gently lifting the peel from the flesh. and dice the tomatoes in ¼-inch pieces. Snap the ends off the green beans and discard the ends.
2. Add all ingredients to the slow cooker. Stir 2 or 3 times with a wooden spoon. Cook covered on low setting 5 to 6 hours.

Serve over mashed potatoes with a side of squash for a fall harvest treat.

Polish Stew

Cooking time: 8–9 hours

Preparation time: 20 minutes

Attention: Minimal

Pot size: 3–6 quarts

Serves 4

1½ pounds Polish sausage

2 medium-sized onions

4 medium potatoes

1 cup shredded Monterey jack cheese

4 cups sauerkraut

1 (10¾-ounce) can cream of celery condensed soup

⅓ cup brown sugar

1. Cut the Polish sausage into ½-inch-thick slices. Peel the onions and chop into ¼-inch pieces. Peel the potatoes and cut into 1-inch cubes. Shred the cheese using a vegetable grater. Drain the sauerkraut.
2. Combine the soup, brown sugar, sauerkraut, sausage, potatoes, and onions in the slow cooker. Cover and cook on low for 8 to 9 hours. Stir in the cheese 10 minutes before serving.

Fruity Beef Stew

Cooking time: 10 hours	
Preparation time: 30 minutes	
Attention: Medium	
Pot size: 6–8 quarts	
Serves 8	

2 pounds beef round roast
2 cups chopped yellow onions
6 cloves garlic
2 teaspoons crushed, dried red peppers
¾ teaspoon turmeric
¾ teaspoon ground cinnamon
¾ teaspoon ground ginger
½ teaspoon salt
2 tablespoons extra-virgin olive oil
2 cups beef broth
1 cup dried pitted dates
1 cup dried apricots
1 tablespoon cornstarch
2 tablespoons water

1. Cut the meat into 1¼-inch pieces. Peel the onion and chop into ¼-inch pieces. Peel and mince the garlic. In a small mixing bowl, combine the red peppers, turmeric, ginger, cinnamon, and salt; coat the meat with this seasoning mixture. In a large skillet heat the olive oil over medium heat until hot, then brown the meat; drain off grease.
2. Place the meat in the slow cooker the with onions, beef broth, dates, and apricots. Cover and cook on low setting for 9 hours. Remove the meat, onions, and fruit. Make a paste out of the cornstarch and water and stir into the juice in the slow cooker. Cook on high setting, stirring periodically, until mixture thickens into a gravy.
3. Add the meat, vegetables, and fruit back into slow cooker. Cover and cook on low setting for 1 more hour.

Serve with Minnesota Wild Rice (page 571) for a nice mix of flavors.

When Roasting Meat

When making a large pot roast, cut the meat into four or six smaller pieces. It will cook faster and get up to the bacteria-killing temperature quicker. Try adding onions between each layer of meat so their flavor saturates the meat.

Savory Garlic Chicken Stew

Cooking time: 6–8 hours
Preparation time: 30 minutes
Attention: Minimal
Pot size: 3–6 quarts
Serves 4

5 cups canned or frozen chicken broth
2 cups water
¼ cup all-purpose flour
8 garlic cloves
½ teaspoon low-fat oil
2 cups fresh carrots, sliced
6 medium golden potatoes
1 medium-sized yellow onion
1 cup fresh celery, sliced
2 pounds fresh or frozen boneless, skinless chicken breasts
1 teaspoon salt
¼ teaspoon white pepper

1. Put the chicken broth, water, and flour in a mixing bowl and whisk quickly until smooth.
2. Peel the garlic cloves and mash individually by placing the side of a large knife over each clove and pressing until the clove "pops," allowing the juice to come out. The cloves do not need to be cut into pieces. Sauté the mashed garlic in oil on medium heat until lightly golden.
3. Peel and cut the carrots and potatoes into 1-inch chunks. Dice the onion with a paring knife until pieces are smaller than ⅛-inch square. Cut the celery into ¼-inch slices. Cut the chicken into 1-inch cubes.
4. Combine all ingredients except the pepper in the slow cooker Stir until ingredients are well mixed and covered with liquid. Cook 6 to 8 hours covered on low heat. Remove cover 15 minutes before serving. Stir well and add pepper.

Although it is excellent served alone, to create a complete meal, ladle the stew over Heavy Brown Bread (page 375). Add color to the plate with a garnish of fresh orange slices and purple grapes.

Cooking time: 8–9 hours

Preparation time: 30 minutes

Attention: Minimal

Pot size: 3–6 quarts

Traditional Beef Stew

Serves 6

2 pounds beef chuck

6 medium carrots

6 medium-sized yellow onions

6 medium potatoes

6 celery ribs

1 (10¾-ounce) can condensed
   tomato soup

1 cup water

¼ cup flour

2 beef bouillon cubes

½ teaspoon salt

½ teaspoon pepper

1. Cut the beef into 1-inch cubes, trimming off all fat. Peel the carrots, onions, and potatoes. Slice the celery and carrots into 1-inch pieces. Quarter the onions and potatoes.

2. Mix the soup, bouillon cubes, water, and flour together in a medium-sized bowl with a fork until the mixture is smooth and the bouillon cubes have dissolved. Place the beef in the bottom of the slow cooker. Cover with the liquid mixture. Add the carrots, onions, celery, and potatoes. Sprinkle with salt and pepper. Cook on low setting for 8 to 9 hours.

Serve with Dilly Mashed Potatoes (page 573) for a flavorful and nutritious meal.

Why the Variations in Cooking Times?

The size of the slow cooker and the quality of meat or the water content of the vegetables can cause food to take more or less time to cook.

New Brunswick Chicken Stew

Cooking time: 6–8 hours

Preparation time: 20 minutes

Attention: Minimal

Pot size: 3–6 quarts

Serves 6

1 stewing chicken
2 quarts (8 cups) water
2 large yellow onions
4 cups fresh tomatoes, chopped
3 medium potatoes
2 cups okra, chopped
2 cups lima beans

4 cups fresh sweet corn
  (about 8 ears)
3 tablespoons table salt
1 teaspoon pepper
1 tablespoon sugar

1. Cut the chicken into pieces and put them in the slow cooker with two quarts of water. Cook covered on high setting for 2 hours. Remove the chicken and set aside to cool.
2. Peel and slice the onions into ¼-inch-thick rings. Cut the tomatoes into ½-inch cubes. Peel and cut the potatoes into ½-inch cubes. Cut the sweet corn from the cob. Chop the okra into ½-inch pieces. Remove the meat from the chicken bones.
3. Add the meat, onions, tomatoes, potatoes, sweet corn, okra, lima beans, salt, pepper, and sugar to slow cooker. Cook covered on low setting for 6 to 8 hours.

The flavor of this stew improves when it is refrigerated overnight and reheated the following day.

Using Aromatics

Turnips, onions, celery, and carrots are known as aromatic vegetables because they smell wonderful when cooked and add a great deal of flavor to meat-based recipes.

Cooking time: 10–12 hours

Preparation time: 15 minutes

Attention: Minimal

Pot size: 3–6 quarts

Serves 6

Apple Cider Beef Stew

2 pounds stewing beef
8 carrots
6 medium potatoes
2 Granny Smith apples
1 small white onion
2 teaspoons salt
½ teaspoon thyme
2 cups apple cider
¼ cup flour

1. Cut the beef into ½-inch cubes. Peel and slice the carrots ⅛ inch thick. Peel the potatoes and cut into ½-inch cubes. Peel the apples and cut into ½-inch pieces. Peel the onion and finely chop.

2. Place the carrots, potatoes, and apples in the slow cooker. Add the meat and sprinkle with salt, thyme, and onion. Pour the cider over the top. Cover and cook on low setting for 10 to 12 hours. Before serving, mix the flour with enough water to make a paste and add mixture to the stew; stir in. Cover and cook on high setting until thickened, about 15 minutes.

Ladle over Dilly Mashed Potatoes (page 573) for an unusual blend of flavors.

Best Meat Cuts to Use

The best cuts of beef for stew meat are chuck, flank, or brisket. The slow cooking tenderizes even the toughest meat while these cuts tend to be well marbled, allowing the flavorful fat juices to permeate the stew.

Layered Beef Stew

Cooking time: 9–10 hours

Preparation time: 20 minutes

Attention: Minimal

Pot size: 3–6 quarts

Serves 6

2½ pounds beef stewing meat

1 large yellow onion

6 medium carrots

4 celery ribs

4 large ripe tomatoes

10 small new potatoes

2 tablespoons Worcestershire sauce

¼ cup red wine

3 tablespoons brown sugar

1 teaspoon table salt

½ teaspoon ground black pepper

¼ teaspoon allspice

¼ teaspoon dried marjoram

¼ teaspoon dried thyme

2 bay leaves

6 tablespoons quick-cooking tapioca

1. Cut the beef into 1-inch cubes. Peel the onion and cut into ¼-inch-thick slices. Peel the carrots and cut in half lengthwise. Remove the leaves from the celery and cut ribs in half. Chop the tomatoes into ¼-inch pieces.

2. Layer all ingredients in the slow cooker in the following order: beef, onions, potatoes, carrots, celery, Worcestershire sauce, red wine, brown sugar, salt, pepper, allspice, marjoram, thyme, bay leaves, tapioca, tomatoes. Cover and cook on low setting for 9 to 10 hours.

Serve with Grandma Dorothy's Peas and Rice (page 569) for a complete meal.

French Countryside Chicken and Pork Stew

Cooking time:	8–9 hours
Preparation time:	20 minutes
Attention:	Minimal
Pot size:	3–6 quarts
Serves 4	

3 pounds pork chops
4 chicken breasts
10 pearl onions
8 ounces (1 cup) fresh
   mushrooms, quartered
4 garlic cloves

1 tablespoon olive oil
2 cups beef broth
¼ cup dry white wine
2 tablespoons Dijon mustard
1 teaspoon flour
1 teaspoon warm water

1. Remove the bones from the pork and cut the meat into ½-inch cubes. Remove the bones and skin from the chicken and discard; cut the chicken into ½-inch cubes. Peel the pearl onions. Clean the mushrooms by wiping with a damp cloth; cut into quarters. Peel the garlic and mince.
2. Sauté the pork, chicken, onions, and garlic in olive oil over medium heat in a large skillet until the meat is browned. Drain off grease and add mixture to the slow cooker. Combine beef broth, wine, and mustard in a medium-sized bowl and pour mixture into the slow cooker. Add mushrooms on top. Cover and cook on low setting for 8 to 9 hours.
3. About 30 minutes before serving, make a paste of the warm water and flour; add to the slow cooker, stirring well. Cook uncovered, stirring occasionally, until a gravy develops.

Top with chopped parsley right before serving.

Preparing Pearl Onions

When using pearl onions, cook them first in boiling water for 3 minutes. Plunge them into cold water. Remove them from the water and cut off the ends before easily removing the stems.

Chicken Peanut Stew

Cooking time: 4–6 hours
Preparation time: 15 minutes
Attention: Minimal
Pot size: 3–6 quarts
Serves 4

4 chicken breasts
1 green bell pepper
1 red bell pepper
2 medium-sized yellow onions
1 (6-ounce) can tomato paste
¾ cup crunchy peanut butter
3 cups chicken broth
1 teaspoon table salt
1 teaspoon chili powder
1 teaspoon sugar
½ teaspoon ground nutmeg

1. Remove the skin and bones from the chicken breasts and discard; cut the meat into 1-inch cubes. Remove the stems and seeds from the peppers and cut into ¼-inch rings. Peel the onions and cut into ¼-inch rings.
2. Combine all the ingredients in the slow cooker; stir until all the ingredients are well mingled. Cover and cook on low setting for 4 to 6 hours.

Sprinkle with chopped peanuts and flaked coconut before serving over freshly cooked rice.

Don't Eat Bay Leaves

Remember, bay leaves add lots of flavor, but you should always remove them before serving a dish. Bay leaves are sharp and dangerous to eat.

Stewed Mushrooms, Peppers, and Tomatoes

Cooking time: 8–9 hours

Preparation time: 20 minutes

Attention: Minimal

Pot size: 3–6 quarts

Serves 8

12 plum tomatoes
2 red bell peppers
2 yellow bell peppers
2 green bell peppers
2 large yellow onions
12 ounces (1½ cups) oyster mushrooms, quartered
6 garlic cloves
2 tablespoons olive oil
3 bay leaves
2 teaspoons dried basil
1 teaspoon salt
1 teaspoon ground black pepper

1. Chop the tomatoes into ½-inch pieces. Remove the stems and seeds from the peppers and cut into ¼-inch-thick strips. Peel the onions and cut into ¼-inch rings. Clean the mushrooms by wiping with a damp cloth; cut into fourths. Peel the garlic and cut into eighths.
2. Heat the olive oil in medium-sized skillet on medium heat. Add the peppers, onions, garlic, and mushrooms and sauté for 5 minutes. Drain off grease. Transfer the vegetables to the slow cooker. Add the spices and tomatoes; stir well. Cover and cook on low setting for 8 to 9 hours.

Serve this to complement Lean, Mean Meat Loaf (page 397).

Shrimp and Clam Stew with Tomatoes

Cooking time: 6–9 hours
Preparation time: 20 minutes
Attention: Minimal
Pot size: 4–8 quarts
Serves 6

½ pound small to medium shrimp
3 cups canned or shelled fresh
   clams
2 medium-sized yellow onions,
   chopped
4 medium-sized ripe tomatoes
2 medium-sized white potatoes
1 medium-sized green bell
   pepper

2 celery ribs
2 medium carrots
4 garlic cloves
1 tablespoon olive oil
1 cup tomato sauce
1 teaspoon dried thyme
½ teaspoon ground black pepper
1 tablespoon hot pepper sauce

1. Boil the shrimp for 10 minutes. Drain and rinse in cool water. Remove the shells and tails. Remove the black veins by running the tine of a fork along the back of each shrimp. If using fresh clams, remove the shells. Peel the onions and chop into ¼-inch pieces. Chop the tomatoes into ½-inch pieces. Peel the potatoes and chop into ½-inch pieces. Remove the seeds and stem from the green pepper and chop the pepper into ¼-inch pieces. Chop the celery into ¼-inch pieces. Peel and chop the carrot into ¼-inch rounds. Peel and mince the garlic.

2. Sauté the onion and garlic in olive oil in a large skillet on medium heat until the onion is translucent and limp. Add the tomatoes, potatoes, green pepper, celery, carrots, tomato sauce, thyme, pepper, and hot sauce; sauté for 5 minutes.

3. Transfer mixture to the slow cooker. Cover and cook on low setting for 6 to 8 hours. Add the shrimp and clams. Cover and cook on high setting for 30 additional minutes.

Chop one bunch of green onions into ¼-inch pieces, including the green stems, and sprinkle on top of the soup before serving with French bread..

CHAPTER 24
Beef

Beef Roast with Dried Fruit

Cooking time:	6–8 hours
Preparation time:	15 minutes
Attention:	Minimal
Pot size:	3–6 quarts
Serves 8	

2 medium-sized yellow onions
1 clove garlic
3–4 pound boneless pot roast
1½ cups mixed dried fruit
1½ cups dried apple rings
¾ cup pale ale
1 cup water
¼ cup packed brown sugar
1 bay leaf
¼ teaspoon ground cinnamon
2½ teaspoons salt
¼ teaspoon ground black pepper

1. Peel and slice the onions about ¼-inch thick. Peel and mince the garlic using a sharp kitchen knife.
2. Place the onions in bottom of the slow cooker. Place the roast on top. Cover with the mixed dried fruit. Mix together the beer, water, garlic, brown sugar, bay leaf, cinnamon, salt, and pepper; pour over the roast. Cover and cook on low setting 6–8 hours.

Remove the bay leaf and top with the apple rings before serving.

Sweetening with Soda

Substitute Coca-Cola® or 7-Up® for the liquid when making your next roast. The sugar adds a caramel-like texture while the flavors meld well with meat and vegetables.

Cajun Vegetable Beef Soup

Cooking time: 8–10
Preparation time: 30 minutes
Attention: Minimal
Pot size: 4–6 quarts
Serves 8

1½ pounds beef brisket
1½ cups chopped green onions
1 cup chopped celery
½ cup chopped fresh parsley
1 teaspoon fresh, chopped mint
1½ cups fresh green beans
3½ cups potatoes, chopped
1½ cups fresh tomatoes, chopped
2 cups fresh green bell pepper, chopped

3 cups turnips, chopped
3 garlic cloves
2 cups Brussels sprouts
1½ cups fresh corn
3½ cups dry white wine
16 cups water
2 tablespoons hot pepper sauce
1 tablespoon soy sauce
1 tablespoon salt

1. Cut the brisket into 1-inch cubes. Remove the roots and the first layer of peel from the onions. Chop the onions, celery, parsley, and mint into ½-inch pieces. Cut the stems off of green beans. Peel and cut the potatoes into ¼-inch-thick slices. Peel the tomatoes and cut into ½-inch pieces. Remove the seeds and stem from the green pepper and cut the green pepper into ¼-inch pieces. Peel the turnips and cut into ¼-inch pieces. Peel the garlic and mince with a sharp paring knife.
2. Combine all ingredients in the slow cooker. Cover and cook on low setting for 8 to 10 hours.

Corn Bread in the Round (page 366) is a must to make this an authentic Cajun dish.

Using Veggies in Converted Receipes

When using strong vegetables such as turnips and rutabaga, reduce the amount in an oven recipe to half for the slow cooker. The slow cooking tends to draw out these flavors, which can overpower the dish.

Grandma Opal's Vegetable Oxtail Soup

Cooking time: 6–8 hours

Preparation time: 20 minutes

Attention: Minimal

Pot size: 3–6 quarts

Serves 6

1 small yellow onion

1 cup carrots, diced

½ cup celery, diced

2 cups white potatoes, cubed

1 pound (16 ounces) canned tomatoes, liquid retained

2 turnips

2 pounds oxtail

2 quarts (8 cups) water

1 teaspoon salt

1 teaspoon celery salt

1 pound (16 ounces) canned whole kernel corn, liquid retained

1. Peel and chop the onion into ¼-inch pieces. Peel the carrots with a potato peeler and cut into ¼-inch pieces. Cut the celery into ¼-inch pieces. Peel the potatoes and cut into ½-inch pieces. Cut the tomatoes into ½-inch pieces, reserving the liquid. Peel and chop the turnips into ¼-inch pieces.
2. Place the meat bones, water, salts, onions, carrots, turnips, and celery in the slow cooker. Cover and cook on low setting for 5 to 6 hours. Take the oxtail out of the slow cooker and remove the meat from the bones; discard the bones and return the meat to the slow cooker. Add the potatoes, tomatoes, and corn, including the liquid from the corn and tomatoes. Cover and cook on low setting for 1 to 2 additional hours.

Slightly Seedy White Bread (page 374) is a good complement to this traditional soup.

Slow to Cook Veggies

Dense root vegetables such as potatoes, carrots, turnips, and rutabagas take longer to cook than meat or other vegetables. Cut them into small pieces and line them on the bottom and along the sides of the food crock to ensure they receive the most heat.

Cooking time: 7–8 hours
Preparation time: 20 minutes
Attention: Minimal
Pot size: 3–6 quarts
Serves 6

Porcupine Meatballs

½ cup chopped yellow onion
½ cup chopped green bell pepper
1½ cups lean ground beef
½ cup uncooked white rice
1 egg
1 teaspoon table salt
½ teaspoon ground black pepper
1 (10¾-ounce) can condensed tomato soup

1. Peel and chop the onion into ⅛-inch pieces. Remove the stem and seeds from the green pepper and chop into ⅛-inch pieces. In a mixing bowl, combine the ground beef, rice, onion, green pepper, egg, salt, and pepper; mix well with your hands until well blended.
2. Shape the mixture into about 24 golf ball–sized balls. Place in the slow cooker. Pour the soup over the meatballs. Cover and cook on low setting for 7 to 8 hours.

Serve with Brussels Sprouts à la Orange (page 549) for a complete meal.

Turkeyloaf?

For a lean alternative, substitute ground turkey for ground beef in your next meatball, chili or meatloaf recipe. It is less fatty and offers similar nutritional value.

Spicy Pot Roast

Cooking time: 8–10 hours

Preparation time: 15 minutes

Attention: Minimal

Pot size: 3–6 quarts

Serves 8

1 yellow onion
4 large white potatoes
4-pound pot roast
1 cup water
¼ cup dry white wine
¼ cup ketchup
2 teaspoons Dijon mustard
1 teaspoon Worcestershire sauce
1 package brown gravy mix
⅛ teaspoon garlic powder
¼ teaspoon ground black pepper
½ teaspoon table salt

1. Peel and chop the onion into ¼-inch pieces. Peel the potatoes and cut in half lengthwise.
2. Place all ingredients except the pot roast in the slow cooker; stir well. Add the pot roast. Cover and cook on low setting 8 to 10 hours.

Mix the liquid from the slow cooker with 2 tablespoons flour to create a luscious gravy.

Freezing Meat Dishes

When browning meat for a dish you plan to freeze, use little or no fat during the cooking process. Cooked, frozen fat can taint the flavor of the meat.

Lean, Mean Meat Loaf

Cooking time: 4–6 hours

Preparation time: 15 minutes

Attention: Minimal

Pot size: 3–6 quarts

Serves 6

2 cups cabbage, shredded
1 medium-sized white onion
1 green bell pepper
1 pound lean ground beef
½ teaspoon caraway seed
1 teaspoon table salt

1. Shred the cabbage into ¼-inch strips with a large kitchen knife. Peel and chop the onion into ¼-inch pieces. Remove the stem and seeds from the green pepper and chop the pepper into ¼-inch pieces.
2. Combine all ingredients in a mixing bowl. Shape into a round loaf. Place loaf on a meat rack or vegetable steamer in the slow cooker. Cook covered on high setting for 4 to 6 hours.

Drizzle Heinz 57 Sauce over the top of the meatloaf before serving for a spicy, tangy flavor.

Keep Meatloaf from Sticking

To keep meatloaf from sticking to the bottom of the slow cooker, place a slice of bacon on the bottom of the cooker before adding the meat mixture.

Slow-Cooked Sauerbraten

Cooking time: 5 hours

Preparation time: 15 minutes

Attention: Minimal

Pot size: 4–6 quarts

Serves 8

2 yellow onions
4-pound beef roast
½ teaspoon table salt
½ teaspoon ground black pepper
2 cups beef broth
⅓ cup brown sugar
⅓ cup cider vinegar
8 gingersnap cookies

1. Peel and chop the onions into 1-inch pieces. Sprinkle the beef roast with salt and pepper. Place the roast in the slow cooker. Add the onion, broth, brown sugar, and vinegar. Cover and cook on high setting for 5 hours.

2. Remove the roast from the slow cooker. Crumble gingersnap cookies and add to the sauce in the slow cooker. Stir slowly for about 10 minutes, or until the sauce thickens. Slice the meat and ladle the sauce over slices.

Serve with Heavy Brown Bread (page 375) for an authentic Bavarian meal.

Preventing Splatters

To keep hot fat from splattering when browning meat, sprinkle flour on the bottom of the skillet before adding the meat. You also can add water as the meat cooks.

A Dilly
of a Pot Roast

Cooking time: 8–10 hours

Preparation time: 20 minutes

Attention: Minimal

Pot size: 4–6 quarts

Serves 6

3-pound chuck roast

1 teaspoon table salt

½ teaspoon ground black pepper

2 teaspoons dried dill weed

¼ cup water

1 tablespoon vinegar

Sprinkle both sides of the meat with salt, pepper, and dill weed. Place the roast in the slow cooker. Pour water and vinegar over the top. Cover and cook on low setting for 8 to 10 hours.

This is excellent served with a sauce made of 1 cup sour cream and 2 teaspoons dill weed.

Cooking time: 8–10 hours

Preparation time: 10 minutes

Attention: Minimal

Pot size: 4–6 quarts

Serves 4

Sparkling Beef Tips

2-pound chuck roast

2 cups fresh mushrooms, sliced

1 (10¾-ounce) can cream of mushroom condensed soup

1 envelope dry onion soup mix

1 cup lemon-lime carbonated drink.

Cut the meat into 1-inch cubes, trimming off the fat as you go. Clean the mushrooms by wiping with a damp cloth; slice ⅛-inch thick. Add all ingredients to the slow cooker; mix well. Cook covered on low setting for 8 to 10 hours.

Serve with Sweet Potato and Apple Bake (page 564) for a good mix of flavors.

Beef Bourguignon

Cooking time: 8–10 hours

Preparation time: 20 minutes

Attention: Minimal

Slow cooker size: 4–6 quarts

Serves 4

2-pound chuck roast
1½ tablespoons flour
4 large yellow onions
1 cup fresh mushrooms, sliced
1 teaspoon table salt
¼ teaspoon dried marjoram
¼ teaspoon dried thyme
¼ teaspoon ground black pepper
1 cup beef broth
1 cup burgundy wine

1. Cut the meat into 1-inch cubes, trimming off the fat as you go. Dredge the meat in flour by pressing the chunks firmly into a bowl containing the flour. Peel and slice the onions into ¼-inch rings. Wash the mushrooms by wiping with a damp cloth; slice ⅛-inch thick.
2. Add all ingredients to the slow cooker. Cover and cook on low setting for 8 to 10 hours.

Serve over wide egg noodles with a side of Cheesy Cauliflower (page 574) for a complete meal.

Cooking time: 8–10 hours

Preparation time: 20 minutes

Attention: Minimal

Pot size: 4–8 quarts

Serves 8

Hungarian Goulash

2 pounds round steak

½ teaspoon onion powder

½ teaspoon garlic powder

½ teaspoon table salt

½ teaspoon ground black pepper

1½ teaspoon paprika

2 tablespoons flour

1 (10¾-ounce) can condensed tomato soup

½ cup water

1 cup sour cream

1. Cut the steak into 1-inch cubes. Mix the meat, onion powder, garlic powder, salt, pepper, paprika, and flour together until meat is well coated. Place in the slow cooker. Pour soup and water over the top. Cover and cook on low setting for 8 to 10 hours.
2. About a half-hour before serving, stir in the sour cream. Cover and cook on low setting.

Serve over cooked elbow macaroni for an authentic look.

Low-Fat Dairy Substitutions

Substitute low-fat sour cream, cream cheese, and hard cheeses for their regular counterparts in any recipe. However, do not substitute fat-free milk products unless the recipe says you can. A certain amount of fat is needed for the milk product to melt correctly in most dishes.

Beefy Spanish Rice

Cooking time: 8–10 hours

Preparation time: 20 minutes

Attention: Minimal

Pot size: 3–6 quarts

Serves 8

1 pound lean ground beef
1 medium-sized yellow onion
1 red bell pepper
1 cup tomato sauce
1 cup water
1 teaspoon chili powder
2 teaspoons Worcestershire sauce
1 cup raw white rice

1. Brown the ground beef in a medium-sized skillet on medium-high heat. Drain off fat and spread the meat on paper towels to soak up more fat. Peel the onion and chop into ¼-inch pieces. Remove the stem and seeds from the red pepper and chop into ¼-inch pieces.
2. Combine all ingredients in the slow cooker. Cover and cook on low setting for 8 to 10 hours.

Serve as a complement to Wisconsin Cheesy Beer Soup (page 330) for a hearty, flavorful meal.

Browning Meat for Recipes

The best way is to brown your meat before placing it in the slow cooker. Simply sauté it in a small amount of oil at a medium-high heat until the surface of the meat is brown. The slow cooker will do the rest.

Japanese Pepper Steak

1 pound steak
2 garlic cloves
1 green bell pepper
1 cup fresh mushrooms, sliced
1 medium-sized white onion

3 tablespoons soy sauce
1 teaspoon ground ginger **or** 2 teaspoons fresh, minced ginger
½ teaspoon crushed, dried red pepper

1. Slice the steak about ½-inch thick. Peel the garlic and mince with a sharp kitchen knife. Remove the stem and seeds from the green pepper and slice lengthwise into ¼-inch strips. Wash the mushrooms by wiping with a damp cloth; slice paper-thin. Peel the onion and slice into ¼-inch-thick rings.
2. Combine all the ingredients in the slow cooker; stir well. Cover and cook on low setting for 6 to 8 hours.

Serve over cellophane noodles for an authentic taste.

Beef Chop Suey

3 pounds flank steak
½ cup chopped celery
1 cup chopped bok choy
1 small chopped onion
½ cup water

2 tablespoons dark soy sauce
1½ tablespoon dark molasses
1 teaspoon hot sauce
1 tablespoon flour
2 tablespoons water

Combine all the ingredients except the flour and 2 tablespoons water in the slow cooker; mix well. Cook on high for 4 to 5 hours. Combine the flour and water, and add mixture to the contents of the slow cooker; stir until thick.

Serve over white rice and sprinkle with sesame seeds.

Vietnamese Sweet-and-Sour Beef

Cooking time: 8–9 hours

Preparation time: 20 minutes

Attention: Minimal

Pot size: 3–6 quarts

Serves 4

2 pounds round steak
2 cups carrots, sliced
2 cups pearl onions
1 medium-sized green bell pepper
2 large ripe tomatoes
2 tablespoons oil
2 (8-ounce) cans tomato sauce
⅓ cup vinegar
½ cup light molasses
1 teaspoon paprika
¼ cup sugar
1 teaspoon table salt

1. Cut the beef into 1-inch pieces. Peel the carrots and cut into ¼-inch-thick rounds. Remove the peels from the onions. Remove the stem and seeds from the green pepper and cut lengthwise into ¼-inch strips. Cut the tomatoes into 1-inch pieces.
2. Place the oil and steak in a skillet. Cook on medium-high heat until the meat is brown, stirring occasionally. Place this and all other ingredients in the slow cooker; stir so ingredients are mingled. Cover and cook on low setting 8 to 9 hours.

Serve with sliced cabbage in a vinegar and oil dressing.

CHAPTER 25
Poultry

Peachy Georgia Chicken Legs

Cooking time: 5 hours
Preparation time: 30 minutes
Attention: Minimal
Pot size: 4–6 quarts
Serves 4

4 ripe peaches
8 chicken drum sticks
1 cup dried prunes

3 tablespoons water
1 tablespoon sugar
salt and pepper to taste

Peel the peaches; cut into 1-inch pieces, removing and discarding the pits. Place chicken drum sticks in the slow cooker. Stir together the peaches, prunes, water, sugar, salt, and pepper in a small bowl; pour mixture over the chicken. Cover and cook for 5 hours on the high setting.

Serve with a fresh green salad.

Barbecued Chicken and Beans Casserole

Cooking time: 8–10 hours
Preparation time: 10 minutes
Attention: Minimal
Pot size: 3–6 quarts
Serves 4

2 cups (16 ounces) canned pork
    and beans
3-pound chicken, cut into serving
    pieces
¼ cup ketchup

2 tablespoons peach marmalade
2 teaspoons dried minced onion
¼ teaspoon soy sauce
¼ cup brown sugar

Place the beans in the slow cooker. Add the chicken pieces on top of the beans; do not stir. Mix the ketchup, marmalade, onion, soy sauce, and brown sugar in a small mixing bowl.; pour mixture over the top of the chicken. Cover and cook on low setting for 8 to 10 hours.

Serve with Orange-Glazed Vegetable Medley (page 567).

Cooking time: 6 hours

Preparation time: 45 minutes

Attention: Medium

Pot size: 4–6 quarts

Heroic Chicken Livers

Serves 4

1 pound chicken livers

¼ pound lean, thick-cut bacon

1 teaspoon whole black peppercorns

1 large leek

½ pound (1 cup) mushrooms, sliced

½ cup flour

1 teaspoon table salt

1 cup chicken broth

1 (10¾-ounce) can golden mushroom condensed soup

¼ cup dry white wine

1. Cut the chicken livers into ½- inch pieces. Cut the bacon into 1-inch pieces. Wrap the whole peppercorns in paper towels; smash the peppercorns with a hammer. Cut the top and roots off the leek, discard them, and thoroughly wash the leek; Chop coarsely. Clean the mushrooms by wiping individually with a moistened paper towel; slice the mushrooms paper-thin.

2. Fry the bacon in a large skillet on medium heat Remove the bacon from the skillet when the bacon is crispy; set the bacon aside and retain the grease in the skillet. Mix together the flour, salt, and pepper. Coat the chicken livers in the flour mixture. Cook the livers in the bacon drippings until golden brown. Remove the chicken livers from the skillet with a slotted spoon and place them in the slow cooker. Place the bacon on top of the chicken livers. Pour the chicken broth into the skillet, mixing to combine with the grease; pour mixture over the chicken livers and bacon. Add the golden mushroom soup, leeks, mushrooms, and wine. Cover and cook on low for 6 hours.

This delicate-tasting dish is best served over thick egg noodles.

Dilled Turkey Breast

Cooking time: 7–9 hours

Preparation time: 30 minutes

Attention: Minimal

Pot size: 8 quart

Serves 8

1 boneless turkey breast
1 teaspoon table salt
½ teaspoon ground pepper
2 teaspoons dill weed, plus extra for garnish
¼ cup water
1 tablespoon red wine vinegar
3 tablespoons flour
1 cup sour cream

1. Sprinkle the turkey breast with salt, pepper, and half of the dill; place in the slow cooker. Add water and vinegar. Cover and cook on low for 7 to 9 hours or until tender.
2. Remove the turkey breast. Turn the slow cooker to high. Dissolve the flour in a small amount of water and stir into the meat drippings in the cooker. Add the remaining dill. Cook on high until the sauce thickens. Turn off heat. Stir in the sour cream.

Slice the turkey breast and drizzle with the sauce before serving. Sprinkle with additional dill weed.

Leftovers Reminder

When you make a turkey or pot roast, cut the leftovers into bite-size chunks and store in the freezer for next week's slow cooker recipe.

Chicken Breast with Mushrooms and Peas

Cooking time: 6–8 hours	
Preparation time: 20 minutes	
Attention: Medium	
Pot size: 2–6 quarts	
Serves 2	

1 small white onion
12 ounces fresh sliced mushrooms
2 tablespoons minced green onion
2 boneless, skinless chicken breasts
3 tablespoons flour
¼ teaspoon ground tarragon
¼ teaspoon salt
½ teaspoon pepper
1 cup milk
½ cup fresh or frozen peas

1. Peel the onion and slice ¼-inch thick. Clean the mushrooms by wiping with a damp cloth; slice paper-thin. Remove the roots and the first layer of peel from the green onions and mince the onions, including the green stems. Place the chicken breasts on the bottom of the slow cooker, then layer the onions, green onions, and mushrooms on top of the chicken breasts. Cook covered on low heat for 4 hours.
2. After the 4 hours are up, blend the flour, tarragon, salt, pepper, and milk by stirring slowly. Pour mixture over the chicken. Add the peas.
3. Cook covered on low setting 2 to 4 hours, until thick, stirring occasionally.

Serve with fresh orange and apple slices.

The Skinny on Skin

Nearly all of the fat in a chicken comes from its skin. You can buy pre-skinned chicken breasts in the grocery store but it's simple to peel the skin off yourself before cooking. (This is also cheaper!) Choose white meat over dark for the leanest meal.

Orange Chicken

Cooking time: 8–9 hours
Preparation time: 30 minutes
Attention: Minimal
Pot size: 4–6 quarts
Serves 6

3 pounds chicken breasts
2 garlic cloves
2 tablespoons diced green pepper
3 medium oranges
1 cup orange juice
⅓ cup chili sauce
2 tablespoons soy sauce
1 tablespoon molasses
1 teaspoon dry mustard
½ teaspoon table salt

1. Remove the skin from the chicken breasts. Peel the garlic and mince with a sharp kitchen knife. Remove the stem and seeds from the green pepper and chop into ¼-inch pieces. Remove the peels from the oranges and separate oranges into slices.
2. Place the chicken breasts in the bottom of the slow cooker. Combine the orange juice, chili sauce, soy sauce, molasses, dry mustard, garlic, and salt in a medium-sized bowl; mix well. Cover and cook on low setting for 8 to 9 hours.
3. Thirty minutes before serving, add the oranges and green pepper to the slow cooker; stir well. Cover and cook on low for the remaining 30 minutes.

Serve over white rice for a light-tasting meal.

To Avoid Splashing Messes

Always add the liquid ingredients last to avoid splashing. You also will have a better idea how much food your meal is going to make by seeing it in "dry" form before cooking.

Cranberry Barbecued Chicken

Cooking time: 6–8 hours
Preparation time: 10 minutes
Attention: Minimal
Pot size: 3–6 quarts
Serves 4

3 pounds chicken breasts
½ teaspoon table salt
½ teaspoon ground black pepper
2 celery ribs, chopped
1 cup barbecue sauce

1 medium-sized yellow onion, chopped
2 cups whole berry cranberry sauce

Remove the skin from the chicken breasts and place the meat in the bottom of the slow cooker. Cover with remaining ingredients. Cover slow cooker and cook on low setting for 6 to 8 hours.

Serve with Cheesy Cauliflower (page 574) for a nice mix of flavors.

Easy Italian Chicken Legs

Cooking time: 8–10 hours
Preparation time: 10 minutes
Attention: Minimal
Pot size: 3–6 quarts
Serves 4

3 pounds chicken legs
1 package dry Italian dressing mix

1 (12-ounce) can or bottle beer, a lager or pilsner is best

Remove the skin from the chicken legs and place the chicken in the slow cooker. Mix the beer with the Italian dressing mix in a medium-sized bowl; pour over the chicken legs. Cook covered on low setting 8 to 10 hours.

Remove the meat from the bones and serve on hard rolls.

Mandarin Chicken Breasts

Cooking time: 6–8 hours

Preparation time: 20 minutes

Attention: Minimal

Pot size: 3–6 quarts

Serves 4

3 pounds chicken breasts
1 medium-sized red bell pepper
1 yellow onion
½ cup chicken broth
½ cup orange juice
½ cup ketchup
2 tablespoons soy sauce

1 tablespoon light molasses
1 tablespoon prepared mustard
½ teaspoon garlic salt
1 cup fresh or frozen peas
1 (11-ounce) can mandarin
　oranges
2 teaspoons flour

1. Remove the skin from the chicken and discard. Remove the stem and seeds from red pepper and cut into ¼-inch strips. Peel the onion and cut into ¼-inch pieces.
2. Place the chicken in the slow cooker. Combine the broth, juice, ketchup, soy sauce molasses, mustard, and garlic salt in a medium-sized mixing bowl; stir until well combined. Pour mixture over the chicken. Add the onions, peas, and green peppers. Cover and cook on low setting for 6 to 8 hours.
3. Thirty minutes before serving, remove the chicken and vegetables from the slow cooker. Measure one cup of liquid from the slow cooker and place it in a saucepan. Discard the remaining liquid. Bring the liquid in the saucepan to a boil. Drain the oranges, retaining 1 tablespoon of the drained juice; mix this juice with the flour. Add mixture to the boiling liquid. Stir in the oranges.
4. Put the chicken and vegetables back into the slow cooker. Pour the orange sauce over the chicken. Cover and cook on low setting for the remaining 30 minutes.

Sprinkle with sesame seeds or chop 4 green onions into ½-inch pieces and sprinkle on top of the chicken before serving.

Tropical Chicken

Cooking time: 7–9 hours

Preparation time: 10 minutes

Attention: Minimal

Pot size: 3–6 quarts

Serves 6

3 pounds chicken breasts
¼ cup molasses
2 tablespoons Worcestershire sauce
2 teaspoons Dijon mustard
¼ teaspoon hot pepper sauce
2 tablespoons pineapple juice
¼ cup dried coconut

1. Remove the skin and bones from the chicken breasts and discard.
2. Combine the molasses, Worcestershire sauce, mustard, hot pepper sauce, and pineapple juice in a small mixing bowl.
3. Brush mixture on both sides of the chicken breasts using a pastry brush. Cover and cook on low setting for 7 to 9 hours.
4. Sprinkle with coconut before serving.

Serve with a medley of fresh tropical fruits: kiwi, papaya, banana, and guava, for example.

Money-Saving Tip

Buy a roasting or stewing chicken for the best value. They are usually bigger, older chickens so the meat is slightly tougher than a broiler-fryer. However, the slow cooking process makes the meat tender and flavorful.

Chicken Fajitas

Cooking time: 6–8 hours

Preparation time: 20 minutes

Attention: Minimal

Pot size: 3–6 quarts

Serves 4

1 pound chicken breasts
1 medium-sized yellow onion
2 garlic cloves
1 green bell pepper
1 red bell pepper
2 tablespoons lime juice
½ teaspoon oregano
½ teaspoon ground cumin
½ teaspoon chili powder
½ teaspoon ground black pepper

1. Remove the bones and skin from the chicken breasts and cut into ½-inch-wide strips. Peel the onion and cut into ¼-inch-thick rings; put the onion in the slow cooker. Peel the garlic and mince with a sharp kitchen knife. Remove the stems and seeds from the green and red peppers and cut into ¼-inch-wide strips.
2. Combine the garlic, lime juice, oregano, cumin, chili powder, and black pepper in a medium-sized mixing bowl. Add the chicken and toss well to coat. Pour the chicken and juice mixture over the onion. Cover and cook on low setting for 6 to 8 hours. About 30 minutes before serving, stir in the green and red pepper strips; continue cooking, covered, on low for the remaining 30 minutes.

Spoon onto warm flour tortillas and top with chopped tomato, sour cream, grated Colby cheese, and guacamole.

Chicken with Black Olives and Artichokes

Cooking time: 5–6 hours

Preparation time: 20 minutes

Attention: Minimal

Pot size: 3–6 quarts

Serves 6

6 chicken breasts
1 medium-sized white onion
6 garlic cloves
1 cup dry white wine
2 cups chicken broth
2 cups water
1 cup canned, sliced black olives, including juice
1 cup canned artichoke hearts, including juice, cut up
1 cup dry shell macaroni
1 envelop dry onion soup mix

1. Remove the bones and skin from the chicken breasts and discard. Peel the onion and slice into ¼-inch-thick rings. Peel the garlic and mince with a sharp kitchen knife.
2. Put the chicken in the slow cooker; top with onion. Combine the wine, broth, water, black olives, artichoke hearts, garlic, and macaroni in a medium-sized mixing bowl; pour mixture over the chicken and onions. Sprinkle the onion soup mix on top. Cover and cook on low setting for 5 to 6 hours.

Serve with Cheddar and Onion Bread (page 371).

Cooking with Rabbit

Rabbit is an excellent meat for slow cooked meals. It is extremely lean and tends to dry out quickly when cooked in an oven or stovetop. Substitute it for pork or chicken in virtually any recipe.

Chicken Cacciatore

Cooking time: 8–10 hours

Preparation time: 25 minutes

Attention: Minimal

Pot size: 3–8 quarts

Serves 4

3 pounds chicken
3 garlic cloves
1 cup fresh mushrooms, quartered
1 medium-sized yellow onion
1 cup sliced black olives
¼ cup flour
2 tablespoons olive oil
6 cups tomato juice
1 (12-ounce) can tomato paste
2 tablespoons dried parsley
2 tablespoons sugar
2 teaspoons table salt
1 tablespoon dried oregano
½ teaspoon dried thyme
1 bay leaf

1. Cut the chicken into serving-sized pieces. Peel the garlic and mince using a sharp kitchen knife. Clean the mushrooms by wiping with a damp cloth and slice into quarters. Peel the onion and slice into ¼-inch-thick rings. Drain the black olives.
2. Place the flour and chicken in a plastic bag and shake to coat. Heat the olive oil in a medium-sized skillet on medium-high heat and brown the chicken. Transfer the chicken to the slow cooker. Combine the remaining ingredients in a medium-sized mixing bowl and pour over the chicken. Cover and cook on low setting for 8 to 10 hours.

Serve over hot spaghetti noodles for an authentic Italian meal.

Cooking time: 6–7 hours
Preparation time: 15 minutes
Attention: Minimal
Pot size: 3–6 quarts
Serves 4

Chicken à la King

4 chicken breasts
1 medium-sized white onion
1 (10¾-ounce) can cream of chicken condensed soup
3 tablespoons flour
½ teaspoon ground black pepper
1 cup fresh or canned peas
2 tablespoons chopped pimientos
½ teaspoon paprika

1. Remove the bones and skin from the chicken breasts and discard. Cut the chicken into 1-inch cubes; place in the slow cooker. Peel the onion and chop into ¼-inch pieces
2. Combine the soup, flour, and pepper in a medium-sized mixing bowl; pour mixture over chicken. Cover and cook on low setting for 5 to 6 hours. Stir in the peas, onions, pimientos, and paprika. Cover and cook on low setting for 1 additional hour.

Cut thick slices of Heavy Brown Bread (page 375) and ladle Chicken à la King over them.

Is the Low Setting Hot Enough to Be Safe?

When set on low, the slow cooker is roughly equivalent to 200 degrees Fahrenheit. The high setting is about 350 degrees Fahrenheit. Meat cooked to 160 degrees is safe from bacteria.

Nebraskan Creamed Chicken Soup

1 cup chicken, cubed
2 celery ribs
4 medium carrots
1 medium-sized white onion
1 small zucchini
½ cup (4 ounces) canned pimientos, diced
1 cup fresh peas
1 cup fresh sweet corn
½ cup uncooked rice
3 cups chicken broth
2 cups prepared Alfredo sauce

1. Chop the chicken into ½-inch pieces. Slice the celery ribs into ¼-inch pieces. Peel and slice the carrots into ¼-inch rounds. Peel and slice the onion into ¼-inch pieces. Chop the zucchini into ½-inch pieces. Dice the pimientos into ¼-inch pieces.
2. Add all ingredients except the Alfredo sauce to the slow cooker; stir gently. Cover and cook on low setting for 8 to 10 hours. A half-hour before serving, stir in the Alfredo sauce. Cover and continue cooking on low.

Serve with fresh fruit for a completely balanced meal.

Bulgur Wheat

Bulgur is a crunchy, nutty wheat grain that can be substituted for rice or pasta in most dishes. To prepare, just pour boiling water over the bulgur and let it sit until the liquid is absorbed.

CHAPTER 26
Pork

Salt Pork in Mustard Greens

Cooking time: 6–8 hours
Preparation time: 20 minutes
Attention: Minimal
Pot size: 3–6 quarts
Serves 4

1 pound salt pork
2 large white onions
4 garlic cloves
4 large bunches mustard greens
6 cups water
1 cup dry white wine
1 tablespoon jalapeño pepper sauce
2 tablespoons soy sauce
1 teaspoon table salt

1. Cut the salt pork into 1-inch pieces. Remove the peel and cut the onions into ¼-inch-thick slices. Peel the garlic and mince with a sharp paring knife. Wash the mustard greens and tear into 2-inch pieces.
2. Mix the water and wine in a separate bowl. Sauté the meat, onions, and garlic in ½ cup of the water and wine mixture in a large skillet on medium-high heat until the onions are limp and transparent. Put all the ingredients in the slow cooker. Cover and cook on low setting for 6 to 8 hours.

Serve with Sweet Potato and Apple Bake (page 564) for a complete meal.

Cooking with Lamb
Lamb is underused in North America yet it has a wonderful flavor. Substitute it for pork in your next slow cooker recipe for an unexpected treat.

Prosciutto, Walnut, and Olive Pasta Sauce

Cooking time: 6–8 hours
Preparation time: 25 minutes
Attention: Minimal
Pot size: 3–6 quarts
Serves 4

½ pound thin-sliced prosciutto
1 red bell pepper
3 garlic cloves
¼ cup olive oil, divided in half
1 cup chopped walnuts
½ cup chopped fresh parsley
¼ cup chopped fresh basil
½ cup chopped black olives, drained

1. Cut the prosciutto into ½-inch pieces. Remove the stem and seeds from the red pepper; cut into ¼-inch strips. Brush the pepper strips with half of the olive oil and bake in a 350-degree oven for 1 hour. Peel and mince the garlic with a sharp kitchen knife. Chop the walnuts, parsley, basil, and olives into ¼-inch pieces.
2. Put the remaining olive oil in a medium-sized skillet and sauté the garlic on medium-high heat until the garlic is brown. Remove and set aside the garlic so it doesn't burn. Add the prosciutto and sauté until crisp. Add the walnuts and sauté until they are brown. Add the cooked garlic
3. Put all ingredients in the slow cooker; stir until well mixed. Cover and cook on low setting for 6 to 8 hours.

Serve over spinach linguine noodles with a side of garlic toast.

Stale Bread
Looking for a different substitute for rice or noodles? Try serving your next dish over a slice of stale bread. Fresh bread gets mushy when it gets wet but stale bread holds up well to being the base of a meal.

Ham and Asparagus Roll-ups

Cooking time: 6–8 hours

Preparation time: 10 minutes

Attention: Minimal

Pot size: 2–6 quarts

Serves 6

12 thin slices ham
24 fresh asparagus spears
12 slices Swiss cheese
1 teaspoon garlic salt
½ cup chicken broth

1. Lay the ham slices flat on a cutting board. Top each with two asparagus spears. Sprinkle with garlic salt. Top each with a slice of Swiss cheese. Roll up so that the asparagus spears stick out of both ends.
2. Put the chicken broth in the slow cooker. Add the ham roll-ups. Cover and cook on low setting for 6 to 8 hours, or until asparagus is soft but not mushy.

Garlic bread and pickled vegetables are the perfect complement to this dish.

The Other White Meat

Although pork is not really "the other white meat," today's pigs are not fat. In fact, pork tends to be leaner than beef. Substitute pork for beef in any recipe but remember to remove the fat from around the edges.

Ham Sandwiches

Cooking time: 8–10 hours

Preparation time: 10 minutes

Attention: Minimal

Pot size: 2–4 quarts

Serves 8

2 pounds ham, cut into slices　　*1 cup brown sugar*
2 cups apple juice　　　　　　 *2 teaspoons Dijon mustard*

Combine the apple juice, brown sugar, and mustard. Put the ham in the bottom of the slow cooker and pour the liquid mixture over the top. Cover and cook on low setting for 8 to 10 hours. Remove the ham and discard the juice.

Make the sandwiches using Heavy Brown Bread (page 375) and Swiss cheese.

Cherry Pork Chops

Cooking time: 4–5 hours

Preparation time: 15 minutes

Attention: Minimal

Pot size: 4–6 quarts

Serves 6

6 pork chops　　　　　　　　　 *1 (21-ounce) can cherry pie filling*
½ teaspoon table salt　　　　　 *1 chicken bouillon cube*
½ teaspoon ground black pepper　 *2 teaspoons lemon juice*

1. Place the pork chops in a large skillet on the stove. Brown on medium-high heat for 5 minutes. Sprinkle with salt and pepper.
2. Mix half of the can of cherry pie filling, the crushed bouillon cube, and the lemon juice in the slow cooker. Place the pork chops on top of mixture. Cover and cook on low setting for 4 to 5 hours.

Heat the remaining half of the cherry pie filling and ladle it onto the pork chops before serving.

Roast Pork with Ginger and Cashew Stuffing

Cooking time: 8–10 hours

Preparation time: 30 minutes

Attention: Minimal

Pot size: 3–6 quarts

Serves 8

¾ cup yellow onion, diced
1½ teaspoons fresh ginger, grated
1 cup cashews, chopped
1 teaspoon orange rind, grated
3 tablespoons parsley, chopped
2 eggs
2 tablespoons butter
4 cups corn bread crumbs
1 teaspoon table salt
1 teaspoon ground black pepper
6-pound pork roast

1. Peel and chop the onion into ¼-inch pieces. Grate the ginger finely with a vegetable grater. Chop the cashews into ¼-inch pieces. Grate the orange rind without peeling the orange. Chop the parsley into ⅛-inch pieces. Lightly beat the eggs with a fork until yolk and whites are well integrated.
2. Melt the butter in a large frying pan on the stove at medium heat. Add the onions, cashews, and ginger and cook for five minutes, stirring. Transfer to the slow cooker and add orange rind, parsley, bread crumbs, salt, pepper, and eggs. Stir well so that all the ingredients are well mixed.
3. Push the stuffing to the sides of the slow cooker and place the pork roast in the pocket. Cook covered on low setting for 8 to 10 hours.

This is a wonderful winter meal when served with Squash Medley Au Gratin (page 568).

Pork Pisole

Cooking time: 5–6 hours
Preparation time: 20 minutes
Attention: Minimal
Pot size: 3–6 quarts
Serves 4

2 pounds pork chops
1 large white onion
1 garlic clove
4 ripe, fresh tomatoes
1 15-ounce can white hominy
1 15-ounce can yellow hominy
2 teaspoons chili powder
1 teaspoon table salt
½ teaspoon thyme

1. Debone the pork chops and cut the meat into 1-inch cubes. Peel and chop the onion into ¼-inch pieces. Peel and mince the garlic using a sharp paring knife. Place the pork in a large skillet on medium-high heat and cook until brown, about 5 minutes (you may need to add a bit of oil if using very lean pork). Add the onion and garlic; turn the heat down to medium and sauté for 5 more minutes.
2. Chop the tomatoes into 1-inch pieces. Combine the pork, onion, garlic, tomatoes, hominy, and spices in the slow cooker. Cook covered on low setting for 5 to 6 hours.

To complement the flavors in this dish, serve it with a salad of field greens with a red wine vinegar dressing.

Save Time
If you don't have a lot of time for food preparation, buy boneless pork chops instead. Many grocery stores now carry pork that is cut into stir-fry strips; these are also a great substitution.

Fall Is in the Air Pork Roast

Cooking time: 8–10 hours

Preparation time: 15 minutes

Attention: Minimal

Pot size: 4–6 quarts

Serves 8

1 cup diced fresh cranberries
1 teaspoon grated orange peel
4-pound pork roast
1 teaspoon table salt

1 teaspoon ground black pepper
¼ cup honey
⅛ teaspoon ground cloves
⅛ teaspoon ground nutmeg

1. Chop the cranberries into ¼-inch pieces. Grate the orange peel while still on the orange by rubbing it over a vegetable grater.
2. Place the pork roast in the slow cooker. Sprinkle with salt and pepper. Combine the cranberries, orange peel, honey, cloves, and nutmeg; mix well. Pour mixture over the pork roast. Cover and cook on low setting for 8 to 10 hours.

Serve with fresh green beans and Dilly Mashed Potatoes (page 573).

Bavarian Pork Chops

Cooking time: 7–8 hours

Preparation time: 15 minutes

Attention: Minimal

Pot size: 3–6 quarts

Serves 6

6 pork chops
2 cups sauerkraut
¼ cup brown sugar

1 envelope dry onion soup mix
1 teaspoon caraway seeds
½ cup water

Place the pork chops in the slow cooker. Drain sauerkraut. Combine the sauerkraut, brown sugar, onion soup mix, caraway seeds, and water in a medium-sized bowl; pour mixture over the pork chops. Cover and cook on low setting for 7 to 8 hours.

Serve with Orange-Glazed Vegetable Medley (page 567).

Peachy Keen Pork Chops

Cooking time: 4–6 hours

Preparation time: 15 minutes

Attention: Minimal

Pot size: 3–6 quarts

Serves 6

6 pork chops
1 teaspoon table salt
½ teaspoon ground black pepper
1 (29-ounce) can peach halves in syrup
¼ cup syrup from peaches
¼ cup brown sugar
¼ teaspoon ground cinnamon
¼ teaspoon ground cloves
1 (8-ounce) can tomato sauce
¼ cup vinegar

1. Place the pork chops in a large skillet on the stove; sprinkle with salt and pepper. Brown for 5 minutes at medium-high heat. Drain off the fat and place the pork chops in the slow cooker. Place the drained peach halves on top of the pork chops.
2. Combine the ¼ cup of syrup from the peaches, the brown sugar, cinnamon, cloves, tomato sauce, and vinegar; pour mixture over the peaches and pork chops. Cover and cook on low setting for 4 to 6 hours.

Offset the sweet taste of this meal by serving it with pickled cauliflower and beets.

The Importance of Texture

To add variety to frequently made dishes, try experimenting with both chunky and smooth kinds of tomato sauce. The change in texture will keep the meal interesting and new.

German-Style
Ham Hocks

Cooking time: 8–10 hours

Preparation time: 15 minutes

Attention: Minimal

Pot size: 3–6 quarts

Serves 4

4 smoked ham hocks
2 cans (15-ounce) sauerkraut,
   liquid retained

4 large white potatoes, peeled
   and quartered
½ teaspoon ground black pepper

Place all the ingredients in the slow cooker including the liquid from the canned sauerkraut. Cover and cook on low setting for 8 to 10 hours. Remove the ham hocks and take the meat off the bones. Discard the bones and return the meat to the slow cooker.

A traditional German meal calls for baked beans and brown beer with this dish.

Cooking time: 7–8 hours

Preparation time: 20 minutes

Attention: Minimal

Pot size: 3–6 quarts

Serves 6

Blueberry Pork Roast

3-pound pork loin
1 teaspoon grated orange peel
2 cups fresh blueberries

½ cup white grape juice
½ cup sugar
1 teaspoon table salt

Place the pork loin in the slow cooker. Grate the orange peel using a vegetable grater. Wash the blueberries and remove the stems. Combine the grape juice, sugar, orange peel, blueberries, and salt; pour mixture over the pork loin. Cover and cook on low setting for 7 to 8 hours.

Complement the sweet flavor of this dish by serving it with Garlicky Spinach and Swiss Chard (page 565).

Cooking time: 7–8 hours

Preparation time: 15 minutes

Attention: Minimal

Pot size: 3–6 quarts

Serves 6

Teriyaki Pork Tips

3-pound boneless pork loin roast
¾ cup unsweetened apple juice
2 tablespoons sugar
2 tablespoons soy sauce
1 tablespoon vinegar
1 teaspoon ground ginger
½ teaspoon garlic powder
½ teaspoon ground black pepper
2 tablespoons flour
2 tablespoons water

1. Cut the pork roast into 1-inch cubes and place in the slow cooker. Combine the apple juice, sugar, soy sauce, vinegar, ginger, garlic powder, and pepper in a medium-sized mixing bowl; pour mixture over the meat and stir well. Cover and cook on low setting for 7 to 8 hours.

2. A half-hour before serving, make a paste of the flour and water and add the mixture to the slow cooker. Stir well so that there are no lumps of flour. Cook uncovered on high setting for 20 to 30 minutes, stirring frequently.

Serve with Lemony Asparagus and Carrots (page 565).

CHAPTER 27
Wild Game

Cabbage on Pheasant

Cooking time: 6 hours
Preparation time: 30 minutes
Attention: Minimal
Pot size: 6–8 quarts
Serves 6

1 pheasant
2 pieces bacon
1 teaspoon ground black pepper
1 medium-sized yellow onion
1 carrot
1 cup hot water
1 medium head red cabbage

1. Cut the pheasant into quarters; brown the pheasant in a medium-sized saucepan with two pieces of bacon. Peel the onion and chop into ¼-inch pieces. Peel and cut the carrot into ¼-inch rounds. Place the pheasant in the slow cooker. Cover with water, onions, and carrots. Sprinkle with pepper. Cook for 5 hours on low setting.
2. Shred the cabbage into ¼-inch-wide pieces. Place the cabbage over the pheasant and cook for 1 additional hour.

Serve with Minnesota Wild Rice (page 571) as the perfect complement.

Can't Find a Pheasant?

Can't find pheasant or partridge in your grocery store and don't have a bird hunter in your family? Substitute readily available game hens. Thaw them completely before stuffing or adding to the slow cooker.

Rabbit Stuffed with Garlic Mashed Potatoes

Cooking time: 8–9 hours
Preparation time: 1 hour
Attention: Medium
Pot size: 6–8 quarts
Serves 6

4 large potatoes
6 cloves garlic
1 tablespoon vegetable oil
2 tablespoons butter
½ teaspoon ground black pepper
1 whole rabbit, cleaned

1. Clean, peel, and cut the potatoes into eighths; boil the potatoes in a medium-sized pot until tender.
2. While the potatoes are cooking, peel and chop the garlic into ¼-inch pieces. Sauté the garlic in the vegetable oil on low heat in a small skillet until lightly golden.
3. Drain the potatoes and add sautéed garlic. Mash the potatoes with the butter, salt, and pepper.
4. Fill the body of the rabbit with mashed potato stuffing. Place the rabbit in the slow cooker with legs folded under the body. Cook on low setting for 8 to 9 hours.

Serve with Lemony Asparagus and Carrots (page 565).

Slow-Baked Meat

Use a vegetable steamer in the slow cooker to "bake" meat. It will keep the meat out of the juice at the bottom of the cooker without hindering the flow of steam.

Wild Duck Gumbo

Cooking time: 9–11 hours	
Preparation time: 1 hour	
Attention: Medium	
Pot size: 6–8 quarts	
Serves 6	

2 wild ducks, cleaned
1 tablespoon vegetable oil
2 tablespoons flour
1 teaspoon table salt
1 garlic clove, minced
2 cups water
2 teaspoons Worcestershire sauce

1 teaspoon hot pepper sauce
¼ cup red bell peppers, diced
⅛ cup jalapeño peppers, diced
2 medium-sized yellow onions
2 stalks celery
½ pound Polish sausage

1. In a large kettle bring 2 quarts of water to boil, then turn off heat. Add the ducks to the water. Cover and let stand for 10 minutes. Remove the ducks from the pot and place on paper towels. This process is called "parboiling"; it removes excess fat from wild poultry and other fatty meats.

2. Heat the oil on low heat in a medium-sized saucepan. Add the flour, salt, and garlic; sauté until brown. Add the two cups water, Worcestershire sauce, and hot sauce. Simmer, stirring constantly, until sauce is thick.

3. Remove the stems and seeds from the peppers; cut peppers into ¼-inch-wide lengthwise strips. Peel the onions and chop into ¼-inch pieces. Chop the celery into ¼-inch pieces. Place the vegetables on the bottom of the slow cooker. Place the ducks on top of the vegetables. Pour the prepared sauce over the ducks. Cover and cook on low setting for 8 to 10 hours. Remove and debone the ducks. Dispose of the skin and cut the meat into chunks. Cut the sausage into ¼-inch pieces. Return the duck to the slow cooker, add the sausage, and cook for 1 hour, or until the sausage is warmed through.

Serve over white rice with a side of Sweet Potato and Apple Bake (page 564).

Swiss-Style Venison Steak

Cooking time: 4–6 hours	
Preparation time: 20 minutes	
Attention: Minimal	
Pot size: 4–6 quarts	
Serves 6–8	

2 pounds venison steak, approximately 2 inches thick
2 cups flour
2 large Vidalia onions
6 fresh, ripe tomatoes
½ teaspoon minced garlic
¼ cup white vinegar
½ teaspoon pepper
1 teaspoon salt
½ cup water

1. Sprinkle flour onto the steaks and pound the steaks with a meat-tenderizing mallet. Continue sprinkling flour and pounding until the meat is covered with as much flour as possible.
2. Lay the steaks in the bottom of the slow cooker. Slice the onions into ¼-inch-thick rings. Slice the tomatoes into 8 wedges each. Mince the garlic using a sharp kitchen knife. Mix together the onions, tomatoes, garlic, vinegar, pepper, salt, and water in a bowl. Add this mixture to the slow cooker. Cook covered on low setting for 4 to 6 hours.

Green Beans in Lemon Honey (page 550) and mashed potatoes are nice complements to the venison and tomato in this recipe.

Venison in Beer Barbecue Sauce

Cooking time: 8 hours

Preparation time: 10 minutes, plus some work the day before

Attention: Minimal

Pot size: 4–6 quarts

Serves 4

3 pounds roast from deer, elk, or moose
2 medium-sized yellow onions
3 cloves garlic
1 (12-ounce) can or bottle brown ale
1 teaspoon table salt
1 teaspoon ground black pepper
2 cups tomato sauce
1 teaspoon Worcestershire sauce
¼ cup brown sugar

1. Cut the meat into 1-inch cubes. Peel the onions and slice into ¼-inch-thick rings. Peel the garlic and crush it by laying a large knife over each clove and pushing until it "pops."
2. In a large bowl, combine the onions, garlic, beer, salt, and pepper. Marinate the meat in this mixture, covered in the refrigerator, for 12 to 24 hours. Turn the meat occasionally during this time.
3. Remove the meat from the marinade and place the meat in the slow cooker.
4. Mix together the tomato sauce, Worcestershire sauce, and brown sugar in a bowl; pour mixture over the meat. Cook covered on low setting for 8 hours.

Serve with a green lettuce salad and assorted cheeses to create a well-balanced meal.

Marinating Meat

Never marinate meat for longer than 24 hours. The meat begins to break down and the texture becomes mushy. The flavors should penetrate after about two hours.

Sweet-and-Sour Venison

Cooking time: 8 hours
Preparation time: 30 minutes
Attention: Frequent
Pot size: 4–6 quarts
Serves 4

2 pounds venison steak
¼ cup flour
¼ cup oil
½ cup warm water
1 teaspoon salt
1 green bell pepper
1 red bell pepper
½ cup fresh, frozen, **or** canned
    pineapple, cut into chunks

Sauce:

2½ tablespoons cornstarch
½ cup pineapple juice
¼ cup white vinegar
¼ cup white sugar
2 tablespoons soy sauce

1. Cut the venison into 1-inch cubes and roll the cubes in flour. Heat the oil in a skillet to medium and place the venison in the pan; brown the meat on all sides. Remove the meat and set it on a paper towel for a few minutes to absorb the grease. Place the meat into the slow cooker with the water and salt. Cook covered on low setting for 6 hours.

2. Remove the stems and seeds from the peppers and chop into 1-inch pieces. Cut the pineapple into 1-inch chunks. Add the peppers and pineapple to the slow cooker. Cook covered 1 more hour on low setting.

3. To make the sauce, combine the cornstarch, pineapple juice, white vinegar, white sugar, and soy sauce in a saucepan and heat on the stove on medium heat until the sauce has thickened. Add to the slow cooker and cook covered on low setting for 1 more hour.

To maintain the "wild" flavor of this dish, serve it over brown rice.

Venison Definition

Venison isn't necessarily deer meat. It also is the term used for elk or caribou meat. These meats can vary widely in taste depending on what the animal has eaten. As a result, they are best served in stews that blend many flavors.

Uncle Mike's Roast Duck

Cooking time: 8–10 hours

Preparation time: 10 minutes

Attention: Minimal

Pot size: 5–6 quarts

Serves 4

1 yellow onion
2 garlic cloves
2 celery ribs
1 3-pound duck, cleaned
1 teaspoon vegetable oil
½ teaspoon salt
½ teaspoon ground black pepper
½ teaspoon poultry seasoning

1. Peel the onion and chop into ¼-inch pieces. Crush the garlic cloves by taking a large knife and placing it on its side on top of each garlic clove; press down until the clove "pops." Chop the celery into ¼-inch pieces. Put the vegetables in slow cooker.
2. Rinse the duck cavity with cold water and swab with vegetable oil by placing the oil on a paper towel and wiping it inside the cavity. Sprinkle the cavity with the salt, black pepper, and poultry seasoning. Place the duck in the slow cooker on top of the vegetables and sprinkle with dried parsley. Cook covered on low setting for 8 to 10 hours.

Serve with German-Style Cooked Cabbage with Onions and Peppers (page 566) for a robust meal.

Oils

For a difference in taste, try using a flavored vegetable oil. You can find all kinds in specialty grocery stores.

Cooking time: 8–10 hours

Preparation time: 15 minutes

Attention: Minimal

Pot size: 5–6 quarts

Serves 4

Game Birds with Sweet Potatoes

3 medium-sized sweet potatoes
1 cup fresh sliced mushrooms
8 breasts from small game birds (pheasant, partridge, grouse, etc.)
⅔ cup flour, plus 3 tablespoons
1 teaspoon salt
1 teaspoon nutmeg
1 teaspoon cinnamon
½ teaspoon ground black pepper
½ teaspoon garlic powder
½ cup whole milk
½ cup orange juice
2 teaspoons brown sugar

1. Peel the sweet potatoes and cut into ¼-inch-thick slices; place them in the bottom of the slow cooker. Clean the mushrooms by wiping with a damp cloth, then cut into ⅛ inch-thick slices.
2. Rinse the breasts and pat dry. Combine the ⅔ cup flour, salt, nutmeg, cinnamon, pepper, and garlic powder. Thoroughly coat the breasts in this mixture. Place the breasts on top of the sweet potatoes in the slow cooker.
3. Combine the milk, mushrooms, orange juice, brown sugar, and 3 tablespoons flour; mix with a fork in a small bowl until the sugar and flour are well integrated into the liquid. Pour mixture over breasts. Cook covered on low setting for 8 to 10 hours.

For a fall harvest meal, serve the breasts over Minnesota Wild Rice (page 571).

Roasted Small Game with Onions

Cooking time: 10–12 hours

Preparation time: 15 minutes

Attention: Minimal

Pot size: 4–6 quarts

Serves 4

4–5 pounds of small game (rabbit, squirrel, etc.)
2 Vidalia onions
1 garlic clove
½ teaspoon table salt
½ teaspoon ground black pepper
1 cup water
2 tablespoons soy sauce
2 bay leaves
1 whole clove
2 tablespoons all-purpose flour
½ cup cold water

1. Cut the meat into serving-sized pieces. Peel the onions and slice into ¼-inch-thick rings. Peel the garlic and slice paper-thin. Place the onion and garlic in the bottom of the slow cooker.
2. Sprinkle the meat with salt and pepper; place in the slow cooker. Add the 1 cup water, soy sauce, bay leaves, and clove. Cook covered on low setting 10 to 12 hours.
3. Remove the rabbit and set aside. Remove the bay leaf and discard. Stir the flour into the ½ cup water until it is well blended. Pour this mixture into the slow cooker and stir until the gravy thickens.

Cut the meat off the bones and serve over mashed potatoes. Don't forget to top it with the luscious, onion-laden gravy!

Cooking time: 6–8 hours
Preparation time: 20 minutes, plus 2–4 hours of marinating time
Attention: Medium
Pot size: 4–6 quarts
Serves 4

Game Birds with Beer and Mushrooms

3 pounds of small game bird breasts (pheasant, grouse, partridge, etc.)
¾ cup teriyaki sauce
½ cup flour
2 teaspoons garlic salt
1 teaspoon ground black pepper
⅓ cup olive oil
1 large yellow onion, sliced
¾ cup fresh mushrooms, sliced
12-ounce can or bottle dark beer

1. Debone the bird and cut the meat into 1-inch cubes. Marinate the meat in teriyaki sauce in the refrigerator for 2 to 4 hours.

2. Combine the flour, garlic salt, and pepper; coat the meat in this mixture. Place the olive oil in a medium-sized skillet. Add the flour-covered meat and cook on medium heat, stirring constantly until the meat is slightly browned. Add the onion and sauté for 3 minutes, stirring constantly. Remove the meat and onions and place in slow cooker. Clean the mushrooms by wiping with a damp cloth; slice paper-thin. Add the beer and mushrooms to the slow cooker. Cook covered on low setting 6 to 8 hours.

For a more delicate-tasting meal, substitute white wine for the beer.

How Much Marinade?

Allow about ½ cup of marinade for each two pounds of meat, fish or vegetables. Always marinate in the refrigerator to avoid bacteria growth. Discard the marinade or cook it to boiling before adding to a recipe.

Holiday Goose
with Cranberries

Cooking time: 8–10 hours

Preparation time: 10 minutes

Attention: Minimal

Pot size: 6 quart oval

Serves 4

1 wild goose, gutted and skinned (note that domestic goose is much greasier and should not be substituted)
½ teaspoon table salt
½ teaspoon ground black pepper
1 (15-ounce) can whole berry cranberry sauce
1 envelope dry onion soup mix
½ cup orange juice

Wash the goose cavity with cold water and sprinkle with salt and pepper. Place the goose in the slow cooker. Combine the cranberry sauce, dry onion soup mix, and orange juice; pour mixture over the goose. Cook covered on low setting 8 to 10 hours.

Garnish with fresh orange slices, baked sweet potatoes, and parsley to create a festive-looking meal.

What If I Get Home Late?

Because the slow cooker cooks using steam and a low temperature, most dishes will stay moist and tasty for several hours after the recommended cooking time.

Chapter 28
Freshwater Fish and Seafood

Cream of Shrimp Soup

Cooking time: 5½ –7½ hours

Preparation time: 30 minutes

Attention: Medium

Pot size: 4–6 quarts

Serves 8

1 pound potatoes
1 white onion
1 celery rib
2 carrots
2 cups water
½ cup vegetable broth
2 tablespoons white wine
¼ teaspoon dried thyme
*½ pound baby shrimp (**or** large precooked shrimp cut into*
½-inch pieces)
2 cups shredded Swiss cheese
1 cup whole milk
½ teaspoon ground black pepper

1. Peel the potatoes and cut into ½-inch cubes. Peel the onions and chop into ¼-inch pieces. Chop the celery into ¼-inch pieces. Peel the carrots and shred using a vegetable grater. Place the potatoes, onions, celery, carrots, water, vegetable broth, white wine, and thyme into the slow cooker. Cook covered on high heat 4 to 6 hours.
2. Use a hand-held mixer to purée the vegetables in the slow cooker; the resulting mixture should be the consistency of baby food. Add the shrimp and cook covered for 30 minutes on low setting. Shred the cheese using a vegetable grater. Add the cheese, milk, and pepper to the soup. Cook covered on low setting for about 1 hour, stirring every 15 minutes, until the cheese is melted.

Garnish with fresh sprigs of cilantro.

Cooking time: 2–3 hours	
Preparation time: 20 minutes	
Attention: Medium High	
Pot size: 4–6 quarts	
Serves 4	

Salmon in White Wine with Dried Peaches

1½ pounds salmon fillets
¼ cup all-purpose flour
2 tablespoons extra-virgin olive oil
1 cup dry white wine
½ cup vegetable stock
1 cup dried peaches, quartered
½ teaspoon freshly ground black pepper

1. Pat the salmon dry with paper towels. Coat with a light layer of flour. Heat the olive oil in a frying pan at medium heat. Add the salmon and brown on all sides. Discard the oil and place the salmon fillets on paper towels to soak up additional oil.

2. Add the wine and vegetable stock to the slow cooker and cook on high setting until it bubbles. Turn the slow cooker to the low setting. Place the salmon fillets in the bottom of the slow cooker. Place the quartered dried peaches on top. Sprinkle with pepper. Cook covered on low setting for 2 to 3 hours.

Serve with fresh steamed broccoli drizzled with fresh-squeezed lime juice.

Minnesota Mock Lobster

Cooking time: 2–4 hours
Preparation time: 15 minutes
Attention: Minimal
Pot size: 4–6 quarts
Serves 6

3 stalks celery
1 medium onion
½ cup water
½ cup lemon juice
2 tablespoons butter **or** margarine
3 pounds frozen torsk fillets
1 teaspoon salt
1 teaspoon paprika
6 lemon wedges
½ cup melted butter

1. Chop the celery into 1-inch pieces. Peel and quarter the onion.
2. Add the celery, onion, water, lemon juice, and butter to the slow cooker. Cook uncovered on high setting until the butter is melted. Stir mixture and turn the slow cooker to low setting. Lay the torsk fillets on the bottom of the slow cooker. Sprinkle salt and paprika over the fillets. Cook covered on low setting for 2 to 4 hours. Serve with melted butter and lemon wedges.

Add color to this main dish by serving it with Lemony Asparagus and Carrots (page 565).

Too Salty?

If the dish tastes too salty, add a teaspoon each of cider vinegar and sugar to the recipe. They will neutralize the salt without adding additional flavor.

Brown Rice Curry with Vegetables and Scallops

Cooking time: 7–9 hours
Preparation time: 30 minutes
Attention: Medium
Pot size: 4–6 quarts
Serves 6

1 large yellow onion
3 cloves garlic
1 tablespoon olive oil
1 pound baby scallops
1½ cups water
1 tablespoon curry powder
½ teaspoon cinnamon
½ teaspoon table salt
2 large potatoes
1 large zucchini
2 large carrots
1 (16-ounce) can tomatoes, liquid retained

1. Peel and chop the onions into ¼-inch pieces. Peel and slice the garlic paper-thin with a sharp kitchen knife. Heat the olive oil in medium-sized skillet; sauté the scallops, onions, and garlic on medium-high heat until the onions are translucent and limp. The scallops should be slightly brown. Drain off the oil and place the scallops, onions, and garlic in the slow cooker.
2. Add the water, curry powder, cinnamon, and salt to the slow cooker; stir well. Cook covered on high setting for 1 hour.
3. Peel and cut the potatoes into 1-inch cubes. Slice the zucchini into ¼-inch-thick pieces. Peel and slice the carrots into ¼-inch pieces. Slice the tomatoes into 1-inch pieces, retaining the juice. Add the potatoes, zucchini, and tomatoes to the slow cooker. Cook covered on low setting for 6 to 8 hours.

Serve with a dry white wine and Italian Beets (page 575).

Shrimp Marinara

Cooking time: 6–9 hours

Preparation time: 20 minutes

Attention: Minimal

Pot size: 3 to 6 quarts

Serves 4

4 large red tomatoes
1 garlic clove
2 tablespoons fresh parsley, minced
½ teaspoon dried basil
1 teaspoon table salt
¼ teaspoon ground black pepper
1 teaspoon dried oregano
1 (6-ounce) can tomato paste
½ pound small- to medium-sized fresh shrimp

1. Chop the tomatoes into 1-inch pieces. Peel and mince the garlic with a sharp paring knife. Mince the parsley by chopping it into very small pieces. Add the tomatoes, garlic, parsley, basil, salt, pepper, oregano, and tomato paste to the slow cooker. Cook covered on low setting for 6 to 8 hours.
2. Cook the shrimp by boiling it in a large kettle for 10 minutes. Rinse with cold water. Remove the shells and tails. Devein by using the tine of a fork to remove the blackish membrane along the back of each shrimp. Add the shrimp to the slow cooker and stir well. Turn the setting to high. Cook covered for 15 minutes.

Serve over linguine noodles. Top with Parmesan cheese and dried parsley flakes.

Preparing Fresh Shrimp

When using fresh shrimp, boil them for 3 minutes. Run under cold water. Remove all of the shell, although you can keep the tail on if you like. Take a small fork and run it along the back of the shrimp to remove the black vein.

Cooking time: 4–6 hours	
Preparation time: 20 minutes	
Attention: Minimal	
Pot size: 3–6 quarts	
Serves 4	

Freshwater Fish Stew

1½ *pounds freshwater fish (walleye, northern, trout, bass, etc.),*
    cleaned, skinned, and deboned
¾ *cup fresh mushrooms, sliced*
1 *clove garlic*
1 *large white onion*
1 *green bell pepper*
2 *small zucchini*
4 *large ripe tomatoes*
2 *tablespoons olive oil*
½ *teaspoon dried basil*
½ *teaspoon dried oregano*
1 *teaspoon table salt*
¼ *teaspoon ground black pepper*
¼ *cup dry white wine*

1. Cut the fish into 1-inch cubes. Clean the mushrooms by wiping with a damp cloth. Remove the stems and slice the mushroom heads paper-thin. Peel and mince the garlic. Peel the onion and slice into ¼-inch-thick rings. Remove the seeds and stem from the green pepper and chop into 1-inch pieces. Cut the tomatoes into 1-inch pieces.
2. Combine all ingredients in the slow cooker. Stir gently because the fish will break up if stirred too quickly. Cover and cook on low setting 4 to 6 hours.

Use shark, sea bass, or other mild saltwater fish to give a lighter flavor to this dish.

Lobster in Havarti and Cognac Cream Sauce

Cooking time: 1–2 hours
Preparation time: 30 minutes
Pot size: 3–6 quarts
Attention: Frequent
Serves 4

1 pound fresh lobster meat (approximately 3 whole lobsters)
4 garlic cloves
1 teaspoon fresh tarragon, chopped
2 cups Havarti cheese, grated
1 cup light cream
¼ cup cognac
1 tablespoon ground black pepper
½ teaspoon table salt
1 egg

1. Cook lobster by immersing them in boiling water head first. Cover and boil about 20 minutes.
2. Remove the meat from the lobster tails and claws and cut into 1-inch cubes. Peel and chop the garlic cloves into paper-thin slices. Chop the tarragon into ¼-inch lengths.
3. Combine the cheese, cream, cognac, garlic, pepper, salt, and tarragon in the slow cooker on low temperature setting; stir constantly with a wooden spoon until all the cheese has melted.
4. Pour the sauce into a blender and add the egg. Purée for 2 minutes on medium speed. Return the sauce to the slow cooker. Add the lobster meat. Cook covered on low setting for 30 to 60 minutes.

Ladle over cooked spinach linguine noodles.

Cooking time: 1½ hours	
Preparation time: 15 minutes	
Attention: Minimal	
Pot size: 3–6 quarts	
Serves 6	

Citrus Fish Fillets

1 fresh orange
1 fresh lemon
1 white onion
5 tablespoons fresh chopped parsley
¼ teaspoon butter
2 pounds fresh fish fillets, skinned and deboned
½ teaspoon table salt
¼ teaspoon ground black pepper
4 teaspoons vegetable oil

1. Before peeling, run the orange and lemon over the smallest teeth on a vegetable grater to yield 2 teaspoons of grated rind from each. Peel the remaining rind from the orange and lemon, discard, and slice the fruit into ¼-inch-thick pieces. Peel and chop the onion into ¼-inch pieces. Wash the parsley under cold water and chop into ¼-inch lengths.
2. Rub the butter on the bottom of the slow cooker. Add the fish fillets. Sprinkle salt and pepper over the fillets. Put the onion, parsley, and grated rinds on top of fish. Drizzle with vegetable oil. Cover and cook on low setting for 1½ hours. Ten minutes before serving, add the orange and lemon slices on top.

Serve with a vegetable medley of broccoli, cauliflower, and carrots slices about ¼-inch thick, steamed and drizzled with lemon juice.

Shrimp Creole

Cooking time: 7–9 hours

Preparation time: 20 minutes

Attention: Minimal

Pot size: 2–6 quarts

Serves 4

1 pound fresh shrimp
1¼ cup yellow onion, chopped
1 medium-sized green bell pepper
1½ cups celery, chopped
6 large ripe tomatoes
1 (8-ounce) can tomato sauce
1 teaspoon garlic salt
¼ teaspoon ground black pepper
½ teaspoon Tabasco or other hot pepper sauce

1. Cook the shrimp by boiling it for 20 minutes. Immerse in cold water until cool. Remove the shells and tails. Devein by using a fork tine to remove the blackish membrane on the back of each shrimp.
2. Peel and chop the onion into ¼-inch pieces. Remove the stem and seeds from the green pepper and chop the pepper into ¼-inch pieces. Cut the celery into ¼-inch pieces. Cut the tomatoes into 1-inch cubes. Add the celery, onion, green pepper, fresh tomatoes, tomato sauce, garlic salt, black pepper, and hot pepper sauce to the slow cooker. Cover and cook on low setting 6 to 8 hours. Add the shrimp, stir well, cover and cook an additional 1 hour.

Serve over long-grain brown rice. Top with fresh chopped chives.

Slow Cooking with Shellfish

To keep shellfish from getting rubbery in a slow cooked meal, add them during the last two hours of the cooking process. Always use fresh shellfish, if possible, as freezing can cause the flesh to toughen.

Vegetable Seafood Chowder

Cooking time: 8–10 hours
Preparation time: 20 minutes
Attention: Minimal
Pot size: 2–6 quarts
Serves 4

3 large potatoes
1 medium-sized white onion
1 cup fresh carrots, chopped
½ cup celery, chopped
1 cup fresh broccoli, chopped
1 cup frozen or fresh peas
1 cup fresh haddock, cubed
2 cups vegetable stock
1 teaspoon table salt
½ teaspoon ground black pepper

1. Peel the potatoes and chop into 1-inch cubes. Peel and chop the onion in ¼-inch pieces. Cut the carrots, celery, and broccoli into ¼-inch pieces.
2. Add all the ingredients except fresh peas and fish to the slow cooker. Cover and cook on low setting for 7 to 8 hours. Add peas and fish, cook for 1 to 2 hours more.

Add 1 additional cup vegetable stock and 1 cup assorted other fresh seafood such as scallops, oysters, shrimp, and shark meat to make this a diverse, surprising treat.

Manhattan Clam Chowder

Cooking time: 8–10 hours

Preparation time: 20 minutes

Attention: Minimal

Pot size: 2–6 quarts

Serves 4

¼ pound bacon

1 large Vidalia onion

2 medium carrots

1 celery rib

8 medium-sized ripe tomatoes

3 medium potatoes

1 tablespoon dried parsley

3 cups fresh or canned clams

½ teaspoon table salt

½ teaspoon ground black pepper

1 teaspoon dried thyme

4 cups water

1. Brown the bacon in a medium-sized skillet on medium-high heat until crisp. Drain the grease. Lay the bacon on paper towels to cool. Crumble the bacon and add it to the slow cooker. Peel the onion and cut into ¼-inch pieces. Peel and slice the carrots into ¼-inch rounds. Cut the celery into ¼-inch pieces. Cut the tomatoes into ½-inch cubes. Peel the potatoes and cut into ½-inch cubes.
2. Add all ingredients to the slow cooker. Cover and cook on low setting for 8 to 10 hours.

Serve with Sweet Corn Pudding (page 575) for a nice blend of flavors.

Cooking time: 7–8 hours	
Preparation time: 20 minutes	
Attention: Minimal	
Pot size: 4–8 quarts	
Serves 8	

Cioppino

12 mussels

12 clams

12 large shrimp

1 pound cod

1 large yellow onion

1 medium-sized green bell pepper

2 medium-sized ripe tomatoes

2 garlic cloves

2 tablespoons fresh minced parsley

3 tablespoons olive oil

2 cups clam juice

½ cup dry white wine

1 bay leaf

1 teaspoon table salt

1 teaspoon ground black pepper

4 soft-shell crabs

1. Leave the mussels and clams in their shells. Remove the shells from the shrimp and devein the shrimp by running a fork tine along the back of each shrimp. Cut the cod into 1-inch cubes. Peel the onion and chop into ¼-inch pieces. Remove the stem and seeds from the green pepper; chop into ¼-inch pieces. Chop the tomatoes into ½-inch pieces. Peel the garlic and mince with a sharp kitchen knife. Mince the parsley with a sharp kitchen knife.

2. Heat the olive oil in a large skillet on medium heat. Add the onions, green pepper, and garlic and sauté for about 5 minutes, or until the onions are translucent; pour into the slow cooker. Stir in the tomatoes, parsley, clam juice, wine, and bay leaf. Cover and cook on low setting for 6 to 7 hours.

3. Remove the bay leaf. Add the salt, pepper, mussels, clams, shrimp, fish, and crab; stir gently. Cover and cook on low setting for 1 hour. Discard any mussels or clams that remain closed.

Serve with Slightly Seedy White Bread (page 374) for sopping up the wonderful juice.

Tuna Tomato Bake

Cooking time: 8–10 hours

Preparation time: 20 minutes

Attention: Minimal

Pot size: 2–6 quarts

Serves 4

1 medium-sized green bell pepper
1 small yellow onion
1 celery rib
2 cups (16 ounces) water-packed tuna, drained
2 cups (16 ounces) tomato juice
2 tablespoons Worcestershire sauce
3 tablespoons vinegar
2 tablespoons sugar
1 tablespoon Dijon mustard
¼ teaspoon chili powder
½ teaspoon cinnamon
¼ teaspoon hot pepper sauce

1. Remove the seeds and stem from the green pepper and chop the pepper into ¼-inch pieces. Peel the onion and chop into ¼-inch pieces. Cut the celery stalk into ¼-inch pieces.
2. Combine all ingredients; mix gently. Cover and cook on low setting for 8 to 10 hours.

Serve as a sandwich spread with Heavy Brown Bread (page 375).

Slow-Baked Fish
To bake fish in a slow cooker, use a vegetable steamer or other rack that keeps it out of the juices. Sprinkle it with lemon or lime juice and cook on low for only a couple hours. The fish is done when it flakes when separated by a fork.

Cooking time: 3–4 hours
Preparation time: 15 minutes
Attention: Minimal
Pot size: 3–6 quarts
Serves 4

Salmon Casserole

8 ounces (1 cup) fresh mushrooms, quartered
1 small yellow onion
1 cup shredded Cheddar cheese
2 eggs
2 cups (16 ounces) canned salmon with liquid
1½ cups bread crumbs
1 tablespoon lemon juice

1. Clean the mushrooms by wiping with a damp cloth; cut into quarters. Peel the onion and chop into ¼-inch pieces. Shred the Cheddar cheese with a vegetable grater. Beat the eggs by stirring quickly with a fork.
2. Put the fish in a medium-sized mixing bowl and flake with a fork, removing any bones. Mix together all the ingredients; pour into the slow cooker. Cover and cook on low setting for 3 to 4 hours.

Serve with Cheesy Cauliflower (page 574) for a nice blend of flavors.

Peppery Salmon Chowder

Cooking time: 6–7 hours

Preparation time: 20 minutes

Attention: Minimal

Pot size: 4–6 quarts

Serves 6

1 pound fresh salmon
1 medium-sized red bell pepper
1 medium-sized green bell pepper
1 medium-sized yellow bell pepper
4 medium potatoes
3 medium carrots
1 celery rib
2 medium-sized white onions
2 cups sweet corn
3 cups vegetable broth
1 teaspoon whole black peppercorns

1. Remove the skin and bones from the salmon and cut the meat into 1-inch cubes. Remove the stems and seeds from the bell peppers and chop the peppers into ½-inch pieces. Leave the peels on the potatoes and cut the potatoes into ½-inch cubes. Peel and chop the carrots and celery into ¼-inch pieces. Peel the onions and chop into ¼-inch pieces.
2. Combine all ingredients in the slow cooker. Cover and cook on low for 6 to 7 hours.

Serve with fresh Zucchini Bread (page 369) for a nice complement to the spicy vegetables in this chowder.

Kids' Favorites

Cooking time: 2–3 hours

Preparation time: 20 minutes

Attention: Minimal

Pot size: 4–6 quarts

Serves 12

Sloppy Joes

1 medium-sized yellow onion

2 celery ribs

2 pounds extra-lean hamburger

2 cups tomato sauce

½ cup can tomato paste

¼ cup white vinegar

3 teaspoons Worcestershire sauce

2 tablespoons brown sugar

1 teaspoon garlic salt

½ teaspoon pepper

1. Peel the onion and chop into ¼-inch pieces. Chop the celery into ¼-inch pieces. Put the onion, celery, and hamburger in a medium-sized skillet on medium-high heat. Cook until the hamburger is brown and no pink remains. Drain off the grease.
2. Combine all ingredients in the slow cooker. Cook covered on low setting for 2 to 3 hours.

Add potato chips and carrot sticks to the plate and you have a true all-American lunch that is perfect for chilly outings or teen get-togethers.

Mini-Bakery

Use the slow cooker as a mini-bakery for young children. Let them mix up a batch of chocolate chip cookies and watch through the glass lid as one or two cookies at a time bake right before their eyes.

Cooking time: 2 hours	
Preparation time: 30 minutes	
Attention: Minimal	
Pot size: 5–6 quarts	
Serves 6–8	

Pizza Meatballs

Meatballs:

½ pound (1 cup) shredded
   Swiss cheese
1 medium-sized yellow onion
½ of a medium-sized green bell
   pepper
2 pounds extra-lean hamburger
2¾ cups bread crumbs
1 teaspoon salt
¼ teaspoon basil
¼ teaspoon pepper
1 cup canned condensed vegetable soup
¼ cup skim milk

Sauce:

1 garlic clove
1 medium-sized yellow onion
6 large ripe tomatoes
1 cup beef broth
½ cup (4 ounces) tomato paste
1 teaspoon salt
1 teaspoon oregano

1. To make the meatballs, cut the cheese into ¼-inch cubes. Peel and chop the onion into ¼-inch pieces. Remove the stem and seeds from the green pepper and chop the pepper into ¼-inch pieces. Mix all the meatball ingredients together well and form into firm balls no larger than 2 inches in diameter. Lay the meatballs in the bottom of the slow cooker.
2. To make the sauce, peel the garlic and slice thinly with a paring knife. Peel and chop the onions into ½-inch pieces. Peel the tomatoes with a sharp paring knife, gently lifting the skin off, quarter them, and mix in a blender on low speed for 2 minutes. Combine all sauce ingredients and pour over the meatballs.
3. Cook covered on low setting for 2 hours.

Make these ahead of time and freeze them. They can be thawed in the microwave for those last-minute lunch demands or as an after-school snack.

Party Snack Mix

Cooking time: 1½ hours

Preparation time: 15 minutes

Attention: Constant

Pot size: 6 quarts

Serves 12

½ teaspoon vegetable oil
4 tablespoons butter (or margarine)
1 teaspoon garlic salt
½ teaspoon onion salt
4 teaspoons Worcestershire sauce
3 cups Corn Chex cereal
3 cups Wheat Chex cereal
3 cups Rice Chex cereal
1 cup shelled, skinless peanuts
2 cups mini pretzel sticks
½ cup Parmesan cheese, grated

1. Put the vegetable oil on a paper towel and spread the oil over the bottom and insides of the slow cooker. Combine the butter (or margarine), garlic salt, onion salt, and Worcestershire sauce in the slow cooker. Heat on high setting until the butter is melted. Mix well and add the Corn Chex, Wheat Chex, Rice Chex, peanuts, and pretzel sticks. Cook uncovered on high setting for 1 hour, stirring every 15 minutes. Reduce to low setting and cook uncovered for 30 minutes, stirring every 15 minutes.
2. Spread the mixture on paper towels. Lightly sprinkle with Parmesan cheese. Let cool before serving.

This nutritious, low-fat treat keeps for weeks in airtight containers, making it the ideal after-school snack.

Caramel Corn with Peanuts

Cooking time: 1½ hours

Preparation time: 15 minutes

Attention: Constant

Pot size: 6 quarts

Serves 12

¼ cup maple-flavored syrup
¼ cup packed brown sugar
1 teaspoon vanilla
3 tablespoons butter (or margarine)
10 cups unsalted, dry popped popcorn
2 cups skin-on Spanish peanuts

1. Combine the maple-flavored syrup, brown sugar, vanilla, and butter or margarine in the slow cooker. Cook uncovered on high setting until the butter (or margarine) melts and the brown sugar is dissolved; stir well. Add the popcorn and peanuts. Cook covered on high setting for 1 hour, stirring every 15 minutes. Cook uncovered on low setting an additional 30 minutes, stirring every 15 minutes.
2. Spread the mixture on lightly greased cookie sheets to cool before serving.

Add almonds or coconut instead of the peanuts.

A Sweeter Treat

For an even yummier snack, experiment with adding chocolate chips or small candy pieces to the caramel corn mixture.

Real Baked Beans and Franks

Cooking time: 7–9 hours

Preparation time: 15 minutes

Attention: Minimal

Pot size: 5–6 quarts

Serves 6

3 cups dried navy beans
6 cups water
1 medium-sized yellow onion
1 large tomato
½ cup brown sugar
½ cup maple-flavored syrup

1 cup ketchup
2 teaspoons dried mustard
2 teaspoons vinegar
1 cup water
12 all-beef hotdogs, cut into
    ½-inch round slices

1. Wash the beans then soak them in 6 cups of water for 12 hours before cooking. Drain and wash the beans again.
2. Peel the onion and cut into ⅛-inch pieces. Chop the tomato. Combine the brown sugar, maple-flavored syrup, ketchup, mustard, vinegar, tomato, and onion in the slow cooker. Cook uncovered on high setting until the brown sugar has dissolved; stir well. Add 1 cup water, beans, and hotdogs. Stir to cover the beans and hot dogs with sauce. Cook covered on low setting for 7 to 9 hours. One hour before serving, remove the cover and continue cooking on low setting.

To add interest to the meal, serve with apple slices sprinkled with cinnamon.

Cracked Crockery

Slow cookers are simple devices that can take a lot of abuse. However, the crockery pot can crack if dropped. It's also heavy and could easily break a toe. If you do inadvertently drop the slow cooker, check it for cracks and make sure it is heating correctly before you use it again.

Cooking time: 8 hours	
Preparation time: 20 minutes	
Attention: Minimal	
Pot size: 3–6 quarts	
Serves 8	

Halftime Chili

2 pounds lean ground beef
1 medium-sized yellow onion
3 medium tomatoes
2 cups (16 ounces) canned or frozen corn
4 cups (32 ounces) precooked or canned red kidney beans
1 cup water
2 tablespoons chili powder
2 teaspoons table salt
1 teaspoon ground black pepper
¼ teaspoon dried red pepper flakes

1. Brown the meat in a large skillet on the stove. Continue browning at medium heat until no pink remains in the meat. Drain off the fat and lay the meat on paper towels to absorb remaining fat.
2. Peel and dice the onion into ¼-inch pieces. Dice the tomatoes into ¼-inch pieces. Drain and rinse the kidney beans. Combine the onion, tomatoes, corn, kidney beans, water, chili powder, salt, black pepper, and dried red peppers; stir to combine. Cook covered on low setting for 8 hours.

Place small bowls of shredded Cheddar cheese, diced jalapeño peppers, sour cream, and diced green onion tops on the table and let kids top their own chili.

Macaroni and Cheese with Hamburger

Cooking time:	3 hours
Preparation time:	20 minutes
Attention:	Minimal
Pot size:	4–6 quarts
Serves 8	

1 pound lean hamburger
6 cups elbow macaroni
2 cups whole milk
2 cups shredded Cheddar cheese
2 teaspoons dry mustard
¼ teaspoon garlic salt
¼ teaspoon ground black pepper

1. Brown the hamburger in a skillet on medium-high heat on the stove. Drain off the fat and spread the hamburger on paper towels to absorb remaining grease. Cook the macaroni in boiling water until soft.
2. Combine the milk, Cheddar cheese, dry mustard, garlic salt, and black pepper in the slow cooker. Cook uncovered on high setting until the cheese has melted completely. Add the cooked macaroni and hamburger; stir well. Cook uncovered on low setting for 3 hours.

Try different pastas such as rotini or alphabet shapes. Substitute hot dog or sausage slices for the hamburger

Using Skim Milk

If a recipe calls for whole milk, half and half, or cream, you can easily substitute skim milk. You will get all the nutrition and most of the creamy taste with much less fat.

Mom's Cure for a Winter Cold: Easy Chicken Noodle Soup

Cooking time:	8–10 hours
Preparation time:	30 minutes
Attention:	Medium
Pot size:	4–6 quarts
Serves 10	

1 chicken, cleaned, with skin and bones
1 medium-sized yellow onion
8 carrots
4 celery ribs
6 cups water
2 chicken bouillon cubes
1 teaspoon table salt
½ teaspoon ground black pepper
8 ounces dried egg noodles

1. Cut the chicken into serving portions—legs, wings, thighs, breasts. Peel and dice the onions and carrots into about ¼-inch pieces. Slice the celery ribs into ¼-inch pieces.

2. Combine the water, bouillon cubes, salt, pepper, and chicken pieces in the slow cooker. Cook covered on high for 4 to 5 hours. Remove the chicken and discard the bones and skin. Place the meat back in the slow cooker. Add the noodles, carrots, celery, and onions in the slow cooker. Cook covered on high setting for 4 to 5 additional hours.

Spicy dill pickles, Cheddar cheese, and saltine crackers are the perfect complement to chicken noodle soup.

Minty
Hot Chocolate . . .

Cooking time: 30 minutes
Preparation time: 5 minutes
Attention: Constant
Pot size: 2–6 quarts
Serves 12

12 cups whole milk
1 cup chocolate syrup
1 teaspoon peppermint extract

Combine the milk, syrup, and peppermint extract in the slow cooker. Cook uncovered on high setting for 30 minutes, stirring every 5 minutes until the chocolate syrup is dissolved.

Use a soup ladle to let kids serve themselves right from the slow cooker.

. . . And
Ooey, Gooey S'mores

Cooking time: 10 minutes
Preparation time: 5 minutes
Attention: Minimal
Pot size: 2–6 quarts
Serves 4

8 graham cracker squares
2 Hershey's chocolate bars without almonds
4 large marshmallows

Preheat the slow cooker on high setting for 10 minutes. Place 4 graham cracker squares on the bottom of the slow cooker. Top each with half of a chocolate bar. Top this with one marshmallow each. Cook covered on high setting for 10 minutes. Add 4 graham cracker squares to the tops to make 4 sandwiches. Press down until the chocolate and marshmallow begin to ooze out of the sandwich.

For a different yet still scrumptious treat, use half of a chocolate bar with almonds or half of a Mounds bar instead of the half all-chocolate candy.

Barbecued Chicken Drummies

Cooking time: 5 hours
Preparation time: 15 minutes
Attention: Minimal
Pot size: 3–6 quarts
Serves 12

1 teaspoon yellow onion, grated
2 garlic cloves
1 cup water
¼ cup honey
2 teaspoons soy sauce
2 tablespoons vinegar
1 cup bottled barbecue sauce
2 tablespoons hot pepper sauce (optional)
½ teaspoon table salt
½ teaspoon ground black pepper
1 teaspoon cayenne pepper (optional)
36 chicken drummies (the fleshy part of the wing that attaches to
    the breast)

Peel and grate the onion using a vegetable grater. Peel the garlic cloves and slice paper-thin. Combine the onion, garlic, water, honey, soy sauce, vinegar, barbecue sauce, hot pepper sauce (if using), salt, black pepper, and cayenne (if using) in the slow cooker. Cook on high setting about 15 minutes, until all ingredients are well combined. Stir well and add the chicken drummies. Cook covered on low setting for 5 hours.

This is a perfect appetizer for slumber parties or teen get-togethers. Add the optional ingredients for older teens to get the flavor of Buffalo wings. Remember to serve them with celery sticks and blue cheese dressing!

Sicilian Potatoes

Cooking time: 4–5 hours

Preparation time: 20 minutes

Attention: Medium

Pot size: 4–6 quarts

Serves 4

1 small yellow onion
4 garlic cloves
4 ripe tomatoes
¼ teaspoon oregano
2 teaspoons salt
3 tablespoons olive oil
14 small new potatoes
6 links Italian sausage

1. Peel and chop the onions and garlic into ¼-inch pieces. Chop the tomatoes into ½-inch pieces. Turn the slow cooker on high setting. Add the olive oil, garlic, and onions. Cook for 10 minutes. Add the tomatoes, oregano, and salt. Reduce heat to low, cover, and cook for 15 minutes.
2. Peel and wash the potatoes. Cut each Italian sausage link into 4 equal pieces. Place the potatoes and sausage in the slow cooker. Cook on low setting for 4 hours, or until the potatoes are tender.

Low-Fat Substitutions
If you want to make these potatoes healthier and lower in fat, use Italian-spiced turkey or chicken sausages instead.

I Did It Myself Ham and Vegetable Soup

Cooking time: 2–3 hours

Preparation time: 10 minutes

Attention: Minimal

Pot size: 2–6 quarts

Serves 8

4 cups water
1 can sliced carrots
1 can corn
1 can peas
1 can sliced potatoes
1 can green beans
1 ham soup bone
A dash of ground black pepper

1. Add the water to the slow cooker and turn on low setting.
2. Empty all ingredients into the slow cooker, including the juices from the canned vegetables; stir well. Cook covered on low setting for 2 to 3 hours.
3. Remove the soup bone and take off all of the meat that hasn't already fallen off. Tear the meat into bite-sized pieces if necessary. Return the meat to the slow cooker and discard the bone.

Even a preschooler will be proud to make this tasty soup—all Mom or Dad did was open the cans! Serve it with cheese sandwiches and olives for a complete do-it-yourself meal.

| Cooking time: 8–10 hours |
| Preparation time: 30 minutes |
| Attention: Minimal |
| Pot size: 3–6 quarts |
| Serves 8 |

Vegetarian Stone Soup

1 large white onion
1 cup rutabaga, chopped
1 turnip
2 large potatoes
1 cup baby carrots
2 celery ribs
1 cup broccoli, chopped

1 small zucchini
1 stone, about the size of an egg
4 cups water
1 cup fresh or frozen green beans
1 teaspoon table salt
½ teaspoon ground black pepper

1. Peel and chop the onion, rutabaga, turnip, and potatoes into 1-inch pieces. Slice the carrots in half. Chop the celery into ¼-inch pieces. Chop the broccoli and zucchini into ½-inch pieces. Clean the stone well—it's best to run it through the dishwasher!

2. Put the stone and water in the slow cooker. Add one ingredient at a time to the slow cooker, stirring as each ingredient is added. Cook covered on low setting for 8 to 10 hours. Remove the stone before serving.

This is a fun party recipe for preschoolers or kindergarteners. Have each child bring one or two ingredients and let them stir their own ingredients into the soup! Serve with crackers and American cheese for a healthy lunch.

Replacing Broccoli

If you don't have fresh broccoli handy, substitute green beans. They hold up well while slow cooking and offer similar nutritional value as broccoli.

Chocolate-Covered Cherries

Cooking time: 1–2 hours
Preparation time: 10 minutes
Attention: Constant
Pot size: 2–6 quarts
Serves 50 as snacks

5 pounds confectioners' sugar
½ pound (1 cup) butter
¼ teaspoon vanilla
1 (12-ounce) can sweetened condensed milk
¾ pound edible paraffin
3 (12-ounce) packages semisweet chocolate chips
1 large jar maraschino cherries (about 200)
Round toothpicks

1. Using your hands, mix together the confectioners sugar, butter, vanilla, and condensed milk. Cover and set aside. Shave the paraffin with a vegetable grater. Place the chocolate chips and paraffin in the slow cooker. Heat on high setting uncovered, stirring periodically, until melted.
2. In the meantime, drain and discard the juice from the cherries. Mold the sugar mixture over the cherries and spear with a toothpick. When the chocolate is melted, dip each of the cherries into the chocolate, then place them on wax paper to harden.

Substitute peppermint flavoring for the vanilla.

Slow-Cooked Candy

Use the slow cooker instead of a saucepan for making basic candies such as caramel apples and candy-coated pretzels. It will melt the ingredients without scorching. It's also safer than a hot stove.

Peanut Butter Crunch

½ cup chocolate-covered toffee

1 (16-ounce) jar crunchy peanut butter

½ cup miniature semisweet chocolate chips

Break the chocolate-covered toffee into small pieces using a wood mallet or cleaver. Place the toffee, peanut butter, and miniature chocolate chips into the slow cooker; mix well. Cook covered on low setting for 1 hour.

Use as a dip for graham crackers or vanilla wafers.

Doubling a Recipe

When doubling or tripling a recipe in the slow cooker, be sure you have a large enough slow cooker. Add enough water for the single recipe then add more later in the cycle if needed.

CHAPTER 30
Hot and Spicy

South o' the Border Chicken Casserole

Cooking time: 4–5 hours

Preparation time: 15 minutes

Attention: Minimal

Pot size: 3–6 quarts

Serves 4

4 boneless, skinless chicken breasts
1 small yellow onion
1½ cups grated Cheddar cheese
12 flour tortillas
1 (10¾-ounce) can cream of mushroom condensed soup
1 (10¾-ounce) can cream of chicken condensed soup
1 cup sour cream
½ cup (4 ounces) canned chopped jalapeño peppers
1 cup salsa

1. Cut the chicken into 1-inch cubes. Peel the onion and grate using the fine side of a vegetable grater. Grate the cheese using the larger side of the vegetable grater. Tear the tortillas into eighths.
2. Combine the onion, cheese, soups, sour cream, and jalapeño peppers in a medium-sized bowl. Make layers in the slow cooker using a third of the torn tortillas, soup mixture, chicken, then salsa. Repeat twice more. Cover and cook on low setting for 4 to 5 hours. Gently stir before serving.

Serve over a bed of lettuce and baked tortilla chips.

Onion Varieties

Onions vary in sweetness. Vidalia tend to be the sweetest, followed by red then yellow. White onions are the least sweet and are better in meat dishes than in soups.

Cooking time: 6–8 hours	
Preparation time: 15 minutes	
Attention: Minimal	
Pot size: 3–6 quarts	
Serves 6	

Mexican Beef

2 pounds round steak
1 yellow onion
4 fresh tomatoes
1 beef bouillon cube
1 (16-ounce) can kidney beans
¼ teaspoon ground black pepper
½ teaspoon garlic salt
1 tablespoon chili powder
1 tablespoon prepared mustard
½ cup (4 ounces) canned chopped jalapeño peppers

1. Cut the beef into 1-inch cubes. Peel and chop the onion into ¼-inch pieces. Cut the tomatoes into quarters. Crush the bouillon cube. Drain the kidney beans.
2. Mix meat, pepper, garlic salt, chili powder, and mustard in slow cooker. Cover with onion, crushed bouillon cube, tomatoes, jalapeño peppers and beans; mix well. Cover and cook on low setting 6 to 8 hours. Mix well before serving.

Serve over white rice with fresh-sliced oranges.

Tomato Types

All tomatoes are not alike. Substitute plum tomatoes for a more robust flavor. Choose golden tomatoes for a more mellow taste. Reserve pricier hot-house tomatoes for recipes in which tomatoes are the main ingredient.

Mexican Chicken Chowder

Cooking time: 7–8 hours

Preparation time: 20 minutes

Attention: Medium

Pot size: 3–6 quarts

Serves 4

1½ pounds boneless, skinless chicken breasts
2 medium-sized white onions
2 garlic cloves
2 celery ribs
½ cup (4 ounces) canned or fresh green chilies, chopped
1 cup (8 ounces) Velveeta cheese, cubed
1 tablespoon olive oil
4 cups chicken broth
1 package dry chicken gravy mix
2 cups milk
2 cups salsa
1 (32-ounce) bag frozen hash brown potatoes

1. Cut the chicken into ½-inch cubes. Peel the onion and cut into ¼-inch pieces. Peel the garlic and mince with a sharp kitchen knife. Cut the celery into ¼-inch pieces. Cut the chilies into ⅛-inch pieces. Cut the cheese into ½-inch cubes.
2. Combine the chicken, onions, garlic, celery, oil, and broth in the slow cooker. Cover and cook on low for 3 to 4 hours.
3. Dissolve the gravy mix in the milk in a medium-sized mixing bowl. Stir into chicken mixture. Add the salsa, potatoes, chilies, and cheese; mix well. Cover and cook on low for 4 hours.

Serve with Corn Bread in the Round (page 366) for an authentic Mexican meal.

Chicken Creole

Cooking time: 6½ –8½ hours

Preparation time: 30 minutes, plus 1 hour soaking time

Attention: Medium

Pot size: 4–6 quarts

Serves 8

4 large chicken breasts (about four cups of meat)
4 tablespoons dehydrated onion
1 tablespoon dehydrated green onion
1 tablespoon dehydrated parsley flakes
1 teaspoon garlic powder
2 cups warm water
2 cups chicken or vegetable stock (or water)
1 cup dry white wine
3 tablespoons steak sauce
2 teaspoons hot sauce
4 cups (32 ounces) canned, peeled tomatoes
½ cup (4 ounces) canned, chopped jalapeño peppers

1. Boil the chicken for 20 minutes in water in a large pot on the stove. Cut the meat off the bones.
2. Mix the dehydrated onions, green onions, parsley, and garlic powder in 2 cups of water and set aside; let this soak for about 1 hour. Combine the water, wine, steak sauce, hot sauce, tomatoes, and jalapeño peppers in the slow cooker. Cook uncovered on high for 30 minutes. Add the soaked dehydrated ingredients to the slow cooker; stir well. Add the chicken and mint to the seasoned water and stir well. Cover and cook on low setting for 6 to 8 hours.

Serve over white rice.

Southwestern Beef Roast with Peppers

Cooking time: 8–10 hours

Preparation time: 20 minutes

Attention: Minimal

Pot size: 3–6 quarts

Serves 6

4 garlic cloves
3 medium-sized yellow onions
1 green bell pepper
1 red bell pepper
1 yellow bell pepper
2 tablespoons jalapeño pepper, minced

5 large ripe tomatoes
1 tablespoon olive oil
3-pound chuck roast
2 cups hot salsa

1. Remove the peel and mince the garlic with a sharp kitchen knife. Remove the peels from the onions and slice into ¼-inch-thick rings. Remove the stems and seeds from the peppers and slice lengthwise into ¼-inch-wide strips. Mince the jalapeño pepper with a paring knife. Chop the tomatoes into ½-inch pieces.
2. Place the olive oil, garlic, onions, bell and jalapeño peppers, and roast in a large skillet on the stove. Cook on medium-high heat until the roast is browned. Flip it so both sides are browned. Scoop the mixture into the slow cooker. Do not drain the oil. Pour the salsa over the ingredients in the slow cooker. Add the tomatoes on top. Cover and cook on low setting for 8 to 10 hours.

Serve with Lemony Asparagus and Carrots (page 565) for a wonderful mix of flavors.

No Time for Browning?

If you don't want to brown meat in a skillet before adding it to the slow cooker, plan to make a thick gravy to serve with it. This will hide the grayish color of the meat.

Cooking time: 4–5 hours
Preparation time: 20 minutes
Attention: Medium
Pot size: 3–8 quarts
Serves 6

Tex-Mex Pork and Potatoes

3-pound pork roast
3 large white onions
4 garlic cloves
10 assorted whole chili peppers
5 medium-sized new potatoes
10 whole cloves
1 cinnamon stick
10 black peppercorns
1 teaspoon whole cumin seeds
2 tablespoons white vinegar

1. Trim the fat from the pork roast. Peel the onions and cut into quarters. Peel the garlic and mince with a sharp kitchen knife. Remove the stems from the chili peppers; cut in half lengthwise. Peel the potatoes and cut in half.
2. Place the pork in the slow cooker. Cover with onions, garlic, chili peppers, cloves, cinnamon, peppercorns, and cumin. Add just enough water to cover ingredients. Cover and cook on low setting for 3 hours.
3. Stir mixture. Add the potatoes. Cover and cook for 1 to 2 hours, or until the potatoes are soft. Ten minutes before serving, remove the spices and add vinegar.

Serve with Cheddar and Onion Bread (page 371).

Mushy Potatoes

Have your raw potatoes gone mushy? They're still good if you use them right away. Remove the peels and slice the potatoes thickly. Put them into a soup or stew and no one will know they were past their prime.

Mexican Pork Carnitas

Cooking time: 4–6 hours

Preparation time: 15 minutes

Attention: Minimal

Pot size: 3–6 quarts

Serves 4

4 garlic cloves
2–4-pound pork butt roast
1 bunch fresh cilantro
1 fresh jalapeño pepper, seeded and chopped
1 (12-ounce) can or bottle lager beer

1. Peel and slice the garlic cloves about ⅛-inch thick. Using a sharp paring knife, cut slices into the butt roast and insert the garlic cloves, one slice in each opening. Place the butt roast in the slow cooker.
2. Chop the cilantro into ¼-inch lengths. Place the cilantro and jalapeño pepper on top of the butt roast. Pour the beer over the top and cook on high setting for 4 to 6 hours. Remove the meat and shred it. Discard the jalapeño pepper and cilantro.

Steam corn tortillas by placing them in the microwave with a cup of water and cooking on high for 20 seconds. Ladle the meat into the tortillas and top with chopped tomatoes and onions.

Quick Marinade
An easy marinade for any meat is half Heinz 57 sauce and half Italian salad dressing. Cut the meat into bite-size pieces and place in a container in the refrigerator for a couple hours before using.

Spicy Chicken Chili Stew

Cooking time: 1–3 hours

Preparation time: 20 minutes

Attention: Minimal

Pot size: 4–6 quarts

Serves 4

4 chicken breasts

1 large white onion

2 stalks celery

2 (4-ounce) cans of tomato paste

2 (12-ounce) cans of tomato sauce

2 (15-ounce) cans of red chili beans, with juice

6 tablespoons chili powder

2 tablespoons cumin

3 teaspoons dried hot red peppers

4 tablespoons hot red pepper sauce

4 bay leaves

8 cups cooked rice

1. Remove the skin from the chicken and boil the chicken for about 15 minutes in water on the stove. Remove the bone and shred the chicken meat, using 2 forks.
2. Peel and chop the onion into 1/8-inch pieces. Chop the celery into 1/8-inch pieces. Place all ingredients in the slow cooker and stir well. Cook on low setting for 1 to 3 hours. Remove the bay leaves.
3. Prepare the rice as per package directions to yield 8 cups cooked. Add the rice to the slow cooker and mix together all the ingredients well.

Instead of adding rice, create a wonderful chicken chili stew by mixing 2 tablespoons of flour with 2 cups of water until well blended; then add the mixture to the ingredients in the slow cooker about 20 minutes before serving.

Freezing Cooked Rice

Cooked rice can be frozen up to six months. The next time you make some for a meal, make twice what you need and freeze the rest in an airtight container. It needs virtually no thawing before being added to a slow cooker recipe.

Hot as a Devil Green Chili

Cooking time: 4–6 hours

Preparation time: 20 minutes

Attention: Minimal

Pot size: 4–6 quarts

Serves 6

1 large yellow onion
4 garlic cloves
4 large potatoes
1 cup (8 ounces) fresh or canned green chilies, diced
1 pound lean ground beef
½ pound ground pork
1½ cups whole kernel corn
3 cups chicken broth
1 teaspoon ground black pepper
1 teaspoon crushed dried oregano
½ teaspoon ground cumin
1 teaspoon table salt
2 teaspoons red pepper sauce

1. Remove the peel from the onion and cut into ¼-inch pieces. Remove the peel from the garlic cloves and mince with a sharp paring knife. Peel the potatoes and cut into ½-inch cubes. Dice the green chilies with a sharp paring knife.
2. Put the meat, onion, and garlic in a large skillet and cook on medium-high heat until the meat is well browned; drain off grease. Put all ingredients in the slow cooker; stir well. Cover and cook on low setting for 4 to 6 hours.

Let people make their own chili tacos by serving this with warm flour tortillas, fresh chopped lettuce, grated Colby cheese, and sour cream.

Cooking time: 10 hours
Preparation time: 10 minutes
Attention: Minimal
Pot size: 3–6 quarts
Serves 8

Super Taco Filling

1 medium-sized yellow onion
1½ cups fresh or canned green chilies, minced
4-pound beef chuck roast
1 envelope dry taco seasoning
1 tablespoon white vinegar
2 teaspoons red pepper sauce
½ teaspoon garlic salt

1. Peel the onion and chop into ¼-inch pieces. Mince the green chilies with a sharp paring knife. Add all ingredients to the slow cooker. Cover and cook on low setting for 9 hours.
2. Remove the meat and shred with a fork. Return the meat to the slow cooker and stir into the other ingredients. Cover and cook on low setting for 1 additional hour.

Let people make their own tacos by serving this with warm flour tortillas, grated cheese, refried beans, shredded lettuce, chopped tomatoes, and sour cream.

Tex-Mex Necessities
Always have plenty of guacamole, salsa, limes, shredded cheese, sour cream, and hot sauce handy whenever you're serving a Tex-Mex inspired meal.

Szechuan Chicken

Cooking time: 7–8 hours

Preparation time: 20 minutes

Attention: Minimal

Pot size: 4–6 quarts

Serves 4

4 chicken breasts
3 green onions
2 garlic cloves
1 tablespoon peanut oil
¼ cup sesame paste
3 tablespoons strong-brewed green tea
2 tablespoons wine vinegar
2½ tablespoons soy sauce
1½ tablespoons rice wine
2 teaspoons crushed red pepper
1 teaspoon dried ginger
½ teaspoon cayenne pepper

1. Remove the skin and bones from the chicken and slice the meat into ¼-inch strips. Remove the roots and first layer of green onion and chop the onion into ¼-inch pieces, including the stems. Peel the garlic and chop into eighths.
2. Place the peanut oil in a medium-sized skillet on medium heat. Add the chicken, sauté until browned and set aside. Add the garlic and onions; sauté until the onions are limp and translucent. Pour into the slow cooker. Add the remaining ingredients; stir well. Cover and cook on low setting for 6 to 7 hours, add chicken and cook for another hour.

Serve over white rice and sprinkle with chopped peanuts.

Cooking time: 8 hours
Preparation time: 30 minutes
Attention: Minimal
Pot size: 6–8 quarts

Barbecueless Chicken

Serves 4

1 whole chicken
½ cup onion, chopped
4 garlic cloves
1 can tomato sauce
¼ cup vinegar
¼ cup dark brown sugar
2 tablespoons Bourbon
1 tablespoon Worcestershire sauce
½ teaspoon table salt
2 tablespoons hot sauce

1. Cut the chicken into serving portions (legs, thighs, wings, breasts).
2. Peel and chop the onion into ¼-inch pieces. Peel the garlic and smash each clove with the broad side of a large knife. Combine the onion, garlic, tomato sauce, vinegar, dark brown sugar, Bourbon, Worcestershire sauce, salt, and hot sauce in a small mixing bowl.
3. Place the chicken in the slow cooker. Pour the prepared barbecue sauce over the chicken. Cover and cook on low setting for 8 hours.

Serve with Corn Bread in the Round (page 366).

Cooking Meat

The smaller the cut of meat the less time it has to cook. If you overcook a bite-size piece of beef, for example, it will fall apart and mix with the other ingredients in the slow cooker. If you're in doubt, add the meat half-way through the cooking process.

Ethnic Cuisine

Congo Stew

Cooking time: 7–9 hours
Preparation time: 20 minutes
Attention: Minimal
Pot size: 3–8 quarts
Serves 8

2-pound pork roast
1 large white onion
1 green bell pepper
2 garlic cloves
2 plum tomatoes
½ teaspoon curry powder
½ teaspoon ground coriander
½ teaspoon ground cumin
½ teaspoon ground black pepper

1 teaspoon crushed red pepper
   flakes
½ teaspoon ground ginger
¼ teaspoon cinnamon
1 bay leaf
1 teaspoon table salt
2 cups chicken broth
1 tablespoon tomato paste
½ cup chunky peanut butter

1. Cut the pork into 1-inch cubes. Peel and chop the onion into ¼-inch pieces. Remove the stems and seeds from the green pepper and chop into ¼-inch pieces. Peel and mince the garlic using a sharp kitchen knife. Chop the plum tomatoes into ¼-inch pieces.
2. Brown the pork in a large skillet at medium-high heat. Add the onions, garlic, curry powder, coriander, cumin, black pepper, and crushed red pepper; stir well and cook for 1 minute. Transfer the mixture to the slow cooker. Add the ginger, cinnamon, salt, bay leaf, chicken broth, and tomato paste. Cover and cook on low setting for 6 to 8 hours.
3. Add the peanut butter and stir well to blend. Stir in the chopped tomato and bell pepper. Cover and cook on low setting for 1 hour.

Add no-salt, skinless peanuts to the top of the bowl before serving.

Mexican Green Chili Burros

Cooking time: 8–10 hours

Preparation time: 15 minutes

Attention: Minimal

Pot size: 3–6 quarts

Serves 4

2-pound beef rump roast
1 cup chopped yellow onions
1 (10-ounce) can diced green chilies
1 (16-ounce) can tomato sauce
1 package taco seasoning mix
1 tablespoon oregano
1 teaspoon garlic powder
8 flour tortillas
½ cup sour cream
1 large green onion, diced
¼ cup chopped black olives

1. Add the meat to the slow cooker. Peel and chop the onions into ¼-inch pieces. Add all ingredients on top of the meat. Cook on low setting for 7 hours. Remove the meat and shred it using 2 forks. Return the meat to the slow cooker and stir together all the ingredients. Cook on low setting for an addition 1 to 3 hours.
2. Serve on flour tortillas that have been warmed in a 250-degree oven for 10 minutes. Top with sour cream, diced green onions, and olives.

Serve on flour tortillas that have been warmed in a 250-degree oven for 10 minutes. Top with sour cream and diced avocado.

Avocados

Avocados are one of the only vegetables high in fat. Substitute cucumber for avocado for a fresh flavor with none of the fat grams. Choose a seedless cucumber and remove the skin before dicing it.

Egyptian Chicken

12 chicken legs
2 medium-sized yellow onions
1 red bell pepper
1 green bell pepper
2 celery ribs
2 cups chicken broth
½ cup crunchy peanut butter
1 teaspoon crushed red chili pepper

1. Remove the skin from the chicken legs. Peel and slice the onion into ¼-inch-thick rings. Remove the stems and seeds from the peppers and slice into ¼-inch-thick rings. Slice the celery into ¼-inch pieces.

2. Combine the onions, peppers, celery, and chicken broth in the slow cooker. Spread the peanut putter over the chicken legs and sprinkle with chili pepper. Place on top of the onions and peppers; do not stir. Cover and cook on low setting for 5 to 6 hours.

Serve with Roasted Garlic (page 302) and Slightly Seedy White Bread (page 374).

Bouillon Cubes

Bouillon cubes will work in place of broth when necessary. When using them instead of homemade broth, be sure to add a little extra of the aromatic vegetables such as onion, celery, and carrots.

Chicken from the French Countryside

Cooking time: 7–9 hours
Preparation time: 45 minutes
Attention: Minimal
Pot size: 6 quarts
Serves 4

1 whole chicken
2 teaspoons table salt
¼ teaspoon coarsely ground
   pepper
4 carrots
1 large Bermuda onion
2 cups fresh green beans

½ cup fresh mushrooms, sliced
8 garlic cloves
2 bay leaves
6 ripe tomatoes
⅓ cup brown rice
½ cup water

1. Cut the chicken into serving portions (legs, thighs, wings, breasts), then rinse off the pieces and dry them. Peel and dice the carrots and onions. Wash the green beans and cut into 2-inch pieces. Clean the mushrooms by wiping individually with a moistened paper towel; slice the mushrooms. Smash, peel, and dice the garlic. Wash, core, and chop the tomatoes into ¼-inch pieces.
2. Place the chicken in the slow cooker. Add the carrots, onions, green beans, mushrooms, garlic, tomatoes, salt, pepper, and bay leaves to the slow cooker. Cover and cook on low for 4 to 5 hours.
3. Stir in the rice and water. Cover and cook on low for 3 to 4 more hours.

Serve on a platter with a dry white wine.

Replacing Fresh Tomatoes
You can substitute one 28-ounce can of peeled whole tomatoes for three fresh tomatoes in any slow cooker recipe. Be sure to include the juice from the can when adding it to the recipe.

Savory Chinese Beef

Cooking time: 6–7 hours

Preparation time: 30 minutes

Attention: Minimal

Pot size: 3–6 quarts

Serves 6

1½ pounds sirloin tip
1 bunch (approximately 8)
   green onions **or** 1 large leek
8 ounces (1 cup) bean sprouts
8 ounces (1 cup) Chinese
   pea pods
1 cup low-fat beef broth
¼ cup low-sodium soy sauce

2 tablespoons cornstarch
2 tablespoons lukewarm water
¼ teaspoon ground ginger **or**
  ½ teaspoon fresh minced ginger
½ teaspoon hot sauce (optional)
1 small can water chestnuts, drained
1 small can bamboo shoots, drained

1. Thinly slice the sirloin tip (slicing is easier if the meat is frozen and then cut when partially thawed). Wash all the fresh vegetables. Cut off the roots at the ends of the green onions (or leek); finely chop the onions (or leek).

2. Place the sliced sirloin in the slow cooker with the beef broth, soy sauce, ginger, and chopped green onions (or leeks). Cover and cook on low for 6 to 7 hours.

3. Uncover and turn setting to high. Mix the cornstarch with the water in a small measuring cup. Stir the cornstarch mixture and the hot sauce into the slow cooker. Cook on high for 15 minutes, or until thickened; stir periodically. During the last 5 minutes of cooking add the remaining canned and fresh vegetables.

For an adventurous audience, serve in individual bowls over Chinese noodles with chopsticks.

Fruit Compote

Nearly any combination of fresh fruits makes a wonderful fruit compote in the slow cooker. Add one cup of sugar for every eight cups of fruit and cook on low until the sauce is thick.

Native American Pudding

Cooking time: 4–5 hours
Preparation time: 45 minutes
Attention: Medium
Pot size: 3–6 quarts
Serves 4

2 tablespoons butter, plus ¼ tablespoon for greasing
3 cups 1 percent milk
½ cup cornmeal
½ teaspoon salt
3 large eggs, beaten
¼ cup packed light brown sugar
⅓ cup molasses
½ teaspoon cinnamon
¼ teaspoon allspice
½ teaspoon ginger

Lightly grease the slow cooker with ¼ tablespoon butter by putting butter on a paper towel and rubbing it along the inside of the slow cooker. Preheat the slow cooker on high for 15 minutes. In a medium-sized saucepan bring the milk, cornmeal, and salt to boil. Boil, stirring constantly, for 5 minutes. Cover and simmer on low for 10 minutes. In a large bowl, combine the remaining ingredients. Gradually whisk the cornmeal mixture into the combined ingredients until thoroughly mixed and smooth. Pour into slow cooker. Cook covered on medium for 4 to 5 hours.

Serve in small bowls with a dollop of low-fat whipping cream.

Cooking time: 8–9 hours

Preparation time: 45 minutes

Attention: Minimal

Pot size: 4–6 quarts

Serves 8

Brazilian Paella

½ pound medium-spicy pork sausage
2–3-pound chicken
2 large yellow onions
1 pound (16 ounces) canned tomatoes
½ teaspoon table salt
½ teaspoon ground black pepper
1½ cups uncooked long-grain brown rice
3 chicken bouillon cubes
2 cups hot water

1. Form the sausage into balls about the size of large marbles. Clean and cut the chicken into serving size pieces. Peel and chop the onions into ¼-inch pieces. Drain the tomatoes, retaining the liquid, and cut into 1-inch pieces.
2. Using a large skillet on medium-high heat, fry the sausage balls until they are well browned and crisp. Place them on paper towels to absorb the grease. Sprinkle the chicken with salt and pepper. Without emptying the grease from the skillet, fry the chicken pieces for about 10 minutes. Place the chicken on paper towels to absorb the grease.
3. Drain all but 3 tablespoons of grease from the skillet. Sauté the onions on medium heat in the skillet until translucent. Add the rice to the skillet and continue to sauté, stirring constantly for 10 minutes.
4. Place the sausage balls, chicken, the onion and rice mixture, tomato juice, and tomatoes in the slow cooker. Mix the bouillon in 2 cups of hot water; add to the slow cooker. Cover and cook on low setting for 8 to 9 hours.

Serve with fresh-sliced oranges and bananas sprinkled with coconut to achieve a true Brazilian flavor.

Mongolian Mixed Meat Stew

Cooking time: 8–9 hours

Preparation time: 20 minutes

Attention: Minimal

Pot size: 3–6 quarts

Serves 8

¼ cup A-1 Steak Sauce
2 chicken bouillon cubes
1 teaspoon table salt
½ teaspoon ground black pepper
1 teaspoon sugar
½ cup hot water
3 pounds chicken thighs

1 pound lean stewing beef
1 medium-sized yellow onion
2 medium potatoes
8 ounces (1 cup) baby carrots
1 (16-ounce) can stewed tomatoes, liquid retained
¼ cup flour

1. Combine steak sauce, bouillon cubes, salt, pepper, sugar, and hot water in the slow cooker; stir well. Remove the skin from the chicken thighs and discard. Cut the chicken meat into 1-inch cubes. Cut the stewing beef into 1-inch cubes. Peel and chop the onions into ¼-inch pieces. Peel the potatoes and cut into ½-inch cubes.

2. Add the chicken, beef, onion, potatoes, carrots, and tomatoes, including juice, to the slow cooker. Cover and cook on low setting for 8 to 9 hours. Before serving, mix the ¼ cup flour with enough water to make a paste; stir mixture into the stew. Cook on high setting uncovered until thick, about 15 to 30 minutes.

Cheddar and Onion Bread (page 371) goes well with this meal.

Freshly Ground Pepper

If possible, use freshly ground black peppercorns when pepper is called for in a recipe. These retain their flavor better than pre-ground pepper and you'll need less of it to get the same flavor.

Portuguese Sweet Bread

Cooking time: 2–3 hours

Preparation time: 10 minutes

Attention: Medium

Pot size: 3–8 quarts

Serves 8

Bread:

½ cup milk

1 package active dry yeast

⅛ cup warm water

¾ cup sugar

½ teaspoon salt

3 eggs

¼ cup butter, softened

3 cups flour

Glaze:

1 egg

1 teaspoon sugar

1. To make the bread, put the milk in a small saucepan on the stove and heat on high until the milk is slightly yellowed. Let the milk cool to room temperature. Dissolve the yeast in warm water in large bowl. Stir in the milk, sugar, salt, eggs, and butter. Beat with an electric mixer until smooth and creamy. Stir in flour. Place the dough onto a lightly floured surface and knead until smooth and elastic, about 5 minutes. Place the dough in a greased bowl; cover and let rise in a warm place for about 2 hours. Shape a round, slightly flat loaf.

2. Grease the slow cooker by putting a small amount of shortening on a paper towel and rubbing it along the inside of the slow cooker. Place the loaf of bread in the slow cooker. To make the glaze, beat the egg until the yellow and white are well mixed brush over the loaf. Sprinkle with sugar.

3. Cover and cook on high setting for 2 to 3 hours. The loaf should be golden.

This is excellent served with Egyptian Chicken (page 492).

Russian Vegetable Beef Borscht

Cooking time: 8–10 hours

Preparation time: 20 minutes

Attention: Minimal

Pot size: 3–6 quarts

Serves 8

1 pound leftover beef roast
½ head cabbage
3 medium potatoes
4 carrots
1 large white onion
1 cup fresh tomatoes, chopped
1 cup green beans
1 cup diced beets
1 cup fresh sweet corn
2 cups beef broth
2 cups tomato juice
¼ teaspoon garlic powder
¼ teaspoon dill seed
2 teaspoons salt
½ teaspoon pepper

1. Cut the beef roast into 1-inch cubes. Slice the cabbage into ¼-inch strips. Peel the potatoes and dice into ½-inch cubes. Peel and slice the carrots into ¼-inch pieces. Remove the skin from the onion and chop into ¼-inch pieces. Chop the tomatoes into ½-inch pieces. Remove the stems from the green beans. Precook the beets by slicing the tops and roots off. Boil in water for ½ hour. Set beets in cool water and use a sharp paring knife to remove the skins. Cut into ½-inch pieces.
2. Add all ingredients to the slow cooker. Add enough water so that the slow cooker is ¾ full. Cook covered on low setting for 8 to 10 hours.

Add a dollop of sour cream to the top of each bowl right before serving.

Polish Sauerkraut Soup

1 pound smoked Polish sausage

5 medium potatoes

2 large yellow onions

3 medium carrots

6 cups chicken broth

4 cups (32 ounces) canned or bagged sauerkraut

1 (6-ounce) can tomato paste

1. Slice the Polish sausage into ½-inch-thick pieces. Do not remove the peel from the potatoes; slice into ½-inch cubes. Remove the peel from the onions and chop into ¼-inch pieces. Peel and slice the carrots ¼-inch thick.
2. Add all ingredients to the slow cooker. Cover and cook on low setting for 8 to 10 hours.

Serve with Heavy Brown Bread (page 375)

Cooking time: 4–5 hours
Preparation time: 15 minutes
Attention: Minimal
Pot size: 4–8 quarts
Serves 8

Pepperoni Rigatoni

12 ounces rigatoni
1 cup fresh mushrooms, sliced
1 large yellow onion
4 garlic cloves
1 medium-sized green bell pepper
2 pounds pepperoni slices
1 (28-ounce) jar spaghetti sauce
3 cups shredded mozzarella cheese

1. Cook the rigatoni in boiling water until soft but not mushy. Clean the mushrooms by wiping with a damp cloth; slice ⅛-inch thick. Remove the peel from the onion and cut into ¼-inch pieces. Remove the peel from the garlic and mince with a sharp paring knife. Remove the stem and seeds from the green pepper; cut into ¼-inch pieces.
2. Add all the ingredients to the slow cooker; stir well. Cover and cook on low setting for 4 to 5 hours.

Serve with a fresh green salad with Italian dressing.

Mushroom Varieties

Different mushrooms have very different tastes. Don't hesitate to substitute exotic dried mushrooms such as wood ear, enoci, and porcini even if the recipe calls for fresh mushrooms.

East Indian Green Curried Chicken

Cooking time: 6½–7½ hours
Preparation time: 20 minutes
Attention: Medium
Pot size: 4–6 quarts
Serves 6

6 chicken breasts
2 fresh green chili peppers
¼ cup fresh mint leaves, chopped
1½ cups unsweetened coconut milk, divided
1½ tablespoons green curry paste
1 cup sliced, canned bamboo shoots
¼ cup fish sauce
1 tablespoon sugar

1. Remove the skin and bones from chicken breast. Remove the stems and seeds from the chili peppers and chop into ⅛-inch pieces. Chop the mint leaves into ¼-inch pieces.
2. Heat ½ cup of the coconut milk and the green curry paste in a medium-sized skillet on medium heat; stir until well blended. Add the chicken and sauté for 10 minutes. Put the chicken breasts into the slow cooker. Stir in the remaining coconut milk, bamboo shoots, fish sauce, and sugar. Cover and cook on low setting for 6 to 7 hours. Stir in the mint and chili peppers. Cover and cook an additional 30 minutes.

Serve with long-grain brown rice.

Stocking Up on Ethnic Staples
If your local grocery store doesn't carry certain ethnic spices or ingredients, you may be able to find them on the Internet or at specialty shops. Just make sure to stock up on shelf-stable necessities so you can make these dishes whenever you like.

Mediterranean Couscous with Vegetables

Cooking time: 6½ –7½ hours

Preparation time: 30 minutes

Attention: Medium

Pot size: 3–8 quarts

Serves 8

2 medium zucchini

6 plum tomatoes

½ pound (1 cup) fresh
   mushrooms

4 garlic cloves

2 medium-sized white onions

2 celery ribs

1 large red bell pepper

2 medium carrots

½ cup black olives, pitted
   and diced

¼ cup minced fresh basil

2 tablespoons olive oil1

½ teaspoons dried oregano
   leaves

1 teaspoon salt

¼ teaspoon cinnamon

¼ teaspoon ground black pepper

3 tablespoons balsamic vinegar

1½ cups whole-wheat couscous

1. Cut the zucchini into 1-inch pieces. Chop the tomatoes into ¼-inch pieces. Clean the mushrooms by wiping with a damp cloth; cut in half. Peel the garlic and mince with a sharp kitchen knife. Peel the onions and chop into ¼-inch pieces. Chop the celery into ¼-inch pieces. Remove the stem and seeds from the bell pepper and slice into ¼-inch strips. Peel and slice the carrots into ¼-inch rounds. Chop the black olives into ¼-inch pieces. Chop the basil into ¼-inch pieces.

2. Heat the olive oil in a large skillet at medium-high heat. Add the garlic, onion, and red pepper. Sauté until the onion is limp and translucent. Add the celery, carrots, mushrooms, zucchini, tomatoes, olives, and half the basil; sauté for 5 minutes. Transfer to slow cooker. Add half the remaining basil, oregano, salt, cinnamon, and black pepper. Cover and cook on low setting for 6 to 7 hours.

3. Stir in the vinegar and couscous. Cover and cook on low setting for an additional 30 minutes.

Serve with pocket bread and hummus for an authentic meal.

Thai Shrimp and Scallop Soup

Cooking time: 8–9 hours

Preparation time: 20 minutes

Attention: Minimal

Pot size: 3–8 quarts

Serves 8

1 small white onion
8 ounces (1 cup) fresh mushrooms, sliced
2 garlic cloves
6 green onions
⅓ cup fresh parsley, chopped
½ pound precooked popcorn shrimp
½ pound baby scallops
6 cups water
½ teaspoon thyme
1 teaspoon table salt
¼ teaspoon ground black pepper
2 teaspoons ground coriander
1½ teaspoons chili powder
1 teaspoon red pepper sauce
1 tablespoon soy sauce
2 cups uncooked white rice

1. Peel the onion and chop into ¼-inch pieces. Clean the mushrooms by wiping with a damp cloth; cut into paper-thin slices with a sharp kitchen knife. Peel the garlic and mince with a sharp kitchen knife. Remove the roots and first layer of skin from the green onions and chop into ¼-inch pieces. Chop the parsley into ½-inch pieces.
2. Combine all ingredients except the parsley, green onions, precooked shrimp, and baby scallops in the slow cooker. Cover and cook on low setting for 7 to 8 hours. Add shrimp and scallops and cook for 1 to 2 hours. Stir in the parsley and green onions right before serving.

Serve with Slightly Seedy White Bread (page 374).

Cooking time: 8–9 hours	
Preparation time: 30 minutes	
Attention: Minimal	
Pot size: 3–6 quarts	
Serves 6	

Turkish Pork Chops

½ teaspoon salt
½ teaspoon pepper
2 tablespoons paprika
½ cup flour
6 lean pork chops
4 medium onions
2 garlic cloves
4 tablespoons butter
1 cup chicken stock

1. Combine salt, pepper, paprika, and flour. Dredge the pork chops by smashing them into the flour. Peel the onions and chop into ¼-inch pieces. Peel the garlic and chop into eighths.
2. Heat the butter in large skillet at medium-high heat. Brown the pork chops. Remove the pork chops and put into the slow cooker. Add the onions and garlic to skillet and sauté until the onions are limp and translucent. Drain off the grease and place the onions and garlic on top of the pork chops. Add chicken stock. Cover and cook on low setting for 8 to 9 hours.

Make a sauce by combining 1 cup sour cream with 1 tablespoon dill. Add dollops of the sauce to the top of each pork chop.

Greek Lamb Chops with Lentils

Cooking time: 7–9 hours
Preparation time: 30 minutes
Attention: Minimal
Pot size: 3–6 quarts
Serves 6

6 medium lamb chops
1 medium-sized yellow onion
4 garlic cloves
3 medium carrots
2 medium-sized ripe tomatoes
1 cup black olives, chopped
1 cup lentils

3 cups water
½ cup vodka
2 tablespoons olive oil
1 teaspoon table salt
½ teaspoon ground black pepper

1. Trim the fat from the lamb chops. Peel and chop the onion into ¼-inch pieces. Peel the garlic and mince with a sharp kitchen knife. Peel and slice the carrots into ¼-inch rounds. Chop the tomatoes into ¼-inch pieces. Chop the olives into ¼-inch pieces.
2. Put the lentils in the slow cooker with the water and vodka. Add the carrots, onions, and tomatoes. Begin cooking on low setting. In the meantime, heat the olive oil in a large skillet at medium heat. Sprinkle the lamb chops with the salt and pepper and place in the skillet. Add the garlic. Cook until the lamb chops are browned on both sides. Transfer to the slow cooker. Sprinkle the black olives on top. Cover and cook on low setting for 7 to 9 hours.

Serve with a fresh green salad with Greek dressing.

If You Substitute Lamb or Veal . . .

Since lamb and veal are inherently tender meats, they need less cooking time than their grown-up counterparts. Decrease the time by half and add the meat later in the cooking cycle.

CHAPTER 32
California Cuisine

Citrus Chicken Breasts

Cooking time: 6–7 hours

Preparation time: 30 minutes

Attention: Minimal

Pot size: 4–6 quarts

Serves 4

4 pounds chicken breasts

4 medium potatoes

2 tablespoons cider vinegar

¼ teaspoon ground nutmeg

1 teaspoon dry basil

2 tablespoons brown sugar

1 cup orange juice

4 fresh peaches

2 fresh oranges

fresh strawberries, for garnish

1. Remove the skin and bones from the chicken breasts and discard. Peel and slice the potatoes ¼-inch thick. Put the potatoes on the bottom of the slow cooker. Place the chicken breasts on top.
2. Mix the vinegar, nutmeg, basil, brown sugar, and orange juice in a small mixing bowl; Pour mixture over the chicken. Cover and cook on low setting for 6 to 7 hours.
3. Using a slotted spoon, remove the chicken and potatoes from the slow cooker and place in a 250-degree oven to keep warm. Peel the peaches and slice ½-inch thick. Peel the oranges and break into slices. Place the peaches and oranges into the slow cooker. Cook uncovered on high setting for 20 minutes. Pour over the chicken and potatoes before serving.

Garnish with fresh sliced strawberries before serving.

Adding Fruit

Cut fruit right before putting it in the slow cooker. Exposure to air can cause the fruit to discolor while mixing it with sugar or other fruits can draw out the juices.

Cooking time: 5–6 hours
Preparation time: 30 minutes
Attention: Medium
Pot size: 4–6 quarts
Serves 6

Spinach Feta Chicken

1 bunch fresh spinach
4 garlic cloves
1 tablespoon extra-virgin olive oil
4 boneless, skinless chicken breasts
½ teaspoon table salt
¼ teaspoon coarsely ground black pepper
¼ cup dry white wine
⅓ cup feta cheese

1. Thoroughly wash and dry the spinach; cut off the stems from the leaves. Peel and finely chop the garlic.
2. Heat a large skillet on medium-high; add the olive oil. Add the chicken and lightly sprinkle with salt and pepper. Sauté until golden brown. Remove the chicken with a slotted spoon or tongs and place the chicken in the slow cooker. Add the wine to the skillet and mix with the drippings; pour mixture over the chicken. Cover and cook on low setting for 5 to 6 hours, or until the chicken is tender and no longer pink in the middle.
3. Add the spinach, cover, and cook for 1 hour on low setting. Transfer the contents of the slow cooker to a serving platter. Crumble the feta cheese on top.

Serve with a side of garlic-buttered penne pasta.

Turkey for Chicken

For a lean alternative in your next chicken recipe, substitute turkey. It has much less fat and much more protein than chicken while often being a better per-pound buy at the grocery store.

Portobello Mushroom Pork Tenderloin

Cooking time: 6–7 hours
Preparation time: 45 minutes
Attention: Minimal
Pot size: 6 quarts
Serves 6

1 pound (2 cups) portobello mushrooms, sliced
2-pound pork tenderloin
½ cup red wine
1 teaspoon table salt
¼ teaspoon pepper

1. Wash and dry the portobello mushrooms; slice into pieces.
2. Broil the tenderloin on high until the top and bottom are golden brown. Place the tenderloin in the slow cooker. Add the wine, salt, pepper, and mushrooms. Cover and cook on low setting for 6 to 7 hours.
3. Remove the tenderloin from the slow cooker and place on a platter. Slice the tenderloin into 1-inch pieces. Pour the mushroom-wine sauce over the tenderloin.

Serve with new potatoes coated in butter and chopped chives.

Slow-Roasting Meats

Rub salt into the surface of a roast before cooking it to enhance the flavor without overdrying the meat. As an alternative, use garlic or onion salt.

Cooking time: 3 hours
Preparation time: 30 minutes
Attention: Medium
Pot size: 3–6 quarts
Serves 4

Halibut with Almonds

4 halibut fillets
2 tablespoons chopped parsley
½ cup butter, divided in half
¼ cup slivered almonds
1 lemon
¼ teaspoon Worcestershire sauce

1. Wash and dry the halibut fillets. Wash and dry the parsley; chop coarsely.
2. Turn the slow cooker on high. Melt half of the butter in the slow cooker and stir in the Worcestershire sauce. Place the halibut fillets on top of the butter. Place a dollop of butter on each fillet. Sprinkle almonds on top of each fillet. Cover and cook on low setting for 2 hours. Sprinkle parsley on top of the fillets and cook covered for 1 more hour on low setting. Cut lemons into fourths and squeeze one quarter onto each fillet right before serving.

Serve with Brussels Sprouts à la Orange (page 549).

Fatty Oils

All oils are 100 percent fat, including butter and margarine. For a healthy diet, use them sparingly and substitute unsaturated vegetable oil or extra virgin olive oil whenever possible.

Salmon with Asparagus

Cooking time: 4 hours
Preparation time: 30 minutes
Attention: Medium
Pot size: 3–6 quarts
Serves 4

1½ pounds asparagus
¼ cup butter, divided
4 salmon steaks
1 teaspoon dried marjoram
1 teaspoon table salt
½ teaspoon ground black pepper

1. Wash and dry the asparagus; cut off the bottom 1 inch (the light pinkish-green part) of the asparagus.
2. Turn the slow cooker on high. Melt half of the butter in the slow cooker. Place the salmon steaks on top of the butter. Sprinkle the spices over the salmon. Place a dollop of butter on each steak. Cover and cook on low for 3 hours. Add the asparagus. Cover and cook on low for an additional hour, or until salmon flakes.

Serve with Hot Fruit Medley (page 592) over vanilla yogurt for dessert.

Add a Little Zest
Citrus goes great with seafood of all kinds. Try squeezing some lemon or lime on any of your favorite fish recipes.

Kiwi Shrimp

1½ pounds raw tiger shrimp, shelled and deveined
¼ cup parsley, chopped
¼ cup lemon juice
2 kiwi fruit
3 cloves garlic
2 tablespoons butter

1. Coarsely chop the parsley. Mix the lemon juice with the parsley; combine mixture with the shrimp, making sure all the shrimp is well covered. Refrigerate overnight.
2. Peel the kiwi and cut into ¼- inch slices. Peel and mince the garlic. Turn the slow cooker onto high. Melt the butter, then add the garlic. Cover and cook for 15 minutes. After the garlic is tender, add the shrimp. Cover and cook on low for 1½ hours, or until the shrimp begins to turn pink. Add the kiwi. Cover and cook for 15 more minutes. Transfer the shrimp and kiwi to a platter.

Serve with Green Beans in Lemon Honey (page 550).

Provincial Zucchini and Tomatoes

Cooking time: 1 hour
Preparation time: 30 minutes
Attention: Minimal
Pot size: 3–6 quarts
Serves 4

2 small zucchini
12 cherry tomatoes
2 garlic cloves
2 tablespoons olive oil
½ teaspoon dried thyme
½ teaspoon table salt
¼ teaspoon ground pepper

1. Wash the zucchini and tomatoes. Trim the ends from the zucchini and cut lengthwise into ½-inch-thick slices. Peel and dice the garlic.
2. Turn on the slow cooker to high setting; add the olive oil and garlic. Cover and cook for 15 minutes. After the garlic is tender, add the zucchini. Reduce heat to low, cover, and cook for 1 hour. Add tomatoes and cook until they are warmed through. Add the thyme, salt, and pepper just prior to serving.

This is a nice complement to Citrus Chicken Breasts (page 508).

Summertime Specialty

Add yellow summer squash to any recipe with zucchini. Those two vegetables work really well together.

Red Cabbage with Apples

Cooking time: 1 hour

Preparation time: 30 minutes

Attention: Minimal

Pot size: 3–6 quarts

Serves 4

1 small head red cabbage
1 medium leek
1 tart apple
2 tablespoons light vegetable oil
¼ cup cider vinegar
2 tablespoons brown sugar
½ teaspoon table salt
¼ teaspoon ground black pepper

1. Core and shred the cabbage into ¼-inch-wide pieces. Cut the end off the leek and cut the leek into slices about ¼-inch thick. Core, peel, and cut the apple into ¼-inch slices.
2. Turn on the slow cooker to high setting. Add the oil and leek. Cover and cook for 15 minutes, or until the leek is tender. Add the vinegar, sugar, salt, and pepper; mix thoroughly. Add the cabbage and apple; reduce temperature to low setting. Cover and cook for 45 minutes, or until the cabbage is slightly tender.

This is a wonderful complement to Portobello Mushroom Pork Tenderloin (page 510).

Minted Green Peas with Lettuce

Cooking time: 1 hour
Preparation time: 20 minutes
Attention: Medium
Pot size: 2–4 quarts
Serves 4

2 cups fresh peas (1 package frozen peas can be substituted)
2 cups red leaf lettuce, shredded
1 teaspoon chopped fresh mint leaves
2 tablespoons butter
½ teaspoon table salt
½ teaspoon sugar
Mint sprigs for garnish

1. Shuck and wash the peas. Wash and tear the lettuce into small pieces, about the size of a quarter. Finely chop the mint leaves.
2. Turn on the slow cooker to low setting. Melt the butter in the slow cooker. Add peas, cover, reduce heat to low, and cook until the peas are tender (approximately 45 minutes). Add the lettuce and chopped mint. Cook uncovered until the lettuce wilts. Add the salt and sugar. Serve in medium-sized serving bowl with mint sprigs for a garnish.

Serve as a complement to Halibut with Almonds (page 811).

Fresh vs. Dry

If you don't have fresh herbs, you can always use dry ones. Just make sure to experiment with the proper amount; some dry herbs have a more concentrated flavor while others have a weaker one.

East Asian Green Beans with Sesame Seeds

Cooking time: 1 hour

Preparation time: 30 minutes

Attention: Medium

Pot size: 2–4 quarts

Serves 4

2 pounds (4 cups) fresh green beans
1 tablespoon soy sauce
2 teaspoons fresh minced ginger
1 tablespoon vinegar
1 tablespoon butter
2 tablespoons water
2 tablespoons sesame seed

1. Wash the green beans, then cut off the stems. Mix the soy sauce, ginger, and vinegar in a small bowl.
2. Turn on the slow cooker to high setting. Melt the butter in the slow cooker. Add the water and green beans; reduce heat to low. Cover and cook for 45 minutes, or until the beans are tender. Add soy sauce, ginger, and vinegar mixture; mix so that the beans are well covered. Sprinkle with sesame seeds.

This is a perfect complement to Spicy Pot Roast (page 396).

Korean Chicken Breasts with Snow Pea Pods

Cooking time: 6 hours

Preparation time: 30 minutes

Attention: Medium

Pot size: 4–6 quarts

Serves 4

4 chicken breasts
6 garlic cloves
1 pound (2 cups) snow pea pods
1 cup soy sauce
¼ cup red wine vinegar
2 teaspoons crushed red pepper flakes
¼ cup sugar
2 tablespoons vegetable oil

1. Remove the bone and skin from the chicken breasts. Peel and mince the garlic. Wash the snow pea pods and the remove stems. Combine the soy sauce, vinegar, red pepper flakes, and sugar in a small bowl.
2. Turn on the slow cooker to high setting. Add the oil and garlic. Cover and cook for 15 minutes. After the garlic is tender, add the chicken and soy sauce mixture. Reduce the heat to low setting. Cover and cook for 5 hours. Add the snow pea pods. Cover and cook on low setting for 1 more hour.

Serve over a bed of Minnesota Wild Rice (page 571).

Curried Chicken Thighs

Cooking time: 6 hours	
Preparation time: 20 minutes	
Attention: Medium	
Pot size: 4–6 quarts	
Serves 4	

1 pound chicken thighs
2 garlic cloves
2 tablespoons virgin olive oil
1 tablespoon dry mustard

3 tablespoons curry powder
1 tablespoon ground ginger
1 cup fresh peas

Remove the skin and bones from the chicken. Peel and mince the garlic. Turn on the slow cooker to high setting. Add the oil, garlic, mustard, curry powder, and ginger. Cook for 5 minutes. Reduce heat to low. Add the chicken. Cover and cook for 5 hours. Add the peas and mix thoroughly with the chicken. Cook covered for 1 hour on low setting.

Serve with Minted Green Peas with Lettuce (page 516) for a nice mix of flavors.

Sole with Red Grapes

Cooking time: 4 hours	
Preparation time: 20 minutes	
Attention: Minimal	
Pot size: 4–6 quarts	
Serves 4	

¼ cup butter
¼ cup lemon juice
¼ cup minced parsley

1¼ pounds sole fillets
1 cup seedless red grapes

Turn on the slow cooker to high setting. Melt the butter in the slow cooker, then mix in the lemon juice and parsley. Add the sole fillets. Cover and cook on low setting for 3 hours. Add the grapes. Cover and cook 1 hour on low setting.

Keep the flavor of this meal light by serving it with Red Cabbage and Apples (page 515).

CHAPTER 33
Potluck Favorites

Squishy, Squashy Succotash

Cooking time:	8–10 hours
Preparation time:	30 minutes
Attention:	Minimal
Pot size:	3–6 quarts
Serves 6	

1½ pounds acorn squash
4 garlic cloves
2 medium-sized yellow onions
2 jalapeño peppers
1 medium-sized yellow bell
   pepper
¼ fresh minced cilantro
2 cups fresh corn kernels

1 tablespoon olive oil
1 teaspoon cumin seeds
1 teaspoon red pepper flakes
1 teaspoon table salt
1 cup water
2 tablespoons tomato paste
1 teaspoon table salt
2 cups precooked lima beans

1. Peel the acorn squash and cut into 1-inch pieces. Peel the garlic cloves and mince with a sharp kitchen knife. Peel the onions and chop into ¼-inch pieces. Remove the stems from the jalapeño peppers and cut the peppers into ¼-inch pieces. Remove the stem and seeds from the yellow bell pepper and cut into ¼-inch pieces. Mince the cilantro with a sharp kitchen knife.
2. Add all the ingredients except the lima beans and cilantro to the slow cooker. Cover and cook on low setting for 7 to 9 hours. Add the cilantro and lima beans; stir gently. Cook uncovered on low setting for 1 additional hour.

Serve with an assortment of pickled vegetables.

Check for Damage
Check for cracks and deep scratches in the crockery food container and cover before using the slow cooker. Because the stoneware is porous, cracks and scratches can harbor dangerous bacteria.

Almondy Rice Pilaf

Cooking time: 6–8 hours
Preparation time: 15 minutes
Attention: Minimal
Pot size: 3–8 quarts
Serves 4

1 medium-sized yellow onion
8 ounces (1 cup) fresh
   mushrooms
2 cups vegetable broth

1 cup raw converted rice
1 cup canned or frozen peas
2 tablespoons butter
½ cup almond slivers

Peel the onion and mince. Clean the mushrooms by wiping with a damp cloth; slice paper-thin. Add all ingredients to the slow cooker. Cover and cook on low setting for 6 to 8 hours.

This makes an excellent side dish to hot sandwiches.

Emma's Seven-Layer Bars

Cooking time: 2–3 hours
Preparation time: 10 minutes
Attention: Minimal
Pot size: 3–6 quarts
Serves 12

¼ cup melted butter
½ cup graham cracker crumbs
½ cup chocolate chips
½ cup butterscotch chips

½ cup flaked coconut
½ cup chopped walnuts
½ cup sweetened condensed milk

Grease the inside of a 2-pound coffee can by putting shortening on a paper towel and rubbing it along the inside of the can. Place the ingredients in the coffee can in the order listed; do not mix. Cover and cook on high setting for 2 to 3 hours. Let cool before removing from the coffee can.

Use pecans instead of walnuts.

Cook's Surprise Meatballs

Cooking time: 4 hours

Preparation time: 45 minutes

Attention: Medium

Pot size: 4–6 quarts

Serves 4

1 large yellow onion
1 green bell pepper
1 red bell pepper
2 garlic cloves
½ cup crushed saltine crackers
1 egg
1 pound ground turkey
1 pound ground beef

1 pound ground pork
1 (6-ounce) can tomato paste
1 teaspoon oregano
½ teaspoon basil
1 teaspoon salt
1 teaspoon ground black pepper
2 tablespoons vegetable oil

1. Peel the onion and chop into ¼-inch pieces. Remove the stems and seeds from the bell peppers and chop the peppers into ¼-inch pieces. Crush the garlic by laying a large knife on its side over the top of each garlic clove; push down until the garlic clove "pops." Crush the crackers using a spoon in a small bowl. Beat the egg with a fork in a small bowl until the egg yolk and white are thoroughly mixed.
2. In a medium-sized bowl, use your hands to mix the meat, egg, tomato paste, onion, red pepper, green pepper, oregano, basil, garlic, salt, black pepper, and crushed crackers. Form into firm balls about the size of golf balls. Place the meatballs on a cookie sheet and bake in a 350-degree conventional oven for about 10 minutes.
3. Put the vegetable oil in the slow cooker. Transfer all the meatballs to the slow cooker and cook covered on low setting for 4 hours.

Serve the meatballs over fresh egg noodles and peas for a complete meal.

Hold the Salt

Resist the urge to salt. Salt draws flavors and juices out of meat and vegetables. Let the flavors release on their own time for the best result. Guests can salt their own dishes if they prefer. They'll also use less than if you add it while cooking.

Barbecued Green Beans

Cooking time: 6–8 hours

Preparation time: 30 minutes

Attention: Minimal

Pot size: 3–6 quarts

Serves 6

1 pound bacon

¼ cup white onions, chopped

2 garlic cloves

2 large tomatoes

½ cup white vinegar

½ cup brown sugar

3 teaspoons Worcestershire sauce

¾ teaspoon salt

4 cups fresh green beans

1. Brown the bacon in a large skillet on medium-high heat until it is crisp. Transfer the bacon to paper towels to cool. Crumble the bacon by placing it between two layers of paper towel and twisting it. Discard all but 2 tablespoons of the bacon drippings.

2. Peel and chop the onions into ¼-inch pieces. Peel and slice the garlic paper-thin with a sharp paring knife. Sauté the onions and garlic in the retained bacon drippings for about 5 minutes, until the onions are translucent. Remove the skillet from the stove.

3. Skin and mash the tomatoes with a large wooden spoon. Remove skin from tomatoes with a sharp paring knife, gently lifting the skin and peeling it off. Add the tomatoes, vinegar, brown sugar, Worcestershire sauce, and salt to the onions and garlic in the skillet; stir well.

4. Clean the green beans in cold water; snap off and discard the ends. Place the green beans in the slow cooker. Pour the mixture from the skillet on top. Stir 2 or 3 times with a wooden spoon. Cook covered on low setting 6 to 8 hours.

This makes an excellent complement to ham or beef pot roasts.

Hot Dog Lentil Soup

Cooking time: 7–9 hours

Preparation time: 30 minutes

Attention: Minimal

Pot size: 3–8 quarts

Serves 8

1 pound all-beef hot dogs
2 medium-sized yellow onions
3 garlic cloves
2 medium carrots
2 ribs celery
2 tablespoons olive oil
8 cups water
2 cups lentils, rinsed and drained
1 bay leaf
1 teaspoon salt
½ teaspoon ground black pepper
2 tablespoons cider vinegar.

1. Cut the hot dogs into 1-inch pieces. Peel and chop the onion into ¼-inch pieces. Peel and mince the garlic with a sharp kitchen knife. Peel the carrots, then chop carrots and celery into ¼-inch pieces.
2. Heat the olive oil in a medium-sized skillet on medium heat. Add the onions, garlic, carrots, and celery; sauté until the onions are limp and translucent. Drain off the grease and put the vegetables in the slow cooker. Add the water, lentils, bay leaf, salt, pepper, cider vinegar, and hot dog pieces. Cover and cook on low setting for 7 to 9 hours.

Substitute Polish sausage or kielbasa for a more robust flavor.

Italian Beef Sandwiches

Cooking time: 8–10 hours

Preparation time: 10 minutes

Attention: Minimal

Pot size: 6 quarts

Serves 6

1 teaspoon salt
1 teaspoon pepper
1 teaspoon oregano
1 teaspoon onion salt
1 teaspoon garlic salt
1 teaspoon basil
1 cup Italian salad dressing
2 cups water
5-pound beef pot roast

Mix the spices with the salad dressing and water in the slow cooker. Place the beef roast in the slow cooker. Cover and cook on low setting for 8 to 10 hours. Thirty minutes before serving, remove the beef and shred it using 2 forks and pulling the meat apart. Return the meat to the broth and stir well. Cook covered on low setting for the remaining 30 minutes.

Cut loaves of French bread into 6-inch-long pieces, then cut each piece down the middle and ladle the meat inside. Add a slice of mozzarella cheese on top of the meat.

Using Fresh Herbs

Add fresh herbs during the last 60 minutes of cooking to ensure they retain their flavor. Dried herbs can be added at the beginning of the process.

Texas Barbecued Beef Sandwiches

Cooking time: 9 hours
Preparation time: 15 minutes
Attention: Minimal
Pot size: 5–6 quarts
Serves 8

4-pound chuck roast
½ cup water
2 cups ketchup
10 ounces cola
¼ cup Worcestershire sauce
2 tablespoons prepared mustard
2 tablespoons liquid smoke
¼ teaspoon Tabasco or other hot pepper sauce
8 hamburger buns

1. Cover and cook the roast with the water in the slow cooker on high setting for 8 hours, or until tender.
2. Remove the roast. Shred the meat, trimming off the fat and discarding it in the process. Place the shredded meat in the slow cooker along with ketchup, cola, Worcestershire sauce, mustard, liquid smoke, and hot sauce. Cook covered on high setting for 1 hour. Ladle over buns to serve.

Potato chips and baked beans make this meal an authentic American potluck event!

Meat Grades
The higher the grade of meat, the more marbling (fat) contained in the cut. For a healthy alternative, use a lower grade of meat and cook it in the slow cooker to tenderize it. Select is the least fatty grade.

Cooking time: 1–2 hours
Preparation time: 15 minutes
Attention: Minimal
Pot size: 4–6 quarts
Serves 8

Ham Barbecue

2 pounds chopped ham
1 bottle chili sauce
½ cup ketchup
½ cup water
¼ cup white corn syrup
8 whole wheat bulky rolls

1. Mix together all the ingredients in the slow cooker. Cook covered on low setting 1 to 2 hours, stirring occasionally.
2. Serve on whole wheat rolls.

Leftover Ham

Ham slices are the perfect "don't know what to make" ingredient. Cube it and add the meat to beans to make soup or cut it into quarters and cook it with potatoes, carrots and onions to create a "mock" ham roast.

Holiday Punch

Cooking time: 1 hour

Preparation time: 15 minutes

Attention: Minimal

Pot size: 3–6 quarts

Serves 4

½ medium-sized orange
1 quart apple juice
1 quart cranberry juice cocktail
1 cup brown sugar
4 cinnamon sticks
4 whole cloves

Peel and cut the orange into ¼-inch-thick slices. Add the apple juice, cranberry juice, and brown sugar to the slow cooker. Cook on low setting, stirring occasionally, until the brown sugar is dissolved. Add the cinnamon sticks and cloves. Cook covered for 1 hour on low setting. Right before guests arrive, add the orange slices.

Use a soup ladle to let guests serve the punch themselves.

Slow Cooker vs. Crock-Pot®?

A slow cooker is any cooking appliance that is designed to cook at a low temperature for several hours. A Crock-Pot® is a trade-marked slow cooker that is manufactured by Rival.

Cooking time: 8–9 hours

Preparation time: 30 minutes

Attention: Minimal

Pot size: 3–6 quarts

Serves 12

Cabbage Rolls

12 large cabbage leaves
1 pound lean ground beef
½ cup cooked white rice
½ teaspoon salt
⅛ teaspoon ground black pepper
¼ teaspoon thyme
¼ teaspoon nutmeg
¼ teaspoon cinnamon
1 (6-ounce) can tomato paste
¾ cup water

1. Wash the cabbage leaves. Boil four cups of water in a saucepan on the stove. Turn off the heat and soak the leaves in the water for 5 minutes. Remove the leaves, drain, and cool.
2. Combine the ground beef, rice, salt, pepper, thyme, nutmeg, and cinnamon. Place 2 tablespoons of the meat mixture on each leaf and roll firmly. Stack the cabbage rolls in the slow cooker. Combine the tomato paste and water; pour over the stuffed cabbage rolls. Cook covered on low setting 8 to 9 hours.

Serve with a selection of pickled vegetables and hard cheeses.

Award-Winning Tuna Noodle Casserole

Cooking time: 6–8 hours

Preparation time: 15 minutes

Attention: Minimal

Pot size: 3–6 quarts

Serves 8

2 cups (16 ounces) water-packed tuna

3 hard-boiled eggs

2 celery ribs

1 medium-sized yellow onion

1 cup frozen mixed vegetables

2 cups cooked egg noodles

1½ cups crushed potato chips

1 (10¾-ounce) can cream of mushroom condensed soup

1 (10¾-ounce) can cream of celery condensed soup

1. Drain the tuna. Chop the hard-boiled eggs into ¼-inch pieces. Chop the celery into ¼-inch pieces. Peel the onion and chop into ¼-inch pieces. Thaw the frozen vegetables overnight in the refrigerator, or thaw them in the microwave. Precook the egg noodles in boiling water. Crush the potato chips while still in the bag.
2. Combine all ingredients except ½ cup potato chips. Put mixture into the slow cooker. Cover with remaining potato chips. Cover and cook on low setting for 6 to 8 hours.

Serve with Slightly Seedy White Bread (page 374).

CHAPTER 39
Hearty Appetites

Southern-Style Barbecued Pork Ribs

Cooking time: 6–9 hours
Preparation time: 20 minutes
Attention: Medium
Pot size: 4–8 quarts
Serves 4

2 pounds pork ribs
1 medium-sized yellow onion
¼ cup fresh green pepper, chopped
1 cup brewed coffee
1 cup ketchup
½ cup sugar
½ cup Worcestershire sauce
¼ cup white vinegar
¼ teaspoon ground black pepper
¼ teaspoon garlic salt

1. Cut the ribs into pieces that will easily fit into the slow cooker. Cover and cook the ribs on low setting for 4 to 5 hours.
2. Cut the onion and green pepper into dime-sized pieces. Combine the coffee, ketchup, sugar, Worcestershire sauce, vinegar, black pepper, garlic salt, onion, and green pepper. Stir until all ingredients are well mixed; pour mixture over the ribs and continue to cook covered on low setting for another 2 to 4 hours.

Corn Bread in the Round (page 366) makes an excellent complement to this dish.

Ribs per Person

Spare ribs are the least meaty of any red meat. The rule of thumb is to buy one pound for each serving. If you're buying country style ribs, you can buy about ¾ pound per person.

Sauerkraut-Stuffed Roast Duck

Cooking time: day 1, 6 hours; day 2, 8 hours

Preparation time: 30 minutes

Attention: Minimal

Pot size: 6–8 quart

Serves 6

1 domestic duck
1 cup vinegar
¼ teaspoon salt
Dash of pepper
2 apples
1 medium yellow onion
1 quart (4 cups) sauerkraut
1 pound pork spareribs

1. Clean and wash the duck, then place it in a large kettle. Cover with water and add the vinegar. Soak for 3 hours. Remove the duck from liquid, dry it off, and season with salt and pepper, cover and place in the refrigerator overnight.
2. While the duck is being soaked, core and chop the apples and chop the onion into ½-inch chunks. Combine the apple, onion, sauerkraut, and spareribs in the slow cooker. Cook for 6 hours, or until the meat from the ribs falls from the bones. Discard the bones and refrigerate the slow-cooker mixture. The next day stuff the sparerib-sauerkraut mixture into the duck. Place the stuffed duck into the slow cooker and cook on medium for 8 hours, or until golden and tender.

Serve with Minnesota Wild Rice (page 571).

High-Altitude Slow Cooking

Since water boils at a higher temperature in high altitudes, you may want to cook most of your dishes on the high setting to ensure they're getting hot enough. You also can easily test the slow cooker by heating water in it and determining the temperature with a thermometer.

Ham Hocks and Beans

Cooking time: 6–8 hours

Preparation time: 15 minutes

Attention: Minimal

Pot size: 3–6 quarts

Serves 4

2 cups dried pinto beans, rinsed
3 smoked ham hocks
4 cups water
1 bay leaf
½ teaspoon ground black pepper

Place all the ingredients in the slow cooker. Cover and cook on high setting for 6 to 8 hours. Remove the ham hocks and take the meat off the bones. Discard the bones and return the meat to the slow cooker; stir well. Remove the bay leaf before serving.

Smoked ham hocks are quite salty, so resist the urge to salt this dish before serving.

A Word on Canned Beans

Remember that canned beans have been precooked. If substituting them in a recipe calling for dry beans, decrease the water by four cups per cup of beans. You also can reduce the cooking time by half.

Sweet and Saucy Beef Roast

Cooking time: 10–11 hours
Preparation time: 30 minutes
Attention: Minimal
Pot size: 4–6 quarts
Serves 6

3-pound chuck roast
1 teaspoon vegetable oil
1 large white onion
1 (10¾-ounce) can cream of mushroom condensed soup
½ cup water
¼ cup sugar
¼ cup vinegar
2 teaspoons table salt
1 teaspoon prepared yellow mustard
1 teaspoon Worcestershire sauce

1. Place the beef roast and oil in a skillet on the stove and cook on medium-high heat until the roast is brown; flip the roast so it browns on both sides. Transfer the roast to the slow cooker.
2. Chop the onion into ¼-inch pieces. Combine the onions and the remaining ingredients in a medium-sized bowl, stirring so they are well mingled; pour mixture over the beef roast. Cover and cook on low setting for 10 to 11 hours.

Serve with Heavy Brown Bread (page 375).

Meat Safety

To prevent bacteria growth, thaw and brown large cuts of meat before putting them in the slow cooker. This gets them into the hot, bacteria-killing temperature zone quicker.

Beef Dumpling Soup

Cooking time: 8–9 hours

Preparation time: 15 minutes

Attention: Medium

Pot size: 3–6 quarts

Serves 6

1 pound lean steak
1 package dry onion soup mix
6 cups hot water
2 carrots
1 celery rib
1 tomato
1 tablespoon fresh chopped parsley
1 cup packaged biscuit mix
6 tablespoons milk

1. Cut the steak into 1-inch pieces. Sprinkle with the dry onion soup mix. Place in the bottom of the slow cooker and add the hot water. Peel the carrots with a potato peeler, then shred the carrots using a vegetable grater. Chop the celery. Peel and chop the tomato into ¼-inch pieces. Add the vegetables to the slow cooker. Cover and cook on high setting for 8 to 9 hours.

2. Finely chop the parsley. In a small bowl, combine the biscuit mix with the parsley. Add the milk and stir until the biscuit mix is moistened. About 30 minutes before serving, drop the batter by heaping teaspoonfuls onto the top of the soup. Cover and cook on high for remaining 30 minutes.

Serve with Cheery Cherry Crispy (page 556) for a wonderful fall meal.

Barbecued Pork and Beans

Cooking time: 4–6 hours
Preparation time: 20 minutes
Attention: Minimal
Pot size: 3–6 quarts
Serves 4

2 tablespoons yellow onion, chopped
1 pound canned or fresh baked beans
4 lean pork chops
½ cup prepared mustard
½ cup prepared ketchup
¼ cup lemon juice
¼ cup sugar

1. Chop the onion with a medium-sized knife into pieces about the size of a dime. Mix with the beans and place in the bottom of the slow cooker.
2. Using a butter knife, spread the mustard and ketchup over both sides of the pork chops. Sprinkle both sides with lemon juice and sugar. Lay the pork chops on top of the beans. If possible, do not layer them. Cook on low heat for 4 to 6 hours.

Serve with steamed broccoli and baked potatoes for a complete meal.

Cooking Dried Beans

Instead of soaking beans overnight, cook them on low in the slow cooker overnight. Add some onion, garlic, salt, and pepper and you have a ready-to-eat-anytime treat. You also can freeze the cooked beans for later use in recipes.

Sausage, Red Beans, and Rice

Cooking time: 6–8 hours

Preparation time: 30 minutes

Attention: Medium

Pot size: 3–6 quarts

Serves 8

1 pound dry red kidney beans
6 cups water
1 meaty ham bone
2 large yellow onions
1 green bell pepper
2 ribs celery
¼ cup chopped fresh parsley
2 cloves garlic
1 teaspoon table salt
½ teaspoon ground black pepper
¼ teaspoon sugar
1 bay leaf
2 pound smoked sausage, cut up
8 cups prepared long-grain white rice

1. Soak the beans overnight in the water. Drain and rinse the beans. Trim the fat from the ham bone. Peel and chop the onions into ¼-inch pieces. Seed and chop the green bell pepper into ¼-inch pieces. Chop the celery into ¼-inch pieces. Chop the parsley into ¼-inch lengths. Peel and slice the garlic paper-thin with a sharp kitchen knife.
2. Put the beans, ham bone, onions, green pepper, celery, garlic, salt, pepper, sugar, and bay leaf in the slow cooker. Cook covered on low setting for 3 to 4 hours.
3. Slice the sausage into ½-inch pieces. Brown the sausage in a medium-sized skillet on medium-high heat on the stove; cook until the sausage is crisp. Drain off the grease and place the sausage pieces on paper towels to soak up remaining grease. Add the sausage to the slow cooker. Cook covered on low setting for 3 to 4 additional hours.
4. Just before serving, remove the bay leaf and add the parsley. Serve over rice.

Easy Steak Stroganoff

Cooking time: 6 hours

Preparation time: 20 minutes

Attention: Medium

Pot size: 3–6 quarts

Serves 4

2 pounds round steak
1 garlic clove
¼ cup flour
½ teaspoon ground black pepper
½ teaspoon table salt
1 small yellow onion
½ pound (1 cup) fresh mushrooms, sliced
3 tablespoons butter
1 tablespoon soy sauce
½ cup whole milk
1 cup water
2 beef bouillon cubes
1 (8-ounce) package cream cheese

1. Cut the steak into 1-inch cubes. Peel and mince the garlic using a sharp paring knife. Mix the steak with the flour, pepper, salt, and garlic. Peel and chop the onion into ¼-inch pieces. Clean the mushrooms by wiping with a damp cloth; slice paper-thin.
2. Add all ingredients except the cream cheese to the slow cooker. Cover and cook on low setting for 6 hours, stirring occasionally. Approximately a half-hour before serving, cut the cream cheese into 1-inch cubes and stir into the slow cooker. Continue stirring until melted.

This is excellent served over wide egg noodles. Sprinkle with parsley and eat with a heavy red wine.

Hamburger Rice Skillet

Cooking time: 6–8 hours

Preparation time:

Attention: Minimal

Pot size: 3–6 quarts

Serves 4

1 medium-sized yellow onion
1 medium-sized green bell pepper
1 clove garlic
4 medium-sized tomatoes
1 pound lean ground beef
1 cup medium-grain dry rice
1 (8-ounce) can tomato sauce
1 teaspoon Worcestershire sauce
½ teaspoon dry crushed basil
1½ cups water
1 teaspoon table salt

1. Peel and slice the onion into rings. Remove the stem and seeds from the green pepper and chop the pepper into ¼-inch pieces. Peel and the mince garlic using a sharp paring knife. Cut the tomatoes into quarters.

2. Combine the beef, onion, pepper, and garlic in a skillet on the stove. Cook on medium-high heat, stirring constantly, until the meat is browned. Drain off the grease and put the meat and vegetables into the slow cooker. Add the rice, tomatoes, tomato sauce, Worcestershire sauce, basil, water, and salt; stir well. Cover and cook on low setting 6 to 8 hours.

Serve with a vegetable medley of broccoli, cauliflower, and carrots drizzled with honey.

Cooking time: 2–3 hours	
Preparation time: 10 minutes	
Attention: Minimal	
Pot size: 1–3 quarts	

Beefy Cheese Spread

Serves 8

3 green onions
3 ounces dried beef
8 ounces cream cheese
½ cup whole milk
1 teaspoon dry mustard

1. Remove the roots and first layer of skin from the green onions; chop the onions into ¼-inch pieces, including the stems. Chop the dried beef into ¼-inch pieces. Cut the cream cheese into ½-inch cubes.
2. Put the cream cheese and milk in the slow cooker. Cover and cook on low setting for 1 to 2 hours, until the cheese is fully melted. Add the mustard, onion, and dried beef; stir thoroughly. Cover and cook on low setting for 1 more hour.

Serve as a spread for sandwiches or as a dip with sourdough bread.

Keep It On!

Never leave food in the slow cooker when it isn't turned on. Any temperature below the low setting on the slow cooker will allow dangerous bacteria to grow.

CHAPTER 35

Summer Tantalizers

Risotto with Fresh Summer Vegetables

Cooking time: 8–9 hours

Preparation time: 20 minutes

Attention: Medium

Pot size: 3–6 quarts

Serves 8

1 tablespoon butter
1 large white onion
1 cup fresh zucchini, chopped
⅓ cup fresh parsley, chopped
1 cup uncooked white rice
4 cups chicken broth
1 cup fresh or frozen green beans
1 cup fresh or frozen snow peas
½ teaspoon table salt
¼ teaspoon ground black pepper

1. Melt the butter in small skillet on medium-high heat on the stove. Peel and chop the onions into ¼-inch pieces. Sauté the onions in the butter for 3 to 5 minutes, until the onions are translucent; drain.
2. Chop the zucchini into 1-inch pieces. Chop the parsley into ¼-inch lengths. Place the onions, zucchini, uncooked white rice, chicken broth, green beans, salt, and pepper in the slow cooker; mix well. Cook covered on low setting 7 to 8 hours, or until the rice is soft. Add the peas and cook 1 to 2 hours more.
3. Add the parsley; stir well. Cook uncovered 15 to 30 minutes.

Serve with assorted gourmet crackers and cheeses.

Brussels Sprouts à la Orange

Cooking time: 2 hours
Preparation time: 15 minutes
Attention: Medium
Pot size: 2–4 quarts
Serves 4

1¼ cup fresh-squeezed orange juice
4 cups fresh Brussels sprouts
½ teaspoon cornstarch
¼ teaspoon ground cinnamon

Squeeze 6 to 8 oranges to make 1¼ cup orange juice; ripe oranges produce the most juice. In the slow cooker, combine the Brussels sprouts, juice, cornstarch, and cinnamon. Cover and cook on low for 1 hour. Uncover and cook on low for 1 additional hour until the sauce has thickened and the Brussels sprouts are tender.

This is the perfect complement to Sparkling Beef Tips (page 399).

Using Frozen Veggies

If using frozen vegetables, thaw them overnight in the refrigerator or for a few minutes in the microwave before adding them to the slow cooker. This will prevent bacteria growth as the food is heating up.

Green Beans in Lemon Honey

Cooking time: 1 hour
Preparation time: 25 minutes
Attention: Minimal
Pot size: 3–6 quarts
Serves 4–6

½ lemon
2 tablespoons butter
3 tablespoons honey
1 teaspoon cider vinegar
½ teaspoon salt
1 tart apple
1 teaspoon cornstarch
1 tablespoon water
3 cups fresh green beans
1 medium yellow onion

1. Slice the lemon into wedges no thicker than ⅛ inch. Combine the butter, honey, vinegar, salt, and lemon slices. Bring to a boil, stirring constantly, for 5 minutes.
2. Core and dice the apple into pieces about ¼ inch square; do not remove the peel. Add to the lemon mixture and cook on medium heat for about 5 minutes.
3. Stir together the cornstarch and water until you have a light paste. Stir this into the apple-lemon mixture. Bring to a boil, then cook on low heat for about 3 minutes.
4. Snap the ends off the green beans and discard. Wash the green beans thoroughly in cold water. Peel and slice onion into ¼-inch rings. Place the green beans and onions in the slow cooker and pour the apple-lemon mixture over them. Cook on low heat for 1 hour.

Even vegetable haters will love this combination of sweet and tart flavors! Use this recipe to complement a grilled steak or pork chops.

Czech Garlic
and Bean Soup

Cooking time: 8–10 hours	
Preparation time: 10 minutes	
Attention: Minimal	
Pot size: 3–6 quarts	
Serves 8	

6 garlic cloves
4 tablespoons chopped fresh parsley
3 tablespoons olive oil
1 pound (2 cups) dry white beans
1 quart (4 cups) beef broth
1 quart (4 cups) water
2 teaspoons table salt
1 teaspoon ground white pepper

1. Remove the skins from the garlic and mince with a sharp paring knife. Finely chop the parsley. Sauté the garlic and parsley in olive oil in a medium-sized skillet on medium-high heat. The garlic should be slightly brown but not hard. Do not drain the oil.
2. Add all the ingredients to the slow cooker. Cover and cook on low setting for 8 to 10 hours.

Serve with Grandma Margaret's Summer Dill Bread (page 373).

Cooking Beans

Any bean recipe gives you two options. Cook it longer and let the beans dissolve for a creamy texture. Serve it earlier in the cooking process, as soon as the beans are completely soft, for more distinct flavors in every bite.

Lemony Chicken and Okra Soup

Cooking time: 7–9 hours

Preparation time: 30 minutes

Attention: Minimal

Pot size: 3–8 quarts

Serves 8

6 chicken breasts
2 tablespoons lemon juice
1 large yellow onion
3 medium tomatoes
2 cups fresh okra, sliced
⅓ cup uncooked long-grain rice
6 cups chicken broth
½ cup (4 ounces) tomato paste
2 teaspoons table salt
¼ ground black pepper
½ teaspoon cayenne pepper
1 teaspoon ground turmeric

1. Remove the bones and skin from the chicken breasts. Rub the chicken with lemon juice, then cut into 1-inch cubes. Peel and chop the onion into ¼-inch pieces. Peel and chop the tomatoes into ½-inch pieces. Wash and slice the okra into ¼-inch rounds.
2. Put all the ingredients in the slow cooker. Cover and cook on low setting for 7 to 9 hours.

Serve with spicy dill pickles and assorted cheeses.

Wild Rice Stuffed Zucchini

Cooking time:	8–9 hours
Preparation time:	20 minutes
Attention:	Minimal
Pot size:	4–6 quarts
Serves 4	

2 small zucchini
1 cup wild rice
1 small yellow onion
½ cup chopped fresh chives
½ teaspoon ground black pepper
½ teaspoon table salt
½ cup shelled, salted, and roasted sunflower seeds

1. Cut the zucchini in half lengthwise and scrape out the inside, leaving about ¾-inch around the sides; discard the insides.
2. Precook the wild rice according to the package directions. Peel and chop the onion into ¼-inch pieces. Chop the chives into ¼-inch lengths. Combine the wild rice, onion, black pepper, salt, and chives in a medium-sized mixing bowl. Use the mixture to stuff the zucchini boats. Sprinkle with sunflower seeds. Place the stuffed zucchini in the slow cooker. Cover and cook on low setting for 8 to 9 hours.

This is a wonderful complement to a grilled steak or pork chops.

Wild Wild Rice

In many states wild rice is a protected crop that can only be raised and harvested by Native Americans. Look for unbroken, dark brown rice for the best flavor and consistency.

Mushroom Vegetable Barley Soup

Cooking time: 3–4 hours

Preparation time: 45 minutes

Attention: Minimal

Pot size: 3–6 quarts

Serves 6

1 pound (2 cups) fresh mushrooms, sliced
4 celery stalks
5 medium carrots
1 cup fresh chopped broccoli
2 cups chopped yellow onion
1½ tablespoons minced garlic
3 tablespoons olive oil
½ teaspoon ground thyme
1 bay leaf
½ cup dry barley
8 cups chicken broth
1 teaspoon salt
½ teaspoon pepper

1. Clean the mushrooms by rubbing with a damp towel, then slice into quarters. Wash the celery, carrots, and broccoli thoroughly in cold water, then cut into ½-inch pieces. Peel the onions and chop into ¼-inch pieces. Peel and mince the garlic.
2. Place the olive oil in the slow cooker. Add the onions and cook on high for about 10 minutes. Add the garlic, thyme, bay leaf, and mushrooms. Cook for about 20 minutes on low heat, stirring occasionally.
3. Add the barley, celery, broccoli, carrots, and broth. Stir in the salt and pepper. Cook covered on low heat for 3 to 4 hours. Remove the bay leaf before serving.

Serve with Zucchini Bread (page 369) for a fun taste combination.

Harvest Vegetable Soup

Cooking time: 6–8 hours
Preparation time: 20 minutes
Attention: Minimal
Pot size: 3–8 quarts
Serves 8

3 cups fresh tomatoes, chopped
2 cups fresh carrots, sliced
2 cups fresh zucchini, sliced
2 cups fresh green beans
1 large onion
1/8 cup diced fresh red bell
   pepper
1 cup fresh, canned or frozen
   whole kernel corn

1 cup fresh or frozen peas
1 bay leaf
1/2 teaspoon thyme (optional)
1/2 teaspoon marjoram
   (optional)
1/2 teaspoon table salt
3 cups water

1. Cut the tomatoes, carrots, and zucchini into 1-inch pieces. Snap the ends off the green beans and discard; cut the green beans into 1-inch lengths. Peel the onion and chop into 1/4-inch pieces. Remove the stem and seeds from the red pepper and chop into 1/4-inch pieces. Combine all the ingredients except the peas in the slow cooker. Stir with a wooden spoon until the ingredients are evenly distributed and covered with liquid. Cover and cook on low heat for 5 to 7 hours. Add the peas and cook 1 to 2 hours more.
2. Remove cover 15 minutes before serving; stir well. Remove and discard the bay leaf.

Because this soup has almost no fat, it makes an excellent first course to a heavier meal such as Southwestern Beef Roast with Peppers (page 480).

Caution When Freezing Soups

When freezing soups, remember that water expands when frozen. Fill the container to within one inch of the top and cover tightly.

Cheery Cherry Crispy

Cooking time: 3–4 hours

Preparation time: 10 minutes

Attention: Minimal

Pot size: 3–6 quarts

Serves 8

⅓ cup softened butter (or margarine), divided
2 pounds fresh cherries
⅓ cup water
2/3 cup packed brown sugar
½ cup quick-cooking oats
½ cup flour
1 teaspoon cinnamon

1. Lightly grease the slow cooker with ½ teaspoon of the butter or margarine. Remove the stems and pits from the cherries and put the cherries in slow cooker. Add water.
2. In a bowl, mix the brown sugar, oats, flour, and cinnamon. Cut in the remaining butter (or margarine) by using a fork and slicing the butter into small pieces; continue doing this until the mixture is crumbly. Sprinkle the crumbs over the cherries. Cook uncovered on low setting for 3 to 4 hours.

This dish works equally well with blueberries or raspberries.

Using Cannned Fruit

If substituting canned fruit for fresh in a dessert recipe, choose fruit in a water base, not syrup. The syrup bases tend to draw the sugar out of the fruit while in the can.

Pistachio-Buttered Vegetable Medley

Cooking time: 2–3 hours

Preparation time: 30 minutes

Attention: Minimal

Pot size: 3–5 quarts

Serves 6

1 cup fresh asparagus tips
3 medium-sized fresh carrots
1 cup fresh green beans
½ cup chopped pistachio nuts
½ cup butter (or margarine), melted
1 tablespoon fresh lemon juice
½ teaspoon dry marjoram

Clean the vegetables and slice into ½-inch pieces. Shell and finely chop the pistachio nuts with a sharp paring knife. Mix the vegetables and nuts together and place in the slow cooker. Add the butter, lemon juice, and marjoram. Cook covered for 2 to 3 hours on low setting. Place the mixture in a serving bowl and top with pistachio nuts if desired.

This is an excellent complement to grilled chicken breasts.

Add Some Tartness

Use lemon juice when cooking vegetables in the slow cooker. Sprinkle a little juice on top and the vegetables will retain their color better. The lemon juice also adds a tang that is a nice substitute for fatty butter.

Romanian Sauerkraut

Cooking time: 4 hours

Preparation time: 30 minutes

Attention: Minimal

Pot size: 3–5 quarts

Serves 6

6 cups sauerkraut
6 ripe tomatoes
1 large yellow onion
1 green bell pepper
2 garlic cloves
1½ pounds kielbasa

1. Drain and rinse the sauerkraut. Chop the tomatoes into ½-inch pieces. Peel the onion and chop into ¼-inch pieces. Remove the stem and seeds from the green pepper and chop into ¼-inch pieces. Peel the garlic and mince with a sharp kitchen knife. Chop the kielbasa into 1-inch pieces.
2. Mix all the ingredients in the slow cooker. Cook covered on low setting for 4 hours.

Serve with an assortment of fresh summer fruits.

Cooking time: 5–6 hours

Preparation time: 30 minutes

Attention: Minimal

Pot size: 2–4 quarts

Serves 6

German-Style Hot Potato Salad

4 slices bacon
½ cup onion, chopped
½ cup celery, sliced
¼ cup diced green pepper
2 potatoes
¼ cup chopped fresh parsley
1 teaspoon sugar
½ teaspoon salt
½ teaspoon ground black pepper
¼ cup white vinegar
¼ cup vegetable oil

1. Fry the bacon in frying pan or cook in the microwave until crisp, then crumble by placing the bacon in a paper towel and wringing it with your hands. Peel and chop the onions into ¼-inch pieces. Chop the celery into ¼-inch pieces. Remove the stem and seeds from the green pepper and chop into ¼-inch pieces. Wash and scrub the potatoes thoroughly; do not peel. Slice about ¼-inch thick. Roughly chop the parsley.
2. Combine all the ingredients except the parsley and bacon; stir well. Cook covered on low setting 5 to 6 hours. Stir in the bacon and parsley before serving.

Use as a side dish when grilling steaks or pork chops.

Discolored Potates

To prevent discoloration, add potatoes to the slow cooker right before turning it on. If you must prepare the slow cooker the night before, layer the potatoes on the bottom of the cooking container so the least amount of air reaches them.

Fresh Zucchini Casserole

Cooking time:	6–7 hours
Preparation time:	20 minutes
Attention:	Minimal
Pot size:	3–6 quarts
Serves 8	

2 cups zucchini, diced
2 cups yellow summer squash, diced
1 large yellow onion
2 cups fresh mushrooms, sliced
2 cups cubed Cheddar cheese
1 package onion soup mix
1 quart (4 cups) fresh or canned spaghetti sauce

1. Clean but do not peel the zucchini and summer squash; chop into bite-size pieces. Peel and chop the onion into ½-inch pieces. Clean the mushrooms by wiping with a damp cloth; slice paper-thin with a sharp paring knife. Cut the cheese into ½-inch cubes.
2. Combine all the ingredients in the slow cooker; mix well. Cook uncovered on low setting 5 to 6 hours. Remove the cover, stir well, and cook 1 hour uncovered on low setting.

Use as a complement to beef or pork roasts.

Lemony Chicken

Cooking time: 8 hours	
Preparation time: 30 minutes	
Attention: Minimal	
Pot size: 4–6 quarts	
Serves 4	

4 chicken breasts
½ teaspoon table salt
¼ teaspoon ground black pepper
2 tablespoons butter
¼ cup sherry
4 cloves garlic, minced
1 teaspoon crumbled dry oregano
¼ cup lemon juice
1 teaspoon grated lemon peel

Wash the chicken breasts; do not remove the bone or skin. Sprinkle the chicken with salt and pepper. Heat the butter in medium-sized skillet. Sauté the chicken until brown. Using a slotted spoon or tongs, transfer the chicken to the slow cooker. Add the sherry to the skillet and stir to loosen the brown bits on the bottom of the skillet (deglaze). Pour the sherry mixture over the chicken. Sprinkle the chicken with the oregano and garlic. Cover and cook on low for 7 hours. Cut the lemon peel into ⅛-inch squares. Add the lemon juice and bits of lemon peel. Cook covered on low for 1 additional hour.

Serve over long-grain brown rice and complement with a variety of pickled vegetables.

Slow Cooking Rice and Pasta

You can cook rice and pasta in the slow cooker although it tends to get mushy over a long cooking cycle. Instead, add precooked rice or pasta during the last half hour of the cooking process.

Pizza-Stuffed Potato Boats

Cooking time: 5–6 hours

Preparation time: 30 minutes

Attention: Minimal

Pot size: 4–8 quarts

Serves 8

4 large potatoes
½ pound (1 cup) pepperoni, diced
1 medium-sized yellow onion
1 cup shredded mozzarella cheese
1 cup spaghetti sauce
¼ cup grated Parmesan cheese

1. Bake the potatoes in the microwave or conventional oven; slice in half lengthwise. Scoop out the insides (do not discard), leaving about ¾-inch of potato all around.
2. Cut the pepperoni into ¼-inch pieces. Peel the onion and chop into ¼-inch pieces. Shred the cheese with a vegetable grater. Mix the left-over potato insides, onion, pepperoni, cheese, and spaghetti sauce in a medium-sized mixing bowl. Put into the potato boats, stuffing firmly. Sprinkle with Parmesan cheese. Place potato boats in the slow cooker. You may have to stack them. Cover and cook on low setting for 5 to 6 hours.

Serve with a fresh green salad and Italian dressing for a completely balanced meal.

Cleaning Roots!

Clean root vegetables thoroughly by scrubbing them with a nail brush or scouring pad designated for that purpose. Because they grow in fertilized soil, they can harbor bacteria on their skins.

Vegetables

Sweet Potato and Apple Bake

Cooking time: 6–8 hours
Preparation time: 30 minutes
Attention: Minimal
Pot size: 3–6 quarts
Serves 8

4 medium-sized sweet potatoes
6 medium-sized apples
2 teaspoons cinnamon
1 teaspoon nutmeg
¼ teaspoon salt
¼ teaspoon vegetable oil
½ cup apple cider

1. Peel the sweet potatoes and cut into ¼-inch slices. Peel and core the apples, then cut into ¼-inch slices.
2. Combine the cinnamon, nutmeg, and salt; mix well.
3. Lightly spread oil over bottom of slow cooker. Add the apple cider to the slow cooker. Layer the sweet potatoes and apples in the slow cooker, alternating the layers: begin with a layer of sweet potatoes, then sprinkle the cinnamon mixture lightly over each layer of sweet potatoes and apples. Cook covered on low setting for 6 to 8 hours.

This is an excellent sweet potato variation for a Thanksgiving feast.

Veggie Water
Next time you are boiling or steaming vegetables, reserve the liquid in a large container in the refrigerator. Use it instead of water in slow cooker recipes to add extra, subtle flavors.

Lemony Asparagus and Carrots

Cooking time: 2–4 hours
Preparation time: 10 minutes
Attention: Minimal
Pot size: 2–6 quarts
Serves 6

2 bunches fresh asparagus
½ pound (1 cup) precleaned
   baby carrots

2 tablespoons lemon juice
1 teaspoon lemon pepper

Clean the asparagus by running under cold water; cut off the bottoms so that no red or white part of the stem remains. Layer the asparagus in the bottom of the slow cooker. Add the baby carrots on top of the asparagus layers. Drizzle the lemon juice on top, then sprinkle with lemon pepper. Cook covered on low setting for 2 to 4 hours.

The beautiful color combination and slightly exotic flavor make this an excellent dish for entertaining.

Garlicky Spinach and Swiss Chard

Cooking time: 4–6 hours
Preparation time: 20 minutes
Attention: Minimal
Pot size: 3–6 quarts
Serves 6–8

1 bunch fresh spinach
1 bunch fresh Swiss chard
3 cloves garlic

½ teaspoon olive oil
¼ cup water

Prepare the spinach and Swiss chard by washing in cold water and removing the stems so that only the tender leaves remain. Peel and slice the garlic paper-thin. Sauté the garlic in the olive oil in small skillet on medium high-heat for 2 to 3 minutes; drain. Add all the ingredients to the slow cooker. Cook covered on low setting 4 to 6 hours.

Press the mixture firmly into small ramekins, discarding the juice that rises to the top. Tip the ramekin over onto a plate and remove the ramekin to create a small "mound of greens."

German-Style Cooked Cabbage with Onions and Peppers

Cooking time: 4–6 hours

Preparation time: 20 minutes

Attention: Minimal

Pot size: 3–6 quarts

Serves 8

1 large cabbage
1 cup celery, sliced
1 green bell pepper
½ red bell pepper
1 yellow onion
¼ cup white vinegar
½ teaspoon table salt
½ teaspoon ground black pepper
1 teaspoon celery seeds
1 teaspoon caraway seeds

1. Cut the cabbage into 12 to 16 pieces with a heavy knife on a firm surface. Slice the celery into ¼-inch pieces. Remove the seeds from the green pepper and red pepper; chop the peppers into ¼-inch pieces. Peel and chop the onion into ¼-inch pieces.
2. Place ingredients in the slow cooker in the following order:
   1. Vinegar
   2. Cabbage
   3. Onion
   4. Red and green peppers
   5. Celery
3. Sprinkle salt, black pepper, caraway seeds, and celery seeds on top. Cook covered on low setting 4 to 6 hours, or until the cabbage is tender and translucent.

The tangy flavors in this dish are a perfect complement to beef or pork roasts.

Orange-Glazed Vegetable Medley

Cooking time: 4–5 hours

Preparation time: 20 minutes

Attention: Medium

Pot size: 3–6 quarts

Serves 8

1 medium parsnip
4 medium carrots
1 medium turnip
1 cup fresh cauliflower pieces
1 cup fresh broccoli pieces
½ cup packed brown sugar
½ cup orange juice
3 tablespoons butter (or margarine)
¾ teaspoon cinnamon
2 tablespoons cornstarch
¼ cup water

1. Peel and chop the parsnip into ½-inch pieces. Peel and slice the carrots into ¼-inch rounds. Peel and slice the turnip into ½-inch pieces. Break the cauliflower and broccoli florets into pieces about the size of a marble.
2. Combine all the vegetables with the brown sugar, orange juice, butter, and cinnamon in the slow cooker. Cover and cook on low setting 4–5 hours. Remove the vegetables and put in a serving dish.
3. Pour the juice from the slow cooker into a saucepan and place on the stove; bring to a boil. Mix the cornstarch and water in a small bowl until well blended. Add to the juices. Boil 2 to 3 minutes, stirring constantly. Pour over the vegetables.

The sweet taste of these vegetables makes this dish a natural complement to lamb or pork.

Squash Medley Au Gratin

Cooking time: 6–8 hours

Preparation time: 30 minutes

Attention: Minimal

Pot size: 4–6 quarts

Serves 8

1 medium to large zucchini
1 medium to large acorn squash
4 large ripe tomatoes
2 medium yellow onions
1 cup shredded mozzarella cheese
½ teaspoon salt
1 teaspoon dried basil

1. Prepare the zucchini by peeling and slicing into ¼-inch-thick rounds. Prepare the acorn squash by cutting into quarters, removing the seeds and "strings," and cutting the "meat" from the rind; cut the meat of the squash into 1-inch cubes. Peel and mash the tomatoes with a wooden spoon. Peel and slice the onions into ¼-inch-thick rings.
2. Layer the ingredients in slow cooker in the following order:
   1. Zucchini
   2. Onions
   3. Acorn squash
   4. Tomatoes
   5. Cheese
3. Sprinkle with salt and basil. Cook covered on low setting 6–8 hours.

This dish can be a meal in itself. It makes a nice fall luncheon.

Grandma Dorothy's Peas and Rice

Cooking time: 3–4 hours

Preparation time: 10 minutes

Attention: Minimal

Pot size: 3–6 quarts

Serves 8

1 medium-sized yellow onion
1½ cups uncooked white rice
3 cups chicken broth
1 teaspoon Italian seasoning
½ teaspoon garlic salt
½ teaspoon ground black pepper
1 cup fresh or frozen baby peas

1. Peel and chop the onion into ¼-inch pieces. Put the rice and onions in the slow cooker.
2. Mix the chicken broth, Italian seasoning, garlic salt, and pepper in a medium-sized saucepan on the stove; bring to a boil. Pour over the rice and onions mix well. Cook covered on low setting for 3 hours, or until all the liquid is absorbed. Stir in the peas. Cook an additional 30 minutes.

Use broccoli instead of peas and garnish with grated Cheddar cheese.

Refrain from Using Canned Veggies

Whenever possible, don't use canned vegetables in a slow cooker recipe. They are precooked and will get very mushy. Carrots and peas will lose their color and can even disintegrate over a long cooking process.

Curried Vegetables and Garbanzo Beans

Cooking time: 9–10 hours

Preparation time: 20 minutes

Attention: Minimal

Pot size: 5–6 quarts

Serves 8

3 medium potatoes
1 pound (2 cups) fresh green beans
1 green bell pepper
½ red bell pepper
1 large yellow onion
2 cloves garlic
4 large ripe tomatoes
2 cups (16 ounces) precleaned baby carrots
2 cups (16 ounces) precooked garbanzo beans
3 tablespoons quick-cooking tapioca
3 teaspoons curry powder
2 teaspoons table salt
2 chicken bouillon cubes
1¾ cups boiling water

1. Peel the potatoes and cut into 1-inch cubes. Slice off the ends of the green beans and cut into approximately 2-inch lengths. Remove the stems and seeds from the red and green bell peppers and chop into ¼-inch pieces. Peel and chop the onion into ¼-inch pieces. Peel the garlic cloves and mince using a sharp, medium-sized knife. Peel the tomatoes and mash in a bowl using a wooden spoon.

2. Combine potatoes, green beans, green pepper, red pepper, onions, garlic, tomatoes, carrots, and garbanzo beans in a large bowl. Stir in the tapioca, curry powder, and salt; mix well, then place mixture in the slow cooker.

3. Dissolve the bouillon in the boiling water; pour over the vegetable mixture. Cook covered on low setting 9 to 10 hours.

Serve this with a pork roast or ham sandwiches for the perfect mix of flavors.

Minnesota Wild Rice

Cooking time: 3–4 hours
Preparation time: 15 minutes
Attention: Minimal
Pot size: 3–6 quarts
Serves 6

½ cup sliced fresh mushrooms
½ cup chopped onion
1 clove garlic
½ cup chopped green bell pepper
1 cup unbroken wild rice
4 cups chicken broth
½ teaspoon salt
½ teaspoon ground black pepper

1. Prepare the mushrooms by wiping with a damp cloth and slicing paper-thin. Peel the onion and chop in ¼-inch pieces. Peel and mince the garlic using a sharp medium-sized knife. Remove the seeds from the green pepper and chop into ¼-inch pieces.
2. Layer the dry ingredients in the slow cooker with the rice on the bottom. Pour the chicken broth over the top. Sprinkle salt and pepper on top. Cover and cook on high setting 3 to 4 hours, or until the liquid is absorbed and the rice is soft and fluffed open.

Unlike its cultivated cousins, wild rice is a very heavy and filling dish. Use this recipe to stuff squash or chicken breasts for a hearty meal.

Power Outage Info

If food is completely cooked and removed from the heat source, such as during a power outage, it will remain safe for up to two hours at room temperature.

Stuffed Acorn Squash with Pecans

Cooking time: 8–10 hours

Preparation time: 15 minutes

Attention: Minimal

Pot size: 2–6 quarts

Serves 2

2 cups cooked wild rice
1 medium-sized yellow onion
1 celery stalk
2 medium acorn squash
½ cup fresh pecan halves, chopped

1. Cook the wild rice as per the package directions to yield 2 cups cooked. Peel and chop the onion into ¼-inch pieces. Chop the celery into ¼-inch pieces. Chop the pecans into ⅛-inch pieces. Slice the tops off the squash and remove the seeds by scraping the inside with a spoon.
2. Combine the wild rice, celery, onion, and pecans; mix well. Scoop the mixture into the cavities of the squash. Place the squash in the slow cooker and cook covered on low setting 8 to 10 hours.

This makes an excellent lunch all by itself. Or serve it with steak for a heavier meal in the fall.

When Preparing Ahead
If you're preparing the food the evening before you will be cooking it, do not add rice or pasta until right before you'll begin cooking. They could absorb juices from the meats and vegetables.

Dilly Mashed Potatoes

Cooking time: 7 hours
Preparation time: 20 minutes
Attention: Medium
Pot size: 3–6 quarts
Serves 6

6 large white potatoes
2 cloves garlic
1 medium-sized yellow onion
6 cups water
1 teaspoon table salt
½ cup skim milk
1 tablespoon butter
2 teaspoons dill weed

1. Wash, peel, and cut the potatoes into 1-inch cubes. Peel and mince the garlic using a sharp paring knife. Peel and chop the onion into ¼-inch pieces. Place the potatoes, onions, and garlic in the slow cooker and cover with the water. Add the salt; stir lightly. Cook covered on high setting for 6 hours, or until the potatoes are tender.

2. Transfer the potatoes from the slow cooker to a large bowl. Drain and discard the liquid in the slow cooker. Add the milk, butter, and dill weed to the potatoes and mash together until there are no lumps. Return the mashed potatoes to the slow cooker and cook covered on low setting for 1 hour.

This makes an excellent complement to a beef or pork roast. The potatoes are excellent without gravy, but the complementary flavors also don't fight with even the richest gravy.

Cheesy Cauliflower

Cooking time: 3–4 hours

Preparation time: 30 minutes

Attention: Medium

Pot size: 3–6 quarts

Serves 8

1 medium head cauliflower
1 small white onion
1 (8-ounce) package of cream cheese
5 ounces processed cheese
¼ pound dried beef, shredded
½ cup dehydrated potatoes

1. Remove the leaves and cut the cauliflower into 1-inch pieces. Place in a pot on the stove and cover with water; bring to a boil. Turn off the heat and let the cauliflower sit (do not discard the water). Peel the onion and chop into ¼-inch pieces. Cut the cheeses into ½-inch cubes. Shred the beef into ⅛-inch-thick pieces.

2. In the slow cooker, combine the cream cheese, processed cheese, cauliflower, and 2 cups of the water the cauliflower was boiled in. Cook on low setting, stirring until the cheese is dissolved and the cauliflower pieces are covered with cheese. Add the dried beef, onions, and dehydrated potatoes; mix well. Cover and cook on low setting for 3 hours.

This is an excellent complement to Lemony Chicken (page 561).

Keep Food Warm

Use your slow cooker as a warming device to keep beverages, rolls, and other food items moist and warm. If breads will be in the slow cooker for a long time, place a cup with an inch of water in the bottom in the slow cooker along with the food.

Sweet Corn Pudding

Cooking time: 2–3 hours

Preparation time: 10 minutes

Attention: Minimal

Pot size: 3–6 quarts

Serves 8

2 (10-ounce) cans whole kernel
   corn with juice

3 (10-ounce) cans creamed corn

2 cups corn muffin mix

¼ pound margarine, softened

8 ounces (1 cup) sour cream

Mix together all the ingredients in a medium-sized mixing bowl. Pour into the slow cooker. Cover and heat on low setting for 2 to 3 hours

Serve to complement Swiss-Style Venison Steak (page 435).

Italian Beets

Cooking time: 9–10 hours

Preparation time: 15 minutes

Attention: Minimal

Pot size: 3–6 quarts

Serves 8

4 medium beets

3 cups water

1 cup Italian salad dressing

¼ cup balsamic vinegar

Remove the tops and stems from the beets. Peel the beets and slice into ¼-inch-thick rounds. Mix together the water, dressing, and vinegar in the slow cooker. Add the beets to the mixture. Cover and cook on low setting for 9 to 10 hours.

This is the perfect complement to Slow-Cooked Sauerbraten (page 398).

Spinach and Brown Rice Hot Dish

Cooking time: 3–5 hours

Preparation time: 15 minutes

Attention: Minimal

Pot size: 3–6 quarts

Serves 6

1 cup frozen or canned chopped spinach
1 small yellow onion
3 cups precooked brown rice
1 cup sharp Cheddar cheese, shredded
3 eggs
1½ cups evaporated milk

1. Thaw the spinach, if necessary. Peel and chop the onion into ¼-inch pieces. Cook the rice according to the package directions. Shred the cheese using a vegetable grater.
2. Combine the eggs and milk in a medium-sized mixing bowl; whisk quickly until well blended and slightly frothy. Add the onion, spinach, rice, and cheese; mix well. Pour into the slow cooker. Cover and cook on low setting for 3 to 5 hours.

Serve as a complement to Peachy Georgia Chicken Legs (page 406).

Romance with a Slow Cooker

French Onion Soup

Cooking time: 6–8 hours

Preparation time: 30 minutes

Attention: Minimal

Pot size: 3–5

Serves 6

3 cups yellow onion, sliced
1 tablespoon sugar
1 quart (4 cups) beef bouillon
¼ cup butter
1 teaspoon salt
2 tablespoons flour
¼ cup Cognac

1. Peel and slice the onions about ¼-inch thick. Place in a medium skillet with butter and cook on medium heat for 15 minutes. When the onions are limp, add the sugar and cook for 5 more minutes.
2. Add all the ingredients to the slow cooker. Cover and cook on low setting for 6 to 8 hours.

Place garlic toast slices covered with Romano and Mozzarella cheese on top of soup. Heat in an oven until the cheese is melted and slightly brown.

Two Slow Cookers are Better Than One
Use two at once. Make your meat dish in one slow cooker while you make the vegetables or even the bread in another. You'll come home to a fully cooked meal with no hassles.

Blue Cheese Soup

Cooking time: 1 hour
Preparation time: 30 minutes
Attention: Minimal
Pot size: 3–8 quarts
Serves 8

½ pound Stilton cheese
½ pound Cheddar cheese
1 medium-sized white onion
2 celery ribs
2 medium carrots
2 garlic cloves
2 tablespoons butter
⅓ cup flour
2 teaspoons cornstarch

3 cups chicken stock
1 cup heavy whipping cream
⅓ cup dry white wine
⅛ teaspoon baking soda
½ teaspoon table salt
½ teaspoon ground white pepper
⅛ teaspoon cayenne pepper
1 bay leaf.

1. Crumble the cheeses into pieces the size of small marbles. Peel and chop the onion into ¼-inch pieces. Clean and chop the carrots and celery into ¼-inch pieces. Peel the garlic and mince with a sharp kitchen knife.
2. Preheat the slow cooker at low setting. Melt the butter in a large skillet on medium heat. Add the onion, celery, carrots, and garlic; sauté until the onion is tender and translucent. Pour into the pre-heated slow cooker. Stir in the flour and cornstarch until no lumps remain.
3. Add the stock, cream, wine, baking soda, and both cheeses; stir until smooth and thickened. Add the salt, white pepper, cayenne, and bay leaf. Cover and cook on low setting for 1 hour. Discard the bay leaf before serving.

Serve as a first course for Spicy Pot Roast (page 396).

Chicken Asparagus Supreme

Cooking time: 5 hours

Preparation time: 20 minutes

Attention: Medium

Pot size: 4–6 quarts

Serves 6

4 chicken breasts
½ cup water
½ cup dry white wine
4 hard-boiled eggs
¾ cup butter
½ cup flour
4 cups milk
½ teaspoon salt, plus extra for sprinkling on chicken
¼ teaspoon pepper, plus extra for sprinkling on chicken
1 cup grated Romano cheese
1 cup canned, chopped pimientos
1 pound fresh asparagus

1. Remove the skin and bones from the chicken breast. Sprinkle each lightly with salt and pepper, then place them in the slow cooker. Cover with water and wine. Cook covered on low setting for 4 hours. Remove the chicken from the slow cooker and discard the liquid.

2. Chop the eggs into ¼-inch pieces. Melt the butter in the slow cooker. Blend in the flour. Add the milk, salt, and pepper, stirring constantly. Add the eggs, cheese, and pimientos. Place the cooked chicken in the slow cooker on top of mixture. Wash the asparagus; cut off and discard the bottom 2 inches of the asparagus. Place the asparagus on top of the chicken. Cook on low for 1 hour, or until the asparagus is tender.

Sweet Potato and Apple Bake (page 564) is a perfect complement to this dish.

Pecan Mushroom Chicken Fettuccine

Cooking time: 5–6 hours

Preparation time: 45 minutes

Attention: Medium

Pot size: 6 quarts

Serves 4

1 pound boneless, skinless
  chicken breasts
1 cup green onions, chopped
2 garlic cloves
3 cups fresh mushrooms, sliced
1 cup chicken broth
½ teaspoon table salt
¼ teaspoon ground black pepper

1 (10-ounce) package of
  uncooked spinach fettuccine
⅔ cup half-and-half
½ cup grated Romano cheese
1 cup chopped, toasted pecans
2 tablespoons fresh chopped
  parsley

1. Cut the chicken into 1-inch cubes. Remove the roots and first layer of skin from the green onions. Chop into ¼-inch pieces, including the tops. Peel and chop the garlic into ¼-inch pieces. Clean the mushrooms by wiping with a damp cloth, then slice paper-thin. Place the chicken, chicken broth, mushrooms, onions, garlic, salt, and pepper in the slow cooker. Cook covered on low setting for 4 to 5 hours.

2. Add the pasta and half-and-half; stir gently. Cover and cook on low setting for 1 hour. Add the cheese once the pasta is tender. Stir until the cheese is fully melted and the sauce has thickened. Garnish with pecans and parsley.

Serve with French bread and Roasted Garlic (page 302).

Replacing Onions

Substitute leeks, rutabagas, or turnips for onions in your slow cooker recipes. They have a more distinct flavor that holds up longer than most onions. They also can turn a basic recipe into something more exotic.

Classic Swiss Fondue

Cooking time: 30 minutes

Preparation time: 15 minutes

Attention: Constant

Pot size: 2–4 quarts

Serves 2

1 garlic clove

1 tablespoon flour

½ cup vegetable broth

⅓ cup evaporated milk

¼ teaspoon brandy or brandy-flavored extract

1 tablespoon fresh Parmesan cheese

2 ounces (¼ cup) Swiss cheese

2 ounces (¼ cup) cream cheese

⅛ teaspoon ground black pepper

⅛ teaspoon ground nutmeg

1 loaf French bread, cubed

1. Peel the garlic and cut in half lengthwise. Rub the inside of the slow cooker with the cut sides of the garlic. Discard the garlic. Whisk the flour and 1 tablespoon of the vegetable broth in a measuring cup until it is well blended. Add the remaining broth and the milk to the slow cooker and cook, uncovered on high setting. Whisk in the brandy and the flour mixture. Cook, stirring constantly, for about 5 minutes.
2. Shred the Parmesan and Swiss cheeses using a vegetable or cheese grater. Cut the cream cheese into 1-inch cubes. Add the Parmesan cheese, Swiss cheese, cream cheese, pepper, and nutmeg to the slow cooker. Cook on high setting, stirring constantly until the cheeses melt and the mixture is very smooth.
3. Turn the slow cooker to the low setting for serving. Serve right inside the slow cooker to keep the fondue from solidifying. Use fondue forks or bamboo skewers to dip the bread.

Preventing Oily Fondue

Naturally aged cheeses tend to separate in the slow-cooking process. Try starting with a base of processed American cheese and adding small amounts of others for flavor.

Tenderloin of Veal

Cooking time: 2 hours

Preparation time: 45 minutes

Attention: Minimal

Pot size: 3–6 quarts

Serves 2

2 pounds veal tenderloin
1 teaspoon table salt
1 teaspoon ground black pepper
2 slices prosciutto ham
8 ounces Brie cheese
¼ cup flour
1 cup butter

4 ounces (½ cup) Morel
  mushrooms, sliced
4 shallots
1 cup cream
1 teaspoon lemon juice
1 cup parsley, chopped

1. Cut the veal into ¼-inch-thick slices and sprinkle each slice with salt and pepper. Pound each slice several times with a meat-tenderizing mallet. Chop the prosciutto ham into ¼-inch pieces and mix with softened and peeled Brie. Spread the Brie and ham mixture onto the veal slices; roll up.
2. Dust the roll-ups with flour. Melt the butter over medium-high heat in a large skillet. Cook the veal rolls until brown on all sides. Put the veal rolls in the slow cooker; retain the veal drippings in the skillet.
3. Clean the mushrooms by wiping with a damp cloth; remove the stems and slice paper-thin. Peel and mince the shallots with a sharp kitchen knife. In the skillet, sauté the mushrooms and shallots in the butter and veal drippings. Add the cream and bring the mixture to a boil, stirring constantly. Pour the sauce over veal rolls. Cook covered on low setting for 2 hours.
4. Coarsely chop parsley. Spoon the sauce over the veal rolls and sprinkle with lemon juice and chopped parsley before serving.

This dish is excellent with garlic spinach: Cook spinach in water with 1 clove minced garlic. Press the water out of the spinach before serving.

Roast Duckling
with Orange Glaze

Cooking time: 6 hours

Preparation time: 20 minutes

Attention: Medium

Pot size: 3–6 quarts

Serves 2

2 cups prepared poultry stuffing
1 duckling, fresh or thawed
½ cup sugar
½ teaspoon salt
1 teaspoon cornstarch
1 (6-ounce) can frozen orange juice concentrate, thawed

1. Prepare the stuffing according to the package directions and stuff into the duckling cavity. Place the duckling breast side up in the slow cooker. Cook covered on low setting for 6 hours.
2. One hour before serving, combine the sugar, salt, and cornstarch. Add the thawed orange juice concentrate. Stir over moderate heat until slightly thickened. Brush the entire surface of the duckling with the glaze. Repeat every 15 minutes for the remaining 1 hour.

Fresh steamed asparagus tips give a pleasing complement in both taste and color to this meal.

Put It All in the Fridge
Food can be stored in the crockery container for up to four days in the refrigerator. However, never freeze food in the container because the crockery may crack.

Quail Baked
in White Wine

Cooking time: 6 hours
Preparation time: 20 minutes
Attention: Minimal
Pot size: 3–6 quarts
Serves 2

2 quail, fresh or frozen (game
   hens can be substituted)
2 garlic cloves
1 small yellow onion
1 tablespoon shortening
2 whole cloves
1 teaspoon black peppercorns

1 bay leaf
1 teaspoon fresh chopped chives
1 cup white wine
½ teaspoon salt
⅛ teaspoon ground black pepper
⅛ teaspoon cayenne pepper
1 cup heavy cream

1. Thaw the quail (if necessary) and clean by running under cold water.
   Peel and chop the garlic and onions into ¼-inch pieces.
2. Melt the shortening in a medium-sized frying pan on medium heat.
   Add the garlic, onions, cloves, peppercorns, bay leaf. Cook for several
   minutes. Add the quail and brown on all sides.
3. Place the quail and the mixture from the frying pan into the slow
   cooker. Chop the chives into ¼-inch pieces. Add the wine, salt,
   pepper, cayenne pepper, and chives to the slow cooker. Cook covered
   on low setting for about 6 hours.
4. Remove the quail and set aside. Remove the bay leaf and discard.
   Strain the liquid, then add the cream to the liquid. Stir well for 5 minutes. Pour over the quail to serve.

*Serve with Orange-Glazed Vegetable Medley (page 567) for a nice
mix of flavors.*

Replacing the Wine

If you don't have wine handy for your recipe, substitute one tablespoon of red or cider vinegar mixed with one cup of water.

Chicken Cordon Bleu

2 whole chicken breasts
4 small ham slices
4 small Swiss cheese slices
¼ cup flour
¼ cup grated Swiss cheese
½ teaspoon fresh or dried sage
¼ teaspoon ground black pepper
1 (10 ¾-ounce) can condensed cream of chicken soup

1. Remove the skin and bones from the chicken breasts. Cut each breast in half and pound with a kitchen mallet until about ¼-inch thick. Place a ham slice, then a Swiss cheese slice on each piece of chicken. Roll up and secure with toothpicks.
2. Combine the flour, grated cheese, sage, and black pepper in a small bowl. Dip the chicken rolls into the mixture. Place in the bottom of the slow cooker. Pour condensed soup over chicken rolls. Cook covered on low heat 4 to 6 hours.

Serve with Curried Vegetables and Garbanzo Beans (page 570) for a truly international meal.

Grate Your Own Cheese
As a time and money saver, buy blocks of cheese and grate them yourself. To keep the cheese from sticking together, add a little cornstarch and toss cheese until mixed through.

Game Hens in Red Wine

Cooking time: 6 hours

Preparation time: 20 minutes

Attention: Minimal

Pot size: 3–6 quarts

Serves 2

2 game hens, fresh or thawed
1 cup flour
½ teaspoon salt
¼ teaspoon ground black pepper
⅓ cup vegetable oil
1 cup sour cream
1½ cups red wine

1. Clean the game hens by running them under cold water. Combine the flour, salt, and ground black pepper. Roll the game hens in the mixture until lightly coated. Heat the vegetable oil at medium temperature in a medium-sized frying pan. Place the game hens in the frying pan and brown on all sides.

2. Place the game hens in the slow cooker on low setting. Pour the red wine on top of the game hens. Cook covered on low setting for 5 hours, add the sour cream and cook for another hour.

Serve with Grandma Dorothy's Peas and Rice (page 569) to make a complete meal.

To Prevent Curdling

To prevent curdling of milk, yogurt, or sour cream, mix it with an equal amount of cooking liquid from the dish being prepared. Consider adding milk products during the last hour of the cooking process and always cook them on the low setting.

Cheese Soufflé

14 slices fresh white bread
3 cups sharp Cheddar cheese, grated
3 cups milk
6 large eggs
2 tablespoons Worcestershire sauce
½ teaspoon table salt
Shortening, for greasing slow cooker
¼ cup butter
½ teaspoon paprika

1. Remove the crusts from the bread and tear the bread into small pieces, about ½-inch squares. Grate the cheese. Put the milk in a medium-sized pot on the stove and cook on high until slightly yellowed. Beat the eggs, milk, Worcestershire sauce, and salt until well blended.
2. Grease the slow cooker by putting the shortening on a paper towel and rubbing it on the inside of the pot. Place half of the bread in the slow cooker. Add half of the cheese and half of the butter. Add remaining bread. Put the remaining cheese and butter on top of the bread. Pour the prepared liquid sauce over everything. Sprinkle with paprika. Cover and cook on low 4 to 6 hours. Do not remove cover until ready to serve.

This is the perfect complement to Roast Duckling with Orange Glaze (page 584).

Using Condensed Milk

Instead of regular milk, cream, or sour cream, substitute sweetened condensed milk in slow cooker recipes. It tends to hold up better over the longer cooking times.

Poached Pears in Red Wine

Cooking time: 4–6 hours

Preparation time: 30 minutes

Attention: Minimal

Pot size: 3–6 quarts

Serves 2

1½ cups dry red wine

1 cup sugar

¼ teaspoon red food coloring

3 small pears

1. Combine the wine and sugar in the slow cooker. Cover and cook about 1 hour, until the sugar is dissolved. Add the food coloring.
2. Peel the pears and slice in half, removing stems and centers. Place in the slow cooker and stir slightly, so the pears are covered with the sugar and wine sauce. Cover and cook on low setting for 4 to 6 hours.

This is the perfect dessert for Classic Swiss Fondue (page 582).

Caramel Rum Fondue

Cooking time: 3–4 hours

Preparation time: 15 minutes

Attention: Medium

Pot size: 3–6 quarts

Serves 8

1 (14-ounce) package caramels

⅔ cup cream

½ cup miniature marshmallows

1 tablespoon rum

Combine the caramels and cream in the slow cooker. Cover and cook on low setting for 2 to 3 hours, or until the caramels are completely melted. Stir in the marshmallows and rum. Continue cooking covered on low setting for 1 hour. Stir before serving.

Serve with fresh sliced apple wedges.

Chocolate Pudding Cake

Cooking time: 3–4 hours

Preparation time: 15 minutes

Attention: Minimal

Pot size: 4–6 quarts

Serves 8

2 cups packaged chocolate cake mix
½ cup instant chocolate pudding mix
2 cups sour cream
4 eggs
1 cup water
¾ cup vegetable oil
1 cup semisweet chocolate chips

1. Combine the cake mix, pudding mix, sour cream, eggs, water, and oil in a medium-sized mixing bowl. Beat with an electric mixer or by hand with a wooden spoon until mixture is creamy. Stir in the chocolate chips.

2. Pour into a 2-pound coffee can. Place the coffee can inside the slow cooker. Cover and cook on low setting for 3 to 4 hours. Because this cake is more moist than others, a toothpick inserted into the center will never come out completely clean. Look for moist crumbs instead of batter to ensure it is done.

Make homemade whipped cream by beating whipping cream on a high speed with a hand mixer. Add a bit of vanilla and confectioner's sugar to give it more flavor.

Cooling Down

Let the slow cooker cool down on its own time. Do not pour cold water into it or immerse it in cold water, as this could cause the crockery pot to crack!

Desserts

Hot Fruit Medley

Cooking time: 3–4 hours

Preparation time: 20 minutes

Attention: Minimal

Pot size: 4–6 quarts

Serves 8

3 fresh grapefruit

3 fresh oranges

2 cups fresh or canned pineapple, cut into chunks

2 fresh pears

2 fresh peaches

3 fresh bananas

1 cup fresh cherries

1 cup seedless grapes

¼ cup sugar

¼ cup water

1 tablespoon lemon juice

1. Peel and section the grapefruits and oranges. Cut the pineapple into chunks about 1 inch square. Peel the pears, peaches, and bananas, then slice into pieces no larger than ¼-inch thick. Remove the pits from cherries.
2. Combine all the ingredients and place in the slow cooker. Cover and cook on low heat 3 to 4 hours, stirring occasionally.

Ladle over low-fat vanilla ice cream for a healthy treat.

Converting Recipes

When converting recipes from the oven to the slow cooker, plan about 8 hours on the low setting for every hour in the oven. Plan about 4 hours on the high setting for every hour in the oven.

Caramel and Peanut Fondue

Cooking time:	1 hour
Preparation time:	10 minutes
Attention:	Constant
Pot size:	1–3 quarts
Serves	8

½ cup butter
½ cup light corn syrup
1 cup brown sugar
½ cup chunky peanut butter

1 can sweetened condensed milk
4 apples, sliced into ½-inch
   wedges

1. Combine the butter, corn syrup, brown sugar, peanut butter, and condensed milk in a medium-sized saucepan on the stove. Bring mixture to a boil, stirring constantly. Continue to boil for 3 minutes.
2. Pour the mixture into the slow cooker. Cook covered on low for 1 hour. Dip the fresh apple slices into the mixture.

This dip also makes an excellent ice cream topping.

Curried Fruit Bake

Cooking time:	3–4 hours
Preparation time:	20 minutes
Attention:	Minimal
Pot size:	3–6 quarts
Serves	8–12

2 cups pitted prunes
2 cups canned or fresh apricots,
   peeled and pitted
1½ cups fresh or canned
   pineapple chunks

1½ cups fresh or canned peaches,
   peeled and pitted
1 cup packed brown sugar
½ teaspoon curry powder
1 (12-ounce) can Ginger Ale

Wash and cut the fruit into 1-inch pieces. Combine all the ingredients in the slow cooker. Cover and cook on low heat 3 to 4 hours.

In the summer, prepare this dessert the night before an event and put it in the refrigerator for a cool, refreshing treat.

Raisin and Orange Baked Apples

Cooking time: 8 hours

Preparation time: 20 minutes

Attention: Minimal

Pot size: 2–6 quarts

Serves 6

6 medium-sized apples
½ cup raisins
3 tablespoons flour
⅓ cup sugar
½ teaspoon cinnamon
⅛ teaspoon salt
1 teaspoon grated orange peel
2 tablespoons butter (or margarine)
⅔ cup water
⅔ cup fresh orange juice

1. Wash and core the apples by taking a paring knife and "digging out" the center of each apple, leaving ½ to 1 inch on the bottom. Start at the top and peel the apples about a third of the way down. Fill the center of each apple with raisins and set the apples in the slow cooker. (You may stack them if necessary.)
2. Using a fork, mix together the flour, sugar, cinnamon, salt, orange peel, and butter (or margarine) in a small bowl until the mixture is crumbly. Sprinkle it over the apples.
3. Mix together the water and orange juice and pour around the apples. Cover and cook on low setting for 8 hours.

There is less chance of the apples falling into pieces if you let them cool slightly before removing them.

Grandma's Apples and Rice

Cooking time: 1 hour	
Preparation time: 15 minutes	
Attention: Minimal	
Pot size: 2–4 quarts	
Serves 8	

1¼ cups uncooked brown rice
1 cup apples, peeled and cubed
4 tablespoons butter, divided
2½ cups chunky applesauce
¼ cup packed brown sugar
1¾ teaspoons ground cinnamon, divided
½ teaspoon salt

Cook the rice according to the package directions. Peel the apples and cut into 1-inch cubes. Stir 2 tablespoons of the butter into the hot rice. Add the applesauce, apples, brown sugar, 1½ teaspoons cinnamon, and salt. Pour into the slow cooker. Dot with the remaining butter and sprinkle with the remaining cinnamon. Cook uncovered on low setting for 1 hour.

Serve in bowls topped with whipped cream.

Seasonal Best

Because there are so many types of apples available year-round, you should always inquire about which ones are in season. This will insure that you are using the tastiest ones in the bunch. Also, try combining different kinds for added flavor and variety.

Rice Pudding

2½ cups cooked white rice
1½ cup scalded milk
3 eggs
shortening for greasing the slow cooker
⅔ cup brown sugar
3 tablespoons soft butter
2 teaspoons vanilla
1 teaspoon salt
1 teaspoon nutmeg
1 teaspoon cinnamon
½ cup raisins

1. Cook the rice according to the package directions to yield 2½ cups cooked rice. Scald the milk by cooking it in a small saucepan on high heat on the stove until it slightly yellows. Beat the eggs in a small bowl with a fork until the whites and yellows are well mixed.
2. Lightly grease the slow cooker by putting shortening on a paper towel and rubbing it on the inside of the slow cooker. Combine all the ingredients. Pour into the slow cooker. Cook covered on high 1 to 2 hours. Stir after first 30 minutes.

Ladle into individual graham cracker crusts to make mini pies.

Cleaning Caution

Do not use detergents or scouring powders with slow cookers. The porous clay cooking crock with soak up the detergent, tainting the flavor of future dishes.

Cooking time: 2–3 hours
Preparation time: 10 minutes
Attention: Minimal
Pot size: 4–6 quarts
Serves 8

Chocolate Peanut Butter Cake

½ cup chopped walnuts
2 cups chocolate cake mix
½ cup water
⅓ cup creamy peanut butter

1. Combine all the ingredients in a medium-sized bowl and beat with a wooden spoon for about 2 minutes.
2. Grease the inside of a 2-pound coffee can, then sprinkle the inside with flour. Pour the batter in the coffee can and cover with aluminum foil. Poke 3 sets of holes in the aluminum foil with a fork. Place the coffee can in the slow cooker. Cover and bake on high for 2 to 3 hours.

Spread a thin layer of peanut butter on each piece right before serving.

A Time-Saver
For an even quicker recipe, buy the walnuts already chopped!

Cinnamon Streusel Pound Cake

Cooking time: 3–4 hours	
Preparation time: 15 minutes	
Attention: Minimal	
Pot size: 4–6 quarts	
Serves 8	

1 (16-ounce) package pound cake mix
¼ cup chopped walnuts
¼ cup brown sugar
1 tablespoon flour
1 teaspoon cinnamon

1. Prepare the cake mix according to the package directions. Grease the inside of a 2-pound coffee can by putting shortening on a paper towel and rubbing it inside the coffee can. Sprinkle the inside lightly with flour. Pour pound cake batter into the coffee can.
2. Chop the nuts into $\frac{1}{16}$-inch pieces with a sharp knife. In a small bowl, combine the brown sugar, flour, nuts, and cinnamon. Sprinkle this mixture over the cake batter.
3. Cover the coffee can with aluminum foil. Poke 3 sets of holes in the aluminum foil with a fork. Place the coffee can in the slow cooker. Cover and cook on high setting for 3 to 4 hours.

This is the perfect complement to eggs and bacon for Sunday brunch.

Adding Frozen Foods
If you must absolutely use frozen foods, set the slow cooker to high for the first two hours then turn it to low to resume cooking. This reduces the chance that bacteria will grow.

Cooking time: 3 hours
Preparation time: 10 minutes
Attention: Minimal
Pot size: 3–6 quarts
Serves 8

Scalloped Fruit Cocktail

3 cups (24 ounces) canned fruit cocktail
8 slices white bread
2 cups sugar
3 eggs
¾ cup butter, melted
¾ cup milk

1. Drain and discard the juice from the fruit cocktail. Mash the fruit with a fork. Remove and discard the crusts from the bread. Tear the bread into ½-inch cubes.
2. Mix all the ingredients in a large mixing bowl, taking care that the eggs are well integrated pour mixture into the slow cooker. Cover and cook on high setting for 2 hours. Turn to low setting and cook covered for 1 additional hour.

Use any canned fruit, such as peaches or pineapple, instead of the fruit cocktail.

Don't Overfill!
Leave at least two inches of space from the food to the top of the slow cooker, especially if the recipe contains a lot of liquid. This will prevent the food from boiling over while simmering.

Pumpkin Pie Pudding

Cooking time: 6–7 hours
Preparation time: 20 minutes
Attention: Minimal
Pot size: 3–6 quarts
Serves 8

2 eggs
1 (15-ounce) can solid-packed
  pumpkin
1 (12-ounce) can evaporated milk
¾ cup sugar

½ cup buttermilk biscuit mix
2 tablespoons melted butter
½ teaspoon nutmeg
2 teaspoons vanilla

Beat the eggs with a fork until slightly frothy. Mix together all the ingredients. Pour into the slow cooker. Cover and cook on low setting for 6 to 7 hours.

Use this as dessert for Day-After Thanksgiving Soup (page 316).

Raisin Bread Pudding

Cooking time: 5 hours
Preparation time: 15 minutes
Attention: Medium
Pot size: 3–6 quarts
Serves 8

8 slices cinnamon raisin bread
4 eggs
2 cups milk
¼ cup sugar

¼ cup butter, melted
½ cup raisins
1 teaspoon cinnamon

Tear the bread into 1-inch pieces and place in the slow cooker. Beat together the eggs, milk, sugar, butter, raisins, and cinnamon. Pour over the bread. Cover and cook on high setting for 1 hour. Reduce heat to low. Keep it covered and cook an additional 4 hours.

Add a drizzle of confectioners' sugar mixed with milk and vanilla to the top of each serving.

Maggie's Favorite Oatmeal Raisin Cookies

Cooking time: 4 hours
Preparation time: 15 minutes
Attention: Frequent
Pot size: 3–8 quarts
Serves 30

½ cup shortening
¾ cup brown sugar
½ teaspoon salt
½ teaspoon cinnamon
½ teaspoon nutmeg
½ teaspoon allspice
1 egg
¾ cup flour
⅜ teaspoon baking soda
⅛ cup buttermilk
½ cup walnuts, chopped nuts
¾ cup rolled oats
¾ cup seedless raisins

1. Combine the shortening and brown sugar in a mixing bowl. Beat well with a wooden spoon or electric mixer, until the batter is smooth and creamy. Add the salt, cinnamon, nutmeg, allspice, and egg. Beat the mixture well, until the batter is smooth and creamy.
2. Mix together the flour and baking soda. Add half this mixture to the batter and beat until creamy. Add the remaining half and the buttermilk. Beat until well mixed.
3. Chop the nuts into about ¹⁄₁₆-inch pieces with a sharp kitchen knife. Add the nuts, oats, and raisins to the batter; mix well with a wooden spoon. The mixture should be firm but not dry. Drop onto the bottom of the slow cooker by rounded teaspoonfuls, about 4 at a time. Cook each batch covered on high for about 15 minutes.

Take two cookies and make a sandwich by spreading vanilla frosting in between.

Fruit Drop Cookies

Cooking time: 4 hours

Preparation time: 15 minutes, plus 1 hour of refrigeration time

Attention: Frequent

Pot size: 3–8 quarts

Serves 30

1 cup diced dates
1 cup candied maraschino cherries
½ cup soft shortening
1 cup brown sugar
1 egg
¼ cup buttermilk
1½ cups flour
½ teaspoon baking soda
¾ cup broken pecans

1. Cut the dates into ¼-inch pieces with a sharp knife. Cut the cherries in half. Beat the shortening, sugar, and egg until smooth and creamy with an electric mixer. Stir in the milk. Combine the flour, baking soda, and salt. Mix with batter, beating until creamy. Stir in the pecans, cherries, and dates using a wooden spoon.
2. Cover the bowl and put the batter in the refrigerator for at least 1 hour. Preheat the slow cooker on high setting. Drop the batter by rounded teaspoonfuls onto the bottom of the slow cooker. Cover and bake each batch 10 to 15 minutes.

Serve with Minty Hot Chocolate (page 468).

Microwave No-No
Don't put the crockery food container in the oven or microwave unless the manufacturers' directions say you can. It could crack or even completely break apart!

Chocolate Coconut and Peanut Clusters

Cooking time: 30–60 minutes

Preparation time: 15 minutes

Attention: Constant

Pot size: 2–8 quarts

Serves 24

2 pounds white candy coating,
  broken into small pieces
2 cups semisweet chocolate chips

½ cup sweet German chocolate
½ cup flaked coconut
3 cups roasted peanuts

Put the candy coating, chocolate chips, and German chocolate in the slow cooker. Heat on high setting, stirring every 10 to 15 minutes until the mixture is completely melted. Stir in the coconut and peanuts; mix well. Drop by teaspoonfuls onto waxed paper. Set in a cool area until the candy is hard.

Add pecans instead of peanuts.

Strawberry Rhubarb Sauce

Cooking time: 7–8 hours

Preparation time: 20 minutes

Attention: Minimal

Pot size: 3–6 quarts

Serves 12

6 cups fresh rhubarb
1 cup sugar
½ white grape juice

1 cinnamon stick
2 cups quartered strawberries

1. Wash the rhubarb and remove the leaves; chop the rhubarb into 1-inch pieces. Place in the slow cooker with the sugar, grape juice, and cinnamon stick. Cover and cook on low setting for 5 to 6 hours.
2. Remove the cinnamon stick. Remove the stems from the strawberries and slice into quarters. Add to slow cooker. Cover and cook on low setting for 2 hours.

Excellent served warm over homemade vanilla ice cream.

Beer Cake

Cooking time: 3–4 hours

Preparation time: 20 minutes

Attention: Minimal

Pot size: 4–6 quarts

Serves 8

²/₃ cup butter

1½ cup brown sugar

3 eggs, beaten

2½ cups flour

1½ teaspoons baking powder

¼ teaspoon baking soda

1 teaspoon cinnamon

¼ teaspoon nutmeg

1½ cups brown ale

1 cup walnuts, chopped

1 cup seedless raisins

1. Mix the butter and sugar in a medium-sized mixing bowl using an electric mixer. The mixture should be light and fluffy. Add the eggs one at a time, mixing well. Combine the flour, baking powder, baking soda, cinnamon, and nutmeg in a bowl; mix well. Pour half this mixture and half the beer into the batter and mix until smooth. Add the remaining flour mixture and beer. Mix until smooth. Fold in the walnuts and raisins.

2. Grease a 2-pound coffee can by putting shortening on a paper towel and rubbing the inside of the can. Lightly sprinkle the inside with flour. Place the batter in coffee can. Cover with aluminum foil. Poke 3 sets of holes into the aluminum foil with a fork. Put the coffee can in the slow cooker. Place the lid on the slow cooker slightly off center so that steam can escape. Cook on high setting for 3 to 4 hours. Remove the coffee can from the slow cooker and allow to cool 15 to 30 minutes before removing the cake.

Who could resist serving this on Super Bowl Sunday as dessert for Halftime Chili (page 465)?

Index

Standard U.S./Metric Measurement Conversions

VOLUME CONVERSIONS

U.S. Volume Measure	Metric Equivalent
⅛ teaspoon	0.5 milliliters
¼ teaspoon	1 milliliters
½ teaspoon	2 milliliters
1 teaspoon	5 milliliters
½ tablespoon	7 milliliters
1 tablespoon (3 teaspoons)	15 milliliters
2 tablespoons (1 fluid ounce)	30 milliliters
¼ cup (4 tablespoons)	60 milliliters
⅓ cup	90 milliliters
½ cup (4 fluid ounces)	125 milliliters
⅔ cup	160 milliliters
¾ cup (6 fluid ounces)	180 milliliters
1 cup (16 tablespoons)	250 milliliters
1 pint (2 cups)	500 milliliters
1 quart (4 cups)	1 liter (about)

WEIGHT CONVERSIONS

U.S. Weight Measure	Metric Equivalent
½ ounce	15 grams
1 ounce	30 grams
2 ounces	60 grams
3 ounces	85 grams
¼ pound (4 ounces)	115 grams
½ pound (8 ounces)	225 grams
¾ pound (12 ounces)	340 grams
1 pound (16 ounces)	454 grams

OVEN TEMPERATURE CONVERSIONS

Degrees Fahrenheit	Degrees Celsius
200 degrees F	100 degrees C
250 degrees F	120 degrees C
275 degrees F	140 degrees C
300 degrees F	150 degrees C
325 degrees F	160 degrees C
350 degrees F	180 degrees C
375 degrees F	190 degrees C
400 degrees F	200 degrees C
425 degrees F	220 degrees C
450 degrees F	230 degrees C

BAKING PAN SIZES

American	Metric
8 x 1½ inch round baking pan	20 x 4 cm cake tin
9 x 1½ inch round baking pan	23 x 3.5 cm cake tin
1 x 7 x 1½ inch baking pan	28 x 18 x 4 cm baking tin
113 x 9 x 2 inch baking pan	30 x 20 x 5 cm baking tin
2 quart rectangular baking dish	30 x 20 x 3 cm baking tin
15 x 10 x 2 inch baking pan	30 x 25 x 2 cm baking tin (Swiss roll tin)
9 inch pie plate	22 x 4 or 23 x 4 cm pie plate
7 or 8 inch springform pan	18 or 20 cm springform or loose bottom cake tin
9 x 5 x 3 inch loaf pan	23 x 13 x 7 cm or 2 lb narrow loaf or pate tin
1½ quart casserole	1.5 litre casserole
2 quart casserole	2 litre casserole